Business Ethics

A MANUAL FOR MANAGING A RESPONSIBLE BUSINESS ENTERPRISE IN EMERGING MARKET ECONOMIES

A publication of the
GOOD GOVERNANCE PROGRAM

D1219850

U.S. DEPARTMENT OF COMMERCE
International Trade Administration
WASHINGTON, D.C.

Library of Congress Cataloging-in-Publication statement
Business ethics : a manual for managing a responsible business enterprise
in emerging market economies / U.S. Department of Commerce,
International Trade Administration.
p. cm.
"A publication of the Good Governance Program"
Includes bibliographical references and index.
1. Business ethics. 2. Business ethics—United States. I. United States.
International Trade Administration.
HF5387.B87129   2004
174'.4—dc22
2002056735

ISBN 0-16-051477-0

Published 2004 by the U.S. Department of Commerce,
International Trade Administration.

For sale by the U.S. Government Printing Office, Superintendent
of Documents
Internet: *http://bookstore.gpo.gov*
Telephone: (202) 512-1800
Mail Stop: SSOP, Washington, DC 20402-0001
Stock number: Stock number 003-009-00731-3

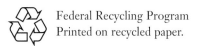

This manual is intended to provide general guidance for businesses and practitioners in better understanding
emerging global standards of responsible business conduct. It is distributed with the understanding that the
authors, editors, and publisher are not engaged in rendering legal, accounting, or other professional services.
Where legal or other expert assistance is required, the services of a competent professional should be sought.
The manual contains information on business ethics program design and implementation that was current as
of the date of publication. While every effort has been made to make it as complete and accurate as possible,
readers should be aware that all information that is contained therein is subject to change without notice.

MESSAGE FROM THE U.S. SECRETARY OF COMMERCE

*B*usiness Ethics: A Manual for Managing a Responsible Business Enterprise in Emerging Market Economies grew out of collaboration between the U.S. Department of Commerce and many dedicated people and organizations. It is intended to provide a practical guide to assist owners and managers in meeting emerging global standards and expectations for an effective business ethics program.

Such a step-by-step guide should have great utility in the emerging market economies that ring the globe. Many are new players in the modern global economy and lack experience in what it takes for free markets to function efficiently and to deliver the jobs, goods, services, consumer choices, and general prosperity that are expected from democratic capitalism. Even developed market economies, moreover, are searching for better ways to meet market challenges.

A fundamental ingredient of any successful market economy is respect for basic human values: honesty, trust, and fairness. These values must become an integral part of business culture and practice for markets to remain free and to work effectively. Private business is at the strategic center of any civil society. It's where people go for a job or to invest savings to realize their aspirations for their families.

Having spent most of my life working in American business, I am compelled to ask, "If businesses fail to honor their responsibilities to society and don't believe in corporate stewardship, who in our society will?" Corporate stewardship protects the whole "human ecology" of the corporation and its communities, nurturing the long-term economic growth of both and of their human resources.

You can apply the manual whether you represent business, civil society, or government and whether your enterprise is large or small. I hope you find the manual easy to use in your development of a business ethics program. We certainly hope that it will stimulate public debate on the importance of business ethics.

Sincerely,

Donald L. Evans
U.S. Secretary of Commerce

ACKNOWLEDGMENTS

*W*e are particularly grateful to Igor Y. Abramov and Kenneth W. Johnson, who were the authors of the manual. In addition, we would like to thank the many businesses and organizations across the globe that have graciously consented to the use of their materials as examples to illustrate the process of designing a business ethics program. This book would not have been possible without the efforts of countless practitioners who have labored to develop international standards of responsible business conduct or business ethics programs for their own enterprises.

Comments and suggestions provided by experts from Armenia, Azerbaijan, Georgia, Kazakhstan, Romania, Russia, the United States, and Uzbekistan on early drafts of this book were critical to its development. We are especially grateful for the insights offered by Gulsum Akhtamberdieva, Anita B. Baker, Ion Pirvu, Kathleen Purdy, Tatiana Raguzina, Rena Safaralieva, Petr Shikirev, Andrew Sommers, Robert Strahota, Jon Thiele, John Truslow, Zhan Utkelov, George Wratney, and several members of the Ethics Officer Association.

We would especially like to thank Matthew Murray for his contributions to the drafting and editing of this manual. We also thank Danica R. Starks, who has served as project coordinator of the book, and Elizabeth Ramborger, John Ward, and William Corley for their contributions to the publication process.

Valuable editorial assistance was provided by the staff of Publication Professionals LLC, who edited the text. The cover and text designs were created by Maureen Lauran. Composition and production assistance were provided by the Typography and Design section of the U.S. Government Printing Office.

Finally, we are grateful for FREEDOM Support Act assistance funds that were extended to the Good Governance Program by the Coordinator for U.S. Assistance to the New Independent States. These funds helped make this book possible.

Susanne S. Lotarski, Ph.D.
Director
Office of Eastern Europe, Russia, and Independent States
International Trade Administration
U.S. Department of Commerce

A project of the

GOOD GOVERNANCE PROGRAM

of the

U.S. DEPARTMENT OF COMMERCE

In consultation and cooperation with:

American Chamber of Commerce in Russia

Casals and Associates, Inc.

Center for Business Ethics and Corporate Governance

Chamber of Commerce and Industry of Romania and Bucharest Municipality

Federal Commission for the Securities Market of the Russian Federation

Russian Chamber of Commerce and Industry
National Fund for Russian Business Culture

Russian-American Business Dialogue
American Chamber of Commerce
Russian American Business Council
Russian Union of Industrialists and Entrepreneurs
U.S.–Russia Business Council

Transparency International, Azerbaijan

FOREWORD

*W*e live in an age of innovation, the growth of free markets, and a world economy. New technologies, roles for government, and players on the global scene offer challenging opportunities, demands, and constraints. More peoples and nations are working together to spread freedom and democratic principles; to nurture free markets; to protect individual property rights; and to encourage respect for human rights, the rule of law, and the environment.

With increasing urgency, market and social forces are rewriting the roles and responsibilities of business as well. Though the profit motive of business is understood and accepted, people do not accept it as an excuse for ignoring the basic norms, values, and standards of being a good citizen. Modern businesses are expected to be responsible stewards of community resources working toward the growth and success of both their companies and their communities.

Government has an important role in the spread of freedom and democratic capitalism. It provides for the essential market-oriented legal framework and reliable dispute resolution processes that allow businesses to compete fairly on the quality, prices, and delivery of their goods and services alone. It enforces laws, regulations, and judgments to safeguard the social order its citizens value. It cannot, however, act alone. Businesses and civil society must also be involved in solutions to community problems. They can help in the fight against the corruption that saps national resources. They must reform the unethical business practices that breed cynicism and distrust in communities.

Businesses are at the strategic center of a civil society, and they have a stake in their communities. They depend on free markets and good public governance for their growth and success, but they are also authors of their own destiny. Through responsible business conduct, they contribute to the essential social capital of trust and fairness that makes good governance and free markets possible.

Markets become free and remain free if their players are responsible and respect the basic values of honesty, reliability, fairness, and self-discipline. The alternatives to responsible business conduct are inefficient markets and costly government regulation. Free flows of capital, talent, knowledge, and creativity are possible where communities are known for transparency, respect for property, a market-oriented legal framework, and reliable dispute resolution mechanisms. The alternatives are a lack of capital, high transaction costs, limited markets, underdevelopment, and poverty.

In short, owners and managers must temper the competitive aspects of capitalism with concerned citizenship. They must take individual responsibility for the decisions and activities of their enterprises and their impact on the culture of their enterprise and its stakeholders. A business needs committed, productive employees, agents, and suppliers to create goods and services. It needs loyal, satisfied customers and consumers to make a profit. It needs people who believe in it and in its prospects enough to invest. It needs to take the long view and to respect the physical environment and the prospects of future generations.

Over the past few decades, governments, international institutions, transnational organizations, organized labor, and civil society have been engaged in an ongoing dialogue into the role of business as responsible stewards. Standards, procedures, and expectations for business are emerging worldwide. Enterprises and markets that are unaware of them, or fail to plan their futures with them in mind, will be unable to participate in the global dialogue and will risk being left behind as the global market economy expands.

Businesses around the world are designing and implementing business ethics programs to address the legal, ethical, social responsibility, and environmental issues they face. By addressing these issues in a systematic way, enterprises can improve their own business performance, expand opportunities for growth, and contribute to the development of social capital in their markets. They can realize specific business benefits, such as:

- Enhanced reputations and good will

- Reduced risks and costs

- Protection from their own employees and agents

- Stronger competitive positions

- Expanded access to capital, credit, and foreign investment

- Increased profits

- Sustained long-term growth

- International respect for enterprises and emerging markets

Enterprises that excel in these areas create a climate of excellence for their employees, shareholders, and communities, and contribute to the economic wellbeing of their countries.

No single volume can tell individual businesses what decisions and activities will foster and meet the reasonable expectations of their stakeholders. Each enterprise faces unique political, economic, social, and technological pressures. Moreover, each has a unique organizational culture that influences all that its members think, say, and do. However, a guide can demonstrate a process through which owners and managers can identify enterprise stakeholders; can foster reasonable stakeholder expectations; and can inspire, encourage, and support responsible business conduct.

Purpose of this Manual

This manual is intended to aid enterprises in designing and implementing a business ethics program that meets emerging global standards of responsible business conduct. Owners and managers can explore the substantial body of global standards, procedures, and expectations described here. They can adopt or adapt them on a sector-by-sector and enterprise-by-enterprise basis, taking into account their particular circumstances, such as applicable laws and regulations, the size of the enterprise, and the enterprise's purpose.

This manual explores how a business ethics program helps owners, managers, and their professional advisers build an enterprise to meet these standards. It builds on three essential concepts to help busy owners and managers design and implement business ethics programs for their unique enterprises.

1. **Responsible business conduct:** the choices and actions of employees and agents that foster and meet the reasonable expectations of enterprise stakeholders.

2. **Responsible business enterprise:** an enterprise characterized by good governance policies and management practices as well as by a culture of responsible business conduct. It is adept at dealing with the challenges and complexities of its business environment, but holds closely to its purpose, core values, and vision.

3. **Business ethics program:** a tool that owners and managers use to inspire, encourage, and support responsible business conduct, by engaging enterprise stakeholders in order to foster and meet their reasonable expectations, and designing structures and systems to guide and support employees and agents.

There is, of course, no one right way to design and implement a business ethics program, let alone to achieve a culture of responsible business conduct. Whatever the size or purpose of the enterprise, however, owners and managers will find value in building an enterprise that sets standards for responsible business conduct, puts them into practice, and learns from experience. This manual distills the experience of business enterprises that have designed and implemented business ethics programs to address a number of issues:

- What it means to be a responsible business
- How to approach responsible business as a strategy
- What structures and systems help management guide employees and agents and foster reasonable expectations among enterprise stakeholders
- How to communicate with stakeholders about enterprise standards, expectations, and performance
- How to align management practices with core beliefs through a business ethics program
- How to evaluate a business ethics program and learn from it

Four distinct but related disciplines have traditionally guided responsible business conduct: business and professional ethics, organizational ethics, corporate social responsibility, and corporate governance. The focus of all four approaches is the governance policies and management practices that inspire, guide, and support responsible business conduct. This manual integrates these four disciplines into a single, systemic discipline: the discipline of responsible business conduct.

To help owners and managers apply the discipline of responsible business conduct, this manual develops a set of tools that will assist them in answering important questions drawn from each of the four traditional approaches to responsible business conduct:

1. Business and professional ethics
   a. What does a business enterprise owe its customers and consumers?
   b. What standards of conduct and performance should an enterprise set for its employees and agents?
   c. What is the role of industry and government in setting business and professional standards?

2. Organizational ethics
   a. What is the optimal mix of values and rules to guide decision-making and action?
   b. What structures, systems, practices, and procedures will best implement the values and rules of the enterprise?
   c. What outcomes should one reasonably expect from an enterprise's decisions and activities, and how can an enterprise track, measure, and report them?

3. Corporate social responsibility

a. Who are the legitimate stakeholders of an enterprise, and what can they reasonably expect?

b. Who speaks for the environment and future generations as stakeholders?

c. What is the role of business in sustainable development?

4. Corporate governance

a. Who can rightfully claim the power to govern an enterprise?

b. How can the board of directors and management best protect the rights of shareholders, especially minority shareholders?

c. How can the board of directors best guide management to meet the reasonable expectations of shareholders?

Organization of this Manual

This manual includes 10 chapters, which are arranged in five parts. The five parts organize the chapters according to the flow of business ethics program design and implementation, from defining key terms and addressing global standards and best practices, through evaluating the business ethics program as a part of organizational learning. Chapters build on each other, but they may be read alone if the reader is interested in a particular topic.

Part I, "The Responsible Business Enterprise," develops a working definition of the responsible business enterprise (RBE). Chapter 1, "Responsible Business Conduct in an Emerging Economy," addresses the challenges business enterprises face, especially in emerging market economies. It concludes that to be part of the solution to the problems facing businesses, enterprises need to improve their business performance, contribute to the social capital of their communities, and work with leaders in government and civil society to develop a market-oriented legal framework and reliable judicial institutions. Chapter 2, "Responsible Management and the Responsible Business Enterprise," describes the emerging global standards of performance and reporting and the benefits of having a business ethics program.

Part II, "The Business Ethics Program," introduces the reader to the elements of a business ethics program and its nature as a business strategy. Chapter 3, "Responsible Business Conduct as Strategy," treats the key concepts and components of a business ethics program and shows how owners and managers can approach a business ethics program as a strategy. Chapter 4, "Creation of a Business Ethics Program," introduces owners and managers to the process of developing, reviewing, and approving a business ethics program.

Part III, "Structuring the Business Ethics Program," details the emerging global standards and best practices of responsible business conduct. Chapter 5, "Standards, Procedures, and Expectations for the Responsible Business Enterprise," discusses responsible board-level governance policies and management-level vision and value statements, and it describes how to implement standards, procedures, and expectations. Chapter 6, "Business Ethics Infrastructure," discusses the structures and systems that owners and managers use to implement a business ethics program. Chapter 7, "Business Ethics Communications and Feedback," discusses the challenges of communicating with an enterprise's stakeholders about standards, procedures, and expectations, as well as about the enterprise's performance.

Part IV, "Putting Business Ethics into Practice," describes how management aligns its practices on an enterprise's core beliefs and follows through on the expectations created through its business ethics program. Chapter 8, "Aligning the Responsible Business Enterprise," examines how an enterprise needs to have the right employees and agents performing the right tasks in pursuit of its purpose. It explores how the RBE responds when things go wrong through the fault of its employees and agents or otherwise. Chapter 9, "Responsible Business Conduct and Practices," pays particular attention to the challenges of being a responsible business enterprise in an emerging market economy, especially dealing with government procurement and contracting, influencing government legislation and regulation, and working with other business leaders and civil society to develop a market-oriented legal framework and reliable judicial institutions.

Part V, "Achieving Responsible Business Conduct," helps owners and managers determine whether their business ethics program is achieving measurable goals. Chapter 10, "Program Evaluation and Organizational Learning," emphasizes the importance of evaluating a business ethics program as an integral part of organizational learning and of what it means to be an RBE.

How to Use this Manual

The audience for this manual includes decision-makers in enterprises of all sorts: business, government, academia, and civil society—and their professional advisers.

Most of the experience in business ethics programs around the globe involves large, often quite complex, enterprises. Owners, shareholder representatives, and managers of such enterprises will find the discussion, worksheets, and sample provisions directly applicable. They may also find that it is in their best interest to encourage or require their suppliers or service providers to design and implement a business ethics program to minimize the risk of supply chain disruption or indirect damage to their reputations.

The bulk of businesses in all economies, especially emerging market economies, consists of small to medium-sized enterprises (SMEs). Owners and managers of SMEs face particular challenges, and most chapters discuss specific issues facing SMEs. Some chapters have tables comparing the best practices of large, complex enterprises and cost-effective solutions for the SME.

Individuals, businesses, and nongovernmental organizations seeking to stimulate a public dialogue on issues and benefits of business ethics will also find this manual useful. It offers a frame of reference for further dialogue. It includes definitions of key terms and concepts. It helps define the role of the private sector in creating transparent markets, strengthening the rule of law, and supporting good public governance.

Although this manual emphasizes responsible business conduct, association members and government officials can also use it as a management tool to order their affairs. The process described here applies to all enterprises having a shared purpose. To be effective, efficient, and responsible, an association or government agency also should understand its relevant context and organizational culture. It also must establish and communicate to its stakeholders its core beliefs, standards, procedures, and expectations. In short, an association or government agency can benefit from designing and implementing an ethics and compliance program similar to the business ethics program described here.

Finally, members of the press and other media can use this manual as a framework to develop a series of articles or programs as features to raise their audiences' awareness of emerging global standards and best practices. As business news events occur, the media can use this understanding to develop and report business events as news items—confident that their readers will appreciate the significance of their reporting. They can then develop an editorial position and can publish a body of opinion-editorial pieces to stimulate national and community dialogue.

When a business enterprise is ready to design and implement its business ethics program, the RBE Worksheets and appendices will aid it in collecting and analyzing the data necessary to build an effective program. The worksheets can be used as checklists to ensure that owners, managers, and working groups taking on this task have considered all relevant circumstances for their enterprise. These circumstances may include fundamental matters such as the political, economic, and social context and organizational culture of the enterprise. An enterprise will be most effective at building a business program if working groups of representative stakeholders are guided by an objective facilitator, whose sole responsibility is to help the group stay on task and consider all relevant points of view.

What sets this manual apart from general management texts and business ethics books is an emphasis on building formal enterprise structures, systems, and practices to achieve responsible business conduct and to embed it in the organizational culture. This manual emphasizes the process by which owners and managers design and implement a business ethics program, recognizing that each enterprise faces unique circumstances. As such, it does not answer specific legal or ethics questions.

What it does provide is a comprehensive framework for addressing ethics, compliance, and social responsibility questions on a strategic basis. It helps owners and managers organize the body of practical wisdom reflected in legal requirements, proposed guidelines, best practices, case studies, and even traditions. It can stimulate and legitimize stakeholder dialogue into matters of significance to all.

The challenges facing business are many, but its importance as the sector of society that generates consumer goods, jobs, wealth, economic progress, and, yes, even tax revenues cannot be underestimated. By working through this manual, business leaders, owners, and managers will construct their own framework for approaching a challenging, complex world more creatively and confidently.

Grant D. Aldonas
Under Secretary for International Trade
U.S. Department of Commerce

Igor Y. Abramov
Director, Good Governance Program
International Trade Administration
U.S. Department of Commerce

Kenneth W. Johnson
Director
Ethics and Policy Integration Centre
Washington, D.C.

CONTENTS

Message from the U.S. Secretary of Commerce   iii
Acknowledgements   v
Foreword   ix
Abbreviations and Acronyms   xxi

I The Responsible Business Enterprise

1 Responsible Business Conduct in an Emerging Market Economy   3

Evolution to a Market Economy
Transition to a Market Economy
The Individual Business in an Emerging Market Economy

SUMMARY   20
RESPONSIBLE BUSINESS ENTERPRISE CHECKLIST   20

2 Responsible Management and the Responsible Business Enterprise   21

Improving Business Performance
Generating Social Capital
Working with Leaders in Business, Government, and Civil Society
Building on the Foundation of Responsible Business Conduct
Adopting Global Standards and Best Practices

SUMMARY   39
RESPONSIBLE BUSINESS ENTERPRISE CHECKLIST   40

II The Business Ethics Program

3 Responsible Business Conduct as Strategy   43

Planning, Strategy, and the Business Ethics Program

Establishing the Nature of the Program
Building a Responsible Business Enterprise
Knowing the Structural Components of the Program
Planning the Business Ethics Program
Engaging the Enterprise's Stakeholders
Adopting a Design, Review, and Approval Process

SUMMARY   63
RESPONSIBLE BUSINESS ENTERPRISE CHECKLIST   64

4   Creation of a Business Ethics Program   65

Planning an Effective Business Ethics Program
Understanding the Program Logic Model
Scanning the Relevant Context
Scanning the Enterprise's Internals

SUMMARY   77
RESPONSIBLE BUSINESS ENTERPRISE CHECKLIST   77

III   Structuring the Business Ethics Program

**5   Standards, Procedures, and Expectations for the
Responsible Business Enterprise**   93

Standards and Procedures
Responsible Governance
Principles for Setting Management Standards, Procedures,
and Expectations
Management Vision for the Enterprise
Management Standards, Procedures, and Expectations
Typical Code of Conduct Provisions

SUMMARY   124
RESPONSIBLE BUSINESS ENTERPRISE CHECKLIST   124

6   Business Ethics Infrastructure   129

Designing Business Ethics Infrastructure
Determining Systems of Authority, Responsibility,
and Accountability

SUMMARY   144
RESPONSIBLE BUSINESS ENTERPRISE CHECKLIST   145

7 | **Business Ethics Communications and Feedback** | 147

Communicating and Providing Feedback
Communicating Standards and Fostering Reasonable Expectations
Ensuring Members Follow Standards and Meet Expectations

SUMMARY 176
RESPONSIBLE BUSINESS ENTERPRISE CHECKLIST 177

IV Putting Business Ethics into Practice

8 | **Aligning the Responsible Business Enterprise** | 185

Understanding the Importance of Alignment
Getting the Right People in the Right Places
Encouraging Employees to Follow Standards and Procedures
Dealing with Mistakes, Misconduct, or Misunderstandings

SUMMARY 204
RESPONSIBLE BUSINESS ENTERPRISE CHECKLIST 205

9 | **Responsible Business Conduct and Practices** | 207

Challenges to the Responsible Business Enterprise
Relationships with Government Officials and Entities
Role of the Private Sector in the Regulatory Process
Government Contracting and Procurement
Role of Voluntary Action
Relationships with Foreign Businesses and Governments

SUMMARY 223
RESPONSIBLE BUSINESS ENTERPRISE CHECKLIST 224

V Achieving Responsible Business Conduct

10 | **Program Evaluation and Organizational Learning** | 229

Ensuring Organizational Learning
Importance of Program Evaluation
Developing a Data Collection Plan
Reporting Program Performance
Conclusion—and New Beginning
RESPONSIBLE BUSINESS ENTERPRISE CHECKLIST 242

Appendices   247

A   Sample Ethical Decision-Making Model   249

B   Basic Guidelines for Codes of Business Conduct   253

C   Sample Integrity Pact   259

D   Sample Declaration of Integrity in Business Conduct   265

E   Sample Supply Chain Management Questionnaire   267

F   Basic Information on the U.S. Foreign Corrupt Practices Act   270

G   Fighting Corruption and Safeguarding Integrity   278

H   Extracts from the U.S. Federal Sentencing Guidelines
for Organizations   285

I   Extracts from the Australian Criminal Code   290

NOTES   293

GLOSSARY   310

RESOURCES AND FURTHER READING   318

PERMISSIONS   325

INDEX   326

ABOUT THE AUTHORS   333

List of RBE Worksheets

1   Business Ethics Program Logic Model   78

2   Relevant Context Data Collection   80

3   Stakeholder Pressure Data Collection   82

4   Organizational Culture Questionnaire   84

5   Questions for the Responsible Business Enterprise   86

6   Sample Outline for a Code of Conduct   125

7   RBE Standards and Expectations Worksheet   127

8   Business Ethics Infrastructure Worksheet   146

9   Communications Needs Assessment Worksheet   178

10   Training Program Outcomes Worksheet   179

11   Communications Infrastructure Worksheet   181

12   Enterprise Alignment Worksheet   206

13   Responsible Business Practices Worksheet   225

14   Organizational Culture Worksheet   243

15   Process Evaluation   244

16   Outcomes Evaluation   245

ABBREVIATIONS AND ACRONYMS

ACFE	Association of Certified Fraud Examiners
AML	anti–money laundering
CEO	chief executive officer
CERES	Coalition for Environmentally Responsible Economies
CSR	corporate social responsibility
FCPA	Foreign Corrupt Practices Act
FSGO	Federal Sentencing Guidelines for Organizations
GPA	Agreement on Government Procurement
GRI	Global Reporting Initiative
ICC	International Chamber of Commerce
IEEE	Institute of Electrical and Electronic Engineers
ILO	International Labor Organization
ISO	International Standards Organization
LCE	large, complex enterprise
NGO	nongovernmental organization
NTT	Nippon Telegraph & Telephone
NYSE	New York Stock Exchange
OECD	Organization for Economic Cooperation and Development
RBE	responsible business enterprise
RICO	Racketeer Influenced and Corrupt Organizations Act
SABA	Strategic Alliance of Business Associations
SAI	Social Accountability International
SEC	U.S. Securities and Exchange Commission
SME	small to medium-sized enterprise
WTO	World Trade Organization

I

The Responsible Business Enterprise

Responsible Business Conduct in an Emerging Market Economy

*T*his chapter explains what it means to be a responsible business enterprise (RBE) in an emerging market economy. It describes the role of responsible business conduct as owners and managers strive to improve business performance, make profits, and contribute to economic progress in their communities.

It lays a foundation for the chapters that follow by examining the legacies of a command economy and the challenges those legacies present to businesses. The chapter concludes that a responsible business can contribute to a successful evolution to a market economy by improving its business performance; by helping build social capital in its economy; and by working with leaders in business, government, and civil society to develop essential market-oriented institutions.

Evolution to a Market Economy

Where a society wants to evolve from a command to a market economy, the challenges presented to individual enterprises can be daunting. All economies face the same fundamental issues of responsible business conduct—product quality, transparency in financial matters, workplace health and safety, protection of the environment, protection of workers, and compliance with laws and industry standards. However, they are magnified in both degree and kind when an entire society is making a rapid evolution toward a market economy.

- **Evolution to a Market Economy**

- **Transition to a Market Economy**

- **The Individual Business in an Emerging Market Economy**

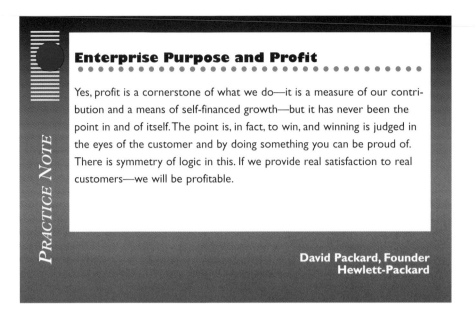

Enterprise Purpose and Profit

Yes, profit is a cornerstone of what we do—it is a measure of our contribution and a means of self-financed growth—but it has never been the point in and of itself. The point is, in fact, to win, and winning is judged in the eyes of the customer and by doing something you can be proud of. There is symmetry of logic in this. If we provide real satisfaction to real customers—we will be profitable.

David Packard, Founder
Hewlett-Packard

RESPONSIBLE BUSINESS CONDUCT IN A MARKET ECONOMY

Whereas the market economy has proved to be an essential condition for meeting the needs of the most people, valuable lessons have been learned along the way, often at great social cost. Societies and individual business enterprises have learned that it matters *how* profits are made, *how* wealth is distributed, and *whether* business can be sustained.

Business enterprises today are expected to meet standards of responsible business conduct that go beyond what had been expected traditionally. Although people more often than not still speak of business in terms of products, jobs, and profits, it is understood and accepted across the globe that a business enterprise remains a member of its community. The pursuit of profits and economic progress is not a license to ignore community norms, values, and standards of respect, integrity, and quality.

Improved business performance, profits, and economic progress come to those who effectively and efficiently foster and meet the reasonable expectations of their primary stakeholders—customers, employees, suppliers, investors, and the environment, as well as the owners and managers themselves (see Box 1.1). Success for any business is ultimately measured in profits and losses, and the socially responsible business generates the capital and revenues required to operate and stay in business over the long haul. The socially responsible business must generate enough revenue to cover the real cost of capital, the risks and uncertainties of future economic activity, and the needs of its workers and pensioners. The socially irresponsible enterprise,

---

BOX 1.1

BUSINESS ENTERPRISE STAKEHOLDERS

Stakeholders are all those involved in, affected by, or able to influence the business enterprise, including:

- Customers and consumers
- Owners, shareholders, and creditors

- Employees and agents
- Suppliers
- Competitors
- Media and advocacy groups
- Government

- Families
- Communities
- Society
- Environment

---

however, fails to cover these costs because it is unable to meet the reasonable expectations of its stakeholders.[1]

For example, an effective, efficient, and responsible enterprise generates revenue by satisfying customers. It attracts capital by meeting investor expectations for return on investment. It increases effectiveness by attracting the best employees. It reduces costs by reducing mistakes, misconduct, and misunderstandings.

An RBE holds some enduring purpose beyond profit to define the enterprise and inspire and guide its employees and agents, because a purpose beyond profit sustains business enterprises.[2] Enterprise purpose, moreover, helps employees and agents have a deeper understanding of the intent

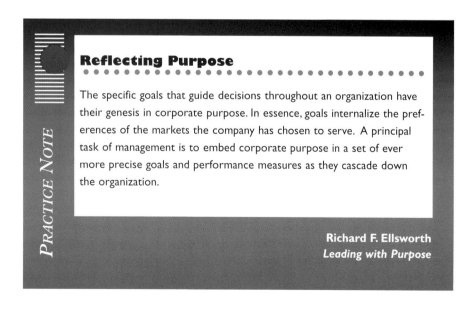

PRACTICE NOTE

Reflecting Purpose

The specific goals that guide decisions throughout an organization have their genesis in corporate purpose. In essence, goals internalize the preferences of the markets the company has chosen to serve. A principal task of management is to embed corporate purpose in a set of ever more precise goals and performance measures as they cascade down the organization.

Richard F. Ellsworth
Leading with Purpose

behind specific goals, measures, and actions. "With this understanding," one author notes, "comes a greater acceptance of and, if they are consistent with the person's values, commitment to the individual goals."[3]

THE BUSINESS ETHICS PROGRAM

An RBE is characterized by responsible business conduct at all four levels of its identity[4] as an enterprise:

1. Compliance with the law
2. Risk management
3. Reputation enhancement
4. Value added to the community

Responsible business conduct includes the choices and actions of owners, managers, employees, and agents that are (a) within their authority, (b) well informed, (c) intended to pursue the enterprise purpose and meet reasonable stakeholder expectations, and (d) sustainable over time. Responsible business conduct allows an enterprise to improve its business performance, make profits, and contribute to the economic progress of its community.

Among the lessons learned by both business and government is that responsible business conduct can be encouraged by the structures and systems, procedures, and practices of responsible business conduct, often called

---

BOX 1.2

TRIPLE BOTTOM LINE

There is a new phrase appearing in business language or "business speak." It is the concept of Triple Bottom Line, a concept that recognises that there are three legs to the measurement of a company's performance—these being financial, social, and environmental. Put in a more friendly way Triple Bottom Line is about "People, Planet and Profits." This concept recognises that a company cannot be judged by financial performance alone. Furthermore, it also recognises that the three legs are linked. It is not sufficient, however, just to talk about Triple Bottom Line as a "nice, warm, fuzzy" concept. For those of us who see this concept as the way of the future it is also necessary to "walk the talk." So this is it—the Hubbard Foods Ltd. Triple Bottom

Line Report—a first attempt to translate this concept into the reality of running a business such as ours.

This report has also taken some soul searching on our behalf and also, I believe, some bravery. In business, we have traditionally been taught to only present the Company in the best possible light, particularly to that important group of stakeholders— the customer. It's hard to be honest and self critical in a public way. It's easy to highlight your successes but hard to highlight your failures and your areas for improvement. In the case of a private company it is also hard to publicly disclose our financial information.

Hubbard Foods Ltd. (New Zealand)
"CEO's Statement"

good corporate governance or *best practices*. Moreover, many businesses now account for the impact they have on all their stakeholders, including their social impact—how they deal with employees, suppliers, and the community—and their environmental impact—how they treat the environment.[5]

A management tool owners and managers use to encourage responsible business conduct is commonly called a *business ethics program*. A business ethics program also helps owners and managers address the *triple bottom line:* the financial, social, and environmental results or impacts of the business's operations (see Box 1.2).

Business owners and managers have learned that a business ethics program helps owners and managers improve their business performance, make profits, and contribute to economic progress by better

- Recognizing political, economic, social, and technological pressures
- Understanding organizational culture: core beliefs, participation, responsibility, knowledge sharing, and methods of dealing with conflict
- Fostering reasonable stakeholder expectations
- Developing responsible management practices to meet stakeholder expectations
- Learning from enterprise decisions and activities

THE GLOBAL MARKETPLACE

The market economy has become increasingly global. Leaders in business, government, and nongovernmental organizations (NGOs) now see global economic development as "the best way to increase prosperity within and among countries, and to create opportunities for millions of people, especially in the developing world, to secure a decent life for themselves and their children."[6] The challenge is to find the right balance between emerging global norms, values, and standards and local cultures, business practices, and community needs.[7]

Businesses in emerging market economies face many challenges, as discussed in more detail later in this chapter. For example, although no society *approves* of paying or accepting bribes, in societies where workers receive lower than subsistence-level pay, "expediting fees" (also known as "bribes") often become unapproved but *accepted* behavior under local custom. In such societies, bribery is so common that even law enforcement officials pay bribes to gain their positions.

While this manual describes processes reflecting emerging global standards, the design and implementation of a business ethics program requires extreme sensitivity to local norms, values, and standards. The program must

PRACTICE NOTE

Cultural Differences

Given the country and industry differences found, from a managerial perspective, it appears to be a mistake to expect all corporate ethics policies to look alike. Careful thought should be given to tailoring the policy to the particular firm, industry, and country. Large multinational firms operating in a number of countries need to consider the general applicability of a code of ethics or ethics training that was developed in the country in which the firm's headquarters is located. If ethical concerns differ by country, then imposing a set of standards developed for one country on another country may be counterproductive. Similarly, expatriates working for multinational firms need to be aware that their own perception of ethical issues may not match that of their native fellow employees.

Bodo B. Schlegelmilch and Diana G. Robertson
"The Influence of Country and Industry on Ethical
Perceptions of Senior Executives in the U.S. and Europe"

recognize that management policies, standards, and procedures will be open to interpretation at all levels of the enterprise. For example, a superficial approach to responsible business conduct condemns bribes and threatens to punish those who pay or accept them. However, a business ethics program takes a comprehensive approach. It recognizes such accepted behavior as part of the challenges facing the enterprise and addresses such issues systemically. In other words, it addresses them at their roots by examining hiring processes, compensation schemes, and training and education; by instituting monitoring, auditing, and reporting mechanisms; and by influencing the legislative or regulatory processes.[8]

A business ethics program does not set up either the enterprise or its employees and agents for failure. Rather, it strives to place the right people in the right positions in the enterprise to foster and meet reasonable stakeholder expectations as the surest means to improved business performance, profits, and economic progress. It scans the relevant context of the enterprise and its organizational culture to identify challenges and to develop responsible ways to meet them. It starts from the assumption that enterprises are integral parts of their communities. It encourages them to work within the community to overcome the challenges of emerging market economies and contribute to community-driven development.

Moreover, a business ethics program takes care not to mistake cultural, legal, or religious differences for a lack of ethics. In Islamic countries, for example, *mudaraba* (reflecting a *Sharia* law requirement that a lender charge no interest) may result in forms of payment that could be mistaken by those unfamiliar with the culture as inappropriate or unethical (that is, as "kickbacks").[9] A common cultural difference is the attitude toward hiring relatives. In some cultures, it is expected that owners and managers will hire relatives as a matter of course. In others, hiring relatives, which is known as *nepotism*, is discouraged or, in some circumstances, prohibited.

RESPONSIBLE BUSINESS AS PART OF THE SOLUTION

As long as businesses concentrate their attention and efforts on dealing with everyday challenges rather than striving to rise above them, they may be part of the problem. For example, although paying a small bribe to get a permit or to evade taxes may be "just the way things are done" or something that "everyone does," businesses that do so may perpetuate business practices and conduct that make the evolution to a market economy more difficult.

The ultimate issue for an RBE in an emerging market economy is whether it sees itself as part of the current problem or part of the solution. We hope this manual inspires all enterprises to see themselves as part of the solution and provides them with a process and a toolkit to develop a road map to guide their employees and agents, improve their business performance, make profits, and increase the prosperity of their communities.

THE SMALL TO MEDIUM-SIZED ENTERPRISE

The "place business should occupy in society"[10] is a particularly challenging issue for the small to medium-sized enterprise (SME).[11] Each SME is unique, often taking on the character of its owners and managers. There is surpris-

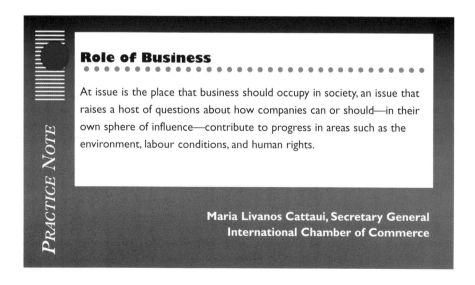

PRACTICE NOTE

Role of Business

At issue is the place that business should occupy in society, an issue that raises a host of questions about how companies can or should—in their own sphere of influence—contribute to progress in areas such as the environment, labour conditions, and human rights.

**Maria Livanos Cattaui, Secretary General
International Chamber of Commerce**

ingly little research into the social responsibility of the SME.[12] Moreover, it is difficult, at best, to generalize the SME experience from country to country or even between regions within a particular country.[13]

SMEs in emerging markets are pioneers; they are plowing new ground as they contribute to developing a market economy. In most economies, they provide the bulk of jobs, especially new jobs, and contribute significantly to the welfare of their communities because they are so closely connected. However, SMEs often lack the capital, staff, or time of large, complex enterprises (LCEs) to address many business issues. For example, tracking and complying with changing laws and regulations are relatively more costly for SMEs. SMEs seldom have the close relationships with government that LCEs have, especially those recently privatized. They are often unable to defend themselves against unreasonable decrees, laws, or regulations or to advocate for changes that would facilitate the transition to a market economy.

Though many of the best practices developed over the past two decades reflect the experiences of LCEs, there are a number of reasons why an SME might profit by adapting what the LCEs have learned:

- The SME of today is more apt to become the LCE of tomorrow by adopting emerging global standards and adapting the best practices of successful LCEs.

- By adopting global standards and adapting best practices where they make sense, owners and managers are able to distinguish their SME from the competition.

- By understanding the basic principles and practices of the emerging global marketplace, owners and managers will be better able to recognize responsible business conduct issues earlier and to work with others to find solutions.

- Especially in a business environment that some perceive as high risk, first impressions count. Developing a business ethics program will help owners and managers present a core set of beliefs and standards more clearly, thus demonstrating to investors and customers their enterprise's commitment to being an RBE in the global marketplace.

- If an SME's people are conversant in the language of emerging global standards and best practices, they will be better able to speak the language of the global markets—and the opportunities to be found there.

Whereas the process of developing standards, procedures, and expectations is the same for all enterprises, the answers for each enterprise will depend on the size and complexity of the enterprise itself. The goal for the SME is not to duplicate the standards, procedures, infrastructure, practices, and expectations of LCEs, but to learn from them—and to improve them.

The CEO statement in Box 1.2, for example, is a part of the report to stakeholders of a 100-person New Zealand food-processing firm.[14]

Moreover, SMEs will find that they need not act alone in adopting the world-class standards, procedures, infrastructure, practices, and expectations described in these materials. Chambers of commerce, business associations, colleges and universities, NGOs, and other professional advisers can use the guide to help SMEs find their way.

Transition to a Market Economy

For the enterprise in an emerging market economy struggling to make payroll, not to mention a profit, global economic development is, at once, an opportunity, a risk, and a challenge. As an opportunity, it offers tantalizing prospects for new markets and access to international capital. The risk, however, is heightened competition and capital flow reversals from the slightest perceived political, economic, or social threat. The challenge is to learn from the experiences of successful businesses in market economies and to adapt them to overcome the legacies of the command economy. By learning from others' experiences (including the mistakes), enterprises in emerging markets can contribute to the development of their own market economies and can join the global marketplace.

A business can influence—but not control—the political, economic, and social contexts in which it operates (its *relevant context*). Business leaders

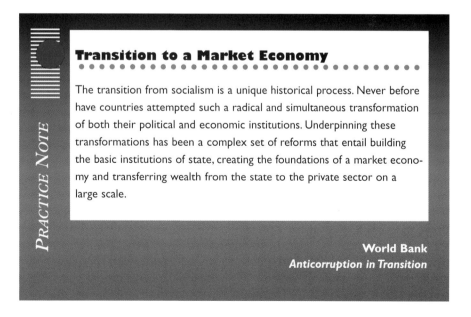

PRACTICE NOTE

Transition to a Market Economy

The transition from socialism is a unique historical process. Never before have countries attempted such a radical and simultaneous transformation of both their political and economic institutions. Underpinning these transformations has been a complex set of reforms that entail building the basic institutions of state, creating the foundations of a market economy and transferring wealth from the state to the private sector on a large scale.

World Bank
Anticorruption in Transition

must work with NGOs and government legislators and regulators to develop a political, economic, and social context in which responsible businesses can compete fairly—and succeed. Businesses and societies that do not meet or aspire to meet these global standards and expectations are unlikely to be ready to participate fully in the global marketplace.

LEGACIES OF CENTRAL PLANNING

Central planning and state-owned production characterized command economies.[15] Resources were allocated by plan instead of by markets. Employment was generally full but effectively rationed through an internal passport system. Capital was allocated centrally through a single institution. Enterprises were responsible for production but not for marketing or pricing. Since planning was based on quantity, not quality, enterprises had little incentive for innovation; indeed, innovation or quality improvement was often punished with higher quotas or standards.[16]

The law restricted or abolished human and property rights and the sanctity of contract. It limited individual rights rather than state power. The legal system lacked procedural and institutional tools to protect individual property and human rights and support the sanctity of contract. The legislative framework was not oriented toward private enterprise, and regulators, judges, and lawyers had little knowledge of, or experience in, free market concepts.[17]

When governments abruptly halted central planning of an entire economy, they left a legacy of cultural, institutional, and economic hurdles for market-oriented reform. The networks of business relationships that form the core of a market economy were largely nonexistent, and enterprises had to develop them without the benefit of markets and supportive institutional and legal frameworks.

Economic Structure Precluded Competition, Entry, and Exit

The competition and innovation to meet the most important needs of customers and consumers, which characterize a market economy, were either unlawful or discouraged in command economies. For relative ease of control, state-owned enterprises tended to be large. New, competitive firms were few and were found more often in the unofficial or "shadow economy." Even state-owned enterprises survived through an informal bartering system, which remains, in large part, to this day.[18] Exit—that is, failure—was seldom feasible because the economy was expected to maintain full employment and because of the official embarrassment that would arise from a failure. There was little competition from foreign producers, since trade relations were governed and restricted by planners.

In many emerging market economies, it is still relatively difficult for a firm to enter the market. The number of procedures, time of entry, and cost of entry vary, but they often greatly exceed what is required to set up an enterprise in a market economy.[19] Enterprises are still expected to provide work and housing to some extent. When the high costs of entry are combined with low levels of "latent entrepreneurship" (an individual preference for self-employment as opposed to employment),[20] domestic competitive forces develop slowly, and open markets become less an opportunity than a threat.

Producers Had Little Contact with Stakeholders

In a command economy, individual enterprises rarely had direct contact with suppliers, customers, or consumers—some of the stakeholders in a business enterprise. For many owners and managers, the concept of a stakeholder is novel, even strange. Entrepreneurs now have to develop these essential relationships, and many others, where none existed before:

- **Customers and consumers.** Recently privatized enterprises had to shift their attention and efforts from satisfying the express preferences of planners—especially in heavy industry—to identifying and satisfying the preferences of customers and consumers.

- **Employees and agents.** In a centrally planned economy, where the quantity of goods produced is more important than their quality or fitness for customer purpose, managers could afford to look at employees as "hands." Independent judgment was often discouraged, and objectivity was seldom valued. People were not expected to bring unique qualities to their jobs. Indeed, until relatively recently, industrial economies saw employees much the same way. In today's market economies, however, a business enterprise needs to tap all the human potential available to it to compete effectively. Enterprises now recognize that they must invest in their employees and agents and "create a work environment that respects the dignity and contribution of each individual."[21]

- **Suppliers and service providers.** With the abolition of central planning, an enterprise needs to develop a chain of suppliers, since it can now choose what suppliers and service providers it wants to work with—and vice versa.

- **Shareholders and owners.** Often, the privatization methods used by many transitioning economies failed to ensure the presence of a *strategic owner*: a single shareholder with sufficient stake to provide motivation for monitoring management effectively. Conversely, some voucher privatization schemes resulted in abusive corporate takeovers whereby an individual was able to purchase small shares of a major state asset at a low cost and to take control of that asset through abuse of the legal process and through corrupt practices. In either event, privatization schemes often failed to require effective corporate governance systems.

Where there is separation of ownership and management without accountability, there is little incentive for managers to make decisions to the benefit of shareholders who have no voice. Managers are, in such cases, able to use the assets of the enterprise to their own purposes.

- **Lenders and investors.** Since in a command economy success for an enterprise was measured by meeting production quotas, businesses had little or no experience with the risk management aspects of lending and investing. Corporate governance encouraging financial transparency is developing slowly, but a continuing barter system makes financial analysis for capital and credit difficult.

- **Government officials and agencies.** Under a command economy, the political system fundamentally favored incumbent firms. At the local level, relationships were very close between politicians or bureaucrats and senior management. Though most state enterprises have by now been privatized, many of these close relationships between politicians and business managers remain in place. In some societies, many large enterprises strive to "capture" the state by securing the passage of laws or by obtaining licenses that benefit them over other enterprises.[22] In others, the state has effectively captured the economy by controlling a dominant crop or natural resource, for example, even though economic resources are nominally owned by the private sector.

Market-Oriented Legislative, Procedural, and Institutional Tools Did Not Exist

A market economy requires a high degree of confidence in the rule of law for business to meet its economic, social, and environmental responsibilities. In many emerging market economies, the vast majority of people do not trust one another. The distrust surrounding the enforceability of contracts, for example, leads to large portions of the population believing that negotiations are not over even after a contract is signed. Transaction costs to protect one party from the other in such circumstances are much higher as a result.

A legal framework oriented toward free markets and reliable judicial institutions is essential for this confidence to develop over time. Such a framework will need

- Contract laws
- Laws regarding the formation, operation, management, and dissolution of corporations
- Laws on privatization
- Real estate laws
- Laws against unfair competition

You Decide

International Labor Organization standards protect the right of workers to bargain collectively. In at least one country in East Asia, employee unions are forbidden by statute. If the employees want to bargain as a group, how should the RBE relate to its workers? Should it bargain with the group of employees?

- Labor–management laws
- Tax laws
- Accounting and auditing standards
- Laws protecting intellectual property rights
- Bankruptcy laws
- Environmental protection legislation and regulation
- Laws ensuring fiduciary responsibilities of managers and directors
- Rules governing the rights and obligations of shareholders, managers, and boards of directors
- Laws permitting class-action suits

You Decide

An electric power distributor is the sole provider in a capital city. It requires customers to sign a contract that binds them, but it sets forth no obligations on the part of the distributor. Are there circumstances under which such a contract should not be enforced?

A confusing, burdensome, or even unfair legislative and regulatory framework drives up the cost of setting up a business, dissuades investors, and provides a fertile ground for corruption. As one researcher observes, "Some critics even believe that regulations are intentionally drafted in a confusing manner to provide officials with more discretion."[23] Such a framework is particularly damaging to the SME. Under such circumstances, responsible business conduct is frequently discarded in favor of survival, or the law is bent or interpreted to fit the circumstances.

Even where laws and regulations are well drafted, they are often enforced unevenly—or ignored by the population—in practice. The failure to enforce the legislative and regulatory framework, *or to comply with it*, contributes to confusion, places the law-abiding enterprise at a competitive disadvantage, discourages investors, and extends a climate of corruption.[24]

Although this manual urges building an RBE from an ethical perspective, it is often the case that the state itself must actively support enterprises that are trying to be responsible but that find themselves at a competitive disadvantage. A key to introducing ethics in an emerging market economy, then, is to build a market-oriented legal framework and reliable judicial institutions. Prescriptive rules, which would be undue government interference in a developed economy, may be necessary to ensure that responsible business conduct becomes a norm, a value, and a standard. The RBE works with other leaders to influence government regulation to that end.

No less important than new laws, one researcher notes, is a judiciary proficient at interpreting and enforcing the law with integrity.[25] The creation of effective dispute resolution mechanisms that can offer businesses transparent, predictable, and cost-effective results is one of the most important steps a government can take to support market processes in an emerging market economy.[26] Finally, government agencies must exercise their authority and responsibility to execute the judgments reached.

Climate of Illegal Activity Persists

A final legacy of central planning is a climate of illegal activity. This legacy stems from the autocratic nature of the state and the unaccountability of its officials in a command economy, the remaining close ties between government and business, the incomplete legal and institutional reforms, the political and economic instability, and the ineffective implementation of market-oriented reforms.[27]

Among the consequences of a command economy was the emergence of an unofficial or "shadow economy," which was, by definition, unlawful. Current entry barriers increase the potential for administrative corruption, where entrepreneurs are tempted to pay bribes to overcome administrative barriers.[28] Higher entry costs are associated with higher corruption and larger unofficial sectors of the economy.

With the collapse of central planning and the lack of external constraints, insiders and managers during the transition to a market economy often took the opportunity to appropriate state-owned enterprises for their benefit, leading to asset stripping and rent diversion. Often, important natural resources or whole industrial sectors were converted by insiders and managers.[29]

DEVELOPMENT OF MARKET-ORIENTED INSTITUTIONS

To raise the living standards of its people, a society must provide the conditions for a functioning market. In a free market, the role of government in the marketplace is limited to protecting it from those who would attack or abuse it. "The state creates and preserves the environment in which the market can safely operate."[30] A free market minimizes the role of command and maximizes the scope for exchange of goods and service to meet important needs through transactions free of duress and not otherwise unconscionable.[31] A suitable institutional framework for a market economy would typically contain at least the following seven components:[32]

1. A transparent regulatory system, including securities regulation
2. A sophisticated accounting and banking profession
3. A stock exchange with meaningful listing standards
4. Labor–management regulations
5. A system of protection for intellectual property
6. Effective legal and judiciary systems
7. A broad-based tax system

Emerging market economies are struggling to provide these conditions to overcome the legacies of central planning, but institutional development takes time to design and implement. How successful an emerging economy is at developing an institutional framework depends, at least in part, on whether (and how long) it had been a sovereign state, how well developed its institutions of public administration were, and how many valuable natural resources it can privatize.[33]

In the meantime, many owners and managers struggle with the question, "What does it mean to be a responsible business?" It is a sign of a healthy dialogue that leaders in businesses, governments, and civil society are asking the same question, not just in emerging market economies, but also across the globe.

The Individual Business in an Emerging Market Economy

The RBE recognizes its many roles and responsibilities in the community—and engages its stakeholders—adding as much value as possible. Through creativity, flexibility, and responsiveness in its day-to-day operations, it can add value to the community in many ways:

- Serving the most important needs of its customers and consumers
- Providing gainful employment for its employees and agents, so that they can provide for their families and be responsible citizens
- Providing an adequate return to investors
- Purchasing goods and services from its suppliers and service providers
- Competing intensely, but fairly
- Forming strategic partnerships and alliances to create new business opportunities
- Supporting community infrastructure through taxes and fees
- Participating in the political process to improve market conditions
- Respecting the environment[34]

The trust-engendering manner in which an RBE engages its stakeholders is a substantial contribution to the community in and of itself. Such enterprises help lay a foundation for a functioning market economy for all.

In an emerging market economy, an RBE must confront and rise above the legacies of a command economy. As a part of the solution to its economy's problems, it can participate in three essential ways: improving its business performance; helping build social capital in its economy; and working with leaders in business, government, and civil society to develop the essential market-oriented legal framework and reliable judicial institutions.

IMPROVING BUSINESS PERFORMANCE

An essential contribution of any business enterprise in the evolution to a market economy is to improve its own business performance.[35] For all business enterprises, this is the first step toward making profits and contributing to economic progress. Performance can be improved by expanding and better engaging stakeholders as follows:

- Establishing clear standards and procedures to guide employees and agents
- Focusing on anticipating and meeting the needs and desires of customers and consumers more effectively and efficiently
- Attracting, hiring, and bringing out the best in employees, suppliers, and service providers
- Establishing internal control mechanisms to build confidence among dispersed owners and investors
- Developing and maintaining strategic alliances with enterprises sharing the same values

These best practices are at the heart of a business ethics program. They can significantly improve an enterprise's prospects for success, as described in more detail in Chapter 2. They can help an enterprise improve its reputation, manage its risk, protect itself from its own employees and agents, strengthen its competitive position, expand its access to capital and credit, increase profits, sustain long-term growth, and gain international respect.

HELPING BUILD SOCIAL CAPITAL

Respect, shared values, and mutual trust among individuals, businesses, NGOs, and government officials are the foundation of a market economy. To compete effectively and sustain economic growth, enterprises need social capital as well as financial capital. To contribute to this social capital, an RBE can

- Make the case in its community for a market economy and the role of responsible business.
- Develop a reputation for meeting the reasonable expectations of its stakeholders.
- Agree to voluntary forms of alternative dispute resolution, such as mediation and arbitration, while domestic courts are formed.
- Take responsibility for its mistakes and misconduct.
- Be willing to be held accountable for its mistakes and misconduct.

- Correct misunderstandings about its decisions and activities.
- Compete fairly with competition, both foreign and domestic.

How effectively, efficiently, and responsibly an enterprise is able to add value to its community depends, in large part, on how much its stakeholders trust one another. As described further in Chapter 2, where market participants and community members cannot trust one another, transaction costs soar. It may be that in markets and communities, especially in emerging market economies, the value an RBE most profitably adds is to be worthy of trust—and to encourage other market participants and community members to be trustworthy as well.

WORKING WITH LEADERS IN BUSINESS, GOVERNMENT, AND CIVIL SOCIETY

An RBE helps government create the conditions for a market economy by promoting responsible business conduct—through self-regulation or by conducting a public dialogue with government officials and NGOs. Even where the legal framework of decrees, laws, and regulations is unfair, supporting the rule of law is an important practice for an RBE. Faced with an unfair legal framework, for example, businesses can work with other businesses and NGOs to point out the ethical dimensions of the decree, law, or regulation and to work for change.

Responsible businesses can serve as a voice for the community. They can work with leaders in government, business, and NGOs to do the following:

- Help develop the necessary institutional and legal frameworks for a market economy.
- Support initiatives to develop good public governance on the part of government itself.
- Strengthen NGOs to provide community-building services that business and government are unable to provide.[36]

In economies where the government is unable to provide the social services a community requires, an RBE can work with other businesses and NGOs to identify community needs and can work with community-based organizations to provide such services. For example, the RBE can contribute supplies or services as a part of community-driven development, or it can contribute funds to community foundations. Some enterprises create their own charity programs or foundations or support volunteer work by employees.

SUMMARY

Across the globe, businesses are expected to be responsible—to improve their performance, to make profits, and to contribute to the economic progress of their communities by learning how to meet the reasonable expectations of their stakeholders: their customers, employees, suppliers, investors, and the environment, among others. Moreover, an enterprise does not cease being a member of its community simply by virtue of entering into business. It is still responsible for meeting community norms, values, and standards.

An RBE in an emerging market economy has many legacies of a command economy to overcome while the state develops a legal framework and institutions that are market-oriented. An RBE can participate in the transition to a market economy by improving its business performance; by helping build social capital in its economy; and by working with leaders in business, government, and civil society to develop the essential market-oriented legal framework and reliable judicial institutions.

RESPONSIBLE BUSINESS ENTERPRISE
Checklist

1. **List as quickly as possible your own heroes or heroines. Is this easy? If not, what does that imply about what it means to be the owner or manager of a responsible business enterprise?**[37]

2. **What challenges does your enterprise face in the years ahead?**

3. **Who are the stakeholders of your enterprise?**

4. **What do you see as the role of business in your society? What, if anything, do you owe your stakeholders?**

5. **What standards and procedures have you established to guide your employees and agents?**

6. **What do your stakeholders expect of your enterprise, employees, and agents? Are they reasonable expectations? What do you do to foster reasonable expectations?**

7. **How do you know what your stakeholders expect? How do you know you are meeting their expectations?**

Responsible Management and the Responsible Business Enterprise

2

*T*his chapter explores how an enterprise becomes a responsible business. It explores how a business ethics program helps the responsible business enterprise (RBE) improve its business performance; help build social capital in its economy; and work with leaders in business, government, and civil society to develop a market framework and the supporting legal infrastructure. It examines specific sets of global standards and best practices of business ethics programs, and it concludes with eight questions that responsible owners and managers must ask themselves for their enterprise.

Improving Business Performance

There is much support for the notion that the discipline of responsible business conduct outlined here contributes to improving business performance and expanding opportunities for growth.[1] Principal benefits coming to an enterprise that implements a business ethics program are

- Enhanced reputation and goodwill
- Reduced risks
- Reduced costs
- Protection from unethical employees and agents
- Enhanced performance, productivity, and competitive position
- Expanded access to capital, credit, and foreign investment
- Increased profits and sustained long-term growth
- Increased international respect

- **Improving Business Performance**

- **Generating Social Capital**

- **Working with Leaders in Business, Government, and Civil Society**

- **Building on the Foundation of Responsible Business Conduct**

- **Adopting Global Standards and Best Practices**

21

Importance of Reputation

Reputation is now more important than ever as a result of an increasing number of laws that regulate our business, higher expectations from our customers and the general public about the way we do business, and a business environment characterized by global expansion, technological advances, and increased competition. But it has always been, and continues to be, our policy to conduct business in compliance with all applicable laws and regulations and in accordance with the highest ethical standards. We expect—as we always have—that UPSers, and the people acting on our behalf, will adhere to these principles.

United Parcel Service Inc.
Code of Business Conduct

ENHANCED REPUTATION AND GOODWILL

An enterprise's reputation for integrity is important for securing the loyalty of customers, for recruiting and retaining the most professional and honest employees, for becoming the business partner of choice, for winning local community acceptance, and for increasing access to capital and credit.

A business ethics program contributes to the enterprise's reputation for integrity. By giving adequate guidance to employees and agents, it ensures that they know what is responsible business conduct. By helping form reasonable expectations among its stakeholders, it minimizes disputes with customers and other stakeholders and increases stakeholder satisfaction.[2]

REDUCED RISKS

Every business, even if it strives to comply strictly with the law, is subject to risks such as these:

- Being exposed to criminal prosecution for bribing a government contracting officer
- Being debarred from government contracting or a strategic partnership for an inappropriate gift or gratuity
- Having to recall products for failure to follow quality standards and procedures

Stakeholder Satisfaction and the Bottom Line

Everyone in business knows it is far easier to retain a loyal customer than to win one. This principle can be extended. According to Frederick Reichheld, U.S. companies lose, on average, 50 percent of their customers every five years, 50 percent of their employees every four years, and 50 percent of their investors every year. But the most successful companies have significantly lower turnovers.

Anita Roddick, Chief Executive Officer
The Body Shop
"A Third Way for Business, Too"

- Having to clean up spills of toxic waste
- Dealing with employee claims of sexual harassment
- Dealing with lost employee time for health and safety problems
- Being placed on a blacklist of international, national, or local organizations

An RBE develops processes with which it identifies, assesses, and manages the full range of factors that might pose a risk to social and financial performance. The processes include assessing risks, establishing adequate standards and procedures, training, and monitoring and auditing systems. These processes help owners and managers plan, organize, and control the day-to-day operations of an enterprise to minimize risks to its capital, earnings, and reputation. They include management of risks associated with accidental losses, as well as operational risks such as those arising from financial mismanagement, fraud and embezzlement, corruption, and loss of reputation.

REDUCED COSTS

By providing employees clear guidelines on how to conduct day-to-day business in compliance with laws and ethics through a business ethics program, the RBE can reduce transaction costs. A business ethics program institutes procedures to detect and to prevent violations of the law and ethics. It provides employees with clear guidelines on a host of day-to-day transactions: how to conduct bids and tenders; how to conclude contracts;

how to use confidential information; how to avoid conflicts of interest; and how to work with customers, suppliers, service providers, and competitors.

The cost of bribery, kickbacks, and other forms of illegal or corrupt conduct is not only the amount paid. The full cost includes management effort to allocate time to work with officials, to maintain a second set of books, and to deal with the threat of extortion and blackmail. The real cost is the risk to reputation and pride in the enterprise and the reduced prospects for participating in a market economy.

PROTECTION FROM UNETHICAL EMPLOYEES AND AGENTS

It is not pleasant to contemplate, but the enterprise itself is often abused by its employees and agents. Embezzlement of enterprise funds is a major example. Cheating on time cards or carrying off supplies and tools, while relatively minor, add up to significant losses sustained every year by businesses—both large and small. It has been estimated that enterprises in the United States lose some 6 percent of their revenues annually to employee misconduct.[3]

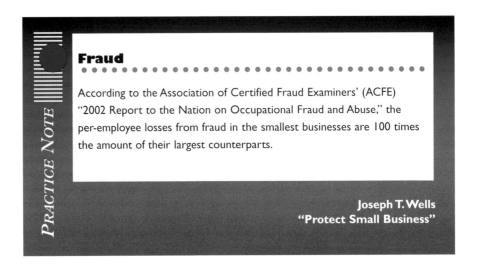

PRACTICE NOTE

Fraud

According to the Association of Certified Fraud Examiners' (ACFE) "2002 Report to the Nation on Occupational Fraud and Abuse," the per-employee losses from fraud in the smallest businesses are 100 times the amount of their largest counterparts.

Joseph T. Wells
"Protect Small Business"

A business ethics program is designed to establish standards and procedures to prevent and detect violations of the trust put in employees. Among these standards and procedures are processes to protect enterprise assets. These specific processes may include establishing standards and procedures, monitoring and auditing systems, and reporting mechanisms.

However, at the heart of a business ethics program is the desire of owners and managers to foster the commitment of their employees to the welfare of the enterprise as a whole. Fostering this sense of loyalty and commitment among employees and agents may be the most effective way in which a business ethics program protects the enterprise from disloyal employees.

ENHANCED PERFORMANCE, PRODUCTIVITY, AND COMPETITIVE POSITION

An RBE increases effectiveness and efficiency by enabling all stakeholders to work together closely on the basis of respect, shared values, and mutual trust. Such efforts lead to what one author calls "invisible savings" by reducing employee conduct that is harmful to the enterprise but difficult to detect.[4] After a business ethics program becomes a part of operations, many of the costs of monitoring and supervision can be reduced.

Product quality may improve and transaction costs, such as contracting, may decline. For example, many large, complex enterprises (LCEs), most of which have business ethics programs, are developing preferred supplier lists to reduce the number of suppliers that they deal with. To ensure that there is no interruption in supplies and services, these LCEs require that their supply chains adopt the same good management practices that they follow, including a business ethics program.[5] See, for example, Box 2.1, which gives in part Gap Inc.'s code of vendor conduct. See Appendix E for a sample supply chain management questionnaire.

Since, in the minds of most employees, ethics are essentially a matter of fairness,[6] a business ethics program often increases employee morale. Better

---

B O X   2 . 1

SAMPLE VENDOR CODE

This Code of Vendor Conduct applies to all factories that produce goods for Gap Inc. or any of its subsidiaries, divisions, affiliates or agents ("Gap Inc.").

While Gap Inc. recognizes that there are different legal and cultural environments in which factories operate throughout the world, this Code sets forth the basic requirements that all factories must meet in order to do business with Gap Inc. The Code also provides the foundation for Gap Inc.'s ongoing evaluation of a factory's employment practices and environmental compliance.

II. Environment

Factories must comply with all applicable environmental laws and regulations. Where such requirements are less stringent than Gap Inc.'s own, factories are encouraged to meet the standards outlined in Gap Inc.'s statement of environmental principles.

A. The factory has an environmental management system or plan.

B. The factory has procedures for notifying local community authorities in case of accidental discharge or release or any other environmental emergency.

Gap Inc.
"The Gap Code of Vendor Conduct"

morale leads to increased productivity and innovation. It strengthens the enterprise's competitive position in its industry.

EXPANDED ACCESS TO CAPITAL, CREDIT, AND FOREIGN INVESTMENT

A business ethics program, including aggressive risk management processes, may increase an RBE's attractiveness to investors. Before making loans, international lending institutions and domestic banks perform due diligence on whether an enterprise is managed well. They look to see whether an enterprise has strong financial supervision and internal controls. A business ethics program is designed to prevent and detect illegal and unethical practices. Financial institutions may view management as a worthy credit risk and allow access to capital at lower rates.

When entering new markets, foreign investors seek reliable partners who demonstrate integrity and operate on a transparent basis. A business ethics program reflecting global norms and values provides a common language between an enterprise and foreign investors. It creates opportunity to build partnerships that are based on respect, shared values, and mutual trust.

INCREASED PROFITS AND SUSTAINED LONG-TERM GROWTH

The discipline of responsible business conduct does not deliver instant results. However, a business ethics program—including infrastructure and processes for continuous monitoring of compliance with law and ethics— should help an enterprise be more reliable and stable over time.

Once an RBE has demonstrated its ability to detect and to prevent violations of the law and ethics, it tends to earn stakeholder confidence. This confidence leads to an increase in the value of shares; to wider access to capital and credit; to new clients, customers, and partners; and to further opportunities for expansion.

INCREASED INTERNATIONAL RESPECT

Adhering to the discipline of responsible business conduct can help enterprises gain access to international markets. It encourages compliance with laws and regulations that require a high level of transparency. When the generally accepted business practices of a community are based on sound standards and reasonable expectations, fair competition is the norm and the RBE can operate on a level playing field. Fair competition may encourage trading partners to reduce trade barriers such as tariffs and quotas.

Recent research suggests that a business ethics program is particularly valuable in times of merger, acquisition, and restructuring.[7] It is thought that the essential elements of a business ethics program may help members of often distinct organizational cultures manage their differences until they find common ground. These elements include core beliefs, standards, and procedures; high-level personnel responsible for the program; and dedicated resources to help employees seek advice. Enterprises undergoing privatization should also consider the advantages of a business ethics program as a means to reduce the risks associated with this transition process.

Generating Social Capital

To define an RBE's social responsibility, we can think in terms of levels of social responsibility and try to appreciate the role of business in generating social capital. Thinking in terms of levels—social responsibility and ultra-social responsibility—reminds us that if a business were to do no more than accomplish its essential business purpose of meeting the important needs of its customers, it would still be making a significant contribution to the common good.[8]

Appreciating the role of business in generating social capital confirms the stake that an RBE has in its communities and reaffirms the essential social value of responsible business.

SOCIAL RESPONSIBILITY

The essential function of any business is to identify and meet the most important needs of its customers. In a free market, it is only by serving customers well that the enterprise will survive and prosper over time. An RBE is an essential part of a market economy, serving the needs of customers while making a profit for its owners and investors. It does so by cooperating well with its primary stakeholders—employees, suppliers, service providers, and investors—as well as many others.

By entering the marketplace, an RBE does not cease to be a member of its community. Being in business is not a license to ignore community norms, values, and standards. An RBE uses good judgment in evaluating the social impact of its goods and services on customers and the community as a whole. For example, although it may be legal to sell a product such as tobacco or alcohol, an RBE will not sell to minors, who may abuse the product. This practice is known as "socially responsible business."

The socially responsible business works hard and competes fairly. It recognizes that to destroy the fabric of a marketplace to make a profit is shortsighted. It does not abuse the public trust or degrade the environment, which

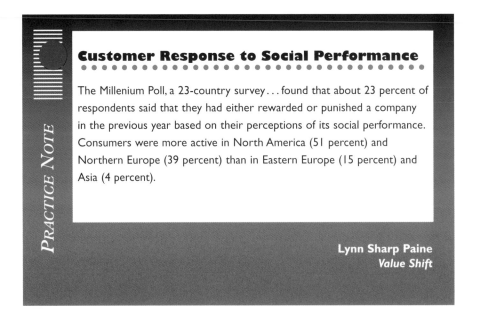

Lynn Sharp Paine
Value Shift

we all rely on. These principles are captured in the following definition of corporate social responsibility:

> A new business strategy in which companies conduct business responsibly by contributing to the economic health and sustainable development of the communities in which they operate, offer employees healthy, safe, and rewarding work conditions, offer quality, safe products, and service . . . are accountable to stakeholders . . . and provide a fair return to shareholders whilst fulfilling the above principles.[9]

As a participant in markets and a member of its community, the socially responsible business expresses its needs and concerns to government when appropriate. It avoids using its economic power to gain competitive advantage through political means.

ULTRA-SOCIAL RESPONSIBILITY

Although the essential purpose of an RBE is to improve its business performance, to return a profit to its owners and investors, and to increase the prosperity of its community by meeting the reasonable expectations of its stakeholders, the RBE is nevertheless concerned about the quality of life in its communities, as the Komatsu code provisions in Box 2.2 illustrate.[10] Its employees and agents also care about the communities in which they and their families live.

Businesses often support literacy programs, local schools and colleges, and local infrastructure, such as water facilities, roads, or parks. They may

You Decide

HIV/AIDS is a growing health problem across the globe. What should the RBE do in the fight against the spread of HIV/AIDS, if anything?

If you believe there is a role for business, does this role represent good business, socially responsible business, or ultra-social responsibility?

BOX   2 . 2

CONCERN FOR THE COMMUNITY

(1) Contribution to the Community

Through its operations as a good corporate citizen, Komatsu responds to the commitment of its stakeholders. Also as a corporate citizen it is expected to contribute to the community. Harmonizing with society is becoming increasingly important.

In an effort to harmonize further with the community, Komatsu Ltd., on its 70th anniversary in 1991, declared its intention to use one percent (1%) of its pre-tax earnings for social contribution. Komatsu will continue to actively work for the community.

Komatsu's purpose and five (5) basic principles concerning social contribution are as follows.

A. Purpose: "Komatsu and its employees, as local community members, will contribute to society"

B. Basic Principles
  1. Consistency
  2. Public interest
  3. Voluntary
  4. Acceptable by employees
  5. Not aimed at advertisement.

(2) Employees' Volunteer Activities

Komatsu will respect employees' self-motivated participation in voluntary charitable activities, and will never require employees to join such activities. Komatsu will prepare various systems to support their participation.

Komatsu Ltd. (Japan)
"Komatsu Code of Worldwide Business Conduct"

---

benefit from these as members of their communities. Supporting literacy programs and education, for example, may lead to better employee applicants. Moreover, in some communities, a socially responsible business is expected or required to contribute a certain percentage of its income to institutions caring for the poor and needy.[11]

In other communities, enterprises support such programs because such involvement makes stakeholders feel better about themselves and the enterprise. For example, one enterprise recently developed a program supporting research on dolphins in the Persian Gulf. Through that contribution to the community, the enterprise not only enhanced its reputation, but also gave great pride to its employees.

Some people confuse this sense of social responsibility with what it means to be a socially responsible business. Nothing could be further from the truth. The important point to remember is that a business is socially responsible simply by virtue of effectively, efficiently, and responsibly meeting the reasonable expectations of its stakeholders.

TRUST AND SOCIAL CAPITAL

Responsible business, as an essential part of a free market, is an investment in growth for a country as well as for an enterprise. Trust cannot be imposed; it must be earned. The RBE makes a singular contribution to the community by positioning itself so that it is able to pursue its purpose as an enterprise over the long run, meeting the most important needs of its customers.

Social capital is "performance-based trust."[12] It is "the ability of people to work together for common purposes in groups and organizations."[13] Each participant in a market or society is responsible for contributing to the pattern of reasonable expectations. In such a community, trust will be rewarded. The RBE strives to be a trustworthy member of its community in order to contribute to its social capital.

Social capital is the foundation of a successful market economy. The benefits of operating in a high-trust environment are many. As one scholar observes, "A high-trust society can organize its workplace on a more flexible and group-oriented basis, with more responsibility delegated to lower levels of the organization. Low-trust societies, by contrast, must fence in and isolate their workers with a series of bureaucratic rules."[14]

Another scholar lists eight studies that demonstrate the link between values in general, trust in particular, and profitability. The link is based on an increase in creativity, support of management decisions, knowledge sharing, and pride, among other factors (see Figure 2.1).[15]

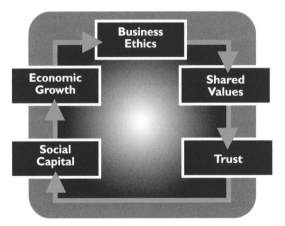

FIGURE 2.1
Links between Values, Trust and Profitability

A climate of trust can be abused, however. Customers who are not attentive may purchase goods or services of poor quality. Employees may steal from their employers. Government agents may take advantage of an enterprise that goes to them for aid. Indeed, it is precisely because people put trust in others that many irresponsible business practices are possible.[16]

The discipline of responsible business conduct described in this manual leads owners and managers to build their enterprises with structures and systems that will compensate for a lack (or abuse) of trust. Over time, such conduct will lead to an organizational culture that is based on shared values and practices; more trust among stakeholders; and more effective, efficient, and profitable performance.

Working with Leaders in Business, Government, and Civil Society

Social capital also accrues through the efforts of civil society: organizations, such as trade groups, business associations, service clubs, charities, university faculty, and other nongovernmental organizations (NGOs) that aim to hold business and government officials accountable. Business enterprises, in general, have the potential to be powerful and influential members of their communities.

The RBE helps create the conditions for good public governance by promoting responsible business conduct—through self-regulation or through public dialogue with government officials. These forms of voluntary action help build social capital—the trust and shared values among individuals, government officials, civil society, the local community, and business that make it possible to work together on a cooperative basis.

Building on the Foundation of Responsible Business Conduct

Though a business enterprise is often portrayed as an isolated entity doing whatever it can to make a profit, the enterprise, whether large or small, is an integral part of its market, its community, and its society.[17] As such, the social responsibilities of a business are to improve its performance, to make profits, and to increase the prosperity of its community by meeting the reasonable expectations of its stakeholders.

RESPONSIBLE BUSINESS CONDUCT IS GOOD MANAGEMENT

Responsible business conduct addresses the issues of ethics, compliance with laws and regulations, and social responsibility. Businesses face these issues every day in a market economy. This manual sees responsible business conduct as a discipline, as something responsible owners and managers can build on, and as an integral part of good management practice. Approaching responsible business conduct as a discipline broadens the thought processes of owners and managers by addressing the issues raised by business and professional ethics, organizational ethics, corporate social responsibility, and corporate governance.

A business ethics program provides a toolkit of leadership and management practices to aid any enterprise—large or small—in the responsible pursuit of its envisioned future. It helps owners and managers ensure that their employees and agents comply with applicable laws and regulations. It also helps them minimize risk to the enterprise, enhance the enterprise's reputation, and bring value to stakeholders by adapting emerging global standards of responsible business conduct and best practices.

SPECIAL OPPORTUNITIES FOR SMALL TO MEDIUM-SIZED ENTERPRISES

Small to medium-sized enterprises (SMEs) have an additional incentive to adopt the discipline of responsible business conduct: to create a wider commercial network. Where owners and managers embrace the global language of responsible business through a business ethics program, a network of business enterprises and supportive NGOs based on shared values is possible. Such a network allows the individual SME to develop some of the synergies and economies of scale that only larger enterprises can afford.

EMERGING GLOBAL STANDARDS

Particularly over the past two decades, a number of prominent business associations, NGOs, and international government institutions have developed a body of global standards for the responsible business. These emerging global standards are of four types:

1. A stakeholder engagement standard (AA1000S)
2. Substantive standards (such as SA8000, Caux Round Table's principles, Interfaith Declaration's principles, and the *Basic Guidelines for Codes of Business Conduct)*
3. Management process standards (such as SA8000, the CERES Principles, and the *U.S. Federal Sentencing Guidelines for Organizations)*
4. Reporting standards (such as the Global Reporting Initiative)

As Figure 2.2 depicts, these standards provide the foundation for establishing the outcomes that can be expected from a business ethics program.

The major standards-setting institutions are of three major types: business associations, stakeholder groups, and international governmental organizations.

Business Associations

Business associations that set standards include the following:

- **Caux Round Table.** A global network of business leaders committed to principled business leadership, the Caux Round Table believes that business has a crucial role in developing and promoting equitable solutions

FIGURE 2.2
Global Standards as a Foundation

to key global issues. The Caux Round Table's *Principles for Business* serves as a guide to sustainable and socially responsible prosperity as the foundation for a fair, free, and transparent society.[18]

- **International Chamber of Commerce.** The International Chamber of Commerce (ICC) champions the global economy as a force for economic growth, job creation, and prosperity. ICC activities cover a broad spectrum, from performing arbitration and dispute resolution to making the case for open trade, the market economy system, and business self-regulation. The ICC's report, *Extortion and Bribery in International Business Transactions*, is another resource that helps fight corruption and commercial crime. The ICC has direct access to national governments and intergovernmental organizations on issues that directly affect business operations.[19]

- **Coalition for Environmentally Responsible Economies.** A U.S. coalition of environmental, investor, and advocacy groups working together for a sustainable future, the Coalition for Environmentally Responsible Economies (CERES) is committed to continuous environmental improvement. It encourages enterprises to adopt the "CERES Principles," a 10-point code of environmental conduct.[20]

- **Institute of Electrical and Electronics Engineers.** The Institute of Electrical and Electronics Engineers (IEEE) is a non-profit, technical professional association of more than 377,000 individual members in 150 countries. Its "Code of Ethics" contains 10 points of agreements to regulate the professional activities of its members.[21] It also has a more detailed "Software Engineering Code of Ethics and Professional

Practices" organized under eight principles.[22] The IEEE has an ethics committee and an ethics hotline.

Stakeholder Groups, Including Nongovernmental Organizations

Stakeholder groups such as the following also set standards:

- **Interfaith Declaration.** The Interfaith Declaration provides principles and guidelines to help practitioners identify the role they and their organizations should play in the community and to support problem solving.[23] Particularly valuable are its "Principles for Global Corporate Responsibility: Benchmarks for Measuring Business Performance."[24]

- **Global Reporting Initiative.** The Global Reporting Initiative (GRI) was established in late 1997 with the mission of developing globally applicable guidelines for reporting on economic, environmental, and social performance, initially for corporations and eventually for any business, government entity, or NGO. Convened by CERES in partnership with the United Nations Environment Programme, the GRI incorporates the active participation of corporations, NGOs, accounting organizations, business associations, and other stakeholders from around the world. The GRI's *Sustainability Reporting Guidelines* represent the first global framework for comprehensive sustainability reporting, encompassing the triple bottom line of financial, social, and environmental issues.[25]

- **Social Accountability International.** A non-profit organization, Social Accountability International (SAI) is dedicated to the development, implementation, and oversight of voluntary verifiable social accountability standards. SAI is committed to ensuring that standards and systems for verifying compliance with such standards are highly reputable and publicly accessible. SAI works to improve workplaces and combat sweatshops through the expansion and further development of the international workplace standard, SA8000, and the associated SA8000 verification system.[26]

- **Global Sullivan Principles.** In 1977, the Rev. Leon H. Sullivan developed the "Sullivan Principles," a code of conduct for human rights and equal opportunity for companies operating in South Africa. To further expand human rights and economic development to all communities, Sullivan created the "Global Sullivan Principles of Social Responsibility" in 1997.[27]

- **International Corporate Governance Network.** A membership association, the International Corporate Governance Network is devoted to improving corporate governance internationally and providing a voice between investors and management. As of 2001, its members owned or managed US$10 trillion.[28]

- **Institute of Directors in Southern Africa.** In July 1993, the Institute of Directors in Southern Africa established the King Committee on Corporate Governance. The King Committee has produced two reports on corporate governance for Southern Africa.[29]

- **Institute of Social and Ethical AccountAbility.** In 1999, the Institute of Social and Ethical AccountAbility launched the AA1000 Framework. AA1000S is an accountability standard designed to help enterprises improve accountability and performance by learning through stakeholder engagement and by integrating their stakeholder engagement processes into daily activities. AA1000S helps users establish a systematic stakeholder engagement process that generates the indicators, targets, and reporting systems needed to ensure the effectiveness of the process in overall organizational performance. AA1000S is designed to complement the GRI's *Sustainability Reporting Guidelines.*[30]

International Governmental Organizations

International governmental groups also set standards as shown below:

- **International Labor Organization.** The International Labor Organization (ILO) is the U.N. agency that seeks to promote social justice and internationally recognized human and labor rights. The ILO formulates international labor standards in the form of conventions and recommendations setting minimum standards of basic labor rights: the freedom to associate, the right to organize, the right to collective bargaining, the abolition of forced labor, the right to equal opportunity and treatment, and other standards regulating conditions across the entire spectrum of work-related issues. Within the U.N. system, the ILO has a unique tripartite structure, with workers and employers participating as equal partners with governments in the work of its governing organs.[31]

- **Organization for Economic Cooperation and Development.** Thirty countries sharing a commitment to democratic government and the market economy form the Organization for Economic Cooperation and Development (OECD). Having active relationships with some 70 other countries, NGOs, and civil society, the OECD has a global reach. It plays a prominent role in fostering good governance in the public service and in corporate activity. The OECD produces internationally agreed-upon instruments, decisions, and recommendations to promote rules of the game in areas where a multilateral agreement is necessary for individual countries to make progress in a globalized economy.

- **U.N. Global Compact.** U.N. Secretary-General Kofi Annan first proposed the Global Compact in an address to the World Economic Forum on January 31, 1999. Annan challenged business leaders to join an international initiative—the Global Compact—that would bring companies together with U.N. agencies, labor, and civil society to support nine principles in the areas of human rights, labor, and the environment. Through the power of collective action, the Global Compact seeks to advance responsible corporate citizenship so that business can be part of the solution to the challenges of globalization. In this way, the private sector—in partnership with other social actors—can help realize Annan's vision: a more sustainable and inclusive global economy.

- **U.S. Department of Commerce.** In cooperation with the Russian Chamber of Commerce and Industry, the U.S. Department of Commerce developed the *Basic Guidelines for Codes of Business Conduct* to reflect extensive input from Russian and U.S. trade organizations and businesses provided in the course of roundtables and discussions conducted in Russia and the United States. The *Guidelines* have served as the foundation for model codes in the Caucasus, Central Asia, Central and Southeast Europe, and Latin America. See Appendix B for the *Guidelines*.

As the result of ongoing global dialogue between these institutions, a body of standards and expectations for responsible business has emerged. These standards address a number of areas of concern to responsible owners and managers:

- Business conduct, including fair competition
- Community relations, including political involvement
- Corporate governance
- Environmental protection
- Human rights
- Marketplace relations
- Workplace relations
- Accountability
- Reporting standards

This manual will refer to these standards often in the practice-oriented chapters that follow.

Table 2.1 identifies a number of emerging global standards affecting different stakeholders.[32] It is organized according to the institutions that sponsor the standards and the major issues they address. The table depicts only the range of international programs and initiatives undertaken to facilitate the widespread adoption of the discipline of responsible business conduct.

TABLE 2.1 Emerging Global Standards and Reporting

Sponsor	Business Conduct	Community	Corporate Governance	Environment	Human Rights	Marketplace	Workplace	Accountability and Reporting
BUSINESS ASSOCIATIONS:								
Caux Round Table	√		√	√	√			√
ICC	√			√	√			√
CERES	√			√	√			√
IEEE	√	√					√	
STAKEHOLDER GROUPS:								
Interfaith Declaration	√			√	√			√
Global Reporting Initiative	√			√	√			√
SAI	√			√	√			√
Global Sullivan Principles	√			√	√			√
International Corporate Governance Network			√					
Institute of Directors in Southern Africa	√		√					
Institute of Social and Ethical AccountAbility								√
INTERNATIONAL GOVERNMENTAL ORGANIZATIONS:								
ILO	√				√			√
OECD	√		√	√	√			√
U.N. Global Compact	√		√	√	√	√	√	√
U.S. Department of Commerce	√	√	√	√		√	√	√

Adopting Global Standards and Best Practices

When an enterprise designs a business ethics program, it is helpful to organize emerging standards and best practices as answers to eight questions owners and managers of any enterprise should ask themselves as they structure the enterprise. In Table 2.2, each question is followed by examples of global standards and best practices that an RBE can use to help develop appropriate answers.[33]

Specific best practices are outlined in the chapters to follow: standards, procedures, and expectations (Chapter 5); business ethics infrastructure (Chapter 6); business ethics communications and feedback (Chapter 7); business ethics alignment practices (Chapters 8 and 9); and business ethics program evaluation and organizational learning (Chapter 10).

All enterprises need to ask themselves each of the questions in Table 2.2. The sample global standards and best practices are drawn from the experiences of LCEs. However, these resources are readily available to all enterprises, including SMEs, on the Internet, and they can aid in working out the answers for individual enterprises and serve to stimulate dialogue and inquiry.

TABLE 2.2 Global Standards and Best Practices: Eight Questions

Questions for the Responsible Business Enterprise	Sample Emerging Global Standards and Best Practices	
What norms, values, and standards should we set to guide our members and foster reasonable expectations among our stakeholders?	• Sound set of core beliefs • OECD Guidelines for Multinational Enterprises	• OECD Guidelines for Corporate Governance • U.S. Federal Sentencing Guidelines for Organizations
What style, structure, and systems of authority and responsibility at all levels should we exercise?	• Leadership styles • Board-level committees • High-level person responsible for program • Executive-level ethics committee	• Ethics office • Individual duty to report misconduct • Australian Criminal Code corporate culture approach
How can we most effectively communicate our standards and procedures and foster reasonable expectations among our stakeholders?	• Executive modeling • Formal communications • Orientation • Ethics training	• Ethics games • Posters • Newsletter • Stakeholder engagement and dialogue
What mechanisms can we establish to know that our members are following our standards and procedures and meeting reasonable stakeholder expectations?	• Independent audit committee • Audit department • Quality monitoring mechanisms • Ethics office	• Organizational ombudsman • Policy prohibiting retaliation • Policy allowing confidentiality and privilege
How can we ensure that we have the right people in the right places while pursuing our purpose as an enterprise?	• Policy on recruiting and hiring • Policy on skills training	• Policy on assigning, promoting, and terminating staff members
How can we encourage our members to follow our standards, procedures, and expectations?	• Recognizing ethical behavior • Rewarding ethical behavior in challenging situations	• Punishing substandard behavior • Establishing compensation schemes, especially bonuses and incentive pay, that promote standards
What do we owe our stakeholders when mistakes, misconduct, or misunderstandings occur involving our standards and procedures or their reasonable expectations?	• Voluntarily reporting mistakes and misconduct • Cooperating with proper authorities	• Correcting harm caused • Conducting required skills and knowledge training
How should we monitor, track, and report our performance as an enterprise and continuously learn from it?	• Establishing program goals and objectives • Developing appropriate action plans • Establishing performance indicators • Developing performance measurements • Instituting data recording, collection, and analysis	• Establishing reporting frameworks and schedules • Identifying reporting targets • Implementing Global Reporting Initiative standards • Developing individual skills of generative learning • Building a culture of knowledge sharing and quality

In actual practice, even the LCEs borrow freely from the documents and experiences of other enterprises. See the Glossary for definitions of key terms.

SUMMARY

There are at least eight practical reasons why owners and managers should embrace a business ethics program as part of its management practice:

- Enhanced reputation and goodwill
- Reduced risks
- Reduced costs
- Protection from unethical employees and agents
- Enhanced performance, productivity, and competitive position
- Expanded access to capital, credit, and foreign investment
- Increased profits and sustained long-term growth
- Increased international respect

An RBE also contributes to the social capital of its community by basing its business conduct on a solid foundation of responsible business conduct. It works with leaders in government, civil society, and other businesses to develop a market framework and the supporting legal institutions.

Over the past two decades, emerging global standards from a number of business associations, stakeholder groups, and international institutions have been addressing the issues of responsible business conduct: ethics, compliance, and social responsibility.

RESPONSIBLE BUSINESS ENTERPRISE
Checklist

1. What responsible business conduct issues does your enterprise face, and how is it organized to deal with them?

2. What does being a socially responsible business mean to you? At what levels does your enterprise perform: socially responsible or ultra socially responsible?

3. How would you describe your enterprise to a stranger? A government regulator? Your family? Are the descriptions different? If so, why?

4. How much social capital is there in your markets? If the level of social capital is low, how does that affect business transactions?

5. What might motivate your enterprise to consider a business ethics program?

6. What benefits might your community see if more enterprises had business ethics programs?

7. How well could owners and managers of your enterprise answer the eight questions for a responsible business enterprise in Table 2.2?

II

The Business
Ethics Program

Responsible Business Conduct as Strategy

3

- **Planning, Strategy, and the Business Ethics Program**

- **Establishing the Nature of the Program**

- **Building a Responsible Business Enterprise**

- **Knowing the Structural Components of the Program**

- **Planning the Business Ethics Program**

- **Engaging the Enterprise's Stakeholders**

- **Adopting a Design, Review, and Approval Process**

*T*his chapter helps owners and managers plan to build a responsible business enterprise (RBE). It provides an approach to designing and implementing a business ethics program, and it describes how having one helps an enterprise improve its performance, make profits, and increase the prosperity of its community by learning to meet the reasonable expectations of its stakeholders. This chapter also addresses the management challenges of designing and implementing such a program.

Planning, Strategy, and the Business Ethics Program

Enterprises of all sizes develop strategies to bring their resources together to achieve their goals and objectives. A business ethics program helps owners and managers improve their business performance, make profits, and contribute to the economic progress of their communities by meeting the reasonable expectations of their stakeholders.[1] A business ethics program also aims to achieve specific expected program outcomes, such as increasing awareness of ethics issues, improving decision-making, and reducing misconduct, which are discussed in more detail in Chapter 4.

To be effective over time, a business ethics program must be a formal plan, because it touches on all aspects of the enterprise—operations, human resources, communications, and marketing to name but a few. Formally planning a business ethics program ensures that owners and managers give due consideration to the enterprise's relevant context, organizational culture, and reasonable stakeholder expectations. This manual provides a systematic approach to guide owners and managers through the process.

Busy managers need not fear that formal planning for a business ethics program will overwhelm daily operations because, as discussed below, they already have many elements in place. The planning process requires targeted stakeholder participation more than a large staff. However, once an enterprise announces its intention to design and implement a business ethics program, it needs to plan well and to base its plan on its core beliefs. A lack of program consistency will hurt employee morale and generate stakeholder cynicism.

Because of resource limitations, most small to medium-sized enterprises (SMEs) use informal program strategy and planning. SMEs are less apt to use formal teams and processes to set goals, objectives, strategies, and action plans than are large enterprises.[2] Nonetheless, they can adapt the processes that follow to meet their circumstances. For example, they can use all of the RBE Worksheets provided in the balance of this manual to direct their thinking, to stimulate dialogue, and to engage their stakeholders.

PRACTICE NOTE

Corporate Social Responsibility (CSR) and the SME

Research on CSR and SMEs is rare, but a 1991 review of research in the U.S. made the following six findings:

- Customer relations (i.e., customer satisfaction) is viewed as the primary social responsibility of small business
- Consumer relations, product quality, employee concern, and profitability are perceived by managers to be key social responsibility areas of small business
- Managers and owners have perceptions of small business social responsibility that are similar to those of nonbusiness people
- Managers of small businesses and large corporations indicate few differences in their perception of acceptable ethical practices
- Social involvement activities by small businesses are informally structured

Judith Kenner Thompson and Howard L. Smith
"Social Responsibility and Small Business"

These worksheets are intended to aid in designing and implementing a business ethics program. They are designed to be consistent with the principles of responsible management developed throughout these materials.[3] A number of worksheets refer to emerging standards and best practices. For example, "Questions for the Responsible Business Enterprise" (RBE Worksheet 5), refers to emerging global standards and best practices. These standards and best practices are developed in detail in the chapters that follow.

Establishing the Nature of the Program

Owners and managers should define and communicate the purpose of the business ethics program as early as possible. Responsible management recognizes that an effective business ethics program touches every decision and activity of the enterprise. It guides patterns of thought, choice, and action that subtly shape the organizational culture of the enterprise. The business ethics program should be based on the core beliefs of the enterprise and should reflect an approach or orientation that will resonate with employees and other stakeholders.

Recent research suggests that "specific characteristics of the formal ethics and legal compliance program matter less than the broader perceptions of the program's orientation toward values and ethical aspirations."[4] This research found that two factors are most important: (1) that ethics is perceived to be important to leadership—from executive through supervisor—and (2) that employees believe they are treated fairly. It is particularly important that enterprise policies and management actions be consistent and that reward systems support ethical behavior.[5]

According to the research, familiarity with a code of conduct is relatively unimportant. Moreover, a program perceived as designed primarily to protect senior managers is clearly harmful and is associated with increased violations of its established standards and procedures.[6] Research and experience over the past 15 years suggest that a primary best practice is to design a business ethics program that goes beyond mere compliance.[7]

The following subsections are intended to help owners and managers define the nature of an enterprise's business ethics program so that it can be as effective as possible.

ORIENTATION OF THE PROGRAM

Program effectiveness is closely related to employees' perceptions of the orientation of a business ethics program. A business ethics program usually has one of four primary orientations. The orientation reflects owner and manager motivations in designing and implementing the program and is an important condition of program effectiveness.

The primary orientations are:

1. A *compliance-based* approach, which "focuses primarily on preventing, detecting, and punishing violations of law"
2. A *values-based* approach, which "aims to define organizational values and encourage employee commitment to ethical aspirations"
3. A *satisfying external stakeholders* approach through which enterprises "hope to maintain or improve their public image and relationships with external stakeholders"
4. A *protecting senior management* approach, which "is introduced in part to protect owners and senior management from blame for ethical failures or legal problems"[8]

These primary orientations are not mutually exclusive. As a single orientation, values-based programs tend to be most effective. However, a business ethics program that includes aspects of compliance-based programs and pays attention to satisfying external stakeholders is also valuable. Employee perceptions that a program is oriented toward protecting senior management from liability or prosecution contribute to employee cynicism and lead to program outcomes that are "significantly more negative."[9]

CONSIDERATIONS FOR THE SMALL TO MEDIUM-SIZED ENTERPRISE

Unlike large, complex enterprises (LCEs), the average SME is closely identified with its owners and managers. Thus SMEs must be particularly alert to designing a well-balanced business ethics program. Often they will be tempted to work out the program on their own and to simply present it to employees and other stakeholders. They have limited resources and staff, and, after all, it is *their* enterprise. Though in many cultures workers expect to be told what to do—even what to think—a program is more apt to succeed where workers are involved enough in its design to feel committed to it and where workers are willing to use individual judgment to apply its standards to the issues they face.

Owners and managers should, therefore, resist this temptation and engage their employees and other stakeholders as much as possible. For example, owners and managers can use an RBE Worksheet in this manual to guide their thinking in designing the program and to stimulate dialogue with their employees and other stakeholders.

Building a Responsible Business Enterprise

Each enterprise has a unique ethical character. This character quietly guides what its members think, say, and do. It influences how external stakeholders view the enterprise. As Figure 3.1 suggests, an enterprise's identity as an RBE has at least four levels: compliance, risk management, reputation enhancement, and value added. Setting objectives in all four levels—and achieving them—is a goal of a business ethics program.

FIGURE 3.1
Levels of an Enterprise's Identity

The identity of an RBE reflects how well it meets its responsibilities as a member of a community. Responsible business conduct—ethics, compliance, and social responsibility—is an essential part of this identity. It influences the way the enterprise sees itself and the way the community views the enterprise. Indeed, how the enterprise deals with responsible business conduct issues may be the most important aspect of defining an enterprise's identity.

A business ethics program provides the essential core of the competitive strategy of an RBE. Programs more limited in purpose—called ethics and compliance programs—typically address the two lowest levels because compliance and risk management are the most obvious levels of identity.

However, a business ethics program addresses the higher levels as well—reputation enhancement and value added—in a systematic way.

A business ethics program helps an enterprise establish the essence of its identity in the community: its core purpose, core values, and envisioned future. It is an effective tool for establishing standards and procedures to ensure that enterprise values are reflected in all that employees and agents think, say, and do. A business ethics program employs a systematic process to reach a wide range of stakeholders more effectively so that it achieves its expected program outcomes. See Appendix A for a sample outcomes-based decision-making model.

COMPLIANCE LEVEL

Compliance means meeting all legal requirements through an effective program to prevent and detect misconduct.[10] The average business enterprise faces myriad legal demands and constraints. Moreover, it is not enough that an enterprise intends to be law abiding. Good intentions alone will not safeguard an enterprise against the risks that its employees or agents will make mistakes or misbehave. Increasingly, compliance requires that an enterprise be able to demonstrate that it pursued management practices that are reasonably calculated to prevent and detect misconduct as a matter of policy. Demonstrating this may take the form of describing the formal structures and systems in place (as in the United States), having a compliance program with respect to competition law (as in the European

PRACTICE NOTE

Categories of Laws Affecting Business

Businesses must comply with these types of laws:

- Principal and agent relations
- Business organization and formation
- Real property law
- Personal property law
- Intellectual property law
- Fair competition law
- Environmental law
- Employment law

- Labor–management law
- Tax law
- Alternative dispute resolution provisions
- Political campaign financing law
- Anti–money laundering law
- Anticorruption law
- Judicial procedure, especially judicial privilege
- International law

Union),[11] or having an organizational culture that does not tolerate or encourage misconduct (as in Australia).

In the United States, the Federal Sentencing Guidelines for Organizations (FSGO) set forth seven minimum steps for an organization to demonstrate that it has an effective program to prevent and detect criminal activity.[12] These steps have come to constitute the minimum characteristics of an effective compliance program. In general, they require that an enterprise set forth adequate standards to guide its employees and agents. These standards must reflect industry standards and government regulations. They must be communicated effectively to employees and agents. The enterprise must have means of knowing whether its employees and agents are following its standards. It must actually enforce them, and it must respond appropriately if they are violated. A high-level person must be responsible for executing the program. No high-level person can be involved in the misconduct.[13] See Appendix H for extracts from the FSGO.

In a similar vein, U.S. law requires many enterprises to have an anti–money laundering (AML) program, which has four elements: (1) standards and procedures, (2) a compliance officer, (3) training procedures, and (4) an external or internal audit. Financial institutions are also required to have a specific customer identification program. Under certain circumstances, foreign individuals and enterprises with no direct contact in the United States will be affected by the procedures of an AML program, as discussed in more detail in Chapter 9. Moreover, many U.S. government agencies, including the Department of Justice, the Department of Health and Human Services, and the Environmental Protection Agency, recommend, or in some circumstances require, compliance programs similar to the FSGO.

Australia has an alternative approach that looks to the culture of the enterprise. This approach is concerned with whether "a corporate culture existed within the body corporate that directed, encouraged, tolerated, or led to non-compliance with the relevant provision" or "failed to create and maintain a corporate culture that required compliance with the relevant provision."[14] See Appendix I for extracts from the Australian Criminal Code on corporate criminal responsibility.

It is generally recognized, however, that these standards and practices are not enough to create an effective business ethics program. They do not address, for example, whether an enterprise is effectively pursuing its core purpose or whether its policies, procedures, and activities are congruent with its core values. With the exception of standards that are designed to prevent breaches of fiduciary duties, these standards and practices do not require that the enterprise meet the reasonable expectations of its stakeholders effectively or well.

RISK MANAGEMENT LEVEL

To make ethics and compliance programs more effective, practitioners argue that enterprises should go beyond legal compliance and should systematically consider the industry and market risks that enterprises face. This involves assessing customer, supplier, and competition risk; examining enterprise policies, processes, and activities; and looking closely at organizational culture to establish whether there is a history of problems, disharmony, and conflict.[15] Often expressed in terms of protecting the reputation of the enterprise, risk management is an important next level.

The consequences for failing to address these risks include, but are not limited to, criminal prosecution, regulatory action, debarment from government contracting, civil lawsuits, compromised strategic partnerships, labor–management disagreements, stakeholder dissatisfaction, and calls from civil society for more regulation.

REPUTATION ENHANCEMENT LEVEL

Damage to the enterprise's reputation has always been viewed as a reason to care about responsible business conduct. More recently, the kind and number of stakeholders that an enterprise needs to be concerned about has expanded to include media, nongovernmental organizations (NGOs), and international institutions. Some enterprises strive to be RBEs simply to avoid criticism from this expanded stakeholder list.

It is more positive and creative to enhance one's reputation by making choices and acting in a manner such that one deserves a good reputation. Hence, enhancing one's reputation among a larger and more diverse group of stakeholders represents a third, more important level of enterprise identity.[16]

VALUE-ADDED LEVEL

Increasingly, responsible business conduct includes adding value to the RBE's community through its decisions and activities.[17] It is understood that the RBE strives to make a profit, but it is also expected to take into account its impact on its stakeholders. For example, many enterprises have quality assurance programs to meet their responsibilities to customers. Though not often considered part of a business ethics program, producing goods and services of low quality may constitute consumer fraud or violate product liability laws (thus violating the compliance and risk management levels). Producing low-quality goods does not enhance the enterprise's reputation—or contribute to employee pride or morale (thus causing the enterprise to fail to meet the reputation enhancement level). And ultimately, producing low-quality goods or services adds little value to the

PRACTICE NOTE

Maintaining Reputation

Nestlé has had to deal with a number of highly contested and sometimes quite acrimonious debates.... Yet I am struck by one fact: our corporate reputation has not suffered in spite of decade-long campaigns and public debate. I am convinced that two elements played in our favor: Nestlé has managed to build that "institutional" trust in broad segments of the public, through an unquestionable priority given to the quality and security of its products, and we have learned over time to show a high degree of consistency in handling difficult issues in a transparent and responsive manner. In other words, trust has been nurtured throughout this period.

Peter Brabeck-Letmathe, Chief Executive Officer
Nestlé
"The Search for Trust"

community for the resources devoted to it (so that the enterprise fails to achieve the value-added level).

As noted in Chapter 1, an enterprise may add value to its community in many ways:

- Serving the most important needs of its customers and consumers
- Providing gainful employment for its employees and agents, so that they can provide for their families and be responsible citizens
- Providing an adequate return to investors
- Purchasing goods and services from suppliers and service providers
- Competing intensely, but fairly
- Forming strategic partnerships and alliances to create new business opportunities
- Supporting community infrastructure through taxes and fees
- Participating in the political process to improve market conditions
- Respecting the environment

To be truly responsible, an enterprise must fully embrace all four levels of identity.

UNDERSTANDING AN ENTERPRISE'S STRENGTHS AND WEAKNESSES

There is no one-size-fits-all business ethics program. The business ethics infrastructure should be designed to encourage responsible choices and actions, such that they become part of the culture of the enterprise itself over time. All enterprises have strengths and weaknesses. It is important to form enterprise strategies with a clear understanding of each.

As Figure 3.2 suggests, the business ethics infrastructure and alignment practices selected by owners and managers must reflect enterprise strengths and must deal with enterprise weaknesses. Owners and managers should design a business ethics program that will accentuate enterprise strengths and will reform enterprise weaknesses. Some apparent enterprise strengths may even be weaknesses, when not kept in perspective.

FIGURE 3.2
Best Practices Reflect Enterprise Strengths and Deal with Weaknesses

Consider, for example, a recently privatized enterprise's reliance on personal relationships with government regulators to propel its success. In the short run, the enterprise may secure contracts or competitive advantages not warranted by the quality of its goods or services. As a result, research and development, quality programs, and effective marketing will tend to be undervalued and underused. When governments change or markets are opened, however, the enterprise will inevitably find itself at a competitive *dis*advantage.

Knowing the Structural Components of the Program

When an enterprise undertakes to design a business ethics program, it seeks answers that go beyond what is required, at a minimum, to comply with law.

It seeks broader, more creative answers based on emerging global standards and best practices.

Every enterprise already has some or all of the structural components of a business ethics program, even though no formal program may exist. All enterprises set standards and procedures that they expect their employees and agents to follow, communicate those standards and procedures, want to know whether their standards are being followed, and respond when standards and procedures are violated or stakeholders complain. What distinguishes the RBE is that its management works consciously to find those structures and systems that will ensure an *effective* program.

A well-designed and implemented business ethics program provides enterprise employees and agents with the guidance and information they need for effective, efficient, and responsible choices and actions. Research and experience over the past few decades suggest that an effective program contains the following nine structural components:

1. Standards and procedures to guide member behavior and foster reasonable stakeholder expectations
2. Adequate structures and systems that provide for authority, responsibility, accountability, and sustainability
3. Communication of standards, procedures, and expectations to the enterprise's members
4. Programs that monitor and audit member conduct
5. Encouragement of members to seek advice and report concerns
6. Due diligence in hiring, especially for sensitive positions in, for example, management, finance, and contracting
7. Encouragement of members to follow standards and procedures
8. Appropriate responses when standards and procedures are violated
9. Regular evaluations of program effectiveness

These nine components are discussed further in the chapters that follow.

Planning the Business Ethics Program

Five principles should drive the planning process and be honored in implementation of the program itself.

DIFFERENTIATE BETWEEN GOVERNANCE AND MANAGEMENT

Owners and managers should sharply differentiate between the governance and management of an enterprise by delineating clear roles, responsibilities, and areas of accountability for policy-makers and managers. Even if the owner is the senior manager or if managers sit on a board of directors, the different roles and responsibilities need to be respected. Governance, for example, takes the broader view: setting policies to guide all employees and agents, including the owners.

The source of a corporate board's authority is the owners of the enterprise.[18] The board is the pivotal authority. Its authority is neither granted nor defined by management. Policies generated by the board control everything, both governance and management.

In practice, however, the board is often considered an adviser to management rather than its source of authority. Indeed, many recent corporate ethics failures in the United States can be traced to the failure of boards to exercise their authority as representatives of the owners. In emerging market economies, lack of a strong voice for shareholders may lead to asset stripping and to rent diversion. As a result, corporate governance is under different stages of review and reform in nations across the globe, and the review is based largely on the distinction between governance on the part of the board and management on the part of executives.

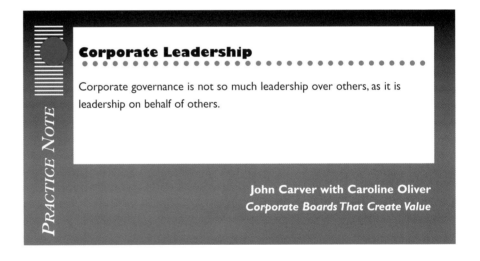

PRACTICE NOTE

Corporate Leadership

Corporate governance is not so much leadership over others, as it is leadership on behalf of others.

John Carver with Caroline Oliver
Corporate Boards That Create Value

BUILD ON STRENGTHS

An RBE strives to be effective, efficient, and responsible through constructive and creative engagement with its stakeholders. To this end, it is helpful to identify and build on the core strengths of the organization. As Figure 3.2 illustrates, an enterprise is a bundle of strengths and weaknesses. The ultimate goal of a business ethics program is to appreciate an enterprise's strengths. This does not mean that weaknesses are ignored.

To the contrary, management applies what it knows about responsible business conduct to compensate for weaknesses. For example, if an enterprise is vulnerable to employee misconduct, the enterprise uses a business ethics program to prevent and detect wrongdoing. If employees are afraid to speak up, the enterprise provides effective mechanisms for employees to seek advice and report misconduct without fear of retaliation.

MOBILIZE THE ENTIRE ENTERPRISE AROUND CORE BELIEFS

Employees and agents can be empowered most effectively and safely when they share core beliefs. In fact, this may be the only way to empower employees and agents responsibly. If becoming an RBE is an enterprise's policy and goal, the effort must be based on core beliefs. An objective of any business ethics program is that every stakeholder, to the appropriate degree, knows the core beliefs that should order the decisions and activities of the enterprise. Every employee and agent should be able to describe the core beliefs that will always guide his or her choices and actions, and should be able to define what constitutes success for the enterprise.[19]

A few inspiring goals can provide further direction to employees and agents. They provide focus of effort and guide the allocation of resources. They order every task and form every structure so that the people involved know exactly how such tasks contribute to achieving the enterprise's goals and why such tasks are consistent with the core beliefs. Perhaps most important is for all people in the enterprise to use a common language that is based on the core beliefs.

DELEGATE AUTHORITY ACROSS ALL LEVELS

To design and implement a business ethics program well, people at all levels of the enterprise must embrace it. A core of people, who are dispersed throughout the enterprise, must be personally responsible for seeing that the project succeeds.

Owners and managers must lead from the front, and it must be clear to all that responsible business conduct is their personal project. The various tasks of designing and implementing the business ethics program must be assigned throughout the enterprise. To do this effectively, owners and managers must know the people and the organizational culture of the enterprise well enough to know whom to assign leadership tasks to—and what results to expect. Moreover, these dispersed leaders must have the authority and resources they need to develop and exercise their responsibilities.[20] Often, owners and managers will have to direct middle management and supervisors to gracefully release key employees from day-to-day operations to support the business ethics program.

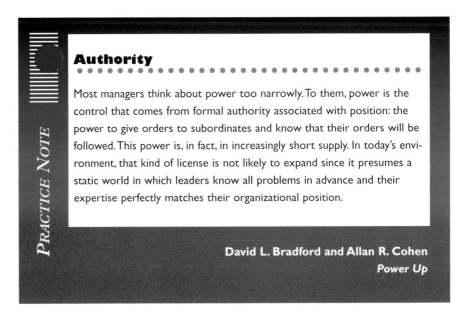

PRACTICE NOTE

Authority

Most managers think about power too narrowly. To them, power is the control that comes from formal authority associated with position: the power to give orders to subordinates and know that their orders will be followed. This power is, in fact, in increasingly short supply. In today's environment, that kind of license is not likely to expand since it presumes a static world in which leaders know all problems in advance and their expertise perfectly matches their organizational position.

David L. Bradford and Allan R. Cohen
Power Up

BUILD IN CONTINUOUS IMPROVEMENT

A business ethics program involves so many levels of the enterprise and so many of its operations and functions that the process itself must be designed for continuous improvement. Moreover, other programs not usually considered part of a business ethics program should be integrated with it:

- Quality management programs
- Preferred supplier programs that help an enterprise integrate responsible suppliers into its operational "family"
- Environmental, health, and safety programs to meet responsibilities to employees and the environment
- Human resource programs to be fair to employees
- Sexual harassment programs to protect employees from abuse
- Labor–management programs to respect employee rights to collectively bargain

This process of continuous improvement requires built-in flexibility and frequent reference to a plan of action, milestones, and interim objectives. As is the case for the other principles, this process should be based on the core beliefs of an RBE itself.

Engaging the Enterprise's Stakeholders

For an enterprise to be responsible, its management must understand what its stakeholders expect and work with them to form reasonable expectations.[21] This is the case for every enterprise, whether it is an LCE or an SME. The discussion that follows addresses specific functions in the business ethics program design and implementation process with the owners and managers of an SME in mind. How they choose, in practice, to staff the functions will depend on the size, complexity, and resources of the enterprise.

An RBE recognizes that its stakeholders cannot be easily labeled. Some employees will also be customers or consumers of its goods or services. They may hold stock or options on stock in the enterprise and may be owners. They may live in communities affected by waste products leaked into the environment by the enterprise. They will have neighbors who have strong opinions about the way the enterprise does business. They look to government to provide good roads and other services, which may be compromised by business bribery and corruption. As one scholar notes, "the notion of 'stakeholder' suggests discrete groups or entities, whereas the primary source of dilemmas in business ethics is the fact that virtually all of us wear (at least) two hats."[22]

To be effective, efficient, and responsible, an enterprise must have core beliefs that include an envisioned future of what its stakeholders can reasonably expect—and how it will be held accountable. The discipline of responsible business conduct helps owners and managers engage stakeholders to foster their reasonable expectations.

ENGAGING STAKEHOLDERS IN THE DESIGN PROCESS

Before turning to the RBE Worksheets described in the following chapters, we must discuss who should be involved in the project of designing and implementing the business ethics program. Engaging stakeholders as early as possible applies the core beliefs and principles of an RBE, leads to better information on which to base design decisions, and builds goodwill with stakeholders. This principle applies to all enterprises—whether large or small. Although an SME may have far fewer stakeholders than an LCE, each of its stakeholders may have far more influence in the success of the SME as a result.[23]

Project objectives will be achieved only if the project is staffed with people who fully subscribe to them, have the knowledge they need when they need it, and are trusted throughout the enterprise. These people undertake a variety of roles and responsibilities, enter and exit the project at various points, and can be thought of as key players, support staff, and stakeholder representatives. They generally maintain their normal duties within the enterprise during the design process.

BRINGING TOGETHER THE KEY PLAYERS

In the early stages of the project, there should be a designated *program catalyst*—usually an owner or the chief executive of the enterprise—who drives the project. His or her involvement will gradually decline as the project progresses, but he or she will retain responsibility to support the significance of the project objectives.

A *project officer* is primarily responsible for developing good ideas and approaches and inspiring people to embrace the eventual plan. He or she plays a prominent and important role in the early stages of the project. Ideally, the project officer is an employee familiar with the operations of the enterprise—but often the skills, time, or effort required to drive the project are not available within the enterprise. The enterprise might then retain a trusted adviser, such as an accountant or attorney, or might employ an independent consultant.

It is valuable for owners and managers to create special *working groups* to develop project objectives, scope of work, and roles and responsibilities.

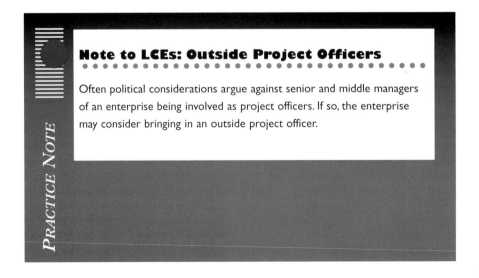

PRACTICE NOTE

Note to LCEs: Outside Project Officers

Often political considerations argue against senior and middle managers of an enterprise being involved as project officers. If so, the enterprise may consider bringing in an outside project officer.

Note to LCEs: Committees and Consultants

Global best practices suggest that the following committees be formed and consultants be hired:

- A **decision-making committee** is regularly briefed on the status of the project and makes the executive-level decisions that arise through the course of the project.
- A **project steering committee** serves as a standing committee to provide information and guidance to the various project agents.
- **Management-level consultants** present the management perspective on the project.
- **Worker-level consultants** present the shop-floor perspective on the project.
- **External stakeholder consultants** present the perspectives of stakeholders outside of the organization.

Such a group (sometimes called a "task force") can serve as adviser, sounding board, and eyes and ears of the project as it progresses. With the assistance of staff, the working group can draft key documents and concept papers.

As the project progresses, the working group can serve as voice of the project. The group can communicate progress to the other stakeholders and test for reaction to date. Its members may be especially effective at evaluating the effectiveness of project communications. Indeed, if properly constituted, the working group can perform much of the reporting function that might otherwise have to be placed on managers.

It is important to organize and build a *project network* to bring in more varied perspectives. Such a network is composed of various designated enterprise and external *stakeholder consultants*, who are individuals respected for their subject matter expertise or are recognized leaders and opinion molders. They become resources to whom the staff or working group can turn for information or reaction.

It is valuable to have *resource teams* available to a working group on short notice, such as legal counsel; environment, health, and safety personnel; and an investor relations team. Individuals or teams can be assigned to research particular elements as subject matter experts.

USING THE RBE WORKSHEETS

At the heart of the design and implementation of a business ethics program is a structured approach to (a) understand the pressures facing the enterprise, its employees, and its agents, and (b) understand its organizational culture, and (c) systematically enhance its strengths and reform its weaknesses through appropriate standards, structures, systems, and practices. The RBE Worksheets described in the following chapters help guide owners and managers through a systematic process of collecting and analyzing data about the enterprise's organizational context and culture. They can then use their findings to answer fundamental questions about how the enterprise should be organized and operated.

To use an RBE Worksheet, representative members of the enterprise and external stakeholders should form a working group. To include more voices, owners and managers might choose additional stakeholder representatives. Role-playing employees are often preferable to external stakeholders to preserve privacy and confidentiality. The average SME might simply invite key stakeholders in for a talk over tea or coffee about their needs and concerns—and how the enterprise might meet them better.

Generally, an RBE Worksheet is a table with multiple elements or cells to stimulate dialogue and decision-making. The working group engages in a facilitated dialogue about each element of an RBE Worksheet, from the

FIGURE 3.3
Extract of RBE
Worksheet 2

RBE WORKSHEET

2 **Relevant Context Data Collection**

RBE Worksheet 2 provides a tool to help owners and managers scan the external context issues an enterprise faces by context element—legal, economic, political, environmental, socio-cultural, and technological—and by the pressures faced in each element—threat, opportunity, demand, constraint, and uncertainty.

In filling out this worksheet, as many stakeholder perspectives as possible should be obtained for each element. For example, the economic element might be filled out as follows:

	Threat	Opportunity	Demand	Constraint	Uncertainty
Economic	New competition enters the market. Competitor introduces new products. Infrastructure is inadequate.	New market is available. Tariffs have been reduced.	Customer expects quality. Industry has standards for certification.	Supply chain is inadequate. Infrastructure is weak.	Value of currency and interest rates may change.

perspectives of the enterprise and its stakeholders. For each element in an RBE Worksheet, there will be at least one item of information of value to the enterprise.

For example, "Relevant Context Data Collection," RBE Worksheet 2 (Chapter 4), is composed of context element and stakeholder pressure cells. In the portion of the worksheet extracted in Figure 3.3, there are cells for five types of pressures: threat, opportunity, demand, constraint, and uncertainty. As the typical enterprise scans its relevant context, it will find *threats* from competition, potentially both foreign and domestic. Another threat might be a stagnant economy or an anticipated rise in interest rates or adverse currency fluctuation. There may also be *opportunities*, such as new products, markets, or strategic alliances. There will be economic *demands* to do certain things, such as meeting new quality standards. There will be some things the enterprise cannot do—that is, *constraints* established by law, reglulations, or industry norms and standards. There will be many economic factors that create *uncertainties*.

A working group should explore each cell, throwing out as many ideas as possible. All members should participate, and no idea should be considered unacceptable. Then they should go back over the ideas and discuss how the ideas may relate to one another. When the ideas themselves have been organized and evaluated, the group can work through their implications by asking, "If _____ is true, what does it mean for our enterprise?"

If subject matter experts are engaged, they should contribute to, but not dictate, the conditions of dialogue. After analyzing the data, the working group should take adequate time to reflect on what it means. The participants might then appoint a smaller team to synthesize what was learned; to make findings, conclusions, and recommendations; and to develop a report for use as a planning document. Routing drafts of the report to all participants helps develop consensus and commitment.

The working group should expect to make a more or less formal presentation of the report to management. The approved report then becomes a key planning document.

TABLE 3.1 Business Ethics Program Development Process	
Step	Direction
1. A high-level decision or commitment to develop the business ethics program is made.	Owners and managers communicate to the enterprise as a whole their commitment to the project and give guidance to key players.
2. A working group develops information requirements.	As the design and implementation project begins, a working group will accumulate data, determine what more information is needed, and identify sources for such information, including external stakeholders.
3. A working group develops an initial draft of a document or concept paper.	When the working group has accumulated the information it needs or has arranged to receive it in due time, it develops the initial draft of a document, such as a code of conduct or a concept paper on, for example, how an ethics office might be structured. Consultant individuals or groups as well as enterprise staff members provide input for the draft.
4. Senior managers review the draft.	Senior managers review the draft and return it with comments. This step is an integral part of the drafting process, and the comments provide a management perspective to the drafting.
5. A working group integrates the managers' comments and produces a second draft.	The working group will redraft the document or concept paper and resubmit it to the senior managers as many times as necessary. Often, the group will find that it needs more information or more perspectives.
6. A representative stakeholder group reviews a later draft and provides comments.	When the document or concept paper nears its final state, the working group can present it to representative stakeholder groups to gauge their reactions—and receive their feedback. This step often provides an excellent opportunity to conduct interviews and focus groups.
7. A working group integrates the stakeholder group's comments and produces a final draft.	By this point, the working group should have all the information it needs and should have considered as many perspectives as possible.
8. Senior managers make a final review of the document or concept.	Senior managers give the document or concept paper a final review and approve it before it is presented to the owners or their representatives. Senior managers are charged with ensuring that the document or concept is sound and consistent with enterprise core beliefs. Often their approval is tentative, pending the development of other documents or concepts.
9. Owners or their representatives review and approve the business ethics program as a whole.	When all documents and concept papers have been assembled, the program should take form, and the owners or their representatives should review and approve the paper.

Adopting a Design, Review, and Approval Process

This manual recommends the process shown in Table 3.1 for developing, reviewing, and approving each element of a business ethics program. As discussed in more detail in Chapters 5 through 8, such elements include a code of conduct and concept papers on specific issues, such as a concept for how a business ethics office might be structured. In the process of creating these documents, any step along the way may be revisited, including the first step, until the document or concept paper is approved as part of a complete system.

SUMMARY

The RBE needs to take a number of practical steps before establishing a business ethics program. Owners and managers must determine the approach and orientation of its business ethics program. They must identify and engage all of an enterprise's stakeholders, foster their reasonable expectations, and order the enterprise's business affairs so that it improves its business performance and increases the prosperity of its community by meeting those expectations.

The responsible business enterprise operates at all four levels of identity: compliance, risk management, reputation enhancement, and value added. It meets all legal requirements through an effective program to prevent and detect misconduct. It works to ensure that its organizational culture does not encourage or tolerate misconduct. It also works to identify and reduce the risks it faces in its markets. In addition, an RBE goes beyond these two lower levels to enhance its reputation and add value to its community.

A business ethics program has nine structural components that reflect global standards and best practices of responsible business conduct:

1. Standards and procedures to guide member behavior and foster reasonable stakeholder expectations
2. Adequate structures and systems that provide for authority, responsibility, accountability, and sustainability
3. Communication of standards, procedures, and expectations to the enterprise's members
4. Programs that monitor and audit member conduct
5. Encouragement of members to seek advice and report concerns
6. Due diligence in hiring, especially for sensitive positions in, for example, management, finance, and contracting
7. Encouragement of members to follow standards and procedures
8. Appropriate responses when standards and procedures are violated
9. Regular evaluations of program effectiveness

Many enterprises have published standards of responsible business behavior. Over the past two decades, in particular, they have developed a body of best practices that enterprises in emerging market economies can consider and adapt for their circumstances.

Checklist

1. How adept is your enterprise at dealing with change?

2. How many of the components of a business ethics program does your enterprise have?

3. What level of identity is your enterprise most concerned about? Compliance? Risk management? Reputation enhancement? Value added?

4. If your enterprise were to initiate a business ethics program, how would it go about engaging its stakeholders?

5. How are important decisions made in your enterprise? Is there a process of engaging stakeholders involved in such decisions?

Creation of a Business Ethics Program

*T*his chapter is intended to introduce owners and managers to the process of developing, reviewing, and approving a business ethics program. It elaborates on the process for designing a business ethics program described in Chapter 3.

The chapter first helps owners and managers develop the measures through which they will evaluate program effectiveness. It will show how to graphically portray the elements of the program in a business ethics program logic model. It then turns to developing a toolkit for owners and managers to use in designing and implementing their business ethics program.

Planning an Effective Business Ethics Program

Before going forward in the design and implementation process, owners and managers need to decide what they are trying to accomplish through their business ethics program. An effective program will have specific, action-oriented, relevant, and timely performance measures. Also, essential to a business ethics program are mechanisms to measure the program's performance. Chapter 10 examines more fully the design of a performance measurement system for a business ethics program.

For the responsible business enterprise (RBE), an effective program is one that achieves expected outcomes and integrates well into the enterprise itself. As one ethics officer in a recent study observed, "Ethics

• **Planning an Effective Business Ethics Program**

• **Understanding the Program Logic Model**

• **Scanning the Relevant Context**

• **Scanning the Enterprise's Internals**

programs become truly effective to the extent that they can evolve and plug into where a company is going."[1] The study concludes that a well-integrated program is one that (a) is aligned with an organization's core beliefs; (b) fits well with organization systems, policies, and practices; (c) addresses leadership priorities as well as employee expectations for ethics; (d) is used by employees at all levels to guide decision-making and action; and (e) becomes a central part of an organization's culture over time.[2]

There are two principal areas to consider in setting business ethics program objectives: (a) how owners and managers think the organizational culture will be affected and (b) what specific outcomes owners and managers desire from the program. Although it is difficult to measure directly the extent to which values such as trust and integrity are shared, there are a number of specific outcomes affecting the organization's culture that can be expected from such a program and that are valuable to monitor, track, and report.

ESSENTIAL CHARACTERISTICS OF ENTERPRISES

A number of elements of organizational culture will give owners and managers a profile of the enterprise to help them design and implement an effective business ethics program. These include five characteristics of a highly effective organization and eight influential cultural factors. When tracked and measured over time, these elements will be extremely valuable in evaluating program success.

Importance of Organizational Culture

The principal predictor of an effective business ethics program is the culture of the organization itself. Responsible owners and managers will shape their management, ethics, compliance, and social responsibility practices to address nuances of the enterprise's organizational culture.

Organizational culture is shaped by the organization's origin and history as well as the values, norms, and attitudes of its owners, managers, and other stakeholders. It is a bundle of assumptions about the way the world works and the beliefs, values, symbols, languages, rituals, principles, rules, and practices that consciously or unconsciously drive the thoughts, feelings, and actions of the enterprise and its stakeholders.

Organizational culture influences what the organization senses, cares about, and is capable of dealing with. It will influence how comfortable employees and agents are with engaging the stakeholders. Culture also is a source of conflict. As one noted scholar observed, "The world is full of confrontations between people, groups, and nations who think, feel, and act differently. At the same time these people, groups, and nations . . . are exposed to common problems which demand cooperation for their solution."[3] Responsible managers are challenged to find the common ground for enterprise stakeholders and to guide their employees and agents to meet their reasonable expectations.

Characteristics of Organizational Culture

The first step in developing measures of an enterprise's organizational culture is to develop a profile of the enterprise as a whole. This profile can be captured in the following five characteristics:

1. Extent to which leaders and members alike embrace the organization's core purpose and values, and are adept at preserving them while stimulating progress

2. Extent to which leaders and members hold themselves responsible—and others accountable—for high standards

3. Extent to which leaders encourage members—and members welcome and accept the opportunity—to participate in organizational affairs

4. Extent to which leaders and members have the knowledge they need when they need it

5. Extent to which conflict and mistakes made in good faith are seen as opportunities for learning and growth[4]

Indicators of Organizational Culture

More specific than the profile described above are a number of measurable indicators of organizational culture, which tend to be closely associated with expected business ethics program outcomes. Eight such influential factors are set forth below:

1. Perceiving that leadership cares about ethics and values as much as the bottom line

2. Feeling safe to deliver bad news

3. Feeling treated fairly

4. Feeling valued as an employee

5. Not feeling pressured to compromise values

6. Believing ethical behavior is rewarded

7. Believing unethical behavior is punished

8. Recognizing whether the enterprise has an employee, community, or self-interest focus[5]

These factors reflect the styles of leadership and sense of fair play that characterize the enterprise. They are visible aspects of organizational culture.

EXPECTED PROGRAM OUTCOMES

The primary purpose of a business ethics program is to help an enterprise address all four levels of its identity as an RBE. The four levels, discussed in detail in Chapter 3, are portrayed again in Figure 4.1. An effective business ethics program will include a performance measurement system that captures program outcomes that reflect the goals and objectives of the enterprise. See Appendix A for a model that employees and agents can use to make decisions with outcomes in mind.

FIGURE 4.1
Levels of an Enterprise's Identity

Tracking the following nine outcomes will help determine whether a business ethics program is effective for all four levels of identity:

1. How often violations of standards, including legal requirements, can be observed (compliance and risk management levels)

2. How often responsible business conduct issues are raised at the workplace (all four levels)

3. How often employees and agents speak in terms of core beliefs and standards (all four levels)

4. How often employees and agents make decisions based on core beliefs and standards (all four levels)

5. How willing employees and agents are to seek advice on standards (all four levels)

6. How willing employees and agents are to report observed or suspected violations (compliance and risk management levels)

7. How satisfied those who reported observed or suspected violations are with management's response (compliance and risk management levels)

8. How committed employees are to the enterprise (value-added level)

9. How satisfied stakeholders are that the enterprise meets their expectations (reputation enhancement and value-added levels)[6]

BENCHMARKS AND BASELINES

When the data are collected and analyzed, they may be used in a number of ways. They can give owners a picture of the culture, program processes, and business conduct of the enterprise. They can be used as baseline data for comparison with subsequent data. They can also be used to compare the findings with those of other similarly situated enterprises (known as *benchmarking*).

The first usage is helpful for owners and managers because it gives them a sense of how their employees and agents view the fundamental workings of the enterprise. Particularly valuable is comparing how managers, supervisors, and workers answer the same questions. Often, the answers are so different that one might wonder if the respondents work for different enterprises. These data also permit comparison between different plants and locations. For large, complex enterprises (LCEs), regional differences can be explored.

Where program evaluation is done on a regular basis—every one to three years, for example—the data serve as *baseline data*. Once a baseline of organizational culture, processes, and expected program outcomes is established, owners and managers can compare later data with the baseline to detect patterns and identify trends over time.

A final use is to compare the organizational culture, program processes, or expected program outcomes with other enterprises that establish benchmarks of practices or conduct. Benchmarking *can* be an effective practice if it compares program processes, such as code of conduct formats, business ethics office organization, or help-line procedures. For analyzing organizational culture or expected program outcomes, however, benchmarking is very difficult to do well, for a number of reasons.

Very little data are available publicly beyond large national surveys for program outcomes. Enterprises that do evaluate their programs for organizational culture and outcomes seldom share the data with the public. Moreover, business ethics programs are so fundamental to the very identity of an enterprise that it would be difficult to make meaningful comparisons that take into account differing organizational culture, program process, and expected program outcomes.

EMPLOYEE MISCONDUCT

According to the National Business Ethics Survey 2003, published by the Ethics Resource Center, 22 percent of all employees surveyed reported having observed at least some misconduct within the past year (4 percent frequently and 12 percent occasionally).

This finding represented a decline from the 31 percent of all employees who observed misconduct in two previous surveys (2000 and 1994).

Ethics Resource Center, 2003
National Business Ethics Survey

Moreover, the real question is why owners and managers would want to spend valuable resources comparing their enterprise with other enterprises since the goal of a responsible business is to meet the reasonable expectations of their stakeholders, not to compare favorably with some other enterprise having different stakeholders. For example, how much comfort will owners and managers derive from finding that their employees observe half the amount of misconduct found by the Ethics Resource Center described in Box 4.1?[7] A favorable comparison alone does not help the enterprise learn what it is doing right, or even whether the data are accurately collected. In a culture of distrust, for example, employees will often refuse to answer a question about misconduct or will answer it incorrectly.

Understanding the Program Logic Model

Before beginning to design and implement a business ethics program, owners and managers must have a firm understanding of what will be required for the program to achieve its expected outcomes effectively, efficiently, and responsibly. A simple, but powerful technique to capture and communicate the *who*, *what*, and *why* of any program is the program logic model.[8]

All management programs have common components. Typically, a situation presents a challenge to the enterprise. Owners and managers establish goals and objectives to meet the challenge. They develop a strategy and an action plan or program to achieve those goals. The action plan or program requires input in the form of resources, contributions, and investment. These resources are used by employees and agents through activities with participants to generate output: goods, services, events, and communications. These activities and their output lead to expected program outcomes, the changes or results in people, enterprises, communities, or societies that occur over the short to long term.[9] See Appendix A for a sample outcomes-based decision-making model.

A program logic model helps planners organize their thinking and encourage stakeholder engagement. It is a particularly effective means of graphically describing the elements of a business ethics program to the owners (or their representatives), senior management, employees and agents, and other stakeholders. A program logic model worksheet (RBE Worksheet 1) is provided at the end of this chapter. Owners and managers can use the program logic model to stimulate dialogue and graphically portray how they envision their business ethics program working. A business ethics program logic model can be completed in four nonlinear steps:

1. **Situation:** Describe the specific problem or issue. For example, a large customer may be requiring its downstream suppliers to comply with global standards. Or, as is currently the case in the United States, regulatory authorities may require that a listed enterprise have some of the elements of a business ethics program.

2. **Outcome:** Determine what the expected program outcomes are. That is, develop the measurable indicators that owners and managers want to accomplish over time that will address the problems or issues of their situation (for example, increased issue awareness or reduced irresponsible behavior). These are the reasons they are pursuing the program.

3. **Process:** Develop the action plans that owners and managers will pursue to design and implement a business ethics program. They will want to address:

    a. **Input:** what they need to invest in terms of resources, including management attention

    b. **Activities:** what needs to be done to achieve the expected program outcomes, such as establishing standards, procedures, and expectations and conducting training and education

    c. **Participants:** the stakeholders who will be involved in each activity

    d. **Outputs:** what will actually be produced, such as, a code of conduct, three specific policies, or 50 percent of all employees trained within the first year

4. **Contributing factors, including assumptions:** Describe the factors and assumptions that owners and managers considered in designing the business ethics program, such as the enterprise's capacity to draft a code of conduct or conduct training, the industry standards that apply, and the aspects of the organizational culture that they need to be concerned about.

Scanning the Relevant Context

Whether an economy is already developed or emerging, owners and managers in that economy should scan the relevant context of their enterprise to identify the pressures it places on the enterprise, its employees, and its agents. These pressures take five forms: threats, opportunities, demands, constraints, and uncertainties.

This section describes the process of collecting the essential items of information about the relevant context that owners and managers need to design and implement an effective business ethics program. It describes two ways policy-makers, owners, and managers can analyze and synthesize these data collected: by *context element* or by *stakeholder*.

IMPORTANCE OF CONTEXT

All enterprises—whether large or small—strive to meet enterprise goals and objectives in a context of legal, economic, political, environmental, socio-cultural, and technological elements. Known as the *relevant context* of the enterprise, these elements bring pressures to bear on the enterprise, its employees, and its agents.

Legal Element

Government creates the legal framework in which market processes operate. As a sovereign entity, a state regulates private activities to protect or promote the general welfare of its citizens and residents. Depending on the level of state involvement in market processes, this regulation will involve, to one degree or another, public health, safety, morality, and dispute resolution.

Government regulation also defines how limited liability businesses, such as corporations, limited partnerships, and joint stock companies, are formed and what the limits of their liability are. Government regulations define the generally recognized corporate governance roles and responsibilities of directors, managers, and shareholders. Indeed, it may be that this tendency to define these roles and responsibilities in such detail is what discourages more discussion of corporate governance in terms of ethics and public policy. The very law that establishes minimum standards often comes to define the ceiling as well.

In emerging market economies, institutions are often not sufficiently independent or strong to enforce the law consistently. Indeed, law enforcement engaging in petty corruption may be a part of the problem.[10]

Economic Element

An RBE must consider the nature of its market and the amount of trust that characterizes exchange transactions. In emerging market economies, the economic system is often unstable and characterized by frequent crises, causing businesses to seek short-term profits at the expense of long-term growth. Instability and lack of trust increase the cost of each transaction as the parties take expensive steps to protect themselves or avoid entering into a transaction at all. Such a climate can also foster a high tolerance for activities that are unethical, such as an individual using an enterprise's assets for personal gain or paying small bribes to move a transaction along. At the same time, the cost of regulation is often so high that shadow markets emerge, making it more difficult for the RBE to compete ethically.

Consumer expectations are a key economic factor. For example, consumers may be more or less discriminating. High quality may be more or less expected. Brand names may be more or less important. Employee economic expectations are also important. For example, employment security and compensation expectations differ significantly depending on where an enterprise is located. Privacy expectations for e-mail usage on company time also differ, as do employee expectations about policies such as the hiring of relatives.[11]

Political Element

In scanning its relevant context, an RBE needs to understand the kind and degree of government influence in the market, how laws and regulations come about, who has practical access to influencing them, and the degree of government control over the economy. Government presence in the trade and investment sector often restricts trade: decreasing competition, creating opportunities for corruption, and increasing costs to business. Regulation in the form of decrees may distort the basic rules set by laws.[12] A principal test is the extent to which consumer interests will be sacrificed to protect producers.

Environmental Element

The physical world in which we live forms the widest relevant context for the business enterprise to consider and its most controversial element. The planet itself is a system of interdependent ecosystems that has evolved over millennia in a process of creation and destruction. Human beings are an integral part of this system and the first to influence consciously its evolution. An RBE is concerned with how to be a part of this process responsibly. It must be adept at recognizing environmental issues and consequences. As a leading textbook notes: "Each [environmental] case, involves a highly individualized set of scientific facts, economic and political issues, and social and natural consequences."[13]

Socio-cultural Element

In addition to organizational culture, each enterprise and its members operate within—and are products of—the broader cultures around them. Culture creates collective patterns of thinking, communicating, and acting that influence the decisions, processes, and activities of the enterprise itself. It influences the mental models that employees and agents bring to the job regarding fundamental issues of concern to managers, including the following five "dimensions of culture," developed by Geert Hofstede:

1. Social inequality, including the relationship with authority
2. Relationship between the individual and the group
3. Concepts of masculinity and femininity
4. Ways of dealing with uncertainty, relating to the control of aggression and the expression of emotions
5. Long-term versus short-term orientation[14]

Culture influences the decisions of owners and managers regarding a range of specific issues, including policies regarding conflict of interest, privacy, and nepotism. Culture also influences the willingness of employees to report misconduct, and the nature of the reward and punishment they will receive.[15]

Technological Element

An important consideration in planning and implementing a business ethics program is the technology available to the enterprise and its stakeholders. Particularly important are computer and telecommunications capabilities. For example, computer capability will influence how easily recordkeeping, monitoring, and auditing can be accomplished. Telecommunications capability will influence how owners and managers exercise control and relay communications.

RELEVANT CONTEXT AND THE SMALL TO MEDIUM-SIZED ENTERPRISE

As we explore the importance of context in this section, it is important to recognize that, while all enterprises need to have a clear understanding of the elements of their relevant context, the issues facing an LCE and a small to medium-sized enterprise (SME) may be dramatically different in kind and in degree of relative severity. For example, Table 4.1 includes a representative sampling of how differently an LCE and an SME might see the issues their relevant contexts present to them.

DATA COLLECTION, ORGANIZATION, AND ANALYSIS

This manual provides two tools to help owners and managers scan the external context issues. RBE Worksheet 2 aids in collecting relevant context data for each context element: legal, economic, political, environmental, sociocultural, and technological. Each of these elements is examined in light of the pressures faced: threat, opportunity, demand, constraint, and uncertainty. RBE Worksheet 3 examines the external context by stakeholder category

TABLE 4.1   Relevant Context Comparison Chart

Element	Typical LCE Issues	Typical SME Issues
Legal	Lacking familiarity with domestic legal institutions, fearing local bias, and paying for third-country arbitration Complying with anticorruption legislation and anti–money laundering regimes in multiple countries and competing with companies in countries without such legislation or where it is not enforced Dealing with technology transfer restrictions and national boycotts	Lacking awareness of rights Lacking access to court systems and coping with delays Dealing with laws and regulations that are disproportionately burdensome for SMEs Dealing with lack of enforcement and administrative corruption in system
Economic	Meeting diverse consumer needs Dealing with advocacy group boycotts against globalization or specific practices Managing the supply chain and creating strategic alliances with companies having shared core beliefs	Lacking bargaining power and sufficient infrastructure Lacking access to foreign markets and the ability to convert currency Lacking resources to identify consumer needs
Political	Imposing proper limits to the influencing of government laws and regulations Dealing with the capture of regulatory government agencies through inappropriate relationships or unduly close industry influence	Having no voice in government decision-making
Environmental	Applying home-country environmental standards when the host country's standards are lower	Remaining competitive when other companies abuse the environment to avoid costly waste disposal
Socio-cultural	Preserving core beliefs of a multinational enterprise in multiple cultures	Coping with a low level of latent entrepreneurship
Technological	Respecting customer privacy in collecting data over the Internet	Lacking access to telecommunications and information technologies

and by the pressures different types of stakeholders bring to the enterprise. Both worksheets are found at the end of this chapter.

This manual recommends that the enterprise form a working group to collect, organize, and analyze the data, using the worksheets as a tool, and to present the findings to the owners and managers.

Scanning the Enterprise's Internals

In addition to scanning the enterprise's relevant context, owners and managers also need to scan the internal structure and dynamics of the enterprise. This manual offers two major tools to help analyze an enterprise's internals. The first is a questionnaire that can be used to develop the organizational

FIGURE 4.2
Organization Culture Profile

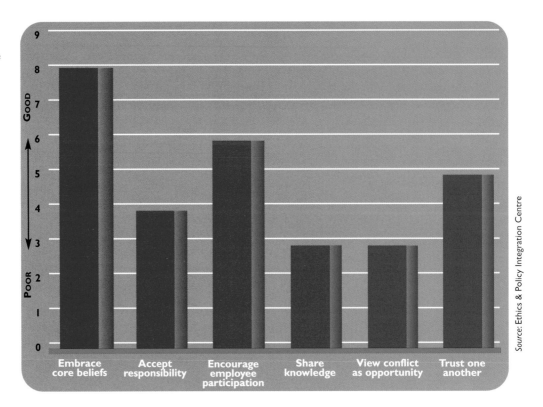

Source: Ethics & Policy Integration Centre

culture profile (RBE Worksheet 4). The second is based on the eight questions listed in Table 2.2 in Chapter 2 (RBE Worksheet 5). Both worksheets can be found in the back of this chapter.

RBE Worksheet 4 can be used as a survey. Owners and managers can average the survey results to develop a profile of the enterprise as seen in Figure 4.2.

RBE Worksheet 5 helps owners and managers answer the eight questions discussed in Chapter 2. Each question is followed by examples of global standards and best practices that can help the RBE adopt appropriate answers.[16] Specific best practices are outlined in the chapters that follow: standards and procedures (Chapter 5), business ethics infrastructure (Chapter 6), business ethics communications and feedback (Chapter 7), enterprise alignment practices (Chapters 8 and 9), and business ethics program evaluation and organizational learning (Chapter 10).

SUMMARY

Before going forward in the design and implementation process, owners and managers need to decide what they are trying to accomplish through their business ethics program. An effective program will have specific, action-oriented, relevant, and timely performance measures of organizational culture and expected program outcomes.

A program logic model helps planners organize their thinking and encourage stakeholder engagement. A program logic model is a particularly effective means of graphically describing the elements of a business ethics program to the owners (or their representatives), senior management, employees and agents, and other stakeholders. Using RBE Worksheet 1, one may capture the essential elements of an entire business ethics program on one page.

This chapter offers a number of worksheets for owner and manager use: RBE Worksheets to scan the external context and the enterprise interior (RBE Worksheets 2–5).

With these processes in mind, Chapter 5 turns to how owners and managers establish enterprise standards of conduct and foster reasonable stakeholder expectations.

RESPONSIBLE BUSINESS ENTERPRISE
Checklist

1. **How well does your enterprise understand its relevant context? What elements offer the most threats and opportunities?**

2. **How well does your enterprise understand its own culture?**

3. **How would your enterprise use the RBE Worksheets?**

Business Ethics Program Logic Model

A program logic model graphically depicts elements of a business ethics program. The model below will assist planners of a business ethics program to organize their thinking and encourage stakeholder engagement. Owners and managers can use the program logic model to stimulate dialogue and graphically portray how they envision their business ethics program working.

Situation	Process			Outcomes			
	Input	**Activities and Participants**	**Ouput**	**Short Term** / **Med. Term** / **Long Term**			**Goal**
The specific problem or issue as framed and deemed worthy of attention	What we invest, such as manager attention, infrastructure, staff, time, budget, reputation	What we do to achieve enterprise goals and objectives, such as engage stakeholders, conduct training, provide advice, monitor and audit, field inquiries, investigate	What we produce and whom we reach, such as code of conduct, training units, help-line, formal inquiries, management response, reports to stakeholders	Measurable indicators of progress toward goals and objectives, such as reduced irresponsible conduct, and increased issue awareness, advice-seeking, reporting of misconduct, satisfaction with management's response, employee commitment, and stakeholder satisfaction			Responsible Business

Contributing factors, including assumptions:
• Enterprise and individual capacity
• Program orientation and level of identity (see Chapter 3)
• Applicable standards of responsible business conduct (see Chapter 2)

• Relevant context (see Chapter 4)
• Organizational culture (see Chapter 4)

A blank worksheet, which may be photocopied for use within your organization, follows on the next page.

Business Ethics Program Logic Model

Situation	Process			Outcomes			
	Input	**Activities and Participants**	**Ouput**	**Short Term**	**Med. Term**	**Long Term**	**Goal**

Contributing factors, including assumptions:

2 **Relevant Context Data Collection**

RBE Worksheet 2 provides a tool to help owners and managers scan the external context issues an enterprise faces by context element—legal, economic, political, environmental, socio-cultural, and technological—and by the pressures faced in each element—threat, opportunity, demand, constraint, and uncertainty.

In filling out this worksheet, as many stakeholder perspectives as possible should be obtained for each element. For example, the economic element might be filled out as follows:

	Threat	Opportunity	Demand	Constraint	Uncertainty
Economic	New competition enters the market. Competitor introduces new products. Infrastructure is inadequate. Civil society advocates against product or practices.	New market is available. Tariffs have been reduced.	Customer expects quality. Industry has standards for certification.	Supply chain is inadequate. Infrastructure is weak.	Value of currency and interest rates may change.

A blank worksheet, which may be photocopied for use within your organization, follows on the next page.

	Threat	Opportunity	Demand	Constraint	Uncertainty
Legal					
Economic					
Political					
Environment					
Socio-cultural					
Technological					

3 Stakeholder Pressure Data Collection

RBE Worksheet 3 helps owners and managers scan the external context by stakeholder category and the pressures stakeholders bring to the enterprise. In this tool, employees are included for balance.

In filling out this worksheet, as many stakeholder perspectives as possible should be obtained for each element. For example, the customers category might be filled out as follows:

	Threat	Opportunity	Demand	Constraint	Uncertainty
Customers	ABC enterprise is a major customer, but it may begin doing more of its contract work in-house.	XYZ Enterprise is a strategic partner and is bidding on a major contract.	Higher quality is demanded by ABC, but also lower prices.	XYZ requires that suppliers meet all International Labor Organization Standards.	XYZ's financial status may be affected if it fails to win contract.

A blank worksheet, which may be photocopied for use within your organization, follows on the next page.

	Threat	Opportunity	Demand	Constraint	Uncertainty
Customers • Major • Minor • Other					
Employees • Managers • Supervisors • Workers • Organized • Families					
Investors • Shareholders • Board • Pension Funds • Activists					
Suppliers					
Competitors					
Community					
Government					
Environment					

4   Organizational Culture Questionnaire

RBE Worksheet 4 may be used in an anonymous survey or as a device to stimulate dialogue. People answering each question should consider the organizational culture extremes and select one number in the range from 1 to 9. The survey results will allow owners and managers to develop a profile of the enterprise.

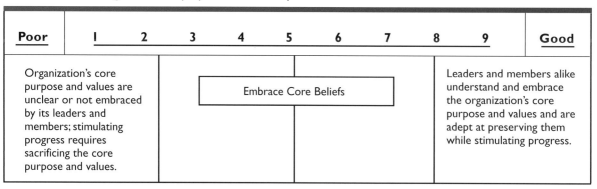

Poor	1	2	3	4	5	6	7	8	9	**Good**

Organization's core purpose and values are unclear or not embraced by its leaders and members; stimulating progress requires sacrificing the core purpose and values.

Embrace Core Beliefs

Leaders and members alike understand and embrace the organization's core purpose and values and are adept at preserving them while stimulating progress.

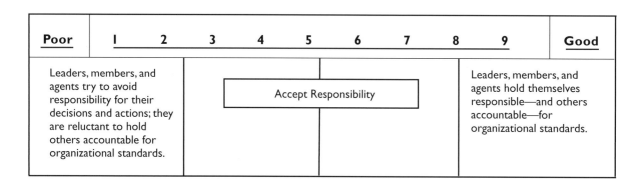

Poor	1	2	3	4	5	6	7	8	9	**Good**

Leaders, members, and agents try to avoid responsibility for their decisions and actions; they are reluctant to hold others accountable for organizational standards.

Accept Responsibility

Leaders, members, and agents hold themselves responsible—and others accountable—for organizational standards.

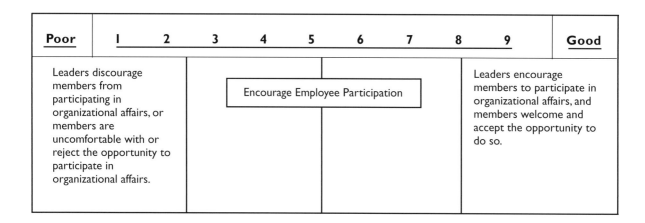

Poor	1	2	3	4	5	6	7	8	9	**Good**

Leaders discourage members from participating in organizational affairs, or members are uncomfortable with or reject the opportunity to participate in organizational affairs.

Encourage Employee Participation

Leaders encourage members to participate in organizational affairs, and members welcome and accept the opportunity to do so.

continued on the next page

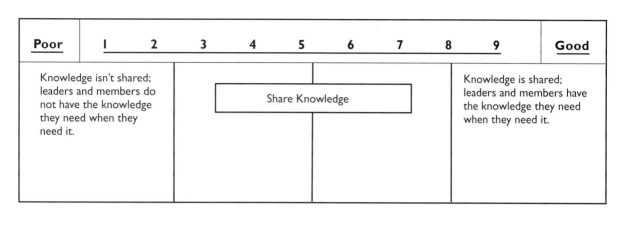

| Poor | 1 | 2 | 3 | 4 | 5 | 6 | 7 | 8 | 9 | Good |

Knowledge isn't shared; leaders and members do not have the knowledge they need when they need it.

Share Knowledge

Knowledge is shared; leaders and members have the knowledge they need when they need it.

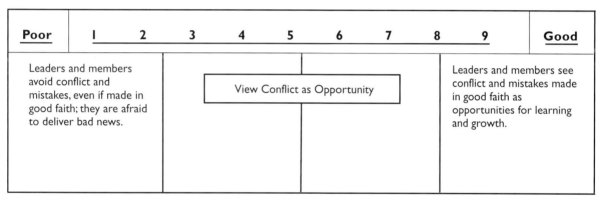

| Poor | 1 | 2 | 3 | 4 | 5 | 6 | 7 | 8 | 9 | Good |

Leaders and members avoid conflict and mistakes, even if made in good faith; they are afraid to deliver bad news.

View Conflict as Opportunity

Leaders and members see conflict and mistakes made in good faith as opportunities for learning and growth.

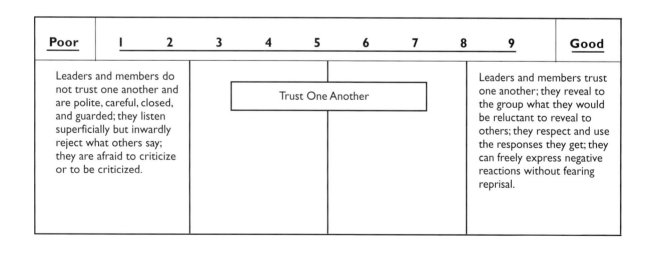

| Poor | 1 | 2 | 3 | 4 | 5 | 6 | 7 | 8 | 9 | Good |

Leaders and members do not trust one another and are polite, careful, closed, and guarded; they listen superficially but inwardly reject what others say; they are afraid to criticize or to be criticized.

Trust One Another

Leaders and members trust one another; they reveal to the group what they would be reluctant to reveal to others; they respect and use the responses they get; they can freely express negative reactions without fearing reprisal.

5 **Questions for the Responsible Business Enterprise**

Owners and managers use this RBE Worksheet to determine what strategies and action plans they should pursue to move from where they are currently to where they believe the enterprise should be. From the myriad standards and best practices known, the enterprise should determine which standards and best practices to adopt. For example, in answering Q.1 regarding standards, the following may be used as a reference:

- Sound set of core beliefs including core purpose, core values, and envisioned future[17]
- Modified OECD Guidelines for Multinational Enterprise/Corporate Governance beyond domestic requirements
- Minimum requirements of U.S. Federal Sentencing Guidelines for Organizations, including all industry standards and government regulations

Owners and managers may find, while analyzing how to fill a gap, that they had set unreasonably high or unnecessarily low expectations in their reference standards. Then, they can go back and reconsider their answers to the question.

	Reference Standards	Current Practices	Gap Analysis
Q.1 What norms, values, and standards should we set to guide our members and foster reasonable expectations among our stakeholders?	• Sound set of core beliefs • OECD Guidelines for Multinational Enterprise/Corporate Governance • U.S. Federal Sentencing Guidelines • Australian corporate culture		
Q.2 What style, structure, and systems of authority and responsibility at all levels should we exercise?	• Sound set of core beliefs • Leadership styles • Board-level committees • High-level person responsible for program • Executive-level ethics committee • Ethics office • Individual duty to report misconduct		
Q.3 How can we most effectively communicate our standards and procedures and foster reasonable expectations among our stakeholders?	• Executive modeling • Formal communications • Orientation • Ethics training • Posters • Newsletter		

continued on the next page

	Reference Standards	Current Practices	Gap Analysis
Q.4 How can we know that our members follow our standards and that reasonable stakeholder expectations are met?	• Independent audit committee • Audit department • Ethics office investigation resources/ availability • Mechanisms free of fear of retaliation • Organizational ombudsman • Policy on retaliation		
Q.5 How can we ensure that we have the right people in the right places while we pursue our purpose as an enterprise?	• Recruiting • Hiring • Skills training • Assignment • Promotion • Termination		
Q.6 How can we encourage our employees and agents to follow our standards and procedures?	• Recognizing ethical behavior equal to standards in tough situations • Punishing behavior not to standards • Consistent compensation schemes, especially bonuses and incentive pay		
Q.7 What do we owe our stakeholders when mistakes, misconduct, or misunderstandings occur that involve our standards and procedures or their reasonable expectations?	• Voluntarily reporting mistakes and misconduct • Cooperating with proper authorities • Correcting harm caused • Conducting training in required skills and knowledge		
Q.8 How should we monitor, track, and report our performance as an enterprise and continuously learn from it?	• Tracking, measuring, and reporting to stakeholders • Establishing program goals and objectives • Developing appropriate action plans • Establishing performance indicators • Developing performance measurements • Instituting data recording, collection, and analysis • Establishing reporting frameworks and schedules		

A blank worksheet, which may be photocopied for use within your organization, follows on the next two pages.

5 Questions for the Responsible Business Enterprise

	Reference Standards	Current Practices	Gap Analysis
Q.1 What norms, values, and standards should we set to guide our members and foster reasonable expectations among our stakeholders?			
Q.2 What style, structure, and systems of authority and responsibility at all levels should we exercise?			
Q.3 How can we most effectively communicate our standards and procedures and foster reasonable expectations among our stakeholders?			
Q.4 How can we know that our members follow our standards and that reasonable stakeholder expectations are met?			

continued on the next page

	Reference Standards	Current Practices	Gap Analysis
Q.5 How can we ensure that we have the right people in the right places while we pursue our purpose as an enterprise?			
Q.6 How can we encourage our employees and agents to follow our standards and procedures?			
Q.7 What do we owe our stakeholders when mistakes, misconduct, or misunderstandings occur that involve our standards and procedures or their reasonable expectations?			
Q.8 How should we monitor, track, and report our performance as an enterprise and continuously learn from it?			

III

Structuring the Business Ethics Program

Standards, Procedures, and Expectations for the Responsible Business Enterprise

*T*he responsible business enterprise (RBE) establishes appropriate standards of conduct for its employees and agents and fosters reasonable expectations among its stakeholders. This chapter describes basic principles and best practices to help owners and managers develop, review, and approve such standards, procedures, and expectations.

Standards and Procedures

The first question owners and managers of an RBE must ask themselves is, "What norms, values, and standards should we set to guide our members and foster reasonable expectations among our stakeholders?"[1] Their answers define how the RBE will improve its performance, make profits, and increase the prosperity of its community by learning to meet the reasonable expectations of its stakeholders. Whether an enterprise is large or small, the question of what standards, procedures, and expectations to establish touches all aspects of an enterprise.

HOW THE RBE DIFFERS FROM OTHER ENTERPRISES

All enterprises set standards and procedures and foster stakeholder expectations. What distinguishes an RBE from other enterprises is that its owners and managers consciously develop the RBE's standards, procedures, and reasonable expectations as the surest

• **Standards and Procedures**

• **Responsible Governance**

• **Principles for Setting Management Standards, Procedures, and Expectations**

• **Management Vision for the Enterprise**

• **Management Standards, Procedures, and Expectations**

• **Typical Code of Conduct Provisions**

route to improving performance, making profits, and contributing to economic progress.

A well-designed and well-implemented business ethics program provides all members of an enterprise with the guidance and information they need for effective, efficient, and responsible choices and actions. Employees and agents need to know what performance is expected of them. They need to know what they should do—and what they shouldn't do—to meet performance goals and objectives. All stakeholders, both internal and external, have expectations of the enterprise, which are more or less reasonable. An effective business ethics program helps owners and managers develop standards, procedures, and expectations that establish the following:

- Who has authority to do what within the enterprise
- Who is responsible for which decisions and activities
- How people will be held accountable for their individual choices and actions
- What stakeholders can reasonably expect from the enterprise

An RBE develops standards, procedures, and expectations with complete understanding of its relevant context and organizational culture.[2]

WHY STANDARDS AND PROCEDURES ARE IMPORTANT

There are many reasons for an enterprise to set standards and procedures for its employees and agents and to foster reasonable expectations among its stakeholders. Standards, procedures, and expectations help focus the energy of employees and agents on achieving enterprise goals and objectives. They let stakeholders know what they can expect.[3] When standards and procedures are clear and stakeholders hold reasonable expectations, relationships based on trust are possible. The enterprise accumulates the social capital it needs to compete effectively, efficiently, and responsibly in global markets.

When standards, procedures, and expectations are not well established, owners and managers may not safely delegate their authority or expect stakeholders to be well served. The enterprise will often find its members operating at cross-purposes, because it is not clear what is expected of them. Its strategies and action plans will lack focus and power. When standards, procedures, and expectations are unclear, it cannot readily measure its performance. Holding an employee or agent accountable for bad faith or poor judgment is unfair if the criteria are uncertain. Stakeholders, both internal and external, may become frustrated, cynical, or distant because their expectations have not been realized. Investor confidence, customer satisfaction, status as a preferred supplier or strategic partner, and employee morale will be at serious risk.

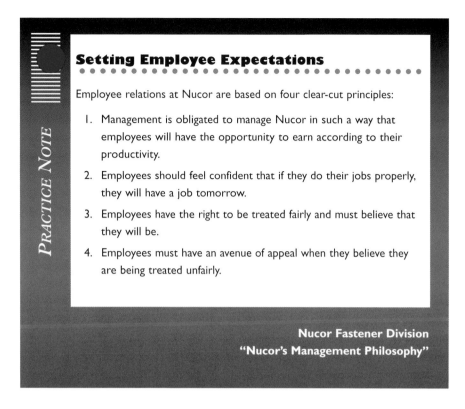

PRACTICE NOTE

Setting Employee Expectations

Employee relations at Nucor are based on four clear-cut principles:

1. Management is obligated to manage Nucor in such a way that employees will have the opportunity to earn according to their productivity.

2. Employees should feel confident that if they do their jobs properly, they will have a job tomorrow.

3. Employees have the right to be treated fairly and must believe that they will be.

4. Employees must have an avenue of appeal when they believe they are being treated unfairly.

Nucor Fastener Division
"Nucor's Management Philosophy"

HOW EMPLOYEE CREATIVITY CAN BE PRESERVED

Standards, procedures, and expectations are more than just control mechanisms. They give the guidance employees and agents need so that they can choose and act confidently. A well-developed set actually provides a sense of stability. If owners and managers honor their own policies, employees and agents can act freely and confidently within defined boundaries. Considerable human potential can be realized because employees and agents no longer fear being punished for violating some standard of which they are not aware. They will have bounded freedom to use their considerable imaginations and talents to perform on behalf of the enterprise.[4]

Standards, procedures, and expectations establish criteria for the development of policies and performance measurement. They are the basis for determining whether choices or actions were made or taken in good faith or reflect good judgment. The confidence and creativity that standards, procedures, and expectations bring to an enterprise and to its employees and agents build trust over time when everyone in the enterprise understands them and acts consistently.

Responsible Governance

There is a flow of authority, responsibility, and accountability throughout all enterprises. At the top of this flow are the owners or their representatives. The owners or representatives of an RBE follow a three-step process to establish policy guidelines for responsible governance. First, they delegate some measure of authority to managers. Next, they establish the purpose of the enterprise, including the value it brings to its community.[5] Third, they establish clear limitations or constraints on the exercise of the authority they granted. These policy categories are comprehensive: they embrace all choices and actions of the enterprise's employees and agents—managers, supervisors, and workers.[6]

Following the responsible governance policies and procedures of the owners or their representatives, managers define methods, activities, conduct, and tasks for employees at all levels and for agents. They define the core beliefs of the enterprise and establish the guidance that employees and agents need to meet reasonable stakeholder expectations.

Where there are owner representatives, such as a board of directors, these representatives also define the purpose, functions, and character of their own governance. These policies define how they will work together and their commitment to doing so.

RESPONSIBLE GOVERNANCE PROCESS

The policy governance commitment statement in Box 5.1 is an example of a general statement that describes the purpose of a board of directors.[7] Three

---

BOX   5 . 1

POLICY GOVERNANCE COMMITMENT

The purpose of the board, on behalf of the shareholders, is to see to it that the company (a) achieves appropriate results for shareholders and (b) avoids unacceptable actions and situations.

1. Accountability Philosophy: The board's fundamental accountability is to the shareholders.

2. Social Responsibility: Although the board accepts as its primary obligation to operate in the best interests of shareholders,

that fidelity is tempered by an obligation to the social order and to be a good member of the community.

3. Directors' Conduct: The board commits itself and its members to ethical, businesslike, and lawful conduct, including members' proper use of authority and appropriate decorum when acting as directors.

John Carver with Caroline Oliver
Corporate Boards That Create Value

> ### BOX 5.2
>
> ## POLICY GOVERNANCE MODEL DELEGATION OF AUTHORITY STATEMENT
>
> ### Delegation to the CEO
>
> The board's sole official connection to the operational company, its achievements, and its conduct will be through a chief executive officer (CEO).
>
> 1. Unity of Control. Only officially passed motions of the board, speaking authoritatively as a group, are binding on the CEO.
>
> 2. Accountability of the CEO. The CEO is the board's only official link to operational achievement and conduct, so that all authority and accountability of management is considered by the board to be the authority and accountability of the CEO.
>
> 3. Nature of CEO Delegation. The board will instruct the CEO through written policies that prescribe the shareholder benefit to be achieved and describe organizational situations to be avoided, allowing the CEO reasonable interpretation of these policies.
>
> **John Carver with Caroline Oliver**
> *Corporate Boards That Create Value*

specific provisions are particularly important: accountability, social responsibility, and directors' conduct. An accountability philosophy statement affirms the board's understanding that its primary responsibility is to the shareholders it represents, not management. A social responsibility statement affirms the board's understanding that, while the board owes faithful attention to the interests of shareholders, it also must pay attention to social order and must see that the enterprise is a good member of a community. Finally, a director's conduct statement commits individual board members to ethical, businesslike, and lawful conduct.

BOARD-MANAGEMENT DELEGATION

In situations when owners are not actively engaged in an enterprise, they or their representatives will delegate a substantial amount of their authority to management. Responsible governance calls for such authority to be delegated to one person. That person, whether called the chief executive officer (CEO), president, or general director, is given the authority to manage everyone else in the enterprise. A sample policy delegating authority to management is set forth in Box 5.2.[8]

Under this arrangement, the lines of authority are clear. The owner representatives have one employee for operational purposes: the CEO. The CEO, in turn, is accountable to the board itself. The CEO will delegate some of his or her authority to other employees through standards, procedures, and expectations, but the CEO remains accountable to the board for all decisions made and actions taken.

OWNER EXPECTATIONS OF MANAGEMENT PERFORMANCE

Owner policies regarding management performance relate to the ends sought for the enterprise. The CEO is not entitled to make any choices or to take any actions that are not reasonably calculated to achieve the designated ends of the enterprise.

Policies Defining Ends

Responsible governance calls for precise definition of the ends of the enterprise. There are three components to an effective ends statement: "first, the *results* for which the [enterprise] exists; second, the *recipients* of those results; and third, the *relative worth* of those results."[9]

At first glance, the *results* component relates to financial performance. Certainly for enterprises whose shares are actively traded results must be related to financial performance. As one scholar, John Carver, notes, however, this is not always the case:

> In some small start-up companies, for example, desired results may include working independently with trusted partners in an exciting field—plus satisfactory financial return. In some family-owned companies, the value owners want is satisfaction of having family members working together in the same business—plus satisfactory financial return.[10]

A range of performance results is possible: market share, long-term capital growth, profits, reliable income, and successful research and development. Owner representatives must take the desires of all owners into account to determine what the desired results of the enterprise are and how to communicate them to employees and other stakeholders.

The *recipients* component seems clear enough, since the owners are the recipients. However, as Carver notes, "owners do not all have the same interests, and the board represents all owners."[11] The board must take into account the diverse interests of the owners. The relative strength of blocs of shareholders must also be considered. Although majority shareholders are entitled to a proportionate share of enterprise results, the board must not disproportionately benefit majority shareholders.

Finally, the *relative worth* component requires that the owner representatives prioritize among the results and recipients it has identified. Rarely will all owners have the same desired performance results. Some, for example, may be willing to forgo current income in favor of capital investment in research and development. Others may be certain that their majority interest entitles them to disproportionate returns or influence over the board. Whatever a given ends statement might contain, management deserves a

---

B O X   5 . 3

MODEL LIMITATIONS POLICY ON BASIC EXECUTIVE CONSTRAINTS

Delegation to the CEO

The CEO shall not cause or allow any practice, activity, decision, or organizational circumstance that is unlawful, imprudent, or in violation of generally accepted business and professional ethics or generally accepted accounting principles.

John Carver with Caroline Oliver
Corporate Boards That Create Value

---

clear statement from the owners or their representatives as to what successful enterprise performance looks like.

Policies Defining Means

When the board is setting management limitations, Carver suggests they set "basic executive constraints" (see Box 5.3).[12] It is up to management to decide how to achieve the ends of the enterprise within the authority granted to it by the board.

Given that the ends of an RBE are ultimately to produce value for the owners, what about the many other considerations of the RBE, such as other stakeholders, the rule of law, and ethical conduct?

These are means issues. They are not the reason for the enterprise's existence, but they suggest how it may obtain its objectives. For example, the enterprise's legal obligations and its relationships with stakeholders, while critical, are not the reason the enterprise exists. To preserve management flexibility, therefore, the board should establish policies that define the boundaries of management authority, rather than offer prescriptions for action.[13]

Carver recommends that the board ask itself, "What management situations, activities, or decisions would be unacceptable to us even if they worked? Even if the ends are being achieved, what risks, ethical violations, and proprieties does the board want to put off limits?"[14] When the board has answered these questions, responsible governance requires that it specify all the limitations it intends to place on management authority. See, for example, the sample means limitations in Box 5.4. The power of this approach is that management authority not expressly limited is, in effect, authorized. Management authority exercised within those boundaries—and reasonably intended in good faith to achieve the ends of the enterprise—has bounded freedom to be agile and creative.[15]

Principles for Setting Management Standards, Procedures, and Expectations

Just as responsible governance at the board level involves setting ends and means for the executive, responsible management establishes a vision for the enterprise; goals and objectives; and standards, procedures, and expectations to guide enterprise employees and agents. As owners and managers establish these, this manual recommends applying the principles described below.

STRIVE TOWARD HIGHER STANDARDS

An enterprise should always strive toward higher standards. Expectations of an enterprise's ethical behavior evolve constantly in response to changing market conditions, both regionally and globally. New values and beliefs emerge not only in the market, but also in the organizational culture and the personal lives of employees. An enterprise should constantly solicit feedback from both internal and external stakeholders to update and modify its business ethics program.

CONSIDER CULTURAL DIFFERENCES

Culture is difficult to measure, and dimensions of culture are even trickier to use in setting standards, procedures, and expectations. However, an increasing number of studies suggest that ethical decision-making processes differ, if not in the result, by country, nationality, and culture. Significant differences have been found in the matters of responsible business conduct, tone taken in addressing issues, and appropriate management responses to employee conduct.[16]

IDENTIFY EXCEPTIONS FROM HOME-COUNTRY STANDARDS

Globalization and the increase of cross-border trade and investment introduce enterprises to a wide range of cultures and values. The globalization process includes increased pressure from civil society, the media, and governments from different nations. Enterprises are expected to abide by the ethical values of their home countries. They must also take into account standards introduced by the forces of globalization, particularly if they operate on a transnational basis.

Sometimes, exceptions to standards, procedures, and expectations must be made when working with actors outside of the enterprise's home country. To do business in other markets without sacrificing their own core beliefs, enterprises must clearly identify when they are making exceptions to home-country standards.

COMMUNICATE WHY

To ensure that the organizational culture is integrated and works toward an enterprise's goals and objectives, owners and managers should communicate not only the enterprise's standards, procedures, and expectations but also the reasons behind them. They should explain why responsible business conduct is important to improving business performance, to making a profit, and to increasing prosperity in the enterprise's community.

Owners and managers should explain to employees and agents why complying with standards, procedures, and expectations is necessary and consistent with the enterprise's core beliefs. For example, simply declaring to an employee that it is unethical to provide confidential information to a third party may be ineffective. Managers should explain that such information could undermine a competitive advantage held by the enterprise and adversely affect its profitability. This explanation will impart perspective to the employee and help him or her understand the purpose behind the rules.

INCLUDE EMPLOYEES IN SETTING STANDARDS

Dialogue is required to set responsible standards, procedures, and expectations that fit the needs of the enterprise and its employees and agents. When developing or modifying a business ethics program, management must understand which responsible business conduct issues are of central importance to employees. Securing employee input is essential. Failure to do so can result in employee cynicism and erosion of trust between employees and management. Ultimately, employees may decide not to comply with enterprise standards and procedures and may fail to pursue the enterprise's purpose, thus causing the enterprise to fail to meet reasonable stakeholder expectations.

CLARIFY OPERATIONAL AND ETHICAL RESPONSIBILITIES

The operational and ethical responsibilities of managers and other employees must be clearly expressed in codes of conduct and other aspects of a business ethics program. The relationship between employees and their supervisors should be governed by two central principles: authenticity and accountability. Authenticity requires honest communication about who is responsible for ethical practices, mistakes, and misconduct. Accountability requires that each party to the relationship accept personal responsibility for what he or she brings to the relationship. An effective business ethics program sets forth these expectations and shows how the enterprise will address mistakes, misconduct, and misunderstandings.

Management Vision for the Enterprise

Responsible management defines the enterprise's core beliefs: its purpose beyond profit, its core values, and its envisioned future. In addition, as developed at length in Chapter 4, owners and managers establish expectations for the business ethics program itself by describing supportive cultural characteristics of the organization and expected program outcomes.

Two researchers, James Collins and Jerry Porras, found that what separates good companies from great ones, in large part, is the vision framework they provide their employees and aligning their choices and actions to that framework.[17] The vision framework that they recommend has three components: a core purpose, core values, and an envisioned future.

CORE PURPOSE

Without losing sight of returning value to the owners, responsible management establishes the fundamental reason for the existence of the enterprise in the form of a purpose statement that inspires its employees and agents. An enterprise purpose beyond profit helps define the enterprise. Unlike goals and objectives, the purpose is never actually achieved. As Collins and Porras describe it, enterprise purpose "like a star on the horizon can never be reached; it guides and inspires forever."[18]

Purpose should be a succinct statement of how the enterprise intends to meet some important need of its community. A purpose statement captures the reasons that employees and agents are eager to go to work. It takes as given that owners want profits and that employees want livelihoods. But one can be certain that most employees do not go to work eager to make more money for the owners or even to earn their next paycheck. They go to work eager to contribute because there is something in the purpose of the enterprise that excites them.

Defining an enterprise's purpose is not an easy process. Collins and Porras suggest describing what the enterprise does in business—its mission, for example—and then asking five times: "Why is that important?" Though deceptively simple, asking "Why is that important?" will help establish the value the enterprise brings to the community. This sense of value added becomes the ordering principle of all subsequent decisions and activities.[19]

CORE VALUES

Responsible management defines four or five values to guide the choices and actions for all employees and agents. These core values should be so fundamental to what the enterprise sees itself to be—and the way that it does business—that they will not be sacrificed for short-term gain.

There is no right set of values for an enterprise. Royal Dutch/Shell, for example, has three core values: *honesty*, *integrity*, and *respect for people*. Chiquita Brands, International, which has plantations around the globe, has four core values: *integrity*, *respect*, *opportunity*, and *responsibility*. Alcatel, a multicultural company with employees in 130 countries, has four values as well: *customer focus*, *innovation*, *teamwork*, and *accountability*.

Core values should reflect the fundamental qualities that the enterprise wants to use to guide employee and agent decisions and activities, but they should not be so far removed from the reality of the enterprise that they are impossible to follow or that they breed cynicism. Moreover, the process of defining core values will influence how they are understood, accepted, and followed. The more stakeholders participate in developing the core values, the more likely these core values are to reflect the enterprise and to be accepted by its members and other stakeholders.

Some enterprises arrive at their core values through a carefully crafted survey of their employees, including interviews and focus groups. Others establish advisory groups at various levels of the enterprise to work with a small working group to draft a set of values for further dialogue. A few enterprises survey all or most of their members plus many other stakeholders.

To bring to the surface enterprise values among employees, ask a simple question such as, "What would you tell a new employee who asks 'What does someone have to do to succeed around here?'" Following through on employee and other stakeholder answers to these questions will lead eventually to four or five values that should guide members of the enterprise.

VISION OF A DESIRED FUTURE

Responsible owners and managers visualize enterprise goals and objectives and the enterprise's role in the community over the long term. Goals should include responsibility to the community and to external stakeholders. They should incorporate relevant political, economic, and socio-cultural considerations. From this vision flow the goals, objectives, and expected outcomes of the enterprise's strategies and action plans.

Research suggests that there are two components to an effective envisioned future: (a) a specific goal that gives direction and meaning to enterprise decisions and activities and (b) a vivid description of the desired future.[20] Box 5.5 shows how Novo Nordisk describes embedding its vision throughout the enterprise.[21]

A good example of describing an envisioned future is the vision of Sony, portions of which are set forth in Box 5.6. This vision was formed in the 1950s, when Japan was still recovering from the devastation of World War II. It contained an audacious long-term goal and a vivid description of the desired future.[22]

BOX 5.5

EMBEDDING VISION IN AN ENTERPRISE

Vision

- We will be the world's leading diabetes care company.
- We will offer products and services in other areas where we can make a difference.
- We will achieve competitive business results.
- A job here is never just a job.
- Our values are expressed in all our actions.
- Our history tells us, it can be done.

The Charter

The Charter describes our Values, Commitments to the Triple Bottom Line, Fundamentals and Methodology—our basic management principles. The full text can be found on the Novo Nordisk corporate website.

Policies

Our Vision expresses the company's key business objectives and guides a set of policies on bioethics, communication, engineering, environment, finance, health and safety, information technology, legal, patents, people, purchasing, quality, regulatory and risk management.

Novo Nordisk
"Novo Nordisk Way of Management"

BOX 5.6

SONY CORPORATION'S VISION

Purpose statement. To experience the sheer joy of innovation and the application of technology for the benefit and pleasure of the general public.

Goal. Become the company most known for changing the worldwide image of Japanese product as being of poor quality.

Vivid description. Fifty years from now, our brand name will be as well known as any on earth . . . and will signify innovation and quality that rivals the most innovative companies anywhere. . . . "Made in Japan" will mean something fine, not shoddy.

James C. Collins and Jerry I. Porras
Built to Last: Successful Habits of Visionary Companies

Management Standards, Procedures, and Expectations

Enterprises of all sorts and sizes are experiencing increasing pressure from home countries, international institutions, and nongovernmental organizations to demonstrate responsible business conduct. Management standards, procedures, and expectations give specific guidance that demands certain activities and restricts others, unlike board-level means limitations, which set limits only.

As discussed in Chapter 3, an RBE functions at four levels of identity: compliance, risk management, reputation enhancement, and value added to the community. Responsible management sets standards, procedures, and expectations at all four levels to give adequate guidance to employees and agents. These standards, procedures, and expectations tend to foster reasonable external stakeholder expectations of enterprise performance.

Standards, procedures, and expectations are often set in a number of basic documents: a set of guiding principles, a code of conduct,[23] and specific policies. Although this chapter discusses how to draft a code of conduct and refers to a number of examples, there is no one right approach. For example, an enterprise can draft the basic documents as separate documents or as a single document.

GUIDING PRINCIPLES

Enterprises will find value in establishing a number of general principles to guide employees and agents. With the core beliefs providing the basis, a statement of general principles aids employees and agents in making choices and taking action. A statement of general principles is more specific than the core beliefs, but it is broader than a code of conduct.

For some enterprises, like Royal Dutch/Shell, its fundamental guiding document is its "Statement of General Business Principles."[24] Another executive-level set of guiding principles to consider is the U.N. Global Compact.[25]

Statements of guiding principles tend to be accessible to employees and agents because they are considerably shorter than the average code of conduct. These principles may be one-sentence statements or short paragraphs, but usually no longer.

Using Royal Dutch/Shell as an example, an enterprise might set forth its basic principles under nine topics: (1) objectives; (2) responsibilities to stakeholders; (3) economic principles; (4) business integrity; (5) political activities; (6) health, safety, and the environment; (7) community, (8) competition; and (9) full relevant disclosure.

Shell begins with a general preamble that states the purpose of the principles themselves. The preamble reads in part as follows:

> Shell companies recognize that maintaining the trust and confidence of shareholders, employees, customers and other people with whom they do business, as well as the communities in which they work, is crucial to the Group's continued growth and success.
>
> We intend to merit this trust by conducting ourselves according to the standards set out in our principles.[26]

The first principle sets forth a general statement of the *objectives* of the enterprise. These closely track its core purpose. The second principle sets forth the *responsibilities* that it believes it owes its primary stakeholders: shareholders, customers, employees, those with whom it does business, and society as a whole, which includes the environment. These descriptions are, for the most part, one or two sentences each. The description of the responsibilities it owes society incorporates a number of the principles of the U.N. Global Compact. Shell sees these five areas of responsibility as inseparable.

The third principle sets *economic* principles to guide its employees and agents (see Box 5.7).[27] Shell notes that profitability and a strong financial foundation are fundamental to meeting its responsibilities. It also notes that pursuit of financial aspects is qualified by social and environmental considerations and an "appraisal of the security of the investment."

Shell's fourth principle addresses its notion of *business integrity*. Shell maintains that its companies "insist on honesty, integrity, and fairness in all aspects of their business and expect the same in their relationships with all those with whom they do business."[28] Going into somewhat more detail than

B O X   5 . 7

ROYAL DUTCH/SHELL'S ECONOMIC PRINCIPLES

3. Economic Principles

Profitability is essential to discharging these responsibilities and staying in business. It is a measure both of efficiency and of the value that customers place on Shell products and services. It is essential to the allocation of the necessary corporate resources and to support the continuing investment required to develop and produce future energy supplies to meet consumer needs.

Without profits and a strong financial foundation it would not be possible to fulfill the responsibilities outlined above.

Criteria for investment decisions are not exclusively economic in nature but also take into account social and environmental considerations and an appraisal of the security of the investment.

Royal Dutch/Shell
"How We Work"

a statement of principle, Shell's business integrity principle expressly addresses bribery, conflicts of interest, and maintaining accurate books and records.

Shell's fifth principle, regarding *political activities*, reinforces its sense of social responsibility and restricts its companies and individual employees in their political activities. However, Shell conspicuously reserves the right to take a public position on matters that affect it or its primary stakeholders.

Shell's sixth principle addresses its commitment to contribute to *sustainable development* and its "systematic approach to health, safety, and environmental management in order to achieve continuous performance improvement." Shell commits to "manage these matters as any other critical business activity, set targets for improvement, and measure, appraise and report performance."[29]

Shell's seventh principle addresses its relationship with the *community*. It expressly notes that its most important contribution is to pursue what we term its core purpose and its envisioned future as a business as effectively as possible. Shell then specifically authorizes community involvement going beyond being a socially responsible business to include ultra-social responsibility where appropriate.[30]

Shell's eighth principle is express support for the *competition* inherent in free enterprise.

Finally, Shell commits to providing *full relevant information* about its "activities to legitimately interested parties, subject to any overriding considerations of business confidentiality and cost."[31]

Shell's "Statement of General Business Principles" covers many aspects of general business conduct and can serve as an excellent guide for an RBE,

CHIQUITA BRANDS' APPROACH TO CORPORATE RESPONSIBILITY

- We take pride in our work, in our products, and in satisfying our customers.

- We act responsibly in the communities and environments in which we live and work.

- We are accountable for the careful use of all resources entrusted to us and for providing appropriate returns to our shareholders.

Chiquita Brands International
"Corporate Responsibility"

even though it does not address a number of the emerging global standards we described in Chapter 2. Nongovernmental organizations (NGOs), while applauding Shell's statement in general, have noted, for example, that it does not specifically address a number of international conventions, notably the Universal Declaration of Human Rights, as well as the Tripartite Declaration of Principles of the International Labor Organization.[32]

Another common approach to a guiding set of principles is to list the enterprise's core values with a number of guiding principles or practices below each value. See, for example, an extract from the Chiquita Brands, International core values statement in Box 5.8.[33] Another example is United Technologies Corporation, which sets forth five "Commitments": "performance, pioneering innovation, personal development, social responsibility, and shareowner value" (see Box 5.9).[34] The value of this approach is that it demonstrates the significance of a few core values, while using principles and practices to define them and to provide concrete examples in one document.

Management may also consider any number of other general principles for ideas. One set to consider is the "Principles for Business" of the Caux Round Table, which are widely considered a good starting point for developing an

UNITED TECHNOLOGIES' PERFORMANCE

Our customers have a choice, and how we perform determines whether they choose us. We aim high, set ambitious goals and deliver results, and we use customer feedback to recalibrate when necessary. We move quickly and make timely, well- reasoned decisions because our future depends on them. We invest authority where it needs to be, in the hands of the people closest to the customer and the work.

United Technologies Corporation
"Our Commitments"

enterprise's sense of ethical and responsible business conduct.[35] Another set of principles to consider is the *Basic Guidelines for Codes of Business Conduct* (reprinted in Appendix B), which can be used as a foundation or guide for developing codes of conduct.

CODE OF CONDUCT

A code of conduct is often the primary means by which management gives guidance to its employees and agents as to what is expected of them by way of business conduct. Indeed, among large enterprises globally, most now have some form of code of conduct.[36]

A code demonstrates management's commitment to meeting all applicable industry practices and government regulations. Its target audience is the enterprise as a whole. Other, more specific policies and procedures will be directed at specific functions, such as procurement or contracting.

A code of conduct addresses minimum standards of conduct and procedures to reduce the enterprise's risk of liability and damage to its reputation. A code of conduct also goes beyond these minimums to guide employees and agents toward enhancing the enterprise's reputation and adding genuine value to its community.

It is important not to place too much significance on a code of conduct standing alone. Most research suggests that a code is important less for its specific provisions than as part of a program or strategy to encourage responsible business conduct. When examining the incidence of misconduct, researchers have found relatively little difference between organizations that have a code and those that do not.[37]

As part of a business ethics program, however, a code is a central component of a process by which the enterprise engages its stakeholders, both internal and external. In recent years, the process of formulating codes of conduct has become more interactive and inclusive. Increasingly, codes are an essential part of an ongoing dialogue designed to shape programs. Indeed, a senior official at Royal Dutch/Shell has declared:

> Shell is increasingly focusing on dialogue, and we have found many NGOs who are willing to enter into debate with us. Discussion based on a broad framework of principles offers a constructive atmosphere for cooperation—and for the compromise that is sometimes necessary in the face of real-life ambiguities.[38]

An enterprise should carefully examine its relevant context when deciding on the scope of its code of conduct. It should consider the priorities of its community and external stakeholders; the state of decrees, laws, and regulations; and industry standards. It should also show respect for national and organizational culture.

Compliance with the Law

When designing a business ethics program, an enterprise must ensure that it complies with all laws and regulations that govern its area of commerce: local, foreign, and international. The codes themselves tend not to set forth the details of the law. However, they will set the general policy of complying with all laws, and they may refer to laws that have specific application to the enterprise's business conduct such as corporate governance, workplace practises, and relationships with government officials. Where more detail is required, these matters will typically be treated in policies and procedures documents. Working closely with legal counsel, an RBE will incorporate changes and amendments to the law and regulations into its business ethics program on a regular basis.

The general nature of a code of conduct—as well as the issues addressed—differ widely between the European Union and the United States. Codes in the United States tend to be more compliance-oriented and are even legalistic, because the laws in the United States tend to leave more business matters to the private sector. They also address the significant risk of litigation. Codes in the European Union tend to be more focused on social responsibility. In part, this difference in focus arises because many matters that are covered in codes tend to be addressed by law and regulation in the United States or by individual or work council contract provisions in the European Union.[39]

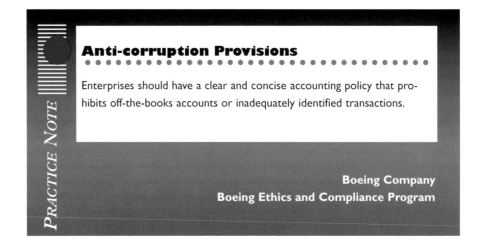

PRACTICE NOTE

Anti-corruption Provisions

Enterprises should have a clear and concise accounting policy that prohibits off-the-books accounts or inadequately identified transactions.

**Boeing Company
Boeing Ethics and Compliance Program**

Compliance with Industry Standards

An RBE is often a member of an industry as well as a community. Owners and managers take into account industry-specific issues and standards and procedures. In doing so, they should strive to achieve the highest standards of compliance in their industry. Improved industry standards increase transparency and trust in the marketplace, and they enhance the reputation of the industry as a whole. For an example of industry standards regarding the scope of a code of conduct, see the New York Stock Exchange's recently promulgated exchange rules (Box 5.10).[40]

Protection of the Environment

A code of conduct should address the enterprise's standards, procedures, and expectations regarding the environment. Governments, local communities,

---

BOX 5 . 1 0

New York Stock Exchange Rules

In November 2003, in response to great turmoil in the U.S. markets, the New York Stock Exchange (NYSE) promulgated a series of requirements to improve the corporate governance practices of companies listed on the NYSE. A listed enterprise is now required to adopt and disclose a code of ethics addressing, at a minimum, the following issues:

- Conflict of interest: Defines conflicts of interest and requires a policy proscribing conflicts and providing a means to report potential ones.

- Corporate opportunities: A policy should prohibit officers, directors, and employees from taking corporate opportunities, using corporate property, position, or information for personal gain, or competing with the company. All employees, officers, and directors owe a duty to advance the legitimate interest of their company.

- Confidentiality: Information entrusted to employees, directors, and officers by the company or customers should be kept confidential, except when disclosure is authorized or legally mandated. Confidential information includes all non-public information that may be of use to competitors or harmful to the company or clients of the company if disclosed.

- Fair dealing: Each employee, officer, and director should deal fairly with the customers, suppliers, competitors, and other

employees of the company. None should take unfair advantage of anyone through manipulation, concealment, abuse of privileged information, misrepresentation of material facts, or any other unfair-dealing practice.

- Protection and proper use of company assets: Employees, officers, and directors should protect company assets and ensure the efficient and legitimate use of all business assets.

- Compliance with laws, rules, and regulations (including insider trading laws): The company should actively promote compliance with laws, rules, and regulations, including insider trading laws.

- Encouraging the reporting of any illegal or unethical behavior: The company should encourage employees to talk to supervisors, managers, or other appropriate personnel about the best course of action they should take when presented with a particular situation. In addition, companies should encourage employees to report violations of laws, rules, regulations, or the code of business conduct to appropriate personnel. To encourage employees to report such violations, the company must ensure that employees know that the company will not allow retaliation for reports made in good faith.

BOX 5.11

FROM THE NTT GROUP GLOBAL ENVIRONMENTAL CHARTER

Basic Principle

To ensure the harmonious coexistence of people with nature and to achieve sustainable growth, we will do our utmost to protect the global environment in all our corporate activities.

Basic Policies

1. Compliance with laws and regulations and fulfillment of social responsibilities

To observe all laws and regulations regarding environmental protection issues and to carry out our responsibilities as global corporate citizens.

2. Reducing environmental loads

To establish action plans for energy conservation (reduction of greenhouse gas emissions), resource conservation (conservation of materials such as paper), and waste reduction, and to strive to make continuous improvements.

3. Establishing and maintaining environmental management systems

To establish an environmental management system enabling each business unit to pursue voluntary environmental protection activities.

4. Developing environmental technologies

To contribute to the reduction of environmental load through various areas of research and development, including multimedia services.

5. Social contribution efforts

To promote daily environmental protection efforts in coordination with citizens and government agencies.

6. Disclosure of environmental information

To enhance both internal and external communications through the disclosure of environmental information.

NGOs, and international institutions are increasingly using their influence to promote sound environmental practices by business.

A code should include a statement that the enterprise will abide by both local and international laws and regulations designed to protect the environment. It should address how the business balances production objectives with environmental protection in general. In more detailed standards, procedures, and expectations, the enterprise might discuss how to reduce waste products, how to avoid polluting air and water, and how to manage and report chemical use and disposal.

An example of the flow from core values regarding the environment through a basic principle and basic policies to principal activities (leading to achieving goals and objectives) is set forth in the Japanese NTT (Nippon Telegraph & Telephone) Group ethical code of environmental issues (see Box 5.11).[41]

Respect for Cultural Norms

A code of conduct should demonstrate respect for the cultural norms of the society in which the enterprise operates—especially if it is a transnational enterprise. Employees and agents bring their beliefs, values, and cultural norms to the job. Each society has cultural practices that are unique, including practice of religion, gender relations, and power relationships in the workplace. An RBE is sensitive to these practices and ensures that its business ethics program takes them into consideration without sacrificing its core beliefs. Implementing and enforcing a code of conduct that does not take these factors into consideration may be seen as unfair and may lead to confusion and frustration.[42]

A number of responsible business conduct issues are unusually culturally sensitive: dealing with conflicts of interest, accepting and giving gifts and gratuities, making facilitation payments, hiring relatives and friends, seeking advice, and reporting misconduct. Reporting misconduct, in particular, touches on deeply held cultural values and even relatively recent histories, as discussed in Chapter 7.

A best practice for dealing with these cultural nuances is to require regional divisions of an enterprise to formulate local policies and to submit them for approval. Provided that the local policy reflects the spirit of the general policy and is applied consistently, regional policies can be effective ways to address cultural differences. Note, however, that the general rule should apply unless a specific local policy has been proposed and approved. An employee or agent should not be able to claim a regional difference without an approved local policy in place.

PRACTICE NOTE

Gifts Given by Motorola

Some business situations call for giving gifts. Motorola's gifts must be legal, reasonable, and approved by local management. Motorolans never pay bribes.

We understand that gift-giving practices vary among cultures. Our local gift policies and guidelines address this.

We will not provide any gift if it is prohibited by law or the policy of the recipient's organization. For example, the employees of many government entities around the world are prohibited from accepting gifts. If in doubt, check first.

Motorola Corporation
"Code of Business Conduct"

Guidelines for Developing a Code

The process for developing a code of conduct is as important as the code itself. Engaging stakeholders, demonstrating management commitment, and honoring core beliefs will lead to a clear statement of what the enterprise values. Moreover, the process is an important step toward reinforcing the desired aspects of organizational culture.

At the end of the process, the code must be comprehensive enough to give guidance on all important matters to employees and agents. It must have had enough participative feedback from internal stakeholders—especially the owners, managers, and workers—that they will recognize it as their own, support it, and be willing to live by it. It must describe external stakeholder expectations well enough that they will recognize the enterprise as a contributing member of the community.

One noted author in this field, W. Michael Hoffman, encourages drafters to be particularly concerned with the tone of the code. He recounts how he was once asked to review a code titled "Our Responsibilities." Though he thought it was a good title, "every rule that followed began with 'it is your responsibility to . . .'" He suggested changing every "your" to "our" to convey the sense that the rules applied to everyone in the company.[43]

Style for a code also depends on the needs and culture of the enterprise. The more readable codes use large type, color, often pictures, and examples or text boxes for frequently asked questions. There are many fine examples on the Internet.

- WMC Resources Ltd., an Australian global mining company, has a very straightforward, colorful, animated code of conduct. It has many pictures and examples presented as drop down pages under five major topics.[44]

- NTT Group, a Japanese telecommunications company, has a detailed environmental code as part of its "Environmental Report 2002." It is organized as eight questions and their answers.[45]

- Guardsmark LLC, a medium-sized U.S. firm, has a short code of conduct that lays out principles organized by values and major topics. All employees review and acknowledge the code annually.[46]

- HCA Inc., a large U.S. health care company, has a comprehensive code of conduct, as well as policies and procedures for implementing its ethics, compliance, and corporate responsibility program.[47]

- United Technologies Corporation, a large, global manufacturing firm, has a code of ethics translated into 27 languages, which describes multiple means for an employee or agent to seek advice or report concerns, including regional and headquarters ombudsman offices.[48]

Expecting Good Judgment from Employess

We are accountable for our actions and their consequences.

Question: I am a geologist in charge of an exploration project. A well-known local politician, who owns a small bankrupt company, has asked me to hire some of the 70 employees he will have to dismiss. In exchange, he has offered to facilitate local government permits for WMC. If I do not accept, he threatens to do the opposite. Should I accept the proposition? Should I accuse him of blackmail?

Answer: You should not accept the proposition. Your discussion with the politician should be documented, and you should seek guidance from the appropriate WMC manager as to the steps to take including going to police or local authorities.

WMC Resources, Ltd.
"Illustrative Examples"

PRACTICE NOTE

A code of conduct should be a practical, easily accessible document. It should be written in plain language, avoiding technical or legal terms. It should be available in the languages key stakeholders understand.[49]

Aspirational versus Obligatory Provisions

Some authors distinguish between code provisions that are aspirational and those that are obligatory. Aspirational provisions are said to be ones that employees and agents are to strive for but for which they will not be held accountable. Obligatory provisions are said to be ones for which employees and agents can be held accountable and ones that will result in punishment if violated.

An enterprise's standards, procedures, and expectations are intended to guide employees and agents in dealing with real-life issues. Owners and managers should expect employees and agents to demonstrate awareness of all relevant standards and to use good judgment. If the underlying standard is to apply good judgment, therefore, we are reluctant to say that any standard worth putting in a code of conduct is purely aspirational. The better view is that if a provision is worth putting in a code, then it should be followed.

For the most specific standards—rules—good judgment seldom leads one to violate a rule. When rules are violated, punishment is appropriate since a clear intention to violate rules exists. For more general provisions such as values or principles, good judgment is still required, and it makes little sense to describe such provisions as unenforceable. Although the employee may not be punished as such, failure to use good judgment should not be tolerated.

Adaptations, Updates, and Improvements to the Code

Though a code of conduct is a fundamental document, it is not static. To be effective, it must anticipate the guidance that employees and agents will need to deal appropriately with the challenges they face. Laws and regulations change. Stakeholder expectations change as well. Through commerce with enterprises from different markets, businesses become exposed to new values and beliefs that can affect the way employees view the enterprise and markets. All these tend to create new gray areas for employees.

An RBE should plan in the code itself to monitor closely changes in its relevant context, organizational culture, and stakeholder expectations and to adapt, update, and improve the code accordingly. The RBE must be able to react quickly to changes that affect the enterprise, its markets, and its communities. It must adapt its code to reflect its relationships with new suppliers, service providers, partners, competitors, and markets.

Code Formats

An author who has tracked the trends in drafting codes of conduct has found that most codes apply one or more of three basic formats: (a) *compliance codes*—specific statements giving guidance and prohibiting certain kinds of conduct; (b) *corporate credos*—broad general statements of corporate commitments to constituencies, values, and objectives; and (c) *management philosophy statements*—formal enunciations of the company or CEO's way of doing business.[50]

An Australian author further distinguishes the formats and objectives of corporate codes of ethics as being of three types: (a) *codes of ethics*—statements of the values and principles that define the purpose of an organization, (b) *codes of practice*—which guide and direct decision-making, and (c) *codes of conduct or behavior*—which prescribe or proscribe certain behavior. "In practice," the author notes, "corporations tend to use varying mixes of each type of code, under various labels."[51]

RBE Worksheet 6, found at the end of this chapter, provides a sample outline for a code of conduct.

RESPONSIBLE BUSINESS CONDUCT POLICIES

Once a set of guiding principles, a code of conduct, or both are developed, the process of establishing adequate standards is not complete. To keep these defining documents relatively concise, enterprises typically publish much of the detail that surrounds specific offices or functions, such as internal audit or government contracting, as policies or procedures. An RBE also address-es specific risk areas and opportunities to enhance its reputation or add value to the community. A number of fundamental issues are noted in RBE Worksheet 6, such as ethics, compliance, and responsibility functions and help-line policy and procedures. There may be many others.

Effective business ethics programs are designed specifically for the day-to-day challenges of the individual enterprise, its management styles, and its organizational culture. For example, the comprehensive business ethics program of HCA Inc., a large U.S. health care company, has 20 ethics and compliance-specific policies and procedures and dozens more related policies and procedures from other departments.[52] These policies include the following:

- Policy and procedure development
- Internal handling of ethics-line calls
- Self-reporting of violations of certain laws and regulations
- Business courtesies to potential referral sources
- Business entertainment
- Vendor-promotional training
- Approval of gifts in recognition of volunteer efforts
- Ethics and compliance officer
- Code of conduct distribution and training
- Records management
- Ethics and compliance program contracts
- Ethics and compliance office quarterly reports
- Training for senior management
- Reportable events

There is no set format for issuing policy and procedures. The form shown in Figure 5.1 is provided courtesy of HCA Inc.[53]

Typical Code of Conduct Provisions

The best way to think about what standards, procedures, and expectations to put in a code of conduct is to try to anticipate, from the points of view of stakeholders, the tough decisions that employees and agents might face. With this approach in mind, consider including the items described below. Examples of how some enterprises addressed certain issues are also included.[54] Using RBE Worksheet 7, provided at the end of this chapter,

FIGURE 5.1
Format Used by HCA Inc. in Issuing Policy and Procedures

Department: _____	Policy Description: _____
PAGE: x of y _____	Replaces Policy Dated: _____
Approved: _____	Retired: _____
Effective Date: _____	Reference Number: _____

Scope: _____

Purpose: _____

Policy: _____

Procedures: _____

References: _____

will help ensure that all necessary standards, procedures, and expectations are considered.

INTRODUCTORY MATERIALS

What materials should be included? And why? Introductory materials are highly dependent on the situation, needs, and culture of the enterprise. They should begin with a declaration of the enterprise's core beliefs, examples of which were described earlier.

An advisable provision to include is a disclaimer. For example, Motorola Corporation avoids creating unrealistic expectations—and unintended liabilities—by placing a disclaimer at the beginning of its code (see Box 5.12).[55] Disclaimers are recommended because some courts have treated similar documents as promises on which stakeholders may justifiably rely.[56]

B O X   5 . 1 2

DISCLAIMER TO A CODE OF BUSINESS CONDUCT

Basic Principle

This Code is neither a contract nor a comprehensive manual that covers every situation Motorolans throughout the world might encounter. It is a guide that highlights key issues and identifies policies and resources to help Motorolans reach decisions that will make Motorola proud.

Motorola Corporation
"Code of Business Conduct"

OWNERS

What relationships and responsibilities to its owners should the enterprise assume? And why? Consider the following:

- Maximizing shareholder value
- Minimizing business risk
- Using business resources prudently
- Engaging in legal and ethical behavior
- Preventing insider trading
- Being responsible to community and environment

CUSTOMERS OR CONSUMERS

What relationship and responsibilities to its customers should the enterprise assume? And why? Here are some examples:

- Providing quality, safe goods and services
- Representing products or services
- Communicating clearly so that there is no misunderstanding
- Protecting confidential information
- Preventing bribes and kickbacks
- Regulating gifts and entertainment
- Including government customer provisions
- Including foreign government customer provisions
- Ensuring accurate billing procedures
- Safeguarding property of others

- Preventing the disparagement of competitors
- Ensuring fair competition
- Acquiring marketing data properly and legally

EMPLOYEES AND THE ENTERPRISE

What relationships and responsibilities to its employees should an enterprise assume? What do the employees owe the enterprise? And why? Issues include these:

- Promoting respect for one another
- Promoting equal opportunity and anti-harassment
- Creating a hassle-free environment
- Respecting right to privacy
- Promoting workplace health and safety
- Maintaining skills and qualifications
- Preventing substance abuse
- Preventing workplace violence
- Regulating use of company funds
- Regulating company e-mail and computer use
- Preventing conflicts of interest
- Regulating outside business activities
- Regulating gifts and entertainment
- Regulating collective bargaining
- Promoting human rights
- Excluding child labor
- Promoting business with the company
- Regulating employment outside the company
- Encouraging self-development and lifelong learning
- Regulating the hire of closely related people
- Ensuring accurate books and records
- Retaining records

PARTNERS, SUPPLIERS, AND SERVICE PROVIDERS

What relationship and responsibilities to its partners, suppliers, and service providers should the enterprise assume? And why? Consider these issues:

PRACTICE NOTE

Anticorruption

3. In its relations with governmental agencies, customers and suppliers, the Company will not, directly or indirectly, engage in bribery, kick-backs, payoffs, or other corrupt business practices. The use, directly or indirectly, of Company funds for political contributions to any organization or to any candidate for public office is strictly prohibited, where such contributions are forbidden by applicable law. Where such contributions are lawful, they must be made in a fair and prudent way and must be approved by the most senior Alcatel officer in the country.

Alcatel Group
"Statement on Business Practices"

- Treating all suppliers fairly
- Regulating the acceptance or offer of gifts and gratuities
- Respecting intellectual property of others
- Protecting proprietary data of others
- Using software for its intended purposes
- Requiring consultants and suppliers to act legally and ethically

COMPETITORS

What do we owe our competitors? And why? Issues include:

- Dealing fairly with competitors
- Winning on product and service merits
- Discouraging comparisons with and disparagement of competitors
- Prohibiting inducement of others to break binding contracts with competitors
- Discouraging the discussion of pricing, costing, marketing, or product plans with competition
- Prohibiting illegal or unethical methods to gather competitive information
- Preventing unfair competition (antitrust)
- Promoting adherence to principles of free competition

PRACTICE NOTE

Business Integrity

Our commitment to business integrity is clear and unequivocal. We do not bribe, nor do we accept bribes. We do not sanction illegal payments of any kind. We investigate all suspicious circumstances. Any employee found to have breached our firm "no bribes" policy is dismissed. We will also prosecute where possible.

Royal Dutch/Shell
"Our Approach to Business Integrity"

COMMUNITY, GOVERNMENT, AND THE ENVIRONMENT

What relationship and responsibilities to its communities, governments, and the environment should the enterprise assume? And why?

- Obeying both the letter and the spirit of law
- Promoting good competitor relations
- Complying with local laws and customs
- Promoting anticorruption practices
- Excluding foreign corrupt practices
- Regulating political contributions
- Regulating political activity
- Including indigenous peoples
- Promoting sustainable development
- Complying with anti–money laundering measures
- Complying with antiboycott laws
- Complying with import–export laws
- Voluntarily disclosing violations
- Cooperating with authorities
- Promoting charitable contributions
- Encouraging employee volunteer work
- Protecting the environment

BUSINESS ETHICS PROGRAM

A business ethic program should cover these issues:

- Ethics and compliance structure and systems
- Responsibility of managers and supervisors
- Need to avoid even the appearance of impropriety
- Monitoring and auditing practices
- Employees' duty to report violations
- Failure to comply
- Failure to detect misconduct
- Methods to seek advice and report misconduct
- Policy concerning false reports
- Enterprise response to reports
- Policy for customer, supplier, and contact agents
- Confidentiality and anonymity policy
- Nonretaliation policy
- Policy for employee misconduct
- Policy for rewarding ethical behavior
- Records retention
- Media contact
- Individual accountability
- Obligation to sign acknowledgment

BUSINESS ETHICS PROGRAM RESOURCES

Resources may include these:

- Ethical decision-making model
- Case studies and examples
- Telephone contact numbers

DESIGN, REVIEW, AND APPROVAL PROCESS

The design, review, and approval process for a code of conduct follows the process described in Chapter 4. The code and supporting policies will not be finally approved until all standards, procedures, and expectations as well as implementing policies and infrastructure have been designed and approved.

SUMMARY

Owners and managers establish standards, procedures, and expectations to answer the fundamental question, "What norms, values, and standards should we set to guide our members and foster reasonable stakeholder expectations?" An effective business ethics program contains standards, procedures, and expectations that establish the following:

- Who has authority to do what within the enterprise
- Who is responsible for which decisions and activities
- How people will be held accountable for their individual choices and actions
- What stakeholders can reasonably expect from the enterprise

Standards, procedures, and expectations are set for all levels of the enterprise—from the owners to the independent agents. Core beliefs and reasonable stakeholder expectations set the fundamental aspirations of the enterprise. Standards, procedures, and expectations are liberating devices as well as control mechanisms. They set boundaries for employees and agents that limit what they can do in pursuit of the enterprise purpose. Provided employees and agents choose and act in pursuit of the enterprise's purpose in good faith—and do not exceed these limits—they are free to use their good judgment in making decisions and acting.

RESPONSIBLE BUSINESS ENTERPRISE
Checklist

1. **What is the core purpose of our enterprise beyond profit?**

2. **What are our core values—those three to five values that we never violate?**

3. **What is our envisioned future of this enterprise? What are our goals and objectives over the next 30 to 50 years?**

4. **What management situations, activities, or decisions would be unacceptable to us even if they worked? Even if the ends are being achieved, what risks, ethical violations, and proprieties do we want to put off limits?**[57]

6 | Sample Outline for a Code of Conduct

RBE Worksheet 6 provides a sample outline of a code of conduct. Discussion points are written to assist a working group tasked with drafting a code of conduct. The worksheet may be photocopied for use within your organization.

Topic	Discussion Points
Title page	Use a title page that captures the nature of the document and sets a theme to run throughout the document. Examples include "Living Our Values" (World Bank Group); "Leading with Integrity" (United Parcel Service); and "The Way We Do Business" (PricewaterhouseCoopers).
Table of Contents	A good code is accessible. For even a relatively simple code, it is wise to include a detailed outline of the contents and page numbers to aid use.
Introductory materials • Letter from owner or chief executive • Statement of code purpose • Statement of core beliefs • Statement of guiding principles • Background or explanatory materials	A letter from the owner or chief executive demonstrates top management's commitment to the ethics and compliance program and develops the theme of the title. A brief but clear statement of the purpose of the code—what it is intended to achieve—is important. A one-page restatement of the core beliefs of the enterprise—core purpose and values, as well as the envisioned future—sets the essential foundation. Use this as another opportunity to reinforce the importance of core beliefs. If the enterprise has developed a set of guiding principles, these may be included as a separate page for emphasis. Background or explanatory materials may address a crisis that spurred code development, what responsible business conduct is all about in general, or the process by which the code was developed. Include anything that readers need to know to understand the importance of the code itself and its place in the broader ethics and compliance program.
Specific guidance provisions organized by relationship or responsibilities to stakeholders • Customers • Shareholders and Investors • Suppliers and service providers • Employees • Enterprise itself • Community • Government • Environment	There are many ways to arrange specific code provisions, but arranging by relationship or responsibilities to stakeholders provides a logical way of organizing guidance and reinforces the sense of responsibility to stakeholders. A reason to refer to these provisions as describing the relationship to stakeholders is to avoid any private legal claims of obligation. Specific issues will necessarily touch on human resource issues: fairness in promotion, termination, sexual harassment, and diversity. A temptation is to treat these issues as separate from ethics issues. They must be included in the ethics and compliance program for it to be effective, because to the employee, ethics often means fairness.

continued on the next page

Topic	Discussion Points
Description of the ethics, compliance, and responsibility program • Responsible executive • Responsible staff • Communications • Monitoring and auditing • How to seek advice and report misconduct • Investigations • Dispute-resolution process • Tracking, measuring, and reporting • Program evaluation and modification process	The code should specifically address ethics and compliance training and education. It should lay the essential foundation for all forms of communication regarding program issues. The code should also encourage employees and agents to seek advice and report misconduct. Because they may turn to the code to make decisions, the code should fully describe the process, including the circumstances under which they can call anonymously or confidentially. Also important is setting broad guidelines for tracking, measuring, and reporting enterprise performance, especially reporting to interested stakeholders.
Supporting and related policies and procedures • Business ethics officer's duties and responsibilities • Due diligence positions • Monitoring and auditing policy • Investigating policy and procedures • Confidentiality policy • Nonretaliation policy • Confidentiality agreements • Education and training policies • Problem reporting and nonretaliation policies and procedures • Help-line policy and procedures • Response, follow-up, and resolution policy	To be usable, a code of conduct needs to address only those matters of general interest or applicability to its stakeholders. Matters relating to specific duties or responsibilities, or more detailed policies or procedures, should be established in separate policies. However, it may be important to note in the code that there are more specific policies and procedures and how to access them. An excellent guide to applicable policy statements, though its emphasis is on health care compliance policies in the United States, is Richard P. Kusserow and Andrew H. Joseph, *Corporate Compliance Policies and Procedures: A Guide to Assessment and Development* (Marblehead, Mass.: Opus Communications, 2000).
Supporting Resources • Guides to ethical decision-making • Contact names and phone numbers • Case studies • Ethics games • On-line resource links • Quick reference guide • Index	This portion of the code provides ready access to important supporting resources and quick reference materials. If a code of conduct is very large or complex because of the needs and culture of the enterprise, consider providing an index.

7   RBE Standards and Expectations Worksheet

RBE Worksheet 7, which may be photocopied for use with your organization, provides a tool for ensuring that all necessary standards, procedures, and expectations are considered. Owners, managers, and staff members should engage their stakeholders to address each element of their standards, procedures, and expectations, along the vertical axis, to ensure that they are consistent with the enterprise's core beliefs and four levels of ethical identity, along the horizontal axis.

	Core Beliefs	Compliance	Risk Management	Reputation Enhancement	Value Added
Introductory materials					
Owners					
Customers or Consumers					
Employees and the enterprise					
Partners, suppliers, and service providers					

continued on the next page

	Core Beliefs	Compliance	Risk Management	Reputation Enhancement	Value Added
Competitors					
Community					
Government					
Environment					
Business Ethics program					
Special ethics, compliance, and social responsibility topics					

Business Ethics Infrastructure

*T*his chapter examines an essential element of a business ethics program: business ethics infrastructure—the structures and systems that help enterprise owners and managers address issues of responsible business conduct.

Designing Business Ethics Infrastructure

One of the most important questions owners and managers of a responsible business enterprise (RBE) must ask themselves is "What style, structure, and systems of authority and responsibility at all levels should we exercise?"[1]

This manual details the best practices that have been developed, particularly over the past two decades, by large, complex enterprises (LCEs). These practices will be valuable for similarly situated enterprises in emerging market economies, which may look to formal structures and systems to help speed the evolution to a free market by improving their own business performance.

Although developed by LCEs, these best practices are also valuable as models for small to medium-sized enterprises (SMEs). By considering the best practices that LCEs, international institutions, and nongovernmental organizations (NGOs) have generated over countless hours of reflection, dialogue, and negotiation, SMEs can design business ethics infrastructure that meets world-class standards but is tailored to the requirements of an SME.

- **Designing Business Ethics Infrastructure**

- **Determining Systems of Authority, Responsibility, and Accountability**

129

IMPORTANCE OF BUSINESS ETHICS INFRASTRUCTURE

When designing business ethics infrastructure, owners and managers will consider the nature of the enterprise—its size, its complexity, and the resources available to it. As stressed in Chapter 3, an enterprise uses infrastructure and formal alignment practices to emphasize enterprise strengths and to compensate for and reform enterprise weaknesses.

Over the past few decades, various offices and committees—for example, the business ethics officer and business ethics council—have developed to serve a number of necessary functions. These offices and committees meet the needs of LCEs, and it is valuable to describe them for those designing and implementing a business ethics program of any size.

An example of how complicated these offices and committees can be is the program of HCA Inc., a large, very complex health care provider. Reflecting its complex organization, the program is overseen by a senior vice president for ethics, compliance, and corporate responsibility, who supervises over 20 individuals in a corporate ethics and compliance department, works with over 20 executives, and provides direction and oversight to over 200 ethics and compliance officers.[2]

At the other extreme, many enterprises have neither dedicated business ethics personnel nor a separate business ethics program.[3] In such cases, companies make business ethics a general management function. They provide no dedicated mechanism for employees and agents to seek advice or report concerns without fear of retribution, especially in cases where management is unable or unwilling to help or is part of the problem.

There is no right way to design and implement a business ethics program. However, *formally* addressing each of the seven levels of responsibility that this manual discusses below will serve an enterprise and its stakeholders well, especially in an emerging market economy.

The reader should also remember that, in describing offices and committees, this manual is really addressing functions. It is important that these functions be performed, not that any particular office or committee be established. If owners and managers adequately address the functions, they can design and implement an effective business ethics program that is relevant to their organizational culture and stakeholder expectations. Failure to address any of these functions will often lead to a significant lack of perspective or capacity to respond to issues and problems related to ethics, compliance, and social responsibility. RBE Worksheet 8, at the end of this chapter, will help owners and managers ensure that all necessary levels of responsibility are considered.

RESPONSIBILITY FUNCTIONS

Leading enterprises, government agencies, and NGOs have found that an effective business ethics program addresses functions at seven levels of responsibility:

1. Overseeing the program at a high level (the responsible officer)

2. Performing or coordinating the specific functions of the business ethics program (the business ethics officer)

3. Advising the responsible officer and business ethics officer and representing the enterprise as a whole (the business ethics council)

4. Advising the responsible officer, business ethics officer, and employees and agents about specific professional ethics, compliance, and social responsibility issues, such as biomedical, engineering, or community issues (the professional ethics council)

5. Linking various levels of the enterprise with a central ethics office (business conduct representatives)

6. Performing related executive and department functions (the chief financial officer; legal counsel; human resources; internal audit; environment, health, and safety; government procurement; and investor relations)

7. Abiding by standards and procedures and striving to meet reasonable stakeholder expectations (every employee and other agent of the enterprise)

Although these functions are discussed separately, the nature of the enterprise and its size, complexity, and resources may argue for combining any number of them. Informal channels and reporting relationships can also be integral parts of the design of a business ethics program.

BUSINESS ETHICS INFRASTRUCTURE FOR THE SME

The average SME may not have enough staff members to dedicate an employee or employees to each of the seven responsibility functions. For example, if an enterprise is large and complex, such as HCA Inc., an RBE may need a central coordinator and many high-level responsible individuals at dispersed facilities or regions. For an SME that has only one location, the function can be served by a high-level individual who has enough time to perform the duties—and is sufficiently detached from the issues raised—that he or she can be an effective channel for employees and agents seeking advice or reporting concerns. Often, for these reasons, owners and managers of SMEs will turn to trusted independent advisers, as Box 6.1, "Ten Ways Small Business Owners Can Prevent and Detect Fraud," suggests.[4]

Table 6.1 describes how a typical SME might staff the seven responsibility functions.

BOX 6.1

TEN WAYS SMALL BUSINESS OWNERS CAN PREVENT AND DETECT FRAUD

1. Hire a CPA to examine the books.
2. Have a written code of ethics.
3. Set a good example.
4. Have reasonable expectations.
5. Treat employees well.

6. Restrict bank account access.
7. Perform regular bank reconciliations.
8. Adequately secure inventory and supplies.
9. Adequately prescreen employee applicants.
10. Give employees a way to report fraud.

Joseph T. Wells
"Protecting Small Business"

Determining Systems of Authority, Responsibility, and Accountability

Support for a business ethics program must start at the top of an enterprise. The following general elements of leadership are typically found in successful programs:

- The owners or owner representatives ensure that the program provides them with adequate information regarding enterprise performance.
- The owners and managers set a tone of support for responsible business conduct.
- A high-level person is responsible for the business ethics program.
- The supervisors are responsible for how things are actually done in the enterprise.[5]

INFRASTRUCTURE FOR OWNER REPRESENTATIVES

A business ethics program provides an information and reporting system for both the owners and the managers. An emerging corporate governance standard is that owner representatives are responsible for ensuring that they receive the information they need to prevent and detect wrongdoing. They may be held individually liable for losses caused by noncompliance with applicable legal standards.[6]

While delegating authority to the chief executive officer (CEO) to conduct day-to-day operations, an RBE's board of directors must provide for systematic and rigorous monitoring of enterprise performance through an information and reporting system. Boards often delegate the authority to

TABLE 6.1 Business Ethics Infrastructure: SME Conversion

Function	Typical SME Staffing
Overseeing the program at a high level (the responsible officer)	Often an owner performs this function, but another highly respected employee who has substantial authority in the enterprise is preferable.
Performing or coordinating the specific functions of the business ethics program (the business ethics officer)	Typically, a respected staff member performs or coordinates the functions of the business ethics officer. An SME can form or join a business association to develop training materials and provide a forum to discuss issues, problems, and solutions related to ethics, compliance, and social responsibility. The SME can employ an independent answering service to provide a mechanism for employees and agents to seek advice or report concerns anonymously. The SME can use an outside service to conduct a periodic evaluation of its business ethics program.
Advising the responsible officer and business ethics officer and representing the enterprise as a whole (the business ethics council)	An SME can conduct regular meetings of all or representative employees for perhaps 30–60 minutes, once a month, to discuss enterprise core beliefs; standards, procedures, and expectations; and current issues of ethics, compliance, and social responsibility. A medium-sized enterprise—especially one with multiple locations—can appoint members to a council that meets regularly by telephone. An SME can form or join a business association to provide a forum to discuss current issues, problems, and solutions related to ethics, compliance, and social responsibility. A college, university, or business development council might host a forum for SMEs. A large enterprise can—and often should—host a forum for its suppliers and service providers.
Advising the responsible officer, business ethics officer, and employees and agents about specific professional ethics, compliance, and social responsibility issues (the professional ethics council)	An SME can conduct regular meetings of all or representative professionals, for perhaps 30–60 minutes, once a month, to discuss core beliefs; standards, procedures, and expectations; and current issues of professional ethics, compliance, and social responsibility. A medium-sized enterprise—especially one with multiple locations—can appoint members to a council that meets regularly by telephone. An SME can form or join a business association to develop training materials and provide a forum to discuss current issues, problems, and solutions related to professional ethics, compliance, and social responsibility. A college, university, or business development council can host a forum for SMEs. A large enterprise can host or sponsor a forum for its suppliers and service providers.
Linking various levels of the enterprise with a central ethics office (business conduct representatives)	For the SME, these representatives may be respected, knowledgeable staff members at various levels or locations who have the right to communicate directly with the owner, owner representatives, responsible officer, or business ethics officer on issues of ethics, compliance, and social responsibility. These business conduct representatives can also conduct training and education and assist in program evaluation at local levels.
Performing related executive and department functions (the chief financial officer; legal counsel; human resources; internal audit; environment, health, and safety; government procurement; and investor relations)	SMEs often use trusted, independent professionals to perform many of these functions. If so, they should participate in the training programs for the enterprise's responsible business conduct and, where practicable, its discussions of current issues of ethics, compliance, and social responsibility. These independent professionals can form their own independent forums to discuss current issues of ethics, compliance, and social responsibility. They may also be engaged to advise SME owners and managers on how to design and implement a business ethics program using this guide and other resources.
Abiding by standards and procedures and striving to meet reasonable stakeholder expectations (every employee and agent of the enterprise)	Individual responsibility of employees and agents applies in all enterprises, regardless of their size. In SMEs, it may be difficult for employees to seek advice or report concerns confidentially and anonymously. Owners and managers of SMEs must work to develop an organizational culture in which employees and agents are able to speak up confidently and safely.

monitor enterprise performance to a committee, sometimes called an audit committee, less often a responsible business conduct committee.[7] Delegation of authority, however, does not relieve the board as a whole of its responsibility.[8] It is important that the audit committee have unrestricted access to necessary records and personnel. A policy that authorizes direct but limited access to the audit committee is set forth in Box 6.2.[9]

An audit committee is usually responsible for arranging for competent independent auditing. In this regard, it should be alert to any conflicts of interest that potential auditors might have, including conflicts stemming from their role as consultants.

Where managers sit on a board, an emerging best practice is for the audit committee to be composed wholly or predominantly of independent directors.[10] If committee members are managers, or are closely allied with managers, the board may be unable to represent the owners without bias in favor of management. This situation is an inherent conflict of interest. Moreover, the confidence of employees and agents to seek advice and report concerns may be compromised for fear of retribution.

HIGH-LEVEL RESPONSIBILITY

A first step toward an effective business ethics program is to assign responsibility for its operation to a specific individual or group of people, which this guide calls a *responsible officer*. A responsible officer may be an individual, a committee, or an individual supported by a committee. An RBE should

---

BOX 6.2

BOARD–MANAGEMENT LINKAGE POLICY

Direct, but limited, access to the board by the Responsible Officer, Business Ethics Officer, or Chair of the Business Ethics Council (individually or collectively referred to as "Senior Ethics Personnel") are exceptions to the exclusive role of the CEO in connecting governance and management.

1. If, after having brought to the CEO's attention any impropriety discovered in the course of his or her work, Senior Ethics Personnel deem that the CEO has failed to address the impropriety (or if the CEO is materially involved therein) he or she must report that impropriety to the Audit Committee [Business Ethics Committee]. *Impropriety*, in this context, means a violation of law; material violation of board policies prohibiting the treatment of stakeholders in an unsafe, undignified, or unnecessarily intrusive manner or causing or allowing conditions that are unsafe, unfair, or undignified to employees; and failure to address recommendations of any external evaluation of the Business Ethics program itself.

2. Senior Ethics Personnel, in all other respects, are subject to the CEO's managerial authority over all staff and have no direct access to the board or board committee.

PRACTICE NOTE

Translating the Vision

It is the job of every single employee to translate the Vision, the Charter, and the Policies into action. However, a particular responsibility for keeping the company's actions attuned to stakeholders' demands lies with the Board of Directors, Executive Management, and cross-organisational committees.

Three committees, each chaired by a member of Executive Management, have specific responsibilities for sustainable development:

- The Environment and Bioethics Committee
- The Social and Industrial Relations Committee
- The Health Policy Committee

These committees' tasks are to identify issues, establish and revise policies, and devise strategies, targets, and action plans within their specific areas. Triple Bottom Line issues are reviewed twice a year at the Board of Directors' meetings.

Novo Nordisk
"Translating the Vision"

avoid creating a situation in which no one is responsible because everyone is responsible. In the pressures of day-to-day operations, it is easy for employees and agents to focus on immediate tasks and goals. A single person needs to be tasked with ensuring that responsible business conduct becomes the norm at the enterprise.

For the business ethics program to be effective, the responsible officer, whether an individual or a group, should have a number of basic characteristics:

- Be at a high level of responsibility in the organization
- Have unrestricted access to the CEO and the board, or a designated board committee
- Have a high degree of trust and respect from senior management
- Have access to the resources necessary to ensure that the organization has an effective program
- Be given incentives and rewarded for proactively carrying out the roles and responsibilities of the office
- Have the skills to operate effectively with the media, public forums, government agencies, and the legal process[11]

Ethics and Business Conduct

The Ethics and Business Conduct Committee is responsible for oversight of the ethics program. The committee is appointed by the Boeing Board of Directors and its members include the company chairman and chief executive officer, president and chief operating officer, presidents of the operating groups, and senior vice presidents. The vice president of Ethics and Business Conduct administers the ethics and business conduct program.

Boeing Company
Boeing Ethics and Compliance Program

It is important that the person or group assigned responsibility for the business ethics program be at a high enough level to demonstrate the owners' and managers' commitment to the program. That person or group should be heard when business strategy and other important enterprise decisions are discussed, because an integral part of management's general responsibility is to ensure that enterprise resources are applied to achieve its goals and objectives. This requires that the person or group have substantial control over the enterprise or a substantial role in making policy.[12]

The responsible officer has three major objectives:

1. Ensuring that the enterprise establishes adequate standards and procedures to guide employees and agents and to create reasonable stakeholder expectations

2. Ensuring that these standards and expectations are institutionalized and enforced within the enterprise

3. Evaluating and reporting on the enterprise's performance against these standards, procedures, and expectations[13]

The reporting relationships of the responsible officer are critical. One key way in which owners and managers demonstrate support for a business ethics program is to demand regular reports on performance. Access of the responsible officer to the board and CEO serves a number of functions: it provides greater opportunity for responsible business conduct to be given

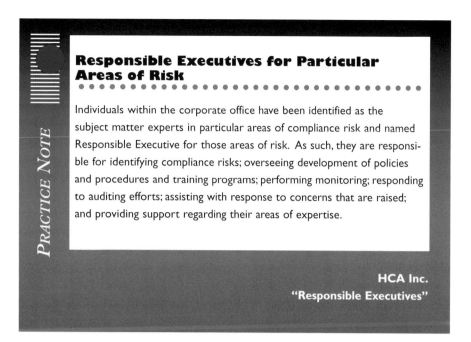

PRACTICE NOTE

Responsible Executives for Particular Areas of Risk

Individuals within the corporate office have been identified as the subject matter experts in particular areas of compliance risk and named Responsible Executive for those areas of risk. As such, they are responsible for identifying compliance risks; overseeing development of policies and procedures and training programs; performing monitoring; responding to auditing efforts; assisting with response to concerns that are raised; and providing support regarding their areas of expertise.

HCA Inc.
"Responsible Executives"

due attention; it reinforces the authority and credibility of the responsible officer; and it provides resources to high-level decision-makers for guidance and support in dealing with difficult issues.

The responsible officer function may be served from any number of positions: an executive, a committee, an individual in charge of a business unit or major function, or someone with a substantial ownership interest.[14] The position may be full-time or part-time, depending on the enterprise.

High-level responsibility may also be assigned for specific areas of ethics, compliance, and social responsibility. For example, in enterprises such as hospitals, one person may be responsible for the organizational ethics program and a medical professional may be assigned responsibility for the biomedical ethics program. In an enterprise that does a lot of government contracting, a high-level person may be assigned to monitor that specific function.

In a highly regulated enterprise, legal demands may be such that a compliance officer should be appointed to deal only with compliance issues, in coordination with the ethics and social responsibility functions. This may be the case, for example, in an economy where the enterprise must be especially diligent against corruption. In another enterprise, issues of responsibility to external stakeholders may be so demanding that a social responsibility officer should be appointed to deal with those issues, in close coordination with the responsible business conduct functions. This may be the case, for example, in an economy where environmental issues or relations with indigenous tribes are common.

BUSINESS ETHICS OFFICER

Independent of high-level responsibility for the business ethics program, a number of specific business ethics staff functions must be accomplished for the program to be effective. It is critical that a specific individual or individuals be assigned responsibility for these functions. Responsibilities for reporting to the owners (or their representatives) are typically retained by the responsible officer. However, a best practice is for both the responsible officer and the business ethics officer to have access to the CEO and board.

Roles and Responsibility of the Business Ethics Officer

The business ethics officer is the staff officer responsible for the day-to-day operations of the business ethics program. Two practitioners have identified the following 12 functions of a business ethics officer:

1. Coordinate development and implementation of the business ethics program.
2. Establish and chair a business ethics council representing all levels of the enterprise.
3. Develop and maintain standards of conduct and procedures, as well as related policies, which will guide employees and agents and will foster reasonable stakeholder expectations.
4. Establish internal reporting channels, including, but not limited to, a help line that employees and agents may use to seek advice and report concerns without fear of retribution.
5. Establish or coordinate monitoring controls and measures to ensure that correct processes are established and followed.
6. Implement or coordinate enterprise-wide communication and training programs to ensure that all employees, agents, and other stakeholders are educated on the standards, procedures, and reasonable stakeholder expectations.
7. Coordinate or conduct inquiries and investigations to ensure proper follow-up on reports and resolution.
8. Delegate authority to conduct appropriate inquiries and investigations (for example, legal, human resources, internal audit) when necessary.
9. Monitor and evaluate the business ethics program for periodic modifications when needed.

10. Maintain a working knowledge of relevant issues, laws, regulations, and emerging standards of ethics, compliance, and responsibility through periodicals, seminars, training programs, and peer contact, including membership in professional associations.

11. Respond appropriately when a violation of these standards is uncovered, including making a direct report to the board or external agency if a violation of law or regulation is involved.

12. Report quarterly to the appropriate board committees on the status of the business ethics program, report to the CEO or appropriate board committees whenever necessary, and report to stakeholders annually.[15]

Location and Centralization of Business Ethics Offices

The functions of the business ethics officer may be performed by one ethics officer out of a central location or may be decentralized. For example, the business ethics officer may be located at headquarters, or each plant may have a business ethics officer. The significant differences relate to responsibility and reporting. In a decentralized program, the local business ethics officer will be personally responsible for the conduct of the program at the local level and be required—and entitled—to report to the CEO and board on issues of responsible business conduct. He or she may also have more responsibility for training and investigations.

The advantages of centralization include a more consistent message, economies of scale in production and distribution, more effective monitoring of the program, and more uniform and efficient enforcement. Advantages of a more decentralized approach include messages that are more tailored to local circumstances, more employee involvement, and more nuanced and inclusive decision-making.[16]

Business Ethics Officer Qualifications

Business ethics officers generally have extensive experience throughout the enterprise over a number of years. They have developed personal networks that allow them to understand and relate well to the enterprise as issues arise.[17] Owners and managers often bring in someone from the outside when there has been a pattern of serious misconduct or when they see the need for significant change in the organizational culture.

In terms of their operational experience, staff members from departments such as general business, finance, internal audit, and human resources tend to be tapped to be business ethics officers. Appointing a lawyer as business ethics officer, especially where legal compliance is a significant program element, often leads to responsible business conduct being treated as simply an extension of the legal function. However, as two lawyers write, "Compliance is not just another legal matter. It is a management responsibility demanding a full range of management resources and skills, and the exercise of those in the day-to-day management of the business."[18]

BUSINESS ETHICS COUNCIL

The business ethics council serves principally as an adviser on setting policy, resolving issues, and monitoring the business ethics program. In larger enterprises, it often consists of representatives of executive management, including finance, general counsel, human resources, internal audit, quality, and public affairs. It is typically chaired by either the responsible officer or the business ethics officer. It is advisable that all levels of the enterprise be represented so that the council's advice fully reflects the enterprise as a whole. Wider participation may also contribute to greater employee acceptance of the program and its message.

A business ethics council should meet on a regular basis, perhaps monthly or quarterly. It raises issues of concern in the enterprise, reviews disposition of help-line requests for advice or reports of concerns, previews training materials, and recommends policy changes or program modifications. It meets on call when there are urgent matters to address, such as unforeseen conduct issues or a compliance violation that may require disclosure to government agencies.

If the business ethics officer is highly respected and has an extensive network of managers and specialists that he or she can turn to for advice, a business ethics council may not be especially valuable. The risk of not having such a council, however, is that the business ethics program lacks the formal acknowledgment that input from all levels of the enterprise is important to management. Also, the lack of a council tends to identify the business ethics program with one person, which may require restructuring the business ethics program when he or she leaves the post.

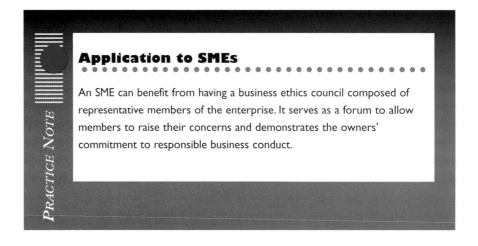

PRACTICE NOTE

Application to SMEs

An SME can benefit from having a business ethics council composed of representative members of the enterprise. It serves as a forum to allow members to raise their concerns and demonstrates the owners' commitment to responsible business conduct.

PROFESSIONAL ETHICS COUNCIL

The business ethics council is concerned with standards of conduct that affect the RBE as a whole. In many enterprises, well-developed bodies of professional ethics standards guide day-to-day operations. For example, biomedical ethics guide health care providers, especially physicians and nurses. Other examples include legal, engineering, accounting, and environmental ethics, but there are many others, including specific social responsibility issues.

In each of these areas, significant issues will arise that require the same sort of consultation and advice process that the business ethics council provides on more general issues. To address these more specific issues, an RBE might establish a professional ethics council. For example, biomedical ethics is such a significant part of hospital operations that hospitals often have a separate biomedical ethics council, which reports directly to senior management on biomedical issues.[19]

If an enterprise wants to contribute to the welfare of its community as a whole, beyond its essential function as a business, it might appoint a community relations committee. Such a committee might identify specific community needs not met by government or civil society, coordinate with NGOs, and organize voluntary employee work projects. It would usually coordinate closely with the public affairs function to further enhance the reputation of the enterprise.

BUSINESS CONDUCT REPRESENTATIVES

An RBE must also determine how best to engage its employees and agents in its business ethics program. If the enterprise is large or complex, local personnel can be appointed to serve as advisers to local managers, employees, and agents and as channels for communication back to a central business ethics office. An SME will generally not make formal appointments of business conduct representatives at individual units since the responsible officer and business ethics officer will generally be able to give each unit adequate attention.

Business conduct representatives generally report directly to both the senior manager at the location and the business ethics officer. They advise managers and other employees on standards, policies, procedures, and the business ethics program as a whole (see Box 6.3). They facilitate the functions of responsible business conduct at the local unit, such as training; monitoring, auditing, and investigating; providing employee incentives and discipline; and evaluating the program. They are responsible for coordinating with other functions at the local level such as legal; environment, health, and safety; quality management; and human resources.

BOX 6.3

BUSINESS CONDUCT REPRESENTATIVES

Business conduct representatives advise employees on standards, policies, procedures, and the business ethics program as a whole. The following question, from the Standards and Ethics Web page of Raytheon, is typical of the issues a business conduct representative deals with:

Q: I was just assigned as the company's in-country program manager for a major foreign government contract. I want to host a business lunch at a local restaurant for a senior official of the Ministry of Defense for the purpose of reviewing contract/program status. Is this permissible?

A: Maybe. You need to review the company's policy on offering business courtesies to customers. Company policy requires that the offer of any business courtesy (including meals) to a foreign government person meet a three element test. First, the proposed gratuity must be legal under the laws and regulations of the person's home country. Second, the gratuity must be a reasonable and bona fide expenditure incurred by or on behalf of the foreign official. Third, the gratuity must be directly related to the promotion, demonstration, or explanation of Raytheon's products or services or performance of a contract with a foreign government. In all cases, business meals being offered to any foreign government person must be approved in advance by your Legal Department Vice President.

Raytheon
"Standards and Ethics"

Business conduct representatives must be familiar with enterprise standards, procedures, and expectations and all communications channels. They must be able to give unbiased advice that will not interfere with the conduct of their primary duties. For this reason, they should not be appointed from the human resources, procurement, or legal units of the enterprise, which are often either the source of the issue or the unit responsible for resolving the issue.

RELATED EXECUTIVE AND DEPARTMENT FUNCTIONS

The business ethics officer is responsible for coordinating the enterprise's ethics, compliance, and social responsibility programs. This task requires that the business ethics program be integrated well with other enterprise functions.

The chief financial officer, for example, is responsible for maintaining the enterprise's financial integrity, including all of its financial practices, books, and records. He or she will also have significant influence in the allocation of resources for business ethics infrastructure, including training.

An enterprise's internal auditor is closely involved in the enterprise's internal controls and processes. (LCEs will often have an audit department.) The internal auditor will be able to provide significant support to the business ethics officer by providing advice on internal controls and processes and by conducting inquiries and investigations.

The business ethics officer will often turn to the chief legal officer for advice on legal requirements of a compliance program, due process requirements of inquiries and investigations, legal risk analysis, and possible program outcomes.

In the minds of many employees, when one speaks of ethics one speaks of "fairness."[20] Many ethics issues, therefore, involve human resources issues: assignments, compensation and benefits, discipline, employee assistance, and promotions. The business ethics officer will need to recognize human resources issues and work with human resources personnel to resolve them.

Other enterprise functions that the business ethics officer will work with closely are training, education, and development; environment, health, and safety; security; quality management; and operations and administration in general.

INDIVIDUAL RESPONSIBILITY

To be a truly responsible business, the enterprise must articulate the responsibilities of all of its employees and agents in a positive, constructive manner. For owners, managers, and supervisors, this effort may involve complete awareness of the business ethics program itself. Owners, managers, and supervisors must demonstrate commitment to the program in all that they say and do. They are responsible for maintaining an organizational climate in which pressures to violate standards are minimized and incentives to achieve enterprise goals and objectives, pursue the enterprise purpose, and meet reasonable

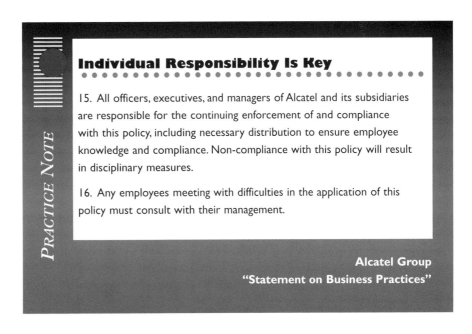

PRACTICE NOTE

Individual Responsibility Is Key

15. All officers, executives, and managers of Alcatel and its subsidiaries are responsible for the continuing enforcement of and compliance with this policy, including necessary distribution to ensure employee knowledge and compliance. Non-compliance with this policy will result in disciplinary measures.

16. Any employees meeting with difficulties in the application of this policy must consult with their management.

Alcatel Group
"Statement on Business Practices"

stakeholder expectations are high. Managers and supervisors may be required to certify regularly that they have no conflicts of interest and that they—and those they manage—are following the business ethics program.

For all employees and agents, their specific responsibilities under the business ethics program may require familiarizing themselves with the standards, certifying receipt of the code and compliance with code requirements, attending scheduled training, participating in feedback sessions and investigations, and seeking advice and reporting concerns.[21] They may also be charged with contributing to an organizational climate in which all employees can work together to achieve the enterprise's purposes.

SUMMARY

Responsible managers consider the strengths and practices of the enterprise when designing business ethics infrastructure. Owners and managers of an RBE design and implement business ethics infrastructure by answering this question: "What style, structure, and systems of authority and responsibility at all levels should we exercise?"

To support employees and agents in their day-to-day conduct of responsible operations, owners and managers establish certain functions and positions, such as high-level oversight of the program; a business ethics staff to administer the program; representative councils of the enterprise and professionals; legal, human resources, and internal audit linkages; and individual responsibilities of staff members. Such infrastructure may be particularly valuable for an enterprise as it participates in the evolution of an emerging market economy.

RESPONSIBLE BUSINESS ENTERPRISE
Checklist

1. How should a board of directors organize itself to best represent the shareholders and provide proper guidance and oversight to management?

2. What style, structure, and systems of authority, responsibility, and accountability should we employ at each level of responsibility in our enterprise?

3. What do we need to do to develop adequate systems to support this infrastructure?

    a. For communications and feedback mechanisms, see Chapter 7.

    b. For management alignment systems and practices, see Chapter 8.

    c. For program evaluation and organizational learning systems, see Chapter 10.

8 Business Ethics Infrastructure Worksheet

RBE Worksheet 8, which may be photocopied for use within your organization, provides a tool for ensuring that all necessary levels of responsibility are considered. Owners, managers, and staff members should engage stakeholders to address each element of their level of responsibility along the vertical axis to ensure that they are consistent with their enterprise standards: their core beliefs and the standards, procedures, and expectations developed in Chapter 5. From this dialogue, they will be able to identify any required elements of the business ethics infrastructure.

Function	Enterprise Standards	Required Infrastructure
Owner representative governance		
Overseeing the program at a high level (the responsible officer)		
Performing or coordinating the specific functions of the business ethics program (the business ethics officer)		
Advising the responsible officer and business ethics officer and representing the enterprise as a whole (the business ethics council)		
Advising the responsible officer, business ethics officer, and employees and agents about specific professional ethics, compliance, and social responsibility issues (the professional ethics council)		
Linking individuals at various levels of the enterprise with a central ethics office (business conduct representatives)		
Performing related executive and department functions (the chief financial officer; legal counsel; human resources; internal audit; environment, health, and safety; government procurement; and investor relations)		
Abiding by standards and procedures and striving to meet reasonable stakeholder expectations (every employee and other agent of the enterprise)		

Business Ethics Communications and Feedback

This chapter examines two essential elements of a business ethics program: (a) communicating standards, procedures, and expectations and (b) learning what is going on in the enterprise. Communication in the responsible business enterprise (RBE) is mutual—that is, owners and managers strive to make sure employees and agents understand their standards, procedures, and expectations, and owners, managers, supervisors, workers, and agents alike have the information they need when they need it. An RBE also engages its external stakeholders in order to foster reasonable expectations and determine stakeholder satisfaction.

Communicating and Providing Feedback

For an enterprise to be responsible, all stakeholders must have a complete understanding of their roles and responsibilities in the workings of its business ethics infrastructure. Moreover, managers must know whether the enterprise's standards, procedures, and expectations are adequate to meet the reasonable expectations of its stakeholders.[1]

This chapter describes the infrastructure and best practices used by an RBE to communicate its standards, procedures, and expectations and to ensure that they are being followed and met. Owners and managers ask themselves two fundamental questions:

- **Communicating and Providing Feedback**

- **Communicating Standards and Fostering Reasonable Expectations**

- **Ensuring Members Follow Standards and Meet Expectations**

1. How can we most effectively communicate our standards and procedures and foster reasonable expectations among our stakeholders?

2. How can we know that our members follow our standards and that reasonable stakeholder expectations are met?[2]

Communicating Standards and Fostering Reasonable Expectations

A primary cultural characteristic of an enterprise is the extent to which knowledge is shared.[3] Communication within an RBE is not top-down but instead flows in all directions. How the elements of a business ethics program are communicated is an integral part of the program itself. The manner in which owners and managers communicate the value they place in the

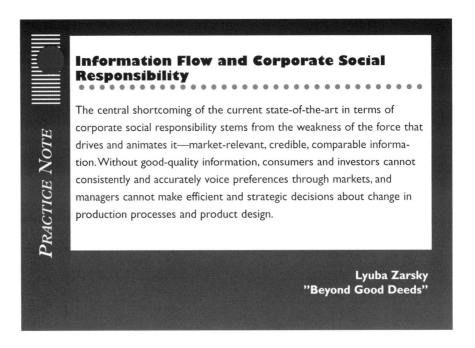

PRACTICE NOTE

Information Flow and Corporate Social Responsibility

The central shortcoming of the current state-of-the-art in terms of corporate social responsibility stems from the weakness of the force that drives and animates it—market-relevant, credible, comparable information. Without good-quality information, consumers and investors cannot consistently and accurately voice preferences through markets, and managers cannot make efficient and strategic decisions about change in production processes and product design.

Lyuba Zarsky
"Beyond Good Deeds"

program through the choices they make, the things they say, and what they do or fail to do will define the program for most other stakeholders.

DEVELOPING A COMMUNICATIONS PROGRAM

For owners and managers to communicate about responsible business conduct, they must be working from a communications program that delivers a clear and consistent message of what it means for the enterprise to be responsible. It must include all enterprise employees and agents and reach beyond them to include all other stakeholders, as appropriate.

Formal communications are the most obvious aspect: program announcements, company newsletters, new employee orientation, training programs, posters, annual and social responsibility reports, speeches, and meetings. Informal communications may include managers explaining how they arrived at a decision, experienced workers telling the newly hired "how things really work around here," and all forms of rumor and gossip. Owners and managers must be alert to both forms of communication. If formal communications tell one story while informal communications tell another, stakeholders often become frustrated and cynical.

In planning the communications program, owners and managers need to identify their stakeholders and prioritize communication efforts among them. They must consider how best to reach particular stakeholders. As with every other aspect of a business ethics program, the communications program must reflect an accurate understanding of the relevant context and organizational culture.

The communications program also needs to address how to solicit and respond to feedback from employees and other stakeholders. Feedback helps the enterprise track whether its standards and procedures are known and followed—and whether reasonable stakeholder expectations are being met.

Know the Audience

For the RBE, the target audience includes all stakeholders. Stakeholders and their interests are identified through the processes of scanning the relevant context and organizational culture described in Chapter 4. Through these processes, owners and managers gain a firm understanding of what is required of the enterprise for its business ethics program to be effective.

Stakeholders, whether internal or external, often have widely differing perspectives on enterprise standards, procedures, and expectations. Communications to stakeholders must be tailored to guide their behavior or foster reasonable expectations accordingly.

Internal stakeholders can be categorized in terms of their interest in ethics:

- Some employees are *ethical enthusiasts*. These employees hold views on corporate responsibility that are strong enough to influence their choice of employer.[4]
- Others are *ethically committed*. These employees have adopted enterprise standards, procedures, and expectations in principle but still require support. They need to be assured that their choices and actions will meet the

enterprise's expectations. They also need to know that if they follow enterprise standards and procedures they can still succeed. For example, most employees will be relieved to know that bribery and other corrupt practices are prohibited by the enterprise, but they will be distressed if owners and managers look the other way when fellow employees continue to bribe purchasing agents to meet quotas or gain bonuses.

- Other employees are *ethically unaware*. These employees are not aware of—or have not yet embraced—these standards, procedures, and expectations and need to be educated about them, employees' individual roles and responsibilities, and the business ethics infrastructure built to ensure that standards, procedures, and expectations are honored.

- Still other employees are *ethically challenged*. They have quietly rejected enterprise standards and procedures because they make lucrative "business as usual" more difficult. These people need to be advised that (a) the enterprise is dedicated to its standards, procedures, and expectations and (b) deviation from them will not be tolerated. Often, these people will self-select themselves out of the enterprise when they come to appreciate that owners and managers are genuinely committed. If not, owners and managers need to lay the foundation to remove or isolate them, as discussed in Chapter 8.

Much the same categorization can be made of external stakeholders. The enterprise message needs to resonate with certain external stakeholders, who can be thought of as potential allies. Some stakeholder advocacy groups, for example, will work cooperatively with an RBE to help it better understand the impact of its activities on others, provided they are convinced that the enterprise is interested in finding mutually satisfactory solutions.[5]

Other stakeholders are well intentioned but hostile to an enterprise because they do not understand its purpose or the challenges facing it. An example is an incident between the advocacy organization Greenpeace and a unit of Royal Dutch/Shell, involving the disposal of a spent deep-sea oil-drilling rig, known as Brent Spar. The conflict revolved around which method of disposal would cause the least environmental damage. Greenpeace was unwilling to consider any method other than land decommissioning. Royal Dutch/Shell had to make the scientific case for its method of disposal and consider "social, ethical, aesthetic, legal and economic factors … in addition to the scientific evidence."[6] In the end, Brent Spar was recycled into a ferry terminal,[7] but all participants in the dispute lost financially and had their reputations damaged: Royal Dutch/Shell, Greenpeace, and the government of the United Kingdom, which had approved deep-sea disposal of the oil-drilling rig.

Finally, some external stakeholders are hostile to capitalism in general. Others object to specific business practices of a particular enterprise. In

Islamic countries, for example, producing pork products or alcohol is unacceptable. Some stakeholder groups remain suspicious of Nestlé (the Swiss food and beverage firm) for marketing infant formula in impoverished countries that did not have the hygiene capabilities and literacy to use the product properly. Other stakeholder groups will never accept tobacco manufacturers or defense contractors as responsible businesses. For an enterprise to engage such stakeholders, an effective communications program must address their concerns as directly as possible, without sacrificing core beliefs. For example, the British American Tobacco social responsibility report describes its social and environmental practices, while acknowledging that some people will never see a tobacco company as inherently responsible.[8]

Assess the Needs

Before designing a communications program, owners and managers must conduct a needs analysis to find out what stakeholders need to know. In general, a need to communicate enterprise standards, procedures, and expectations to employees and agents is clear. It is not likely that most employees or many stakeholders will read the various business ethics program documents cover to cover. And even if some stakeholders do, owners and managers will want to emphasize regularly their commitment to abiding by the program.

Owners and managers need to know much more than the target audiences to design an effective communications program. As depicted in RBE Worksheet 9, at the end of this chapter, management should use a number of standard assessment tools such as interviews, focus groups, surveys, document review, and direct observation to ask the following questions:[9]

- What kinds of responsible business conduct issues do employees and other stakeholders face or are they concerned about?
- What do employees and other stakeholders need to know to be able to fulfill their roles and responsibilities and have reasonable expectations of the enterprise?
- How do employees and other stakeholders learn what is expected of them and what they can expect?
- What communications methods are available to the enterprise to reach specific stakeholders?
- What are the criteria by which successful communications will be evaluated?

Using RBE Worksheet 9 in conjunction with other worksheets, such as RBE Worksheet 2 and RBE Worksheet 4 (see Chapter 4), will help management determine *what* needs to be communicated to *whom* and *how*. With the information obtained, a working group can develop a plan to design a comprehensive communications program.

Typically, the most important stakeholders to reach will be customers, employees, and agents. Next in priority may be financial stakeholders, such as owners and investors, and then, specific stakeholder advocacy groups. Management needs to conduct this analysis carefully to ensure that its message about standards, procedures, and expectations is communicated as effectively and efficiently as possible. Perhaps most important for long-term program success is consideration of the criteria that will be used to determine whether the program is successful. At a minimum, it should be clear to management that the communications program contributes to achieving the expected outcomes of the overall program.[10]

The product of this needs analysis should be a summary report describing the program situation, target audiences, objectives, program resources and constraints, and expected outcomes. The next step is to design a communications program by using the summary report.

COMMUNICATING STANDARDS, PROCEDURES, AND EXPECTATIONS

Standards, procedures, and expectations of responsible business conduct should be communicated through as many means as are likely to be well received by the target audience. Some means are dictated by law, such as annual reports to shareholders or environmental impact assessments to government agencies. Others are dictated by custom or practice, such as an enterprise newsletter or Web site. Some are emerging best practices, such as the Global Reporting Initiative and AA1000S, a framework for accounting for organizational performance.[11]

An important part of any communications program is training, education, and development. For the RBE, training must be comprehensive. For an enterprise to be responsible as a whole, each of its employees and agents must have the skills, knowledge, understanding, and attitudes necessary to work together to achieve enterprise goals and objectives.

Promoting the Program through Management Speeches

There is no doubt that when owners and managers speak employees and other stakeholders listen—at least to some degree. Employees and other stakeholders are also alert to what is *not* said, as much (or more) than what is said. Owners and managers need to be particularly alert to the risk of mentioning enterprise core beliefs or the business ethics program only on special occasions. Employees and agents will note that the enterprise's purpose, values, and standards are rarely discussed. For example, one chief executive officer (CEO) was famous for referring to the business ethics program only once a year. It escaped few employees that, while he lauded the program on the day set aside to honor it, he never referred to, or inquired after, it at any other time.

Especially when introducing a business ethics program, managers need to accept that their message may be greeted skeptically. That is a reason Chapter 3 urges that the business ethics program be treated with all the seriousness of a strategy.

Distributing Statements, Codes, Standards, Procedures, and Expectations

As stressed in Chapter 5, the documents that establish responsible business conduct standards, procedures, and expectations are only the start of a business ethics program. To the extent employees and other stakeholders were formally involved in writing the basic documents setting forth guidance and establishing expectations, the communications process has begun. Indeed, the mere act of appointing workers as project consultants, described in Chapter 3, begins communicating how seriously management takes its business ethics program.

Distributing copies of the responsible business conduct standards, procedures, and expectations to each employee and agent, and requiring them to acknowledge receipt, is a major step. For the newly hired in an enterprise, the documents establishing standards, procedures, and expectations for responsible business conduct should be among the first matters addressed during orientation. Some enterprises discuss their core beliefs as early as the recruiting process. One enterprise, Guardsmark, includes a copy of its code as a part of the employment contract. In the European Union, where employee contracts are used to set forth employment terms and conditions, employees often must stipulate compliance with a code for it to be applicable.[12]

Some companies distribute wallet-size cards with enterprise core beliefs and business ethics contact information to all employees. Others put such information on the back of employee identification cards.

Posting Summaries or Lists of Principles

A cost-effective means of reinforcing the message of responsible business conduct is to post enterprise core beliefs in lobbies, meeting rooms, and work spaces, as well as on bulletin boards. When one enterprise was responding to a responsible business conduct crisis, a manager began each meeting by reciting the enterprise business principles or core values. Other enterprises have required that all meetings begin with specific safety briefings, including designated escape routes, to reinforce the core values of employee health and safety.

Posting is a means of communicating, but owners, managers, and supervisors need to make sure the message is actually understood. For example, one worker, when asked what "quality" meant, replied, "I don't know, but my supervisor told me that if anyone asked, I should point to the poster on the wall."

Posting on a Web Site

Increasingly, standards, procedures, and expectations for responsible business conduct are posted on the enterprise Web site or intranet. This information usually includes the enterprise core beliefs, statement of business principles, and annual report. Increasingly, Web sites include the entire code of conduct, contact information for key figures in the business ethics program, and information about how to seek advice and report concerns. A few organizations now post a social responsibility report, which will be discussed in more detail in Chapter 10.

Publishing Articles and Newsletters

Articles or columns about responsible business conduct can be placed regularly in enterprise publications. In larger enterprises, the business ethics program may have its own newsletter. Whatever the medium, articles may address issues of particular concern to management. These issues include areas of serious risk, patterns of behavior that cause concern, or opportunities for enhancing enterprise reputation or adding value that managers want to be sure employees do not miss.

A particularly sensitive question is how to address incidents that have led to the disciplining of an employee. There is no better way to demonstrate management's commitment to responsible business conduct standards, procedures, and expectations than to disclose publicly how managers dealt with a difficult situation—particularly when the matter involved a senior executive.

While recognizing the value in addressing real-life issues and describing real-life responses, managers must consider the privacy rights of the employee before publishing details of the incident. It is often possible to describe the situation and management's response, including disciplinary action, without including identifying information. If the enterprise is small enough, or the event notorious enough, however, the employee's identity may be clear to all employees. The same may also be true when an employee is rewarded for some ethically exemplary decision or action. In many organizational cultures, individual rewards or rewards for reporting concerns about another member of the group would degrade the harmony of the group itself.

Making Ethics Brochures Readily Available

Where there are matters of particular concern to management, employees and agents may be given brochures to address them. Among many others, topics may include dealing with conflicts of interest, accepting or declining gifts and gratuities, meeting stakeholder expectations, and seeking advice and reporting concerns. Such brochures should be placed in racks located in places where employees congregate. They may stimulate dialogue. The numbers that are taken from racks are also a rough indicator of issues employees want to know more about.

CREATING A TRAINING PROGRAM

Making speeches and distributing written materials are necessary elements of getting the message out, but they are not enough. All employees—from senior managers to workers—need time on the job to review responsible business standards, procedures, and expectations; to explore issues of responsible business conduct; to learn how the program structures and systems work; to understand their roles and responsibilities; and to develop the necessary ethical reasoning and dialogue skills.

Designing a training program requires the same attention to objectives and outcomes as does the design of the business ethics program as a whole. It requires attention to the situation, resources available, activities and participants, target audiences, outputs, and expected outcomes. Without this attention to detail, neither the business ethics program nor the communications program or training program has any criteria for evaluation. In short, it is not clear to all what success looks like.

Demonstrating Management Commitment

Few decisions symbolize management's commitment to its business ethics program more than devoting time, on a regular basis, to training in responsible business conduct. Beyond the skills, knowledge, and understanding developed through such training, the mere fact that management dedicates valuable employee time to such training goes a long way toward demonstrating that it is serious about its standards, procedures, and expectations becoming part of the organizational culture—instead of just a collection of policies sitting on a shelf.

Rescheduling busy day-to-day operations to accommodate regular employee training also conveys an important message from managers and supervisors to their workers. Where training is treated as an integral part of the enterprise, employees tend to value it more than where training is treated as an irritant or necessary evil.

Reinforcing Core Beliefs and Organizational Culture

Training should be designed as an essential link between the enterprise's core beliefs, the business ethics program, and the expected program outcomes. As such, training in responsible business conduct is one of the key activities to list in the program logic model developed in Chapter 4 (RBE Worksheet 1).

The training program should reflect the organizational culture of the enterprise. The enterprise needs to project the expected behavior through the training program. Training should also contribute to the expected outcomes of the business ethics program. If an expected program outcome, for example, is that employees come to recognize issues of responsible business conduct more readily and talk about them in terms of enterprise core beliefs, standards, and procedures, then training composed primarily of lectures will not succeed. Where employees are not used to being asked how they would address important issues, let alone raise them, training will need to demonstrate how it is done—and engage the employees as their comfort level increases.

Designing the Program

Training program objectives depend on relevant context, organizational culture, goals and objectives, and expected outcomes for the business ethics program as a whole. Designing the training program begins with the summary report of the communications needs assessment (RBE Worksheet 9). The training program should be based on enterprise core beliefs. It must reflect the pressures of the enterprise's context and its organizational culture. Its primary objective is to make a positive contribution toward achieving expected program outcomes.

At a minimum, training sessions should require employees to become familiar with applicable laws and regulations, as well as with the enterprise's procedures for reporting and investigating concerns about responsible business conduct. The training should enhance the ethical awareness of employees and should uncover ethical issues and concerns that relate to their needs as well as those of the enterprise. It should include an examination of the criteria for ethical decision-making. See Appendix A for an example of an outcomes-based decision-making model.

A training program may cover a number of topics for each expected program outcome. Using RBE Worksheet 10, found at the back of this chapter, program designers can ensure that training objectives contribute to achieving expected outcomes of the business ethics program. Put together a training program team composed of representative members of the enterprise and representatives of external stakeholders such as customers.

All participants should leave the training program confident that they know what the enterprise expects of them and what they can expect from the enterprise in turn. They should be able to recognize issues of responsible business conduct and have the confidence—and courage—to make the right decision, explain that decision to the appropriate people, and act accordingly. They should understand how the business ethics program relates to strategic issues for the RBE as a whole.

For a training program to contribute to expected outcomes, it requires a heavy emphasis on dialogue and decision-making about issues of responsible business conduct. Beyond developing listening and feedback skills and good judgment in enterprise members, the training program must convey management's sincere desire to know whether its standards and procedures are being followed and whether its stakeholder expectations are being met. The program must also convey management's commitment to support employees and other stakeholders who seek advice and report concerns. This task requires not only encouraging individuals who are inclined to come forward but also explaining to those who do not why their silence is detrimental to enterprise performance.

A typical expected outcome is that employees and agents will use good judgment in addressing issues of responsible business conduct. For the RBE, ethical decision-making is a form of action learning.[13] It is a tool that employees and agents use to learn how to pursue the purpose of the enterprise and meet the reasonable expectations of stakeholders. At a minimum, management might provide a decision-making process that, in a specific incident, enables its employees and agents

- To define the issues of ethics, compliance, and responsibility
- To demonstrate a grasp of all relevant and material facts, including the stakeholders involved and their interests
- To point to the applicable standards, procedures, and expectations, including decrees, laws, and regulations
- To describe the range of options available
- To explain why, based on these considerations, they made a particular choice or acted in a particular manner

Many ethics and policy decision-making models are available on the Internet. They range from simple, five-step models to multiphase frameworks that include decision criteria.[14] The better models are based on well-developed skills in critical thinking. Trainers can introduce the process through lecture and then break the participants into small groups to apply it in a case study. See Appendix A for an approach to ethical decision-making that reflects the approach recommended by this manual.

A long-term expected program outcome should be an organizational culture in which owners and managers have the information they need to make intelligent decisions for the enterprise. To achieve this, employees must leave training believing that they will not be punished for bringing bad news to management.

Participants must also leave training firmly convinced that, should they make a mistake, they will not be punished if they can demonstrate that they followed the enterprise decision-making process. Employees or agents should not be punished for making a mistake if they can demonstrate that they

- Recognized the issue
- Had a reasonable grasp of the relevant facts
- Considered enterprise standards, procedures, and expectations
- Explored the range of options available
- Could justify the choice they made or action they took

DELIVERING THE TRAINING PROGRAM

A number of principles characterize effective training programs on responsible business conduct. First, a program should project the core beliefs of the enterprise—not just teach them. Second, owners and managers should be involved in the training in significant, visible ways. Third, the program should recognize the personal values of individual stakeholders but not rely on them. Fourth, the program should be comprehensive, not limited to specific training in responsible business conduct. Finally, it should include action planning and follow-up to reinforce the lessons learned.

Reflecting Core Beliefs

Where expected program objectives include issue recognition, dialogue, and ethical decision-making, the training program should develop those skills and provide the knowledge necessary to apply them. For adults, who tend to learn best while doing, the best training method is often a balance

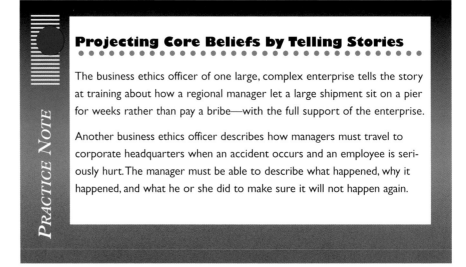

PRACTICE NOTE

Projecting Core Beliefs by Telling Stories

The business ethics officer of one large, complex enterprise tells the story at training about how a regional manager let a large shipment sit on a pier for weeks rather than pay a bribe—with the full support of the enterprise.

Another business ethics officer describes how managers must travel to corporate headquarters when an accident occurs and an employee is seriously hurt. The manager must be able to describe what happened, why it happened, and what he or she did to make sure it will not happen again.

of lectures—to introduce or review standards, procedures, and expectations—and facilitated case studies.

In developing those skills and passing on this knowledge, the program needs to project the core beliefs of the enterprise and the expected program outcomes. Abstract standards, procedures, and expectations take on meaning for employees when relayed in terms of the enterprise's core beliefs. It is one thing to discuss rules governing bribery and corruption because they are in the code of conduct. It is another thing to tell stories about how those rules are applied in practice.

Involving Owners and Managers

Because all training must reflect the relevant context and organizational culture of the enterprise, the precise way to involve owners and managers cannot be specified. A key requirement is that stakeholders, especially employees, believe that management fully supports the training.

Management involvement takes many forms. Some enterprises use cascade training, in which the CEO trains his or her direct subordinates. They, in turn, train those who report to them and so on down the chain of management until supervisors train their workers. This method has the advantage of actively involving managers, which tends to demonstrate commitment. A disadvantage may be that the presence of managers may stifle active involvement of the employees when candid discussion of issues is in order or when the culture of the enterprise is to remain silent on important issues.

Another option is a video of the CEO introducing the training by declaring his or her personal commitment to the training program. Owners and managers may also visit the training, observe it, or be available to answer questions as they arise during the course of the program. In any event, employees are unlikely to value training that management does not appear to support.

Recognizing Personal Values

One of the controversies surrounding training in responsible business conduct is whether one can—or should—teach ethics to adults. It is unlikely that ethics training will change the outlook of most employees. Personal values are usually set in youth—families, schools, churches, and peers subtly guide children as they grow to adulthood. But the purpose of business ethics training is not so much to change adults as it is to support them, admonish them, or reinforce their understanding of management's commitment to enforcing its standards, procedures, and expectations.

Trainers can be confident that what adults bring with them to the enterprise does not include knowledge of enterprise standards, procedures, and expectations. Moreover, it is unlikely that most employees—including owners and managers—are skilled at making the best choice among options where the problem involves complex pressures arising from the relevant context. For some employees and agents, no amount of training is going to change them. Such cases are less a matter of training than of having the right people performing the right tasks, which is addressed in Chapter 8.

For the training to be effective, it must appeal to what motivates the participants. The ideal situation permits an appeal to a participant's sense of community. Where participants feel that they share a purpose, values, and a vision of a desired future, trainers may stress responsibilities to stakeholders. But more often, participants respond to a sense of urgency. This sense can be created by recounting stories about what happened when employees and agents violated standards—and the impact on both the enterprise and the individuals involved.

One cost-effective way of creating a sense of urgency is to develop a "parade of horribles" by collecting headlines of powerful enterprises and individuals who have been prosecuted or held liable for misconduct. "The Bigger They Are, the Harder They Fall," said the headline of one recent working paper, which estimated that "the loss of confidence following the collapse of Enron and WorldCom will cost the U.S. economy $37 billion to $42 billion" in reduced gross domestic product.[15] Since these two enterprises, Enron and WorldCom, were accused of major accounting fraud, their stock values have dropped to a fraction of their former values, and senior executives have been indicted. Few responsible business conduct trainers now miss an opportunity to refer to Enron to demonstrate what can happen if managers act irresponsibly—what has come to be known as the "Enron Effect."

Making Training Comprehensive

Training should take place at all levels of the enterprise. From senior managers and owners to workers on the shop floor, every employee and agent should receive training in responsible business conduct specific to his or her level of responsibility. All employees and agents should review enterprise core beliefs, standards, procedures, and expectations, including policies relating to their individual responsibilities.

Managers and supervisors need additional training to reflect their roles and responsibilities as integral parts of the business ethics program. They may need to gain understanding of the issues that affect their performance such as conflicts of interest, anticorruption measures, or emerging global standards. In particular, they must understand that enterprise standards, procedures, and expectations are never to be violated to meet individual and enterprise performance objectives. They must fully appreciate their roles and responsibilities in nurturing an organizational culture in which employees and agents can seek advice and report concerns so that management has the information it needs to guide the enterprise. Finally, they must learn not to fear evaluation of their units' performance, if the enterprise is to learn from experience.

Agents, including consultants, sales agents, brokers, partners, franchisees, and closely allied suppliers and service providers, should be exposed to the enterprise core beliefs; applicable standards, procedures, and expectations; and specific policies relating to their roles and responsibilities.

Training should address pursuing the enterprise's purpose and meeting stakeholder expectations. A training program begins with basic employee recruiting materials and procedures, and never truly ends. Though the emphasis of a business ethics program is on issues of ethics, compliance, and social responsibility, this focus is primarily on reinforcing an enterprise-wide sense of responsibility to the enterprise and its stakeholders in pursuit of the enterprise's purpose.

For example, concerns such as customer service, quality management, fair dealing with suppliers and service providers, environmental protection, proper relationships with government officials, and individual responsibility for developing a healthy workplace require attention to issues far beyond business ethics. Nevertheless, such issues have substantial elements of responsible business conduct. Although basic training in workplace skills is not specifically training in responsible business conduct, ensuring that employees and agents have the requisite skills, knowledge, understanding, and attitudes to pursue the enterprise's purpose and meet reasonable stakeholder expectations *is* responsible business conduct. Preaching a core value of customer service when employees know they do not have the ability to provide it will build, at best, frustration and cynicism.

In short, the training program should ensure that training in responsible business conduct begins with the earliest opportunity to orient the newly hired or retained and continues to transfer to the workplace as long as the employee remains a stakeholder.

Incorporating Action Planning and Action Learning

One way to make training meaningful is to have participants, individually or as members of a team, develop an action plan for the next three to six months based on what they learned. For senior employees, this action plan may reflect an assessment that some aspects of an enterprise's business ethics program require more support in practice. An example might be recognition that more training is required during the ensuing months on the issue of gifts and gratuities. Another might be a need to develop a division policy on wastewater disposal.

Copies of these action plans should be retained by the business ethics officer or another appropriate officer. Follow-up questionnaires requesting progress reports should be sent regularly. Tracking progress on action plans can give indirect feedback or function as a performance evaluation item. It also has the effect of reinforcing perceptions of management's commitment. An important way to demonstrate management commitment is to include participation in the training and action planning as express elements of performance evaluation.

USING THE MODES OF TRAINING

The training program should use all modes appropriate to the organizational culture and stakeholder needs. In general, training should be as interactive, realistic, and relevant to day-to-day jobs as possible. In a recent study, one researcher found that European "training objectives typically include illumination of the company's and individual's values while in the United States the emphasis is on increasing knowledge of company standards and/or the law."[16] The level of difficulty should challenge but not overwhelm participants.

Some modes of training that enterprises may consider include:

- **Lectures and presentations.** The classic method that adults are familiar with from their school days, lectures are the most effective way to reach a number of people with fairly straightforward information. In the initial rollout of a code, for example, lectures may be the most effective mode of explaining where the code fits into business performance. This mode is also an effective way to describe other resources and ways to access them. If an objective of the training program is to develop dialogue and decision-making skills, it is doubtful that lectures will be effective. Indeed, this mode may be counterproductive if it reinforces an organizational culture in which employees do what they are told and avoid the risks of making decisions.

- **Case studies and scenarios.** After participants understand the purpose of the training and the resources available, issues of responsible business conduct can be effectively introduced through the study and analysis of cases that have actually occurred to the enterprise or to other similarly situated enterprises. Trainers might also develop their own scenarios to raise a number of issues. Case studies and scenarios help develop dialogue and decision-making skills. Case studies take more time to pass on information than do lectures. But analyzing a situation to isolate an issue, to develop the realistic options available, and to justify a decision to others in a relatively risk-free environment is invaluable. This mode

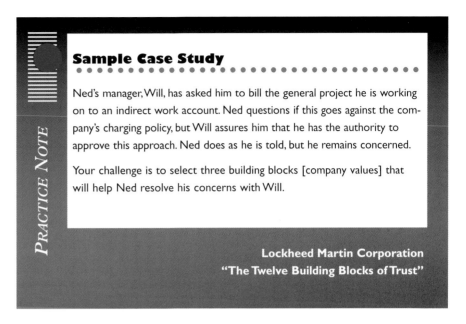

Sample Case Study

Ned's manager, Will, has asked him to bill the general project he is working on to an indirect work account. Ned questions if this goes against the company's charging policy, but Will assures him that he has the authority to approve this approach. Ned does as he is told, but he remains concerned.

Your challenge is to select three building blocks [company values] that will help Ned resolve his concerns with Will.

Lockheed Martin Corporation
"The Twelve Building Blocks of Trust"

also develops the important skills and attitudes of listening and of giving and receiving feedback.

- **Ethics games.** Many larger enterprises, including Citigroup, Lockheed Martin, and Boeing, have developed games to raise awareness of issues of ethics, compliance, and social responsibility; to develop good reasoning skills and judgment; to stimulate dialogue; and to demonstrate management commitment.[17] In general, the games involve dividing employees into small teams and placing before them a situation that raises a discrete issue of ethics, compliance, or social responsibility. The teams are given a few minutes to reach a consensus choice among the four or five alternative responses available to them. Teams are then asked to justify their choice. These games usually stimulate heated discussion. Each answer has a predetermined value in points. A particularly valuable element is that members of senior management sit as an "appeals board" in the event a team disputes the correctness of the answers or their predetermined point values. Participants are then able to observe how senior managers make and justify their decisions.

- **Other modes.** Many companies are now offering quite sophisticated Web-based training.[18] This mode may be relatively cost-effective. Videos and self-paced studies may be purchased off the shelf and may expose participants to the basics. These products, while useful, lack the familiarity that customized materials would offer. Yet, such materials do tend to reinforce the notion that the enterprise is engaging in an emerging global effort, and thus they might add some sense of importance to the training.

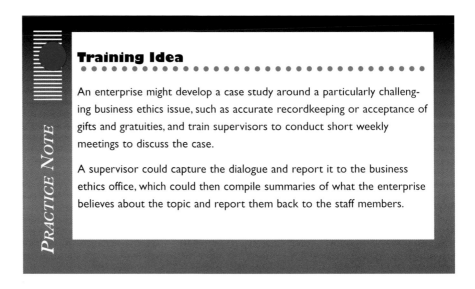

Training Idea

An enterprise might develop a case study around a particularly challenging business ethics issue, such as accurate recordkeeping or acceptance of gifts and gratuities, and train supervisors to conduct short weekly meetings to discuss the case.

A supervisor could capture the dialogue and report it to the business ethics office, which could then compile summaries of what the enterprise believes about the topic and report them back to the staff members.

UPDATING AND MODIFYING THE TRAINING PROGRAM

The training program should be modified over time to ensure that its content contributes to pursuit of the enterprise's purpose and helps meet reasonable stakeholder expectations. Also, it should be reviewed to ensure that the delivery methods are the most effective available. As the relevant context of an enterprise, its organizational culture, and its stakeholders' expectations change over time, the training program must adapt as well. This effort requires considering feedback from the training program.

Training provides useful feedback to managers on the ways in which the business ethics program is being received. It helps uncover sensitive areas such as insufficient guidance for employees or unreasonable stakeholder expectations, legal issues, unfair treatment of employees, and difficult working conditions. Feedback might reveal that trainers focus on issues that do not reflect the real-life concerns of the participants. It might also show that the sessions need more trainer–trainee interaction or that the materials are dull and do not encourage interaction. If feedback shows that participants need a better understanding of complicated issues, such as conflicts of interest, there may be specific real examples or case studies from the enterprise's experience that could address these concerns.

There are several methods for collecting feedback from training programs. Traditionally, training administrators ask trainees to fill out an evaluation form asking whether they found the training useful and what, if anything, they learned. At the end of the training, administrators should ask participants questions such as:

- How would you rate the overall effectiveness of the training?
- Were the materials helpful and relevant?
- Were the right issues discussed?
- What other topics would you like to discuss in the next training session?

Training administrators might also ask participants to take quizzes before, during, and after the training to determine what they learned.

The action-planning process described earlier is probably the most valuable, though time-consuming, process of collecting feedback because it tracks whether training actually transferred to the workplace.

MANAGING TRAINING ADMINISTRATION

Owners and managers demonstrate their commitment to the business ethics program by managing the training program well. Good management requires that adequate time be allocated to training, that training records be well maintained, and that training participation be an element of performance evaluation.

Generally, three to four hours of training per employee, at a minimum, is required to roll out a new business ethics program. Thereafter, annual training of from one to three hours is the norm. In the United States, it is common for all employees and agents to be required to attend the training. In Europe, training tends to be more targeted and to take place at higher management levels.[19] Whatever the target audience, no training exceptions can be granted without bringing management's commitment into question. Additional training should be provided for people in sensitive positions, such as government contracting, sales and marketing, and human resources.

Good records management requires that training administrators record participation in training; participant feedback; action planning follow-through; and issues of ethics, compliance, and responsibility identified during the training.

Ensuring Members Follow Standards and Meet Expectations

IMPORTANCE OF FEEDBACK

Few stakeholders of an enterprise would disagree with the proposition that owners and managers have legitimate needs for information about compliance with its standards, procedures, and expectations. They need this information to guide employees and agents and to foster reasonable stakeholder expectations.

The abiding issue for a business ethics program is how to garner this information through processes that are consistent with the enterprise's core beliefs. The ideal form is free-flowing communication between owners and managers, employees and agents, and other stakeholders about all the matters needed for the enterprise to meet the reasonable expectations of its stakeholders effectively and efficiently. Often, however, either mechanisms to accommodate free-flowing communication are not readily available or there is not enough trust between stakeholders for such communication to take place. Under such circumstances, owners and managers must design and implement other control mechanisms. This section describes the issues, policies, and processes of maintaining internal control and engaging external stakeholders.

In general, owners and managers use five methods to track what is going on in the enterprise:

1. Monitoring ongoing operations
2. Auditing books, records, and process documentation
3. Responding to employees and agents seeking advice and reporting concerns
4. Investigating incidents and reports
5. Engaging stakeholders

All these methods require infrastructure. Management needs to design a monitoring, auditing, and investigation framework that is consistent with the management alignment processes described in Chapter 8. Engaging external stakeholders is not as well defined as the other methods, but enterprises have found a few techniques, such as stakeholder surveys, to be valuable. RBE Worksheet 11, at the end of this chapter, is also a useful tool for ensuring an effective infrastructure is in place.

MONITORING

Monitoring enterprise performance is an essential management task. An RBE plans its work by assigning individual and group responsibility. It sets performance expectations for individuals and groups to guide their efforts toward achieving the enterprise's goals and objectives. Employees and agents are held accountable as individuals and groups for achieving assigned objectives while following the enterprise's standards, procedures, and expectations. Whether set for individuals or for groups, performance expectations must be specific, measurable, achievable, relevant, and time-specific.

In an RBE, processes and projects may be monitored continually. Good monitoring requires consistently measuring performance and providing ongoing feedback to employees and agents as to how well their performance

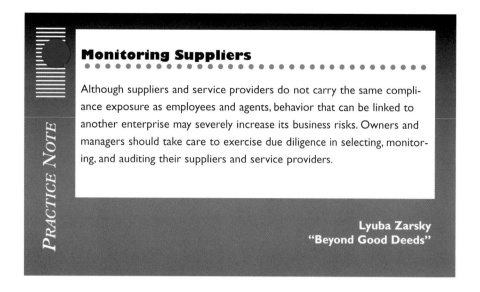

PRACTICE NOTE

Monitoring Suppliers

Although suppliers and service providers do not carry the same compliance exposure as employees and agents, behavior that can be linked to another enterprise may severely increase its business risks. Owners and managers should take care to exercise due diligence in selecting, monitoring, and auditing their suppliers and service providers.

Lyuba Zarsky
"Beyond Good Deeds"

complies with enterprise standards and procedures and meets stakeholder expectations. Continual monitoring enables unacceptable performance to be identified before it fails to meet stakeholder expectations.

The best operational example is the total quality management process, whereby individuals and teams set performance standards, continually collect data, and use quality tools to measure performance and analyze the data to resolve problems and improve processes.

Issues of responsible business conduct may be approached in a similar manner. Where risks have been identified, such as conflicts of interest, fraudulent consumer transactions, inaccurate books and records or expense accounting, or bribes and corruption, an RBE establishes structures and systems to monitor performance on a regular basis. It does not wait for reports of misconduct. It requires regular reports, examines accounts and records, and tracks patterns and trends as good management practice. Other forms of monitoring are performance evaluations and exit interviews.

AUDITING

Whereas monitoring is an aspect of good management practice for all managers and supervisors, auditing is a more formal process. It is a review of employee or agent performance by an independent agent. This independent agent may be either internal or external to the enterprise, but it is not a part of the enterprise's operational management.

Internal audit serves as the primary means by which owners and managers review and evaluate the enterprise's internal control structure.

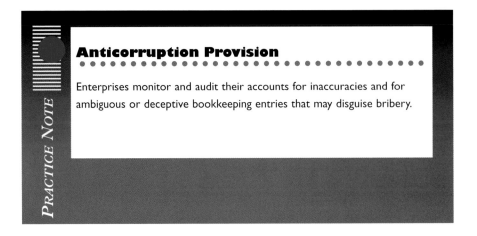

PRACTICE NOTE

Anticorruption Provision

Enterprises monitor and audit their accounts for inaccuracies and for ambiguous or deceptive bookkeeping entries that may disguise bribery.

Although this charter is very broad, in practice the traditional focus had been on financial data. External auditors perform formal audits of financial statements to meet the needs of external stakeholders: investors, creditors, and regulators.

More recently, the traditional focus has expanded to include reviewing the systems established to ensure compliance with an enterprise's standards, procedures, and expectations. Operational audits are often performed by internal auditors, to determine whether the enterprise complies with its standards and procedures. They may be done on a regular basis or in response to specific reports or concerns.

EMPLOYEES SEEKING ADVICE AND REPORTING CONCERNS

Among the surest sources of information about what is going on in an enterprise—especially behavior that violates enterprise core beliefs, standards, procedures, and expectations—are employees and agents. Most employees and agents recognize management's legitimate need for such information, if the enterprise is to meet the reasonable expectations of its stakeholders. Nonetheless, standards, procedures, and expectations that encourage employees and agents to seek advice and report concerns can raise issues of conflicting loyalties to the enterprise and to peers, and, in many emerging market economies, may raise historical memories of betrayal.

Reporting concerns about the business conduct of co-workers is hard for most employees. Indeed, research suggests that substantial numbers of employees, even in developed economies, are extremely reluctant to report their concerns.[20] Many put loyalty to friends and colleagues above loyalty to the enterprise. Many do not trust that managers—or their peers—will not retaliate against them if they report their concerns.

As two authors have observed:

> Both the law and popular opinion have always been ambivalent about whistleblowers, whether in the elementary school yard, universities, the military or other government agency, or in private life. Are they malcontents, troublemakers, and snitches? Or are they brave, ethical individuals who, unlike their fellow beings, coworkers, or superiors, want their company to act legally and ethically as well?[21]

A business ethics program helps employees and agents understand why it is important that they communicate their concerns to management, how they should report their concerns, and why it is safe to do so.

Under a business ethics program, employees and agents are more sensitive to the types of behavior that constitute misconduct or illegality. They are more likely to view reporting misconduct as one of their obligations to the enterprise, their fellow employees, and enterprise stakeholders. As recent research displayed in Figure 7.1 demonstrates, if enterprises have in place at least four elements of a business ethics program, 78 percent of employees are willing to report misconduct. Only 52 percent are willing to do so where only written standards are in place, and only 39 percent where none of the four elements were present.[22] (The four elements were written standards of business conduct, training on standards of conduct, an ethics office or telephone advice line, and a means to report misconduct anonymously.)

In an organizational culture that encourages dialogue, questions, and delivery of bad news, employees find it easier to confront issues of responsible business conduct, to seek advice and report concerns, and to make ethical decisions. In many enterprises, however, employees are uncomfortable with coming forward, especially to report their concerns involving other employees. Owners and managers need to make the case for coming forward in terms that resonate with their employees. For example, a manager in a Far Eastern cultural context explained why employees should report their concerns about business conduct by analogy, pointing to how employees would take action to protect their families if there was broken glass in their homes.[23]

Reporting Violations

Ideally, owners, managers, and supervisors maintain an open-door policy for employees and agents who have concerns that involve responsible business conduct. Often, however, employees and agents are reluctant to bring "bad news" to managers and supervisors. To encourage them to come forward, an enterprise should establish discreet procedures for employees to seek advice and report concerns.

FIGURE 7.1
Variations in Employee
Willingness to Report
Misconduct

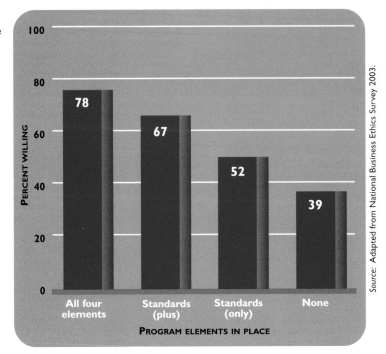

Source: Adapted from National Business Ethics Survey 2003.

Suggestion boxes, help-lines, and whistle-blowing protection all facilitate reporting of questionable conduct. Reports may also be received from individuals who come to the business ethics office and register a concern. The identity of reporters should be kept confidential (to the extent that the law provides), and sources should not be held liable, discriminated against, or harassed for reporting their concerns.

Once the business ethics officer receives a report, it is important that the enterprise follow through. The officer should

- Record the reported concern
- Evaluate the concern and develop an action plan for dealing with it
- Initiate or coordinate an investigation or inquiry, if appropriate
- Take appropriate action on findings and conclusions
- Track reported concerns for patterns and trends
- Make recommendations based on lessons learned

Critical to the success of the business ethics program is feedback to the reporting source of the steps taken to investigate the matter, what was found, and what corrective steps—if any—were or will be taken. In many surveys of employee attitudes, when reasons are given for why an employee observing misconduct did not report it, second only to fear of retaliation is the sense that management would not do anything with the information anyway.[24]

Protecting Employees and Agents from Retribution

All reporting procedures should be designed to leave reporters free from fear of retribution. Managers, supervisors, and other employees should understand that direct or indirect retribution for voicing a concern or complaint is not to be tolerated. Retribution by either managers or peers discourages others from reporting their concerns. An RBE, therefore, should have a strict policy that discipline will be imposed for any instance of retribution.

Occasionally, an employee or other agent reporting concerns may make a mistake or abuse the reporting process and cause an investigation that does not lead to further action. Behavior that abuses the reporting process will often violate enterprise core beliefs; however, managers should counsel, but not punish, such a reporter. Maintaining absolute certainty among employees and agents that they can report concerns without fear of retribution is so important that managers should not risk losing that confidence by punishing anyone who used a reporting process. If the enterprise reserves the right to punish those who abuse the process, the published standards, procedures, and expectations will have to leave that possibility open. Where trust in management is not the norm, reporting sources may be uncertain about just how safely they can make reports.

Moreover, it is difficult, at best, to prove that a reported concern was an abuse of the process. Even if a case can be made, it may raise significant questions in the minds of potential sources about just how safe the process is. In Box 7.1, the last sentence may be seized on by employees as a reason not to report their concerns unless they are certain of all the facts. In short, for all the satisfaction owners and managers may retain in being able to punish someone who abuses the process, the cost in terms of employee confidence in the reporting process is too high to pay.

Although the individual should not be punished to preserve confidence in the business ethics program, other steps can be taken to limit harm to other individuals or to the enterprise. The abusing person or the victim may be reassigned, for example.

Using a Help-Line

A help-line is a dedicated telephone line that gives employees and agents direct access to the business ethics officer. It should be free of charge to the caller. The number should be widely distributed; everyone should have access to the number. If the enterprise uses an answering machine for the number after normal business hours, the machine should be placed in a private, secure location.

BOX 7 . 1

REPORTING CONCERNS

Taking action to prevent problems is part of the Motorola culture. If you observe possible unethical or illegal conduct, you are encouraged to report your concerns.

Retaliation against any employee who honestly reports a concern to Motorola about illegal or unethical conduct will not be tolerated. It is unacceptable to file a report knowing it to be false.

Motorola Corporation
"Code of Business Conduct"

A help-line may be operated by a commercial service with instructions from the enterprise. Typically, under such a service, a source may call anonymously to report concerns. If the source is willing to be contacted for more information but wishes to maintain his or her anonymity, he or she will be given an identification number and will be told to call back at a particular time.

Maintaining Confidentiality and Security

It is difficult for an employee or agent to choose fidelity to enterprise standards, procedures, and expectations over loyalty to his or her friends or colleagues. When an employee or agent decides to report concerns, he or she must believe that it is the right thing to do. Managers owe reporting employees and agents as much security as possible when they report their concerns.[25]

An emerging best practice is to establish a policy authorizing certain business ethics personnel to promise reporting employees and agents that their identities and information will remain confidential. Whether they can make a promise of confidentiality that courts of law will respect, known as a *privileged communication*, depends on the laws of the jurisdiction. Managers must consider that if they promise confidentiality to a reporting source but are then required to disclose the source's identity, others may not come forward to report their concerns.[26]

Distinguishing between Ethics and Personnel Issues

Experience with help-lines demonstrates that more than half of all calls will be about personnel matters. Owners and managers will be tempted to require that such callers be directed to call human resources. They should resist this temptation for two reasons. First, in the minds of employees, when managers speak of ethics, they are talking about fairness, so employees see personnel matters as ethics issues. Second, when management rejects a call to the help-line for whatever reason it risks the reputation of the help-line as an effective and safe way for employees and agents to seek advice or report concerns. Other employees will only hear that a fellow employee made a call to the help-line and was rejected, but not learn management's reasons why, however valid.

In establishing reporting guidelines, however, management must distinguish between matters of responsible business conduct and grievances of union-represented employees. A grievance issue arises when there is a difference in interpretation or implementation of a collective bargaining agreement or an individual labor contract. A department other than the business ethics officer will typically address grievances.

THE ORGANIZATIONAL OMBUDSMAN

In a number of large, complex enterprises (LCEs), a specific office, called the *ombudsman*, has been established to advise employees and agents of their rights and duties regarding responsible conduct. In the business enterprise context, the ombudsman is a separate means by which employees and agents can seek advice and report their concerns.[27]

The ombudsman was originally a Scandinavian office created to investigate citizen complaints against governments or otherwise trusted to look after the affairs of others. Today, the position of an organizational ombudsman in a business ethics program has evolved to be an independent, neutral, and alternative office where employees and agents can go to seek advice and report concerns. *Independent* means the ombudsman is not a part of day-to-day staff or operations management. *Neutral* means it does not function as an advocate for the enterprise or individual. *Alternative* means the ombudsman does not duplicate any other enterprise function, such as investigations. With few exceptions, the ombudsman is authorized to refer reports of misconduct for investigation only with the express consent of the reporting source.

In some jurisdictions, enterprises can claim that the ombudsman can make an enforceable promise of confidentiality. The enterprise will not be deemed to have notice of the concern until the source registers his or her concerns with the enterprise or authorizes the ombudsman to do so. However, as managers review standards, procedures, and expectations, an ombudsman may contribute what he or she has learned about employee concerns, provided that he or she does not compromise the anonymity and confidentiality of the sources.

POLICIES AND PROCEDURES FOR INVESTIGATIONS

It is critical to the success of a business ethics program that reported concerns be investigated. Managers may learn of concerns suggesting that a violation of standards, procedures, and expectations has occurred from a variety of sources, including the help-line. Once on notice, an RBE must take all reasonable steps to determine what happened and how the problem might be avoided in the future.

In developing an investigative plan, managers need to consider the laws of the jurisdiction in which they operate. These laws will affect who conducts the investigation and what rights are afforded to the subjects of the investigation. Investigations should always be conducted with a view to possible government prosecution or civil litigation.

Investigations will typically involve document review and witness interviews. Employees should be instructed to cooperate fully with the investigation, including preserving all relevant documents and materials. The investigator must be alert to avoiding the appearance of influencing witnesses or appearing to speak for the enterprise or another witness. A typical procedure is shown in Box 7.2.

EXTERNAL STAKEHOLDER ENGAGEMENT

Increasingly, nongovernmental organizations (NGOs) hold enterprises accountable for unethical behavior and demand best practices. International institutions are developing policies requiring greater transparency and

---

BOX 7.2

INVESTIGATIVE PROCEDURES

A typical investigative procedure works as follows:

- A call is made to the business ethics officer to report misconduct.

- The business ethics officer registers the report.

- The business ethics officer creates a plan for resolving the matter.

- The plan includes analyzing facts, developing assignments, conducting interviews, and disclosing information to select individuals.

- If the business ethics officer requires additional help from special departments, he or she coordinates other resources, such as legal, internal audit, human resources, or security.

- The business ethics officer devises a written schedule for completing the investigation and standards for the disclosure of information.

- The business ethics officer remains in close contact with individuals involved in the investigation and periodically requests information and details on proceedings.

- At the conclusion of the investigation, the business ethics officer presents a summation of the findings to the enterprise's managers and the board of directors.

- Owners or senior managers decide what corrective action should be taken, including whether the matter should be voluntarily disclosed to a government agency or other stakeholders.

encouraging official investigations of misconduct. Local communities are less willing to host an enterprise known for corrupt or irresponsible practices.

These trends provide owners and managers with the incentive and opportunity to secure feedback from external stakeholders. Feedback mechanisms include media reviews, stakeholder satisfaction surveys, conferences, and discussion groups. The focus of such efforts should be to ascertain how well the enterprise is fostering and meeting stakeholder expectations. Also important is public perception about how responsible the enterprise is or how consistent its business practices are with its core beliefs.

Anita Roddick, founder and CEO of The Body Shop, described an integrated process recently:

> So how can loyalty be built and maintained by British business and what, if any, is the role of government in assisting this process? I believe the key to loyalty is trust, and trust flows from a high level of commitment to transparency and a genuine desire to engage on a human level. In The Body Shop this means putting a lot of effort into assessing the quality of relationships with stakeholders, through systematic dialogue involving opinion surveys and focus groups. It also means active, audited disclosure of social and environmental performance so that everyone involved with the business can judge progress (or lack of it) for themselves. It means being open about our company values, campaigning on issues such as human rights and animal welfare—issues we know our customers and employees care about. Make no mistake, this is not done simply for the fun of it. It works for us because it is genuine, but it also helps us run a better and a more successful company, with very loyal employees and customers.[28]

Meetings with external stakeholders are an effective way to secure feedback. An RBE can sponsor such meetings to demonstrate its initiative and interest. An owner or senior manager should lead the meetings. Local community, government, and NGO representatives may be invited. Questions, comments, and suggestions should be encouraged.

Monitoring media coverage of business is an essential means of securing feedback from the public and making appropriate adjustments to the business ethics program. In recent years, the media have become better informed about how to measure whether leaders of an enterprise are committed to responsible business conduct. Through the media, a business can capture the perceptions of the public regarding its expectations of business and its role in the community.

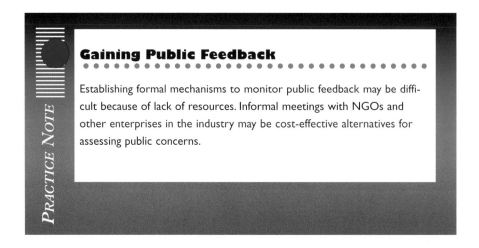

Gaining Public Feedback

Establishing formal mechanisms to monitor public feedback may be difficult because of lack of resources. Informal meetings with NGOs and other enterprises in the industry may be cost-effective alternatives for assessing public concerns.

Finally, as discussed in Chapter 10, an RBE engages its stakeholders by monitoring, tracking, and reporting its performance in areas of concern to its stakeholders, especially civil society. The reaction of civil society and the media to the enterprise's social responsibility reports is valuable information and invites further dialogue.

SUMMARY

It is vital to the welfare of the enterprise and its ability to meet the reasonable expectations of its stakeholders that owners and managers know whether enterprise standards and procedures are being followed and whether reasonable stakeholder expectations are being met. The source of this information, in all cases, is the stakeholders of the enterprise: employees, agents, customers, suppliers, and regulators, to name but a few.

Owners and managers of an RBE should develop a plan to communicate with stakeholders the enterprise's standards, procedures, and expectations. They can do so by answering two fundamental questions:

1. How can we most effectively communicate our standards and procedures and foster reasonable expectations among our stakeholders?

2. How can we know that our members follow our standards and reasonable stakeholder expectations are met?

To communicate enterprise standards, procedures, and expectations, owners and managers use all manner of vehicles: formal and informal communications; training, education, and development; and stakeholder engagement.

To ensure that management knows what is going on in the enterprise, owners and managers establish various mechanisms, as appropriate to the relevant context and organizational culture: monitoring, auditing, reporting, and stakeholder surveys.

RESPONSIBLE BUSINESS ENTERPRISE
Checklist

1   Who in our enterprise has responsibility for ensuring that the core beliefs of the enterprise are documented and disseminated to employees, agents, and other stakeholders?

2.   How do our owners and managers communicate enterprise standards, procedures, and expectations to our employees, agents, and other stakeholders?

3.   Can owners and managers reasonably expect employees and agents to report observed misconduct? If not, why not? If not, what other mechanisms are in place, or should be in place, so that owners and managers know what is going on in the organization?

Communications Needs Assessment Worksheet

RBE Worksheet 9, which can be photocopied for use with your organization, assists owners and managers in conducting a needs analysis to find out what stakeholders need to know. Use the standard assessment tools (interviews, focus groups, surveys, document review, and direct observation) to answer the questions listed.

	Interviews	Focus Groups	Surveys	Document Review	Direct Observation
What kinds of responsible business conduct issues do employees and other stakeholders face or are they concerned about?					
What do employees and other stakeholders need to know to be able to fulfill their roles and responsibilities and have reasonable expectations of the enterprise?					
How do employees and other stakeholders learn what is expected of them and what they can expect?					
What communications methods are available to the enterprise to reach specific stakeholders?					
What are the criteria by which successful communications will be evaluated?					

RBE WORKSHEET

10   Training Program Outcomes Worksheet

Using RBE Worksheet 10, training program designers can work from expected outcomes of the business ethics program through general and specific training topics to formulate specific training program objectives. In filling out RBE Worksheet 10, which may be photocopied for use within your organization, treat each cell opposite a program outcome separately.

Performance Measures	General Training Topics	Specific Topics	Training Objectives
Amount of observed violation of enterprise standards, including legal requirements	• Enterprise core beliefs • Risks to the enterprise when standards are violated • Personal and organizational responsibility and accountability • Difference between personal morality and enterprise standards • Policy on rewarding responsible behavior and punishing irresponsible behavior		
Awareness of issues of responsible business conduct at work	• Enterprise expectations for employee behavior • Stakeholder expectations • Enterprise standards and policies • Recognition of ethics, compliance, and responsibility issues		
How often employees and agents speak in terms of core beliefs and standards	• Ethics and policy theory • Dimensions of culture • Value of diversity • Listening and giving feedback		
How often employees and agents make decisions in terms of core beliefs and standards	• Ethics, compliance, and responsible decision-making • Strategic planning based on core beliefs		
How willing employees and agents are to seek advice on standards	• Individual responsibility to seek advice • Communication channels		

continued on the next page

continued on the next page

Performance Measures	General Training Topics	Specific Topics	Training Objectives
How willing employees and agents are to report observed or suspected violations	• Individual responsibility to report concerns • Communication channels • Policy on confidentiality • Policy against retaliation		
How satisfied those who reported observed or suspected violations are with management's response	• Manager or supervisor training on advising employees • Policies on confidentiality and nonretaliation • Help-line protocols		
How committed employees are to the enterprise	• Core beliefs about stakeholder expectations • Individual and enterprise roles and responsibilities to stakeholders • Opportunities to enhance enterprise reputation • Opportunities to add value to the community • Individual or team skills, knowledge, understanding, and attitude development		
How satisfied stakeholders are that the enterprise meets their expectations	• Core beliefs about stakeholder expectations • Individual and enterprise roles and responsibilities to stakeholders • Opportunities to enhance enterprise reputation • Opportunities to add value to the community • Individual or team skills, knowledge, understanding, and attitude development		

RBE WORKSHEET

11 Communications Infrastructure Worksheet

RBE Worksheet 11, which may be photocopied for use within your enterprise, provides a tool for ensuring consideration of all necessary infrastructure to communicate and solicit feedback about enterprise standards, procedures, and expectations. Owners, managers, and staff members should discuss with their stakeholders each issue along the vertical axis to ensure that they are consistent with their core beliefs and the reference standards and best practices developed in this chapter. From this dialogue, they will be able to identify any required business ethics infrastructure.

	Enterprise Core Beliefs	Reference Standards or Best Practices	Current Structure and Practice	Required Infrastructure
Means of communicating standards and procedures and establishing expectations				
Monitoring and auditing procedures and dialogue mechanisms				

IV

Putting Business Ethics into Practice

Aligning the Responsible Business Enterprise

8

*T*his chapter discusses the basic concepts and practices of responsible management. The responsible business enterprise (RBE) aligns its management practices with its core beliefs, standards, procedures, and expectations, supported by its business ethics infrastructure.

Understanding the Importance of Alignment

Core beliefs, standards, and procedures; reasonable stakeholder expectations; and business ethics infrastructure alone do not make an enterprise a responsible business. The essence of an RBE is that it consistently improves its business performance, makes profits, and increases the prosperity of its community by meeting the reasonable expectations of its stakeholders in pursuit of its purpose as an enterprise.

BUSINESS ETHICS PROGRAMS AND BUSINESS PLANNING

Research and experience suggest that the most helpful aspect of a business ethics program may be that it supports management practices that align enterprise strategies and management practices with core beliefs, standards, procedures, infrastructure, and expectations.[1] A business ethics program is a fundamental aspect of organizational development that provides the foundation for other important aspects of business planning such as a business plan, marketing strategy, investment prospectus, and proposal for a strategic

- **Understanding the Importance of Alignment**

- **Getting the Right People in the Right Places**

- **Encouraging Employees to Follow Standards and Procedures**

- **Dealing with Mistakes, Misconduct, or Misunderstandings**

185

PRACTICE NOTE

Alignment: the Ultimate Measure of Success

Success for a business ethics program comes when the core beliefs, standards, procedures, and stakeholder expectations desired by owners and managers become an integral part of everything that owners, managers, supervisors, other employees, and agents think, say, and do: when core beliefs, standards, procedures, and stakeholders' expectations become "the way we do things around here."

alliance. In all these instances, the enterprise must be able to demonstrate a consistent theme in thought, communication, and action. Each of the five elements below, for example, should be based on the preceding ones and, ultimately, on the core beliefs of the enterprise as developed in Chapter 5:

1. Mission
2. Goals and objectives
3. Strategies, programs, and action plans
4. Performance measures
5. Decisions and activities

In the case of a business plan, for example, all of the elements lead to an integrated approach to the four components of a business plan: (a) description of the business, (b) marketing plan, (c) financial management plan, and (d) management plan. A business plan not based on these elements would be necessarily incomplete.

FUNDAMENTAL QUESTIONS

Three fundamental questions address the alignment practices of an RBE:

1. How can we ensure that we have the right people in the right places while we pursue our purpose as an enterprise?
2. How can we encourage our employees and agents to follow our standards and procedures?
3. What do we owe our stakeholders when mistakes, misconduct, or misunderstandings occur that involve our standards and procedures or their reasonable expectations?[2]

Owners and managers can use Worksheet 12, the enterprise alignment worksheet, to assist in answering these questions.

Getting the Right People in the Right Places

Having the right people in place allows an enterprise to face a changing world confident that it can succeed, regardless of the pressures its relevant context might present. To accomplish this, management needs to attract the right people, train them properly, position them well, and treat them fairly. It also needs to see that the "wrong" people are not in a position to distract the enterprise from pursuing its purpose and meeting the reasonable expectations of its stakeholders.

HAVING RESPONSIBLE OWNERS, MANAGERS, AND SUPERVISORS

Emphasis on having the right people in the right places begins with owners, managers, and supervisors. Responsible owners and managers need to be people who embrace an RBE's core beliefs. If an RBE's purpose is to be a global energy company, as at Royal Dutch/Shell, then they are passionate about delivering energy on a global scale. If the enterprise's values are integrity, contribution to society, responsibility to customers and employees, and the unequivocal pursuit of quality and excellence, those values naturally guide everything owners and managers think, say, or do. If the envisioned future of the enterprise is to become the company that most changes the worldwide image of Japanese products as being of poor quality, as at Sony, that is the owners and managers' picture of where the enterprise is going and their part in it.

Owners, managers, and supervisors set the tone for all that happens—and does not happen—in their enterprise. Employees and agents watch to see if they "pay attention to ethics, take ethics seriously, and care about ethics and values as much as the bottom line," as one recent study confirmed.[3] Over time, their behavior molds the organizational culture that orders "the way we do things around here," regardless of what the formal documents of the enterprise might say.

Owners, managers, and supervisors are in positions that have authority and require discretion. The decisions they make and the activities they sponsor or condone involve great risk and opportunity for the enterprise. As a result, mistakes, misconduct, or misunderstandings involving owners, managers, and supervisors—especially senior managers—may have far-reaching implications at all four levels of enterprise identity:

1. **Compliance level**. Prosecutors are far more likely to prosecute an enterprise for criminal misconduct if senior managers are involved; they are more likely to find that the organizational culture of the enterprise is a

factor, as well. In the United States, a disproportionate number of small to medium-sized enterprises (SMEs) are prosecuted for misconduct.

2. **Risk management level.** Risk to the enterprise may be dramatically higher if senior managers or those with substantial discretion are involved, often costing into the millions of dollars.

3. **Reputation enhancement level.** The damage to the reputation of the enterprise, especially when senior managers are involved, may be irreparable. In recent years, for example, enterprises with household names have ceased to exist or are struggling to recover from lapses in responsible business conduct at the level of senior management. Such lapses are even more devastating for the SME closely connected to its community, where word travels fast.

4. **Value-added level.** An RBE strives to add value to its community while drawing on the resources of the community. If senior managers violate the trust placed in them by an enterprise's stakeholders, the enterprise may never be able to repair the damage done to the trust, social capital, or resources of the community.

What makes any person a "right person" for a particular enterprise, then, are the responsible criteria of the enterprise itself: its core beliefs, its established standards and procedures, and the reasonable expectations of its stakeholders. Applying these responsible criteria to all hiring, placement, and retaining decisions leads to consistency in action and fairness.

HIRING THE RIGHT PEOPLE

Where the responsible criteria of the enterprise are clear, owners and managers can use people who exemplify the criteria to recruit and evaluate

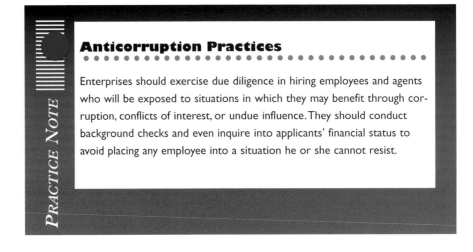

Anticorruption Practices

Enterprises should exercise due diligence in hiring employees and agents who will be exposed to situations in which they may benefit through corruption, conflicts of interest, or undue influence. They should conduct background checks and even inquire into applicants' financial status to avoid placing any employee into a situation he or she cannot resist.

PRACTICE NOTE

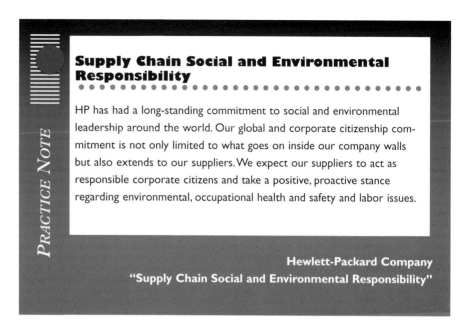

PRACTICE NOTE

Supply Chain Social and Environmental Responsibility

HP has had a long-standing commitment to social and environmental leadership around the world. Our global and corporate citizenship commitment is not only limited to what goes on inside our company walls but also extends to our suppliers. We expect our suppliers to act as responsible corporate citizens and take a positive, proactive stance regarding environmental, occupational health and safety and labor issues.

**Hewlett-Packard Company
"Supply Chain Social and Environmental Responsibility"**

potential employees. By hiring people who embrace the responsible criteria of an enterprise, owners and managers take a large step toward having an effective business ethics program. It takes only one employee or agent to destroy the reputation of an enterprise. Hiring the wrong people increases the risk of criminal and civil liability and increases the costs of defending the enterprise or correcting any harm done. All of these risks adversely affect the prospects for improving business performance, making a profit, and increasing prosperity in the community. In some cases, as recent examples in Asia, Europe, and the United States, have shown, the bad acts of a few employees (often senior managers) can bring an enterprise to near financial ruin.

To exercise due care, an enterprise must balance the reasonable expectations that applicants, employees, and agents have that an RBE will respect their privacy as individuals. Depending on the applicable employment protection laws, an RBE may screen prospective employees. Owners and managers should carefully research what screening processes an RBE may use in considering applications.

Owners and managers should also exercise due diligence in selecting their strategic alliances, the entities with which they merge, the entities they acquire, their joint venture partners, and their suppliers and service providers. See Appendix E for a sample supply chain management questionnaire, which one company uses to qualify its suppliers.

PLACING PEOPLE IN THE RIGHT POSITIONS

All enterprise positions are not the same as far as level of responsibility is concerned. Owners and managers must take care to ensure that their people are able to assume the level of responsibility that their positions demand. As the level of responsibility increases, so too must the competency and responsibility of the person occupying the position.

This is particularly the case if the position has substantial discretionary authority, such as the high-level personnel discussed in Chapter 6: a director, an executive, an individual in charge of a business unit or major function, or someone with a substantial ownership interest. But this principle also applies to other positions such as plant and sales managers and employees who advise the public or have authority to set price levels or negotiate contracts, especially for government contracts.

Where high-level personnel are involved in misconduct, the enterprise itself is at greater risk. Government prosecutors, sentencing judges, the media, and the public, which might be inclined to treat an isolated incident of misconduct by lower-level personnel as an individual shortcoming, are more apt to attribute the misconduct of senior personnel to the enterprise as a whole.

FIGURE 8.1
Observed Misconduct by Actions of Top Management

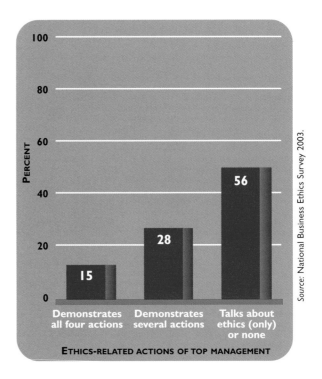

Source: National Business Ethics Survey 2003.

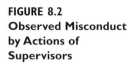

**FIGURE 8.2
Observed Misconduct
by Actions of
Supervisors**

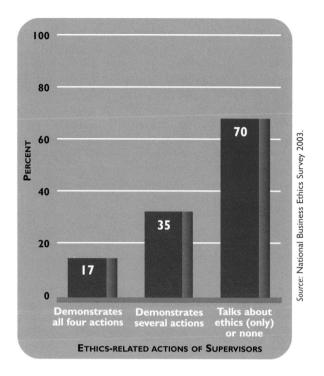

Source: National Business Ethics Survey 2003.

Moreover, the conduct of managers and supervisors is a key indicator of the effectiveness of the business ethics program. As recent research displayed in Figure 8.1 shows, where top management demonstrates four ethics-related actions, only 15 percent of employees say that they observed misconduct. The number climbs to 28 percent where management demonstrates fewer ethics-related actions and jumps to 56 percent where top managers only talk about ethics or take no action at all.[4] (The four ethics-related actions are talking about the importance of ethics, keeping promises and commitments, setting a good example, and keeping employees informed.)

Figure 8.2 shows that the outcomes are even more dramatic for supervisors: only 17 percent of employees observed misconduct where supervisors demonstrated all four ethics-related actions, but 35 percent observed misconduct where supervisors demonstrated fewer ethics-related actions, and 70 percent observed misconduct where supervisors only talked about ethics or took no action at all.[5] (The four ethics-related actions for supervisors are slightly different from those for top management: supporting employees who follow ethics standards is substituted for keeping employees informed.)

These associations between the ethics-related actions of managers and supervisors and expected program outcomes held true for the following

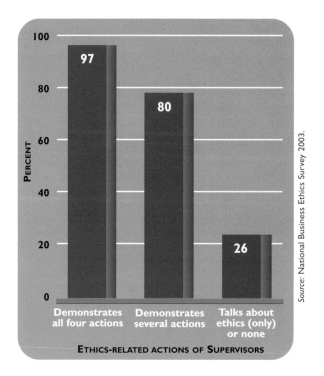

FIGURE 8.3
Employee Satisfaction with Organization by Actions of Supervisors

Source: National Business Ethics Survey 2003.

outcomes as well: less feeling of pressure to compromise standards, more satisfaction with management's response to reported concerns, more sense that managers and supervisors are held accountable, and more satisfaction with the enterprise as a whole. Having the right people in the right places is essential for an enterprise to be a responsible business enterprise. Figure 8.3 addresses employee satisfaction with the organization.

RETAINING THE RIGHT PEOPLE

Responsible people want to use their skills and knowledge in pursuit of a purpose they value. Compensation is important, but the sense of being a responsible member of a responsible enterprise has value in and of itself. As one researcher noted, "The right people will do the right things and deliver the best results they are capable of, regardless of the incentive system."[6]

Having hired the right people, an RBE strives to assign them work they find worthwhile and challenging. It is *irresponsible* to assign a person who lacks the required capabilities to a responsible position.

Often the people most taken for granted are the good people who are trying to do the right thing and succeed. Owners and managers must be alert to practices that reward unscrupulous employees, while leaving conscientious

PRACTICE NOTE

Values

Defining who we are and how we are different from other companies is important to us. These values define our differences and give meaning to our work. They begin to describe what we mean by the "Herman Miller Way." Our future depends on how well we live out these fundamental values. As we do business in an increasingly competitive environment, will our deeds match our words? We believe that if these values become second nature to us and guide our actions, we will deliver extraordinary value to our customers. Moreover, if we make a meaningful contribution to their businesses and their lives, we will flourish and thrive.

Herman Miller Japan Ltd.
"A Different Kind of Company"

employees feeling unrecognized and frustrated. Examples of this situation abound: sales commissions based on total sales that do not account for customer returns or complaints are but one. Managers who engage in "creative bookkeeping" to meet enterprise goals or objectives—and are consistently rewarded for their "performance"—are another.

DEALING WITH THE WRONG PEOPLE

From time to time, owners and managers make mistakes and hire or retain someone who does not share the reasonable criteria of the enterprise. He or she may be unable or unwilling, even with intense management guidance and training, to follow enterprise standards and procedures or contribute to meeting reasonable stakeholder expectations.

When owners and managers make mistakes in hiring, an RBE does neither these employees, their fellow employees, nor the enterprise any favor by having them remain in place. Where management's commitment is clear, employees and agents will often "self-select" themselves out of the enterprise. If they do not, owners and managers must take steps to remove them from the enterprise. This task is not a matter of discipline, although enforcing standards and procedures through discipline is one way to encourage responsible behavior.

Often, the owner or senior manager is the "wrong person." This situation is a particular challenge for those who rely on SME goods or services, especially if the good or service requires the expertise of the owner. Large, complex enterprises (LCEs) may lose a critical part of their supply chains. Here, of course, the entire enterprise is at risk of being prosecuted or debarred from preferred supplier lists. More often, the best employees and agents seek employment elsewhere rather than have their livelihoods placed at risk, if they have the chance.

Sometimes other stakeholders, such as suppliers and even customers, may be the wrong people. As discussed in Chapter 9, it is responsible management to know your customer. See Appendix E for a sample supply chain management questionnaire.

Encouraging Employees to Follow Standards and Procedures

Many management practices support responsible business conduct. These supportive management practices fall in three categories:

1. Recognizing employee contributions
2. Rewarding ethical behavior
3. Punishing unethical behavior

NEED FOR RECOGNITION

The single most important thing that responsible owners and managers can do to encourage responsible business behavior is to recognize the contributions their employees and agents make in pursuit of the purpose of the enterprise. Where managers have tasked employees with challenging work, they should recognize and commend successful completion. Even failure, where it is the result of a good faith effort to contribute, should be addressed favorably, especially if the employee has learned something from it and has shared the experience with other employees.

Performance evaluations are an important means of recognizing employee and agent behavior. Core beliefs, standards and procedures, and reasonable stakeholder expectations should be important elements of the evaluation process. Employees will notice if owners and managers say these are important but do not care enough to have reports on whether their subordinates comply with them. Managers and supervisors will also notice that they are not evaluated on whether they promote the responsible criteria among their subordinates.

REWARD SYSTEMS

An important principle of management is that employees tend to do what is rewarded. If managers want responsible employee and agent behavior that meets standards and procedures and that contributes to meeting reasonable stakeholder expectations, they should pay close attention to what they reward. Few managers plan to reward unethical behavior, but many do. Few managers plan to discourage ethical behavior, but many often do.

Commission schemes are the classic way that managers reward unethical behavior and discourage ethical behavior. If a value of the enterprise is customer service or excellence, the enterprise should aspire to customer satisfaction. However, sales agents and their managers are often compensated not by how well their customers are satisfied, but by how much product is sold. For example, there are numerous instances of sales agents receiving large bonuses based on the volume of their sales, without regard for the number of product returns or customer complaints (see Table 8.1). In one case, a sales agent, knowing that he was being transferred to another region, colluded with customers to order more products than were needed so that he would receive a bonus that the agent following him would otherwise have received. It is obvious that this "reward system" discourages ethical behavior and encourages unethical behavior.

Employees are quite skilled at finding out what is required for success in an enterprise. Although a code of conduct may say that customer service is a value, even one manager saying, "Do whatever it takes," dilutes the message. Sometimes the signal may be more subtle. For example, when an employee's success results from unethical behavior, recognizing his or her efforts can lead to cynicism at best, and other employees joining in at worst.

There is much opposition to rewarding ethical behavior explicitly. First, there is a widespread sense that one should not reward people for doing what

TABLE 8.1 Compensation Scheme Comparison	
Poor compensation scheme: Employees paid a commission based on their sales irrespective of product returns or customer complaints.	**Ethical result:** Employees may use any tactic necessary to increase volume because this scheme rewards quantity over quality. Such schemes can lead to low-quality service, high product returns, channel stuffing,[7] and in some cases fraud.
Good compensation scheme: Employees paid a year-end bonus that requires reaching targets of quality, customer satisfaction, and customer feedback for product improvement set 9 to 12 months in advance.	**Ethical result:** Employees are rewarded for focusing on projects that produce long-term results. Such schemes encourage employees to consider the big picture and to work with other employees during their day-to-day work life.

they should be doing anyway. Second, in organizational cultures that have a strong group orientation, as discussed in Chapter 4, rewards to an individual may be resented and may even make the individual uncomfortable. In such cultures, a reward to an individual may disrupt the harmony of the group.

The first point merits some further thought. As the sales bonus scheme above reflects, managers often reward people for doing what they should have done all along—in this case, selling products. What is the justification for such incentives? Perhaps to spur employees beyond what would otherwise be the minimum acceptable standard of performance. Here is where rewards for ethical behavior make a lot of sense.

If employees honestly fill out expense reports, as some authors suggest, the behavior is so much the norm, that it makes no sense to reward it.[8] However, consider the employee who reports an apparent violation of standards and procedures for the welfare of the enterprise when other employees do not. Without reports from employees who know what is actually going on in the enterprise, owners and managers might learn of problems too late to prevent serious misconduct or lessen the harm done. Although reporting concerns may be expected of all employees, it is not the norm in most enterprises. Substantial minorities of employees say they would never report misconduct they observed to managers.[9] Many others are as concerned about retaliation from their peers as they are about retaliation from managers.

Whatever the specific circumstances may be—and with due regard to the organizational culture—ethical behavior that goes beyond the norms of

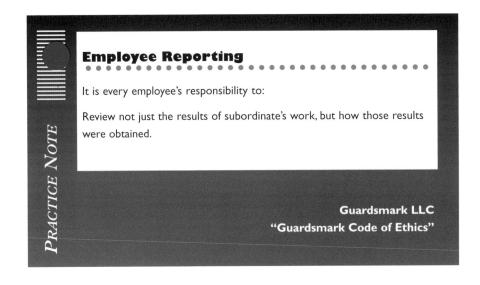

PRACTICE NOTE

Employee Reporting

It is every employee's responsibility to:

Review not just the results of subordinate's work, but how those results were obtained.

Guardsmark LLC
"Guardsmark Code of Ethics"

conduct in the enterprise should be rewarded. Rewarding employees for reporting concerns makes a lot of sense if it is not the norm, and owners and managers should plan for it. The reward may be as simple as recognition. The reward may also need to be made in private. The behavior should certainly be reflected in performance evaluations.

DISCIPLINE SYSTEMS

Recognition and reward are two means of encouraging employees and agents to follow standards and procedures. But what should owners and managers do when standards and procedures are violated? They need to take all necessary steps to get the violator's attention and to prevent further violations, up to and including dismissal and reporting to law enforcement. They need to do this to protect the enterprise and its stakeholders from further harm.

Take the example of a sales agent who earns bonuses through collusion or by offering improper discounts. Fairness requires that the violator knew or should have known that the choice or action was inconsistent with enterprise core beliefs, standards and procedures, or reasonable stakeholder expectations. It is not fair to discipline an employee or agent for violating norms he or she had no reason to know existed. Fairness also requires that the employee or agent be given the opportunity to explain his or her actions. The discipline, if any, must be proportionate to the offense and legally administered.

But fairness is a concept that has a broader application. It is not fair to the enterprise or its stakeholders, including fellow employees, to fail to enforce standards and procedures. First, irresponsible behavior does not help other employees meet the reasonable expectations of stakeholders. Second, a single act of misconduct may result in prosecution of the enterprise, civil claims, loss of reputation, and removal from preferred provider lists and strategic partnerships. Finally, if environment, health, and safety standards and procedures are violated, the welfare of other employees and the community is put at risk.

Allowing standards and procedures to be violated with impunity sends a powerful message. When managers fail to enforce their own standards, they signal that they do not believe in those standards. Moreover, there is no reason why stakeholders should believe that the one violated standard is the only one in which managers do not believe. The whole set of values may come into question because of one failure to act.

Such questions arise particularly where employees perceive a double standard. Recent research suggests that employee perception of a business ethics program as primarily protecting owners and managers is the single most harmful factor to the prospects of the program's success.[10] If ordinary employees are punished for violating a standard but senior managers are not, the entire business ethics program may be regarded as simply one more way to protect owners and managers.

One final consideration is to avoid the temptation to punish all employees for the violations of some of them by setting new standards or procedures. Often, if managers are uncomfortable with confronting an employee or agent about his or her behavior, they instead admonish the group as a whole or establish another standard or procedure designed to encourage the desired behavior.

Dealing with Mistakes, Misconduct, or Misunderstandings

Despite the best efforts of owners and managers, sometimes things go wrong. Even the most responsible business enterprises make mistakes. Standards and procedures will be violated, and reasonable stakeholder expectations will be dashed. Owners and managers deal with these challenges. In the words of one author, "they don't kid themselves."[11]

Owners and managers need to plan for mistakes, actual misconduct, and stakeholder misunderstanding of the enterprise's decisions and actions. At a minimum, they need to establish standards and procedures for dealing with such matters. Managers should be trained on how to exercise crisis management. And when something goes wrong, owners and managers need to determine what happened—and why. They need to determine what steps to take to mitigate further harm or exposure: corrective action, restitution, voluntary disclosure, or any number of other remedial actions to compensate harmed stakeholders or prevent further violations.

Moreover, stakeholders that have been harmed by an enterprise's misconduct expect that they will be informed of a violation of standards that affects them, as well as that all harm done will be corrected, if possible. Failing to meet those expectations sends an undesirable message from owners and managers: *Our core beliefs are negotiable. Our standards apply only if they are not too costly. Failing to meet the reasonable expectations of our stakeholders is acceptable, if we can avoid getting caught.*

DEALING WITH MISTAKES AND FAILURES

In many offices, one will find a sign that reads "To err is human, to forgive divine—neither of which is the policy of this company." However, an RBE recognizes that the employee who never fails is probably not contributing his or her fullest in pursuit of the enterprise's purpose. Much can be learned from failure, provided that the effort was intended to achieve enterprise ends and that the means were well chosen and within enterprise boundaries.

You Decide

In one plant where a number of employees were consistently late, the supervisors gave lectures nearly every day to the team as a whole about the importance of being on time. Eventually, they began to demand that employees arrive early just so that the late ones would be "still late, but on time."

This practice was considered unfair by the responsible employees and was ignored by the irresponsible ones, who continued being late.

What does this tell us about the culture of the enterprise?

BOX 8.1

MODEL POLICY STATEMENT

Employees and agents are expected to accept full responsibility for their decisions and activities on behalf of the enterprise, but management will support choices or actions applying the standards and procedures of the enterprise in good faith, even if they result in mistake or failure.

An RBE fosters an environment in which the creativity and enthusiasm of its employees and agents are encouraged even in the face of mistakes and failure. There is no surer way of preventing creativity than to punish employees for mistakes made in good faith.

The policy statement in Box 8.1 affirms management's commitment to expect the best from employees and agents while providing responsible criteria for evaluating their choices and actions. It reinforces the responsibility that employees and agents assume: to make responsible choices and to take responsible actions to achieve the ends of the enterprise. It is also a liberating policy, which tends to free employees and agents from the fear of unfair criticism or punishment if they make mistakes or fail.

A responsible response to mistakes of employees includes an evaluation of what happened, and why. It includes a sincere effort to learn from mistakes or failure. Managers may need to modify the standards and procedures that failed to prevent the misconduct. They may choose to retrain or educate the employee or other agent, or they may reassign the person, especially if that person is in a position that has substantial discretionary authority.

DEALING WITH MISCONDUCT OR SERIOUS HARM TO STAKEHOLDERS

It is important to distinguish mistakes from misconduct. Misconduct is intentional, negligent, or reckless disregard for the core beliefs, established standards and procedures, and reasonable expectations of the stakeholders of the enterprise. It also involves violating standards or procedures, including the admonition to obey the letter and spirit of the law.

For example, it is no excuse that a choice or action, such as bribing a government official to make a sale, might contribute to achieving the financial ends of the enterprise in the short run. First, it is not clear that making sales through bribery ever contributes to the welfare of an enterprise in either the short or the long run. Bribery often benefits only the employee. Second, owners and managers set the standard precisely because they decided that bribery raises an unacceptable risk to the enterprise. To fail to enforce the standard is to accept a risk that they had determined was unacceptable.

Owners and managers respond to misconduct in the same way they respond to a mistake—by evaluating what happened and why. This response includes a sincere effort to learn from what went wrong. In addition, the perpetrator may be disciplined or terminated as the law permits.

When the misconduct is a violation of law or a stakeholder is seriously harmed, a number of other steps must be considered.

Voluntary Disclosure

When an employee or agent violates the law on behalf of the enterprise, both the individual and the enterprise may be open to prosecution. As a matter of responsible policy, owners and managers must consult with local counsel regarding the advisability of voluntary disclosure to the government. Voluntary disclosure is not an easy step to take if it appears that the government is unaware of the violation or if the rule of law is not the norm. There are good reasons in most economies, however, for an RBE to establish a policy of voluntary disclosure.

First, employees need to know what the policy is and how seriously owners and managers take their admonition to obey the law. Without such clarity, owners and managers may be encouraging a pattern of misconduct from which they will be unable to escape. Second, in many jurisdictions, voluntary disclosure will be treated as good corporate citizenship, and punishment may be limited to the individual alone. In some places, the law of a jurisdiction mandates disclosure and lack of disclosure is a separate violation. In other places, the government promises more lenient treatment if disclosure is voluntary.

Finally, the risk of prosecution and harsh penalties against the enterprise often increases dramatically if the government discovers the violation and learns that the enterprise concealed it.

As two authors note, there are a number of potential dangers in failing to voluntarily disclose a violation: if the government discovers a violation, damage to the credibility of the enterprise may be irreparable. Government agencies are more likely to prosecute if the government discovers a violation. The failure to disclose is more likely to be seen as a cover-up, perhaps to protect senior management. If a subsequent violation occurs, the failure to disclose may be used against the enterprise at the later trial. The authors conclude, "Accordingly, even where the [enterprise] believes that the government is unlikely to eventually discover the violation, it is often in [its] best long-term interest to report the violation to the government."[12]

Where the rule of law is not the norm, owners and managers must carefully examine the relevant context of the enterprise in establishing its policy and seek professional advice. There are situations, to be sure, in which voluntary disclosure will simply open the enterprise to more administrative corruption. Nevertheless, owners and managers must also consider the organizational culture and the effect that failing to take responsibility for misconduct will have on the attitudes of employees.

Where extortion by agency officials can be expected when an RBE reports its' misconduct, it is important that an RBE not deal with this situation in isolation. If extortion is expected, owners and managers should plan to work with trade associations and nongovernmental organizations (NGOs) to reduce their exposure. Since a primary tool in the fight against corruption is transparency, trade associations and NGOs can support enterprises that voluntarily disclose their misconduct by issuing their public statements targeting the offending agency or by otherwise bringing pressure to bear on the agency to reduce extortion. In a climate of such intense attention, especially media scrutiny, an RBE may be less vulnerable to agency extortion.

In any event, responsible managers must establish a policy to govern how they will deal with misconduct before it happens, when their judgment is clearest. In this way, they can identify gaps in capability. In addition to developing a crisis action plan, for example, owners and managers may identify a critical need for a spokesperson or adviser on media relations.

COOPERATION WITH THE GOVERNMENT

Accepting responsibility and voluntarily disclosing misconduct to the government may be followed by a government inquiry or investigation. Or the government may make unannounced visits to the enterprise. Responsible managers establish policies to address these contingencies and set procedures for employees and agents to follow.

How the enterprise responds to government requests has potentially serious legal implications. Responsible managers will establish a policy that governs how the enterprise will respond to government requests. Such a policy supports employees and agents in making the responsible decision to cooperate.

The standards and procedures should be developed with legal counsel familiar with the laws and practices of the jurisdictions in which the enterprise does business. If there is substantial potential for government investigations, audits, or compliance visits, owners and managers should ensure that responsible employees are identified and that their responsibilities are clear. Whom they should contact for advice, including legal counsel, should be clear as well. Having such policies and procedures helps ensure that employees act responsibly and avoid mistakes that may be costly to the enterprise.

Corrective Action

As a general principle, an RBE takes all appropriate steps to cure any harm it has caused stakeholders. These steps include compensating victims, stopping operations, recalling products, restoring the environment to its previous condition, and taking steps to prevent future harm. The enterprise may undertake community service to repair the harm caused by the misconduct.

Where further harm can be predicted, such as health problems that can take decades to manifest themselves, an RBE may set up a trust fund for stakeholders damaged by its misconduct.

HANDLING MISUNDERSTANDINGS AND OTHER CRISES

Sometimes a crisis is not of the enterprise's making. What does an RBE do when accused of shortcomings it did not commit? Responsible management works through such misunderstandings. The general principle is to learn how to pursue the enterprise's purpose and meet reasonable stakeholder expectations by engaging stakeholders when appropriate.

For example, in a famous case in the United States in 1982 involving the pain remedy Tylenol, the manufacturer, Johnson & Johnson, was faced with seven deaths linked to adulterated Tylenol capsules. It chose to avoid risk to its customers, consumers, and reputation by removing millions of dollars of the product from the market.

During an intense period of information gathering and deliberation, two independent management teams considered as many as 150 alternatives for dealing with the crisis. Managers took the dramatic step of recalling 31 million bottles, which cost the enterprise more than $100 million. Johnson & Johnson redesigned the packaging of its product, and just six weeks later Tylenol was back on the shelves. Eventually, it recovered and even increased its market share. Although the experts were predicting that Tylenol, as a brand, would not last a year, "What those experts failed to anticipate was the public reaction to what was perceived as a deliberate act of corporate responsibility that was beautifully executed and skillfully followed up with a well-designed recovery plan."[13]

The decision to recall Tylenol was based on the Johnson & Johnson "Credo," first drafted in 1943 (see Box 8.2).[14] Although the decision was made by the chief executive officer, it reflected the organizational culture of the enterprise as a whole. As one observer noted, "Without a set of values and guiding principles deeply ingrained throughout the organization, it is doubtful that [Johnson & Johnson's] response would have been as rapid, cohesive, and ethically sound."[15]

JOHNSON & JOHNSON'S CREDO

We believe our first responsibility is to the doctors, nurses and patients, to mothers and fathers and all others who use our products and services. In meeting their needs everything we do must be of high quality. We must constantly strive to reduce our costs in order to maintain reasonable prices. Customers' orders must be serviced promptly and accurately. Our suppliers and distributors must have an opportunity to make a fair profit.

We are responsible to our employees, the men and women who work with us throughout the world. Everyone must be considered as an individual. We must respect their dignity and recognize their merit. They must have a sense of security in their jobs. Compensation must be fair and adequate, and working conditions clean, orderly, and safe. We must be mindful of ways to help our employees fulfill their family responsibilities. Employees must feel free to make suggestions and complaints. There must be equal opportunity for employment, development, and advancement for those qualified. We must provide competent management, and their actions must be just and ethical.

We are responsible to the communities in which we live and work and to the world community as well. We must be good citizens—support good works and charities and bear our fair share of taxes. We must encourage civic improvements and better health and education. We must maintain in good order the property we are privileged to use, protecting the environment and natural resources.

Our final responsibility is to our stockholders. Business must make a sound profit. We must experiment with new ideas. Research must be carried on, innovative programs developed, and mistakes paid for. New equipment must be purchased, new facilities provided, and new products launched. Reserves must be created to provide for adverse times. When we operate according to these principles, the stockholders should realize a fair return.

Johnson & Johnson
"Our Credo"

MODIFYING THE BUSINESS ETHICS PROGRAM

Finally, where mistakes, misconduct, and misunderstandings occur, the responsible business constantly evaluates its performance. It uses such incidents as opportunities to learn how the business ethics program is performing. The essential question is, "Does this enterprise have an effective business ethics program?"

The questions for self-governing organizations discussed in Chapters 2 and 4 also apply to a review of any significant incident:

- Were adequate standards, procedures, and expectations established?
- Were responsible managers involved or did they meet their responsibilities?
- Were the standards, procedures, and expectations effectively communicated?
- How did the enterprise detect the incident and could it have been prevented or detected earlier?

- Are the employees and agents involved capable of meeting the standards, procedures, and expectations? Do they have the necessary skills, knowledge, understanding, and attitudes?
- What was done to encourage employees and agents to comply with the standards, procedures, and expectations? What more could be done?
- Was the enterprise's response appropriate?
- How should the incident be treated when evaluating the overall business ethics program?

SUMMARY

Responsible management practices are critical to the success of an RBE in improving its business performance, increasing the prosperity of its community, and contributing to the social capital in its markets by learning to meet the reasonable expectations of its shareholders. Owners and managers of an RBE develop responsible management practices by answering these three questions:

1. How can we ensure that we have the right people in the right places while we pursue our purpose as an enterprise?
2. How can we encourage our employees and agents to follow our standards and procedures?
3. What do we owe our stakeholders when mistakes, misconduct, or misunderstandings occur that involve our established standards and procedures or their reasonable expectations?

To have the right people in the right places in the enterprise involves using the enterprise's core beliefs, standards and procedures, and reasonable stakeholder expectations to establish responsible criteria. An RBE uses these responsible criteria to recruit, hire, retain, assign, and dismiss employees and agents, especially managers and supervisors.

To encourage employees and agents to follow enterprise standards and procedures, pursue the enterprise's purpose, and meet reasonable stakeholder expectations, responsible managers evaluate decisions and activities according to the responsible criteria, and they reward and discipline employees and agents as appropriate.

When things go wrong for an RBE, responsible managers address mistakes, misconduct, and misunderstandings. They learn from mistakes and failures made in good faith. They confront misconduct and respond appropriately. They discipline employees and agents, and they voluntarily disclose to, and cooperate with, government authorities, as appropriate.

RESPONSIBLE BUSINESS ENTERPRISE
Checklist

1. How carefully do we align our management practices with our core values?

2. What are our policies regarding recruiting, hiring, training, and employing our work force?

3. What risks do we foresee in our business climate, and what is our plan for dealing with them in the event of a crisis?

4. What strategic alliances can we forge to see that we do not have to deal with these crises in isolation?

12 Enterprise Alignment Worksheet

RBE Worksheet 12, which may be photocopied for use within your organization, provides a tool to help owners and managers consider all enterprise alignment issues. Owners, managers, and staff members should work together to compare and contrast current management practices with enterprise standards. Expect significant give and take as to what the relevant current standards and practices actually are. This discussion is part of the dialogue and engagement process the RBE wants to foster.

	Enterprise Core Beliefs	Reference Practices	Current Practices	Required Changes
Having the right people in the right places				
Encouraging compliance; building commitment				
Responding appropriately to mistakes, misconduct, and misunderstandings				

Responsible Business Conduct and Practices

*U*sing the tools contained in this manual, the responsible business enterprise (RBE) has set standards and procedures to guide employees and agents, fostered reasonable expectations among its stakeholders, built supporting business ethics infrastructure, and aligned its management practices with its core beliefs. This chapter applies these elements of a business ethics program as the foundation for five specific areas of business conduct and practice that challenge an RBE, especially, but not exclusively, in emerging market economies. By developing responsible business practices in those five areas, the RBE can be part of the solution to the challenges facing business in all markets.

Challenges to the Responsible Business Enterprise

There are a number of issues of responsible business conduct to which the owners and managers of an RBE need to give special attention:

1. Relationships with government officials and entities
2. Role of the private sector in the regulatory process
3. Government contracting and procurement
4. Role of voluntary action
5. Relationships with foreign governments and businesses

- **Challenges to the Responsible Business Enterprise**

- **Relationships with Government Officials and Entities**

- **Role of the Private Sector in the Regulatory Process**

- **Government Contracting and Procurement**

- **Role of Voluntary Action**

- **Relationships with Foreign Governments and Businesses**

These five issues are central to what it means to be a responsible business enterprise. The discussion in this chapter, along with RBE Worksheet 13 at the end of the chapter, will help owners and managers establish responsible standards, procedures, and expectations and compensate for weaknesses through business ethics infrastructure, communications and feedback, and enterprise alignment. The chapter will also help create reasonable expectations for external stakeholders: government, other businesses, civil society, and the community as a whole.

Relationships with Government Officials and Entities

Governments establish the necessary conditions for economic stability, social progress, and environmental protection by adopting laws, policies, and practices that help markets perform independently, free of undue government interference. These conditions, sometimes referred to as "good public governance," help an economy grow according to market principles. Just as an RBE has a vital interest in good corporate governance, the private sector as a whole has a vital interest in supporting trustworthy, stable, accountable, and reliable governments capable of good public governance.

Good public governance respects human and property rights, supports the sanctity of contracts, protects residents, provides infrastructure that speeds the transportation of goods and services and supports the transmission of knowledge, and establishes a market-oriented legal framework and reliable judicial institutions that allow its residents to resolve conflicts. Good public governance is founded on a transparent relationship between government and the private sector.

REDUCING CORRUPTION, BRIBERY, AND EXTORTION

To create the conditions necessary for good public governance, one must address the problem of corruption, from both the demand side and the supply side. Both government and the private sector are responsible for creating conditions for transparent business, and they should repudiate all corruption, bribery, and extortion. Leaders in business and government should work together to combat corruption.

One means of private–public sector cooperation is for business enterprises to recommend standards, procedures, and expectations to help the government administer laws and regulations in a transparent, accountable, and fair manner. Business leaders and government officials should have an ongoing public dialogue about issues that contribute to corruption, such as monopoly practices, discretionary fees, onerous taxes, and regulations and licenses that impede business and entrepreneurship. This dialogue should

---

BOX 9 . 1

GOVERNMENT ANTICORRUPTION POLICIES

Government anticorruption policies take many forms:

- Commercial codes governing contracts and dispute settlement

- Law enforcement and judicial procedures promoting due process and the rule of law

- Independent systems promoting and ensuring the integrity and efficiency of agencies

- Civil service reforms and competitive wages

- Systems promoting integrity of capital markets and transparency on issuance of securities

- Systems promoting predictable and transparent procurement and privatization

- Improved and standardized public accounting, auditing, and management systems

- Effective bankruptcy and insolvency laws

- Limits on discretionary authority tending to administrative corruption

- Oversight mechanisms and appellate remedies

- Protection for whistleblowers and the media

- Disclosure of and access to public records

- Encouragement of civil society participation in anticorruption efforts

U.S. Department of State
"Recognizing and Making Anticorruption Issues Part of the
Business–Government Dialogue"

---

aim to ensure that government administrative processes at all levels are fair, transparent, competitive, and informed. Box 9.1 lists some of the anticorruption and good governance policies that emphasize transparency, due process, and accountability.[1] See also Appendix F for a more comprehensive list of guiding principles for fighting corruption in government.

Government administrative, licensing, inspection, and certification procedures intended to regulate business often create obstacles to business. For example, governments sometimes require several official signatures to complete the simple act of registering and opening a business. Such administrative obstacles increase opportunities for public officials to demand bribes and favors. As Table 9.1 shows, while opportunities for bribery and extortion vary somewhat from market to market, the average proportion of bribes spent on each type of public service varies substantially.[2]

Bribery, kickbacks, and other forms of illegal or corrupt conduct increase costs for an enterprise not only because of the payments involved but also because it requires management time and effort to work with officials, maintain secret accounting books, and address threats of extortion and blackmail. To reduce such obstacles, business leaders and government officials should work together to establish regulatory practices that reduce administrative discretion and promote transparency and efficiency.

TABLE 9.1   The Average Proportion of Bribes Spent on Each "Service"

Country	Connection to Public Services	Licenses	Taxes	Government Contracts	Customs	Courts	Health/Fire Inspections	Legislation Influence	Other	Total
Armenia	10.9	9.8	30.6	5.8	14.0	4.7	2.9	3.2	18.0	100.0
Azerbaijan	9.2	20.2	31.6	17.4	8.6	6.0	4.3	2.4	0.1	100.0
Belarus	9.6	30.4	28.2	7.3	7.1	3.6	13.6	0.2	0.0	100.0
Bulgaria	17.7	22.6	14.1	6.6	11.9	13.6	8.2	2.8	2.6	100.0
Croatia	9.1	6.7	7.3	44.7	10.7	8.8	4.1	4.0	4.5	100.0
Czech Republic	8.3	16.3	7.2	43.0	6.4	6.5	9.2	1.6	1.6	100.0
Estonia	2.0	26.5	6.4	34.5	15.2	2.5	4.2	5.9	2.8	100.0
Georgia	11.0	18.3	29.3	3.6	9.6	11.3	10.4	6.6	0.0	100.0
Hungary	7.3	43.6	10.9	11.1	14.2	3.1	3.3	1.4	4.9	100.0
Kazakhstan	10.7	23.2	20.3	5.3	14.4	12.7	9.5	1.3	2.8	100.0
Kyrgyzstan	5.0	15.2	53.5	6.5	6.8	4.5	7.4	1.1	0.0	100.0
Lithuania	14.0	8.5	16.3	5.0	15.1	8.7	17.6	4.3	10.6	100.0
Moldova	14.9	29.7	21.4	3.9	10.4	9.0	7.0	1.6	2.2	100.0
Poland	7.4	26.1	8.8	17.7	15.8	9.9	5.7	4.3	4.3	100.0
Romania	16.1	39.8	6.3	7.8	15.2	5.2	5.7	3.4	0.6	100.0
Russia	11.7	20.4	18.5	11.3	8.8	11.1	11.6	2.8	3.7	100.0
Slovakia	5.7	33.2	10.1	18.3	11.8.	12.9	4.3	1.3	2.5	100.0
Slovenia	6.5	24.9	4.3	36.3	8.7	5.3	5.8	8.2	0.0	100.0
Ukraine	10.3	21.3	25.8	10.4	12.2	6.8	9.7	2.5	1.1	100.0
Uzbekistan	8.5	18.0	27.9	15.4	10.9	5.2	12.0	0.9	1.2	100.0
Overall	10.6	22.0	19.4	14.6	12.2	7.9	7.8	2.6	2.9	100.0

Source: Joel S. Hellman et al., "Measuring Governance, Corruption, and State Capture" Policy Research Paper 2312 (Washington, D.C.: World Bank, 2000)

Business associations in some emerging market economies have succeeded in influencing governments to adopt one-stop registration for new businesses. In the Russian Federation, for example, the Business Partnership of Seversk (Tomsk Oblast), a nongovernmental organization (NGO), has worked with municipal authorities to increase transparency and to reduce administrative barriers. With input from the NGO, government authorities simplified procedures for leasing public property, which included streamlining procedures to resolve disputes and eliminating illegal fees. A database of federal and local laws and regulations was developed, and the business community has received training in current laws and regulations related to business operations and business rights and responsibilities.[3]

To facilitate good public governance, the RBE can adopt standards, procedures, and expectations for conducting business with government officials and entities as part of its business ethics program. They should be based on knowledge of and respect for the specific rules that govern the conduct of

Transparency and Government Revenue

In 1998, when Newmont Mining Corporation began its joint-venture Batu Hijau copper mine in Indonesia, it created a program to promote transparency in revenue-sharing payments to host governments. With its first royalty payment, Newmont placed a full-page advertisement in local and regional newspapers detailing the amount of money transferred to the national government. For subsequent payments, totaling more than $38 million by the first quarter of 2002, the company generated news coverage detailing the royalty payment, transfer documents, and deposit account number. Legally, a percentage of royalties is to flow back to the region of impact but, in reality, it is often delayed or not sent at all. At first, regional authorities, whose receipt of mining royalties was suddenly exposed to public scrutiny, reacted by attempting to deny the payments. Over the course of a year, however, both local and regional authorities used the increased transparency and media coverage to pressure the national government to return funds more quickly to the region.

Juliette Bennett
"Multinational Corporations, Social Responsibility, and Conflict"

public officials.[4] These standards, procedures, and expectations should make clear that employees and agents must abide by all laws and regulations, especially refraining from bribery and other forms of corrupt conduct intended to influence official decisions.

ENCOURAGING GOVERNMENT STANDARDS AND PROCEDURES

Responsible business leaders should encourage governments to adopt formal programs to guide the choices and actions of civil servants through established standards, procedures, and codes of conduct. These standards and procedures should address issues such as values of public service, conflicts of interest, use of public office for private gain, and acceptance of political contributions and bribes. Government standards and procedures help ensure that government officials uphold the law and avoid even the appearance of impropriety. Creating clear standards and procedures to which public officials are held accountable helps instill respect and public confidence in government institutions.

Government officials should be encouraged to go beyond simply setting standards and procedures. Civil servants should be hired and assigned transparently and should receive compensation adequate to support their families properly without resorting to corruption. Training and education should be provided to raise awareness of the devastating impact of corrupt practices on the functioning of public governance, as well as on economic growth and social capital. Oversight mechanisms to monitor and audit government functions at particular risk to corruption are essential, especially where civil servants are reluctant to report their concerns. Finally, these standards and procedures must be enforced, and the government must respond appropriately when bribery and corruption are uncovered.

Business leaders must also recognize, however, that good public governance requires resources. Reasonable civil servant compensation, for example, tends to reduce corruption, but it must be paid, in part, with the taxes that businesses pay. Failure to pay business taxes when the government is trying to reform makes reform efforts virtually fruitless. Being part of the solution to this challenge of developing a market economy requires paying the enterprise's fair share of the cost of government.

Role of the Private Sector in the Regulatory Process

The ultimate objective of good public governance is to create conditions under which markets function independently and facilitate fair competition. These conditions help innovative, effective, and efficient enterprises succeed and grow while preventing inefficient enterprises from looting public resources. They create opportunities for increased investment and trade.

Under conditions of good public governance, the private sector has a vital role in influencing the government to adopt laws, regulations, and practices designed to enable the market to function independently. This activity should be conducted on a transparent basis designed to benefit all stakeholders in the development of a market economy and civil society.

IMPROPERLY INFLUENCING GOVERNMENT

There are several obstacles to good public governance, including practices that enable enterprises to influence government policy improperly. Enterprises operating in many markets have adopted the practice of forming patron relationships with individual public officials as a means of securing government contracts and preferential treatment.

Many large and successful enterprises strive to "capture" the state by securing the passage of laws or obtaining licenses that benefit them over other enterprises. What many think of as state capture is the effort of a firm to shape the laws, policies, and regulations of the state to its own advantage by providing illicit, illegitimate, and non-transparent private gains to public officials.[5] Such practices may offer short-term gains, but they are a major source of business risk and market instability.

State capture is also a cause of poor public governance, because decrees issued to benefit one enterprise or organization injure the economy as a whole by undermining competition. An enterprise that engages in state capture has a stake in maintaining conditions of poor public governance, including weak state institutions and ambiguous laws and regulations. State capture seriously impedes the development of the rule of law. It creates conditions under which effective and efficient enterprises support ineffective and inefficient enterprises. World Bank studies show an association between state capture and poor governance in emerging market economies.[6]

PROPERLY INFLUENCING GOVERNMENT

To foster stable conditions for economic growth, responsible business leaders should help establish clearly defined laws and practices regulating how businesses might influence government decision-making. RBEs conduct their business with government on a transparent basis. They organize themselves around issues of mutual concern with other enterprises to lobby the government under applicable laws and procedures.

Business associations provide a structure that enables private-sector leaders to find one voice and coordinate efforts. They provide the opportunity and leverage to influence lawmakers in an ethical and democratic

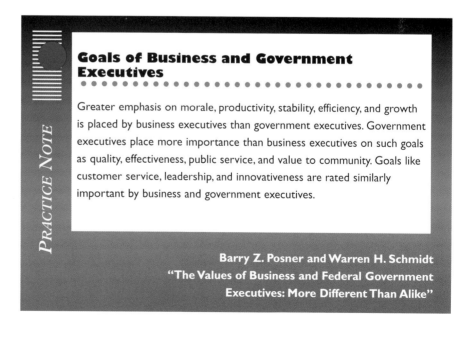

PRACTICE NOTE

Goals of Business and Government Executives

Greater emphasis on morale, productivity, stability, efficiency, and growth is placed by business executives than government executives. Government executives place more importance than business executives on such goals as quality, effectiveness, public service, and value to community. Goals like customer service, leadership, and innovativeness are rated similarly important by business and government executives.

Barry Z. Posner and Warren H. Schmidt
"The Values of Business and Federal Government Executives: More Different Than Alike"

manner. RBE leaders work with their business associations and trade groups to demand accountability of government and to create conditions for fair competition.

To maximize their leverage and influence, RBE leaders develop a national business agenda that promotes the goals and incorporates the interests of both large enterprises and small to medium-sized enterprises (SMEs)—and the public interest.[7] This agenda identifies policy and legal reforms that are required of government to create the conditions necessary for all transparent enterprises to compete and succeed. RBEs publish their goals and strategies in the media in order to reach out to other businesses and solicit feedback from external stakeholders and civil society.

Private-sector lobbying efforts by RBEs promote and instill good public governance and respect for the rule of law. When a particular law or regulation is damaging to the market, RBEs seek to amend or replace it in a manner that respects the legislative process.

To strengthen this process, business associations often adopt a legislative advisory program, which analyzes current legislation and assesses whether it meets the requirements and the needs of business. As part of such a program, the associations provide legislators with objective and accurate information regarding market conditions to assist in their decision-making processes. For an example of such a program, see Box 9.2.[8]

RBE leaders work closely with civil society—including chambers of commerce, trade associations, industry associations, community advocacy groups, public interest groups, and other NGOs—to form alliances that help promote the national business agenda. Civil society "includes organizations, structures, and networks separate from the legislative, administrative, and judicial power of the state and, many would argue, from business but inter-

---

BOX 9.2

INTERNATIONAL CENTER FOR ENTREPRENEURIAL STUDIES

The International Center for Entrepreneurial Studies has established an innovative program in Romania called the Strategic Alliance of Business Associations (SABA). SABA consists of 44 chambers of commerce and trade groups. SABA brings together large enterprises and small to medium-sized enterprises (SMEs) that have similar concerns and priorities. It helps these enterprises create a national platform for their objectives. It also educates members on changes in business laws and regulations. SABA has helped establish an SME development agency in Romania with wide participation from entrepreneurs. The SABA program is a model for promoting the collective private-sector interests of large enterprises and SMEs in economic reform.

acting with both in a variety of ways."[9] The groups that make up civil society often act collaboratively for the common good to "stimulate democratic action, and to analyze and educate public debate."[10]

NGOs have a stake in the success of RBEs as entities that operate on a legal and transparent basis and fulfill their social responsibilities. Some NGOs specialize in working with the private sector to shape legal and government reform. NGOs also bring business and government leaders together to educate and train them in areas where they should work together on a more cooperative basis. On controversial issues, NGOs can serve as mediators between private- and public-sector representatives.

Government Contracting and Procurement

When an RBE conducts business directly with a government official or entity, whether as a contractor, supplier, or in some other capacity, it should take steps to ensure that its relationships are transparent and ethical. It should abide by all laws; refrain from engaging in bribery, cronyism, or coercion; and avoid even the appearance of impropriety. By so doing, the RBE minimizes the risk of penalties, fines, and other forms of sanction for misconduct.

The success of public projects rests on sound government procurement practices that promote integrity, respect, fairness, and transparency. These practices also help create conditions for good public governance and the development of a market economy. See Box 9.3 for a sample policy.

CHALLENGES IN GOVERNMENT CONTRACTING

The process of government contracting and procurement poses a risk of corruption from both the demand side and the supply side. Corruption distorts the process by favoring one enterprise or group of enterprises over another. An obvious example is a contract for government procurement awarded to an enterprise in response to a bribe. Corruption can occur at any point in the process, starting from design and preparation, when selection of the technical criteria, the due date for submission of offers, the time of delivery of the project, and the parties invited to tender may distort the process.

Under such conditions, a responsible enterprise cannot compete successfully for government contracts, even when it outperforms other companies in terms of quality and price. Nevertheless, when seeking a government contract, an RBE abides by all applicable laws, regulations, and stipulations of the tender. It ensures that all statements, communications, and representations to government officials are truthful and accurate.

MODEL PROCUREMENT STANDARDS

The World Bank Group, which lends to governments to finance major restructuring of industries and development of infrastructure, has five basic guidelines that govern its procurement policies:

1. All goods and services needed to carry out the project must be procured with special consideration for economy and efficiency.

2. The loan must be used to purchase only those goods and services needed to carry out the project.

3. All qualified bidders from the bank's member countries have an equal opportunity to compete to participate in the bank's projects.

4. The borrower must encourage the development of local contractors and manufacturers in borrowing countries.

5. The procurement process must be transparent.[11]

Other examples of government procurement policies that ensure transparency and due process in government contracting can be found in some international procurement agreements, most notably the World Trade Organization (WTO) Agreement on Government Procurement (GPA).[12]

The GPA is an accord entered into by 28 WTO member countries to provide market access to each other's government procurement of goods and services. It calls for governments to maintain transparency in government procurement by establishing standards in procurement procedures. These standards are designed to ensure consistency and predictability for enterprises. For example, the GPA sets guidelines for governments to publish notices of procurement opportunities. The notices are required to contain basic information necessary for enterprises to assess their interest in an opportunity and to prepare meaningful bids. The GPA sets out minimum time periods—usually 40 days—in which interested suppliers must submit bids. It also requires that technical specifications be prepared in terms of performance rather than design or descriptive characteristics and not be developed or applied as inappropriate obstacles to international trade.

The GPA addresses other procurement procedures, including qualification procedures, contract award decisions, and publication of procurement laws and regulations. It also seeks due process for suppliers, who are provided the right to learn from procuring entities the reasons that their bids or qualification applications are unsuccessful. The GPA also requires governments to maintain independent and impartial review bodies to hear supplier complaints.

BOX 9.3

BUSINESS ETHICS AND CONDUCT IN CONTRACTING WITH THE UNITED STATES GOVERNMENT

10. Government rules on gifts and gratuities (broadly defined to include entertainment and business meals) are very restrictive. Employees shall not offer or give a gift or gratuity to any government employee, except where clearly permitted by applicable government regulations (for example, 32 Code of Federal Regulations Part 40). Guidance with respect to the applicable regulations can be obtained from the operating unit Business Practices/Compliance Officer. Furthermore, employees shall not offer or give, directly or indirectly, anything to a government employee who is a procurement official or who performs a procurement function except: (a) beverages at a business meeting, (b) light snacks for a business meeting where government employees in travel status are in attendance, and (c) promotional items displaying the company logo and having a truly nominal value, such as baseball caps or pads of paper. Any exceptions must be approved in writing by the UTC Vice President, Business Practices.

14. Employees shall not offer or give entertainment, gifts, or gratuities to representatives or employees of higher tier government contractors other than customary business courtesies that are reasonable in frequency and value. Offering or giving any payment, gift, or other thing of value to such a person for the purpose of obtaining or acknowledging favorable treatment (a "kickback") is a crime.

15. Even though not otherwise prohibited, employees will not offer or give to any representative or employee of a higher tier government contractor any entertainment, gift, gratuity, or anything else of value that such representative or employee is known to be prohibited from accepting under the policies of the higher tier government contractor.

16. Consultants performing work related to a government contract or subcontract shall be required by contract to comply with the laws and regulations relating to government contracting and with this Policy Statement. This Policy Statement shall be incorporated in the standard terms and conditions for all such consultant contracts, and each such contract shall expressly provide for termination in the event the consultant violates either the laws or regulations relating to government contracting or this Policy Statement.

Implementation

All organizations in the Corporation that contract directly or indirectly with the federal government of the United States are required promptly to maintain current, detailed procedures and policies, including an ongoing program of communication and training, to insure compliance with this Policy Statement and with the laws and regulations governing contracting with the government. Such procedures and policies shall expressly designate the department or activity responsible for implementing each element of the detailed policies and procedures.

United Technologies Corporation
"Code of Ethics"

INTEGRITY PACTS

Another means of ensuring more transparency in government procurement and contracting is called an *integrity pact*, a concept developed by the NGO Transparency International in the mid-1990s. In the context of government procurement, an integrity pact is a formal pact or agreement between a government office inviting tenders and the enterprises intending to participate. By signing such an agreement, an enterprise commits itself to participate in the tendering process in a legal and transparent way. In particular, it pledges not to offer, pay, accept, or seek bribes of any kind during the tender. The government office, in turn, commits that its officials will not demand or accept any bribes.

The key component of an integrity pact is transparency. All offers and payments made by an enterprise should be reported to members of the pact. The pact has preapproved sanctions for violations. Sanctions include denial or loss of the contract, forfeiture of bid security, liability for damages, or blacklisting by the government office.[13]

Use of the integrity pact is slowly developing on a global basis, hindered by the expertise and funds needed to encourage governments and enterprises to enter into the agreement. Transparency International has facilitated integrity pacts in Argentina, Benin, Colombia, and Panama.[14] See Appendix C for a sample integrity pact.

Role of Voluntary Action

The private sector has an economic interest in creating a trustworthy, stable, and reliable government capable of good public governance. Business enterprises, in general, have the potential to be powerful and influential members of their communities.

Beyond the contributions they make in producing goods and services to meet the needs of customers and consumers, businesses provide livelihoods for employees, other agents, and suppliers. Business enterprises pay taxes that support good public governnance, but they can do much more as responsible members of their communities.

LEVELING THE BUSINESS PLAYING FIELD

Declarations of integrity are a form of voluntary action by enterprises designed to help promote a transparent business environment through responsible business conduct. They document a coalition of enterprises that are committed to fair business practices and showing leadership in this direction. Such declarations offer a means of bringing enterprises together with civil society and government officials and entities with the goal of developing a more transparent investment climate. See Appendix D for an example of a declaration of integrity.

Industry-specific declarations of integrity may be an especially effective means of promoting responsible business conduct. In developing market economies, many industries, professions, and chambers of commerce accomplish much the same effect through codes of conduct that they voluntarily adopt and follow.

A prominent example in the United States is the Defense Industry Initiative, which was formed in 1986 to improve the responsible business conduct of defense contractors following a series of defense contracting scandals. To avoid further government regulation, prominent defense contractors voluntarily subscribed to designing and implementing business ethics programs, to reporting on their performance, and to meeting to share best practices annually.

In emerging market economies, codes of conduct are being developed in many industry sectors, including engineering and banking.

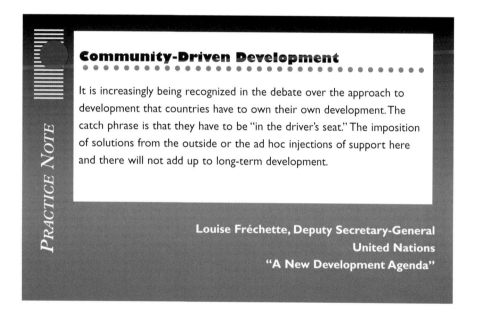

PRACTICE NOTE

Community-Driven Development

It is increasingly being recognized in the debate over the approach to development that countries have to own their own development. The catch phrase is that they have to be "in the driver's seat." The imposition of solutions from the outside or the ad hoc injections of support here and there will not add up to long-term development.

Louise Fréchette, Deputy Secretary-General
United Nations
"A New Development Agenda"

PARTICIPATING IN COMMUNITY DEVELOPMENT

An RBE may also contribute to its community by participating in community economic development projects. Such projects promote cooperation between business and the local community. An enterprise that engages in a community economic development activity designs programs to train and employ local citizens. Through such projects, a multinational enterprise partners with locally owned enterprises and franchises to help develop successful business strategies. Such actions enhance an enterprise's reputation and goodwill in the community.

Another avenue for an RBE is to work with a community foundation and local government to support community-driven development. Development projects are designed to meet important community needs by engaging the community itself with help from donors to a local community foundation. The role of enterprises, both foreign and local, is increasing as foreign donors, in particular, see the value in local communities fashioning their own solutions to local problems.[15]

An RBE may encourage its employees to support philanthropic initiatives or to take part in volunteer programs. The RBE might also institute a release-time policy, giving employees paid leave to take part in voluntary initiatives during business hours. Such an initiative will reinforce the enterprise's commitment to supporting employees and the community.

FORMING CHARITABLE FOUNDATIONS

Leading multinational enterprises establish charitable foundations that donate funds to entities whose missions are consistent with the enterprise's values and vision. Such foundations provide funding for educational institutions and students through grants and scholarships, to improve the quality of education.

Relationships with Foreign Governments and Businesses

When engaging in international business, enterprises face government officials and entities, laws, customs, and cultural practices different from those in home markets. An enterprise will face new and different ethical dilemmas, which are shaped by local law, customs, and practices. An enterprise that seeks to conduct business in a foreign market or to form a joint venture with a foreign partner must first become knowledgeable of the local customs and practices. Differences in values and notions of responsible business conduct between joint venture partners, for example, often lead to "communication, cooperation, commitment, and conflict resolution problems..., which in turn cause interaction problems that adversely influence joint venture performance."[16]

While consciously striving to understand cultural and legal differences, an RBE remains focused on and committed to its core beliefs and standards, procedures, and expectations of responsible business conduct. It abides by the laws of its home country and all applicable foreign laws, whichever are stricter. It develops a strategy to remain loyal to its core beliefs and standards while adapting to the culture and expectations of local markets.

COMBATING BRIBERY OF FOREIGN OFFICIALS

When doing business abroad, an enterprise should be aware of the strict rules and regulations that govern bribery in international transactions. In 1997, 34 nations signed the Convention on Combating Bribery of Foreign Public Officials in International Business Transactions. This convention, established by the Organization for Economic Cooperation and Development (OECD), went into effect in 1999, and requires signatory nations to make the payment of bribes to foreign government officials a criminal offense. Before the adoption of the OECD convention and its implementing legislation, many nations allowed their enterprises to deduct the costs of bribing foreign government officials from their taxes.

Now enterprises operating in foreign markets are under increasing scrutiny and regulation in their home countries. For example, U.S. firms are governed by the Foreign Corrupt Practices Act (FCPA), which makes it unlawful to bribe foreign government officials to gain a business advantage. U.S. firms that conduct business internationally usually find it advisable to maintain rigorous corporate compliance programs to ensure that they comply with the FCPA and the laws of the other nations that are party to the OECD Convention.

The FCPA prohibits U.S. enterprises from using intermediaries such as an independent agent, joint venture, or foreign enterprise to make corrupt payments on the U.S. enterprise's behalf. These provisions require U.S. enterprises to develop business relationships with reputable and qualified partners and representatives. They encourage these enterprises to practice due diligence when working with foreign enterprises.

Due diligence may come in the form of investigating foreign representatives and joint venture partners to determine their status as a local business. The FCPA encourages enterprises to be aware of red flags. These indicators include unusual payment patterns or financial arrangements, a history of corruption, a refusal to pledge to uphold legitimate business practices, and a lack of transparency. Failure to comply with these provisions could lead to fines or imprisonment under U.S. law. See Appendix F for a detailed description of the Foreign Corrupt Practices Act.

ADHERING TO ANTI-MONEY LAUNDERING PROVISIONS

Using legitimate business to conceal the illegitimate origins of large sums of money—money laundering—has a destabilizing effect on the enterprises involved, on domestic financial institutions, and on society as a whole. An economy that enables laundering of illegitimate funds is vulnerable to organized crime infiltrating financial institutions and legitimate businesses and aggravating corruption in government. An emerging market economy may be tempted to risk these disasters for the immediate flow of cash through the economy. However, having an image as a haven for money laundering will make it much harder to develop a reputation as a stable and secure environment for investment.[17]

Enterprises working with a foreign partner, or even with a domestic partner that has connections with U.S. financial institutions, should be aware that the anti–money laundering regimes and reporting of suspicious activity that have been required for several years have been extended to additional categories of financial institutions. Under U.S. Treasury regulations that have been promulgated, have been proposed, or are pending, financial institutions required to have an anti–money laundering program include not only banks, savings associations, and credit unions, but also securities brokers and dealers, casinos, operators of credit card systems, businesses engaged in vehicle sales, pawnbrokers, private bankers, and a number of other entities.

While many countries, including emerging market economies, have similar anti–money laundering provisions, the U.S. provisions may affect foreign operations through requirements for due diligence for correspondent accounts and private banking accounts. Under these regulations, a broad range of financial institutions outside of the United States are subject to exercising due diligence under the U.S. anti–money laundering regime if they maintain a correspondent account in the United States. Under some circumstances of enhanced due diligence, U.S. and other financial institutions may be required to gather detailed information before doing business with enterprises or individuals.

Even when an RBE is not technically a financial institution, the basic "know your customer" rule is responsible business conduct. This rule is important for an emerging market economy, in particular, to gain international acceptance. For example, an international body combating money laundering, the Financial Action Task Force on Money Laundering, advocates countermeasures that would restrict financial transactions with some countries. It has recommended or considered such restrictions for a number of countries thus far.[18]

PROTECTING THE ENVIRONMENT

Finally, when engaging in business in a foreign market, an enterprise should be particularly sensitive to issues involving protection of the environment. At a minimum, an RBE abides by the local laws and regulations designed to protect the environment. An enterprise has a social responsibility to examine the impact its operations may have on the local environment and adopt global best practices for protecting the environment.

Global best practices may be more demanding than local practices, but in a global environment, an RBE is expected to adopt the more stringent environmental protection requirements of the host government or its home government. Doing so often requires an RBE to self-regulate, because in emerging market economies the desire to attract foreign direct investment may encourage governments to be somewhat less inclined to enforce their own standards.[19]

SUMMARY

Responsible owners and managers apply all the perspectives, practices, and principles developed in the earlier chapters to meet the challenges that their markets present. Five issues are particularly challenging for enterprises in emerging market economies, although they are present in all markets:

1. Relationships with government officials and entities
2. Relationships with foreign governments and businesses
3. Role of the private sector in the regulatory process
4. Government contracting and procurement
5. Role of voluntary action

Business leaders and government must work together to develop the institutions, laws, regulations, and practices that contribute to good public governance and independent markets. Particular attention should be given to reducing corruption in the forms of bribery and extortion. Government must reduce the opportunities and motivations for corruption. This objective can be achieved through both good corporate governance and good public governance, applying the lessons of Chapters 5 through 8 of this manual.

An RBE is alert to opportunities to improve the business environment through its own responsible business conduct and through its association with other enterprises, civil society, and government. All enterprise decisions and activities aim to improve the RBE's business performance; to help build social capital in its economy; and to work with leaders in business, government, and civil society to develop the essential market-oriented legal framework and reliable judicial institutions.

RESPONSIBLE BUSINESS ENTERPRISE
Checklist

1. What is our policy for working with government officials and entities?

2. What does an evaluation of our government's policies tell us?

3. How are we involved in working with other enterprises, civil society organizations, and government to improve market conditions?

Responsible Business Practices Worksheet

RBE Worksheet 13 provides a tool to help owners and managers consider the responsible business practices discussed in this chapter. The worksheet may be photocopied for use within your organization. Owners, managers, and staff members should work together to compare and contrast current management practices with enterprise standards, procedures, and expectations or the reference standards discussed in this chapter. Expect significant give and take about what the relevant current standards and practices actually are; this discussion is part of the dialogue and engagement process an RBE wants to foster.

	Compliance	Risk Management	Reputation Enhancement	Value Added
Relationships with government officials and entities				
Role of the private sector in the regulatory process				
Government contracting and procurement				
Role of voluntary action				
Relationships with foreign governments and businesses				

V

Achieving Responsible Business Conduct

Program Evaluation and Organizational Learning

*T*his manual concludes by discussing the basic concepts and practices of evaluating a business ethics program as an integral part of organizational learning. The purpose of this chapter is to demonstrate the power of program evaluation and to re-emphasize the role of the individual enterprise as part of the solution to the challenges facing business in all markets, especially emerging market economies.

Ensuring Organizational Learning

Organizational learning is an integral part of how a responsible business enterprise (RBE) improves its business performance, makes profits, and increases the prosperity of its community through its decisions and activities. For an RBE, organizational learning is a way of life that enables it to adapt to the conditions facing it and learn how to "continuously expand its capacity to create the future it truly desires to live."[1] Organizational learning is essentially a characteristic of an RBE's organizational culture, as described in Chapter 4. Organizations share this information consciously on one level, record it in documents on another, but ultimately store it in their cultures.[2] If the drive to learn has not developed in the organizational culture, then management admonitions to generate, share, or access knowledge will be for naught.

This chapter addresses the last of the eight fundamental questions owners and managers must ask

- **Ensuring Organizational Learning**

- **Importance of Program Evaluation**

- **Developing a Data Collection Plan**

- **Reporting Program Performance**

- **Conclusion— and New Beginning**

themselves: "How should we monitor, track, and report our performance as an enterprise and continuously learn from it?"[3]

A business ethics program is an integral part of how an enterprise learns as an organization. It is a form of action learning—a process and culture of learning by doing.[4] By evaluating program performance, an enterprise determines:

- How it learns what it needs to know (relevant context and internal scanning),[5]
- How it gathers, stores, and shares information and knowledge (standards and procedures, infrastructure, communications, program evaluation, and organizational learning),[6]
- How it uses information and applies that knowledge to pursue the enterprise purpose and meet reasonable stakeholder expectations (enterprise alignment practices).[7]

The goal of a business ethics program is to help owners, managers, employees, and agents work together to pursue the purpose of the enterprise and to achieve its goals and objectives. As the author cited in Box 10.1 argues, this is an essential management process.[8] To benefit from a business ethics program, then, an RBE needs to have a firm understanding of how its decisions and activities affect its stakeholders.

Specific expected program outcomes were developed in Chapter 4 and are discussed later in this chapter. Once a business ethics program is in place for some period of time, owners and managers need to ask themselves how the enterprise performed. This manual recommends that owners and managers ask a number of questions, including the following:

- How well did we face the pressures of our relevant context, and what pressures will we face in the years ahead?
- How well did our organizational culture perform, and how has it changed over the relevant period?
- Did we set and adequately communicate appropriate standards and procedures for our employees and agents, and are they following them?
- Have we fostered reasonable expectations among our stakeholders, and have we satisfied them?
- Is our business ethics infrastructure supporting our strengths and compensating for our weaknesses?
- Are our management practices aligned with our core beliefs and consistent with our standards, procedures, and expectations?
- Have our expected program outcomes been realized?

- What have we learned through the business ethics program over the relevant period?
- Where do we go from here?

An effective business ethics program will have the necessary feedback mechanisms built into the program through its evaluation processes. These mechanisms enable an RBE to collect new information; integrate that information with existing skills, knowledge, understanding, and attitudes; and put what has been learned into practice. The measure of success for a business ethics program is an organizational culture fully committed to enterprise core beliefs, standards, procedures, and expectations, as they develop over time.[9]

Importance of Program Evaluation

An RBE undertakes the design and implementation of a business ethics program in order to perform certain processes and achieve certain outcomes. Responsible owners and managers evaluate and learn from these processes and outcomes. They track how well the processes work, how many of the expected program outcomes are achieved, and what the enterprise learns along the way to justify the time, effort, and resources the enterprise puts into the program. They are also concerned with the quality of the enterprise's stakeholder engagement.[10]

ENTERPRISES SHOULD EVALUATE THEIR PROGRAMS

As a matter of good management, owners and managers should regularly evaluate any strategy, program, or plan of action they undertake. It is irresponsible to dedicate significant management attention and resources to a program without evaluating its performance to determine whether it is a worthwhile endeavor.

Owners and managers can use an outcomes-based evaluation of a business ethics program in at least four ways: to provide accountability to stakeholders, to monitor and track changes in the organizational culture, to improve program quality, and to reallocate resources toward more or less intensive programs.

PROGRAM EVALUATION AND THE SMALL TO MEDIUM-SIZED ENTERPRISE

Because of resource limitations, most program evaluations in a small to medium-sized enterprise (SME) will be informal. Owners and managers will be less apt to use formal teams and processes to set objectives and evaluate performance. They will adapt the processes that follow to meet their circumstances. For example, often they will have spoken to people they trusted to establish objectives instead of convening a team. They will work with small groups or individuals to evaluate performance.

The test of an effective evaluation is not whether any specific process is followed, but whether adequate information and essential knowledge is gained. Provided that owners and managers ask the questions this manual recommends and engage their stakeholders as effectively as possible, they can be sure that they can work within their resources and with their staff to have as effective, efficient, and responsible an enterprise as possible.

MEASURING PROGRAM PERFORMANCE

To sustain the confidence of stakeholders in any business ethics program, an enterprise should evaluate the process and outcomes on a routine basis. Evaluating program processes answers the question, "Did we do what we said we would do?" Evaluating program outcomes adds the question, "Did the changes we expected occur?"[11]

Evaluation processes reflect the same dynamics addressed in designing and implementing the business ethics program. They depend on the relevant context and organizational culture of the enterprise and the reasonable expectations of its stakeholders. They can be of varying intensity. They can be more or less informal.

DEFINING THE PURPOSE OF PROGRAM EVALUATION

The first step for owners and managers to take in evaluating a business ethics program is to agree on the questions they want answered. In the early years of the business ethics program, owners and managers may be primarily concerned about process: "Is the enterprise establishing standards, procedures, and expectations?" "Is the training being accomplished effectively?" "Are reports to stakeholders being well received?"

Management's ultimate purpose in having a business ethics program, however, is not simply to have a code of conduct or to conduct ethics, compliance, and responsibility training. Owners and managers will eventually want to know the answers to outcome questions:[12]

- Is there less misconduct?
- Are employees and agents able to recognize responsible business conduct issues?
- How often do employees and agents speak in terms of standards, procedures, and expectations?
- How often are decisions made with reference to standards, procedures, and expectations?
- How willing are employees and agents to seek advice?
- How willing are employees and agents to report concerns?
- How satisfied are those who report their concerns with management's response?
- How committed are employees to the enterprise?
- How satisfied are stakeholders with the enterprise?

SCANNING THE RELEVANT CONTEXT

Before proceeding to determining which aspects of process and program outcomes to evaluate, owners and managers need to conduct a scan of the enterprise's relevant context. A significant part of the scanning process is engaging stakeholders and determining their reasonable demands for information. Only by being alert to the demands of stakeholders can the enterprise determine which outcomes should be evaluated, which indicators will be most effective (and credible), and how and to whom to report its findings. The AA1000S framework, discussed in more detail at the end of this chapter, provides a standard for quality in engaging stakeholders.

TRACKING ORGANIZATIONAL CULTURE

Although changing organizational culture need not be a reason for having a business ethics program, by its very nature such a program will make subtle changes to the organizational culture. Moreover, certain cultural aspects will influence the process and its prospects for success. For example, there is a close relationship between program success and perceptions that owners and managers care as much about ethics and values as the economic bottom line.[13]

For these reasons, it is critical that the enterprise track a number of key aspects of organizational culture. In Box 10.2 are eight factors that can be tracked routinely. Factors such as these can be tracked using the organizational worksheet provided at the end of this chapter (RBE Worksheet 14).

EVALUATING THE PROCESS

Process evaluation looks at how the program works: whether resources are being used well, whether assigned activities are being performed, and whether specific outputs are produced.

Many general management evaluation models, especially in the arena of continuous quality improvement, are process models, including the International Organization for Standardization (ISO) management systems models. The ISO 9000 series for quality certification does not define quality; instead, it examines whether the processes that have been shown to lead to quality goods and services have been followed. The same is true for the ISO 14000 series for environmental management. It does not define what protecting the environment is; instead, it determines whether management systems are in place to protect the environment.

In the arena of social reporting, the Global Reporting Initiative also does not set standards, but it does provide a comprehensive, even exhaustive, framework for what should be reported.[14] AccountAbility, formally known as

BOX 10.2

MEASURABLE FACTORS OF ORGANIZATIONAL CULTURE

These eight factors can be tracked routinely:

1. Perceiving that leadership cares about ethics and values as much as the bottom line

2. Feeling safe to deliver bad news

3. Feeling treated fairly

4. Feeling valued as an employee

5. Not feeling pressure to compromise values

6. Believing that ethical behavior is rewarded

7. Believing that unethical behavior is punished

8. Recognizing whether the enterprise has an employee, community, or self-interest focus

---

the Institute of Social and Ethical AccountAbility, sets no specific standards for a responsible business enterprise either, but it does provide a framework for planning and reporting in a manner designed to give external stakeholders confidence in the report (AA1000S).[15]

The process evaluation worksheet (RBE Worksheet 15) at the end of this chapter can be used by evaluators to develop a plan to collect and analyze information. For example, when communicating standards and procedures is the process the enterprise is evaluating, RBE Worksheet 15 helps examine a number of specific questions: who was involved and affected, when, and where. It can be used to look at training expenses, the number of employees trained per year, participant satisfaction with the training, and performance on action plans following training. Process evaluation also leads to consideration of more subjective indicators, such as activity successes, challenges, unexpected developments, and insights.

DEFINING EXPECTED PROGRAM OUTCOMES

Owners and managers need to define outcomes they can measure. As discussed in Chapter 4, there are at least nine commonly expected outcomes for the time and effort that managers put into a business ethics program (see Box 10.3). At the end of this chapter is an outcomes evaluation worksheet (RBE Worksheet 16) to assist owners and managers in developing an outcomes evaluation plan.

A number of emerging global standards discussed in Chapter 2 set specific standards for enterprises to meet. Among them are the Caux Round Table *Principles for Business*, U.N. Global Compact, Organization for Economic Cooperation and Development (OECD) *Guidelines for Multinational Enterprises*, U.S. Department of Commerce *Basic Guidelines for Codes of Business Conduct*, and

---

BOX 10.3

MEASURABLE PROGRAM OUTCOMES

1. Violating enterprise standards

2. Being aware of ethics, compliance, and responsibility issues

3. Speaking in terms of core beliefs and standards

4. Making decisions in terms of core beliefs and standards

5. Being willing to seek advice on standards

6. Being willing to report observed or suspected violations

7. Being satisfied with management's response

8. Increasing employee commitment to enterprise

9. Increasing stakeholder satisfaction with the enterprise (including a proxy for the environment)

Interfaith Declaration *Principles for Global Corporate Responsibility.* From these standards, the responsible business can derive outcomes for its business ethics program.

Developing a Data Collection Plan

There are a number of classic data collection methods for evaluators to consider in collecting data for the relevant context scan, organizational culture tracking, and process and outcome valuation. As indicated in Table 10.1, these methods include interviews (including focus groups), surveys, document review, and direct observation. Each has its strengths, weaknesses, and resource demands.[16]

BOX 10.4

MODEL SURVEY QUESTIONS

- How often did you refer to this company's code of responsible business conduct in the past year?

- If you attended responsible business conduct training in the past year, how useful did you find it?

- How often would you say this company—as a whole— lives up to its own values? [List values]

- How committed to living the values of this company would you say senior management is?

- If you had questions about whether a choice or action meets this company's standards, procedures, or expectations of responsible business conduct, where would you go for advice? [List available sources]

- If you observed employee or agent conduct that violated the law or this company's code of responsible business conduct, what was it? [List major types of misconduct]

- If you did report your concerns about misconduct, how satisfied were you with management's response?

TABLE 10.1 Commonly Used Data Collection Methods	
Interviews (including focus groups)	Interviews are a series of questions—typically semistructured or unstructured—conducted in person or over the telephone. Focus group interviews are an approach that takes advantage of small-group dynamics to conduct interviews with a small group of people (usually eight to 12 individuals). Interviews are useful for in-depth information and are particularly appropriate for investigating sensitive topics.
Surveys	Surveys are standardized written instruments that contain several questions about the issues to be evaluated. These questions can include a combination of types of questions—for example, single, direct questions; a series of questions about the same topic; and unstructured open-ended questions. Surveys can be conducted by mail, in person, over the telephone, through the Internet, or in a centralized activity as part of an event. Surveys are usually considered an efficient data collection strategy.
Document review	Document review is a review of enterprise records that provide both descriptive and evaluative information of the program process and its outcomes. These reviews can focus on the frequency with which specific behaviors occur.
Direct observation	Director observation is firsthand observation of interactions and events that provide descriptive or evaluative information. Observations are usually guided by predetermined protocols or observation guides to focus the information gathered. Observations will be valuable in situations in which self-reports or existing data may not be accurate or in which professional judgment is helpful.

Source: Adapted from Reisman and Mockler, A Field Guide to Outcome—Based Program Evaluation

The primary concern is to develop a cost-effective collection plan that encourages employees and agents to be forthcoming and give evaluators, owners and managers, and stakeholders a clear picture of what is going on in the enterprise. Surveys and document review are valuable for collecting standardized data very cost-effectively (Box 10.4 lists some model survey questions).[17] However, they offer no opportunity to follow through on the information gathered. Where the evaluators need the opportunity to follow leads gained from initial impressions or responses, interviews, focus groups, and direct observation are better methods, though generally more expensive. Unless people outside the enterprise are involved in collecting the data, it is difficult to ensure the anonymity or confidentiality often required to secure candid responses.

It is beyond the scope of this manual to discuss issues of validity, reliability, and cultural sensitivity or how to construct questions for surveys and interviews, but excellent discussions are available, including the work that this subsection is based on.[18]

Reporting Program Performance

As they develop a plan to evaluate business ethics program performance, owners and managers need to determine whether the evaluation is intended only for internal consumption or for wider distribution. Since the enterprise cannot report on performance that it has not evaluated, owners and managers must determine the outcomes of legitimate interest to stakeholders and the methods of evaluation and reporting that stakeholders will trust.

REPORTING TO EXTERNAL STAKEHOLDERS

Coupled with the increased activism of civil society, there is an emerging trend among enterprises to report more about their impact on society to more people. One term for this is *triple bottom-line reporting*. Triple bottom-line reporting requires enterprises to evaluate their social and environmental performance to the same degree that they evaluate and report economic performance.[19]

Reporting on an enterprise's performance and impact on society is becoming more common—and expected. Beyond publicizing the enterprise's role in the economic, social, and environmental evolution of its community, expanded reporting requires the enterprise to integrate social and environmental considerations into its strategic and operational decision-making. Considering what outcomes to measure and report, what indicators to measure, how to analyze the data, and how to report data can produce synergies that can be quite energizing—in the long run—for the enterprise.

BUILDING REPORTING CREDIBILITY

There are no generally accepted standards for reporting on business ethics program performance, especially the topics of social and environmental performance. A number of international initiatives are under way

---

BOX 10.5

AA1000S PROCESS PRINCIPLES

Fundamental Principle

　Accountability

Operating Principle

　Inclusivity

Scope and Nature of Process

　Completeness

　Materiality

　Regularity and timeliness

Meaningfulness of Information

　Quality assurance

　Accessibility

　Information quality

Management of Process on an Ongoing Basis

　Embeddedness

　Continuous improvement

Institute of Social and Ethical Accountability

---

to develop such standards, but it will take years to develop a consensus, if one is even possible.

AccountAbility's AA1000S framework is intended to standardize evaluation reporting processes and assurance. It does not provide a prescriptive framework for the resolution of conflicts between an enterprise and its stakeholders (and conflicts between its stakeholders), but it does provide a process for enterprises to begin engaging their stakeholders in order to find common ground and build trust.

AA1000S is based on the fundamental principle of accountability to stakeholders. From that principle, a number of evaluation principles and processes flow. These principles are listed in Box 10.5. Although AA1000S does not have outcome standards per se, the stakeholder engagement process itself will affect an RBE and its community.

DETERMINING FORMAT

Program evaluation is of most value to an enterprise and its stakeholders when presented in a high-quality, useful format. In drafting the evaluation, it is important to remember that many people will see program evaluation as a threat, because it may reflect adversely on their performance. Evaluators should expect to meet such resistance unless the enterprise has developed an organizational culture of continuous learning and sharing of information.

There is no established format for the evaluation report. A typical format is shown in Box 10.6.[20]

MODEL REPORT FORMAT

1. **Executive summary.** Give a one to four-page summary of the key points of the report. Since many people will read only the executive summary, it is important to include all of the important points. Include basic information on the purpose of the evaluation, key findings, any recommendations, and contact information. Refer to the body of the report for other information.

2. **Purpose.** Explain why the evaluation was conducted. What are the broad questions the evaluation is trying to answer? Who requested or initiated it?

3. **Background.** Provide readers with adequate background information about the program's structure, history, and goals and objectives. What do they need to know in order to understand the evaluation?

4. **Methodology.** Explain the evaluation design, including the data collection tools and sampling method (include data collection instruments as attachments).

5. **Summary of results.** Start with the bottom line: What are the summary conclusions? What are the answers to the key questions the evaluation set out to answer?

6. **Principal findings.** Provide more detail on the findings that support the summary conclusions. This section will probably include charts or tables illustrating the findings.

7. **Considerations or recommendations.** Draw from the findings their implications for the program, the enterprise, or its stakeholders.

8. **Attachments.** Include attachments as appropriate.

Jane Reisman and Richard Mockler
A Field Guide to Outcome-Based Program Evaluation

REPORTING CONTENT

The content of an evaluation report is driven by the purpose of the evaluation. The Global Reporting Initiative sets forth an exhaustive set of elements for enterprises to report on, as described in Box 10.7.[21] Few organizations, even the largest multinationals, issue such an exhaustive report, but this framework is a useful checklist for planning purposes even for SMEs.

Conclusion—and New Beginning

The question, "How should we monitor, track, and report our performance as an enterprise and continuously learn from it?" tests the resolve of an RBE. Often owners, managers, and supervisors are not confident or courageous enough to want to know how they are really doing.

ORGANIZATIONAL LEARNING

An RBE measures its performance as an enterprise for at least four reasons: to provide accountability to stakeholders, to monitor and track changes in the organizational culture, to improve program quality, and to allocate resources toward more or less intensive programs.

BOX 10.7

GLOBAL REPORTING INITIATIVE REPORT CONTENT

1. **Vision and strategy.** Description of the reporting organization's strategy with regard to sustainability, including a statement from the chief executive officer.

2. **Profile.** Overview of the reporting organization's structure and operations and of the scope of the report (22 items).

3. **Governance structure and management systems.** Description of organizational structure, policies, and management systems, including stakeholder engagement efforts (20 items).

4. **Content index.** A table supplied by the reporting organization identifying where the information listed in the Sustainability Reporting Guidelines 2002 is located within the organization's report.

5. **Performance indicators.** Measures of the effect of the reporting organization divided into integrated, economic (10 core, 3 additional); environmental (16 core, 19 additional); and social performance indicators (24 core, 25 additional).

Global Reporting Initiative
Sustainability Reporting Guidelines 2002

An RBE can use the worksheets in this manual to develop a plan to monitor, track, and report on its performance as an enterprise. The plan should address the quality of the evaluation process itself as well: how well it was planned and executed, whether it secured the intended information, how well the information secured was used, and what the impact of the evaluation process was on all stakeholders.

In the final analysis, however, an RBE benefits from learning how to deal with the myriad changes confronting it. Through a business ethics program, an RBE becomes adept at organizational learning. It learns how to constructively influence its relevant context, develop its organizational culture, improve its business performance, contribute to the social capital of its community, and work with community leaders to encourage the development of a market-oriented legal framework and reliable judicial institutions.

NEW BEGINNING

An RBE uses its business ethics program to learn how to contribute to developing social capital in emerging market economies, rather than being a part of the problem. This may well be the most important value that any citizen can contribute to any community.

We hope this manual inspires owners and managers to see themselves as part of the solution to the problems in their economies. It provides them with a process and toolkit to develop a road map to guide their employees and agents and to meet the reasonable expectations of their stakeholders. Then, when they have decided what makes sense for their enterprises in their communities, they may use the 16 RBE Worksheets and best practices to develop their core beliefs, standards and procedures, infrastructure, communications, and management practices. By putting a business ethics program in place, RBEs can improve business performance, make profits, and contribute to economic progress in their communities by meeting the reasonable expectations of their stakeholders.

RESPONSIBLE BUSINESS ENTERPRISE
Checklist

1. **What processes do we have in place to determine whether the programs we have designed and implemented are being accomplished?**

2. **What processes do we have in place to monitor and track our organizational culture?**

3. **What processes do we have in place to determine whether our business ethics program has achieved our expected program outcomes?**

RBE WORKSHEET

14 Organizational Culture Worksheet

Evaluators can use RBE Worksheet 14, which may be photocopied for use within your organization, to develop a plan to monitor, track, and measure the organizational culture. Evaluators will work with enterprise stakeholders to determine which cultural factors might be measured and how they might be measured. For example, to measure whether "leadership is perceived to care about ethics and values as much as the bottom line," evaluators may determine that three indicators apply:

1. Employee perceptions of leadership, determined through interviews, focus groups, and a survey
2. Statements made by leadership, determined through a review of leadership communications and interviews in its communications department
3. Intentions of leadership, determined through interviews with key personnel

	Interviews	Focus Groups	Surveys	Document Review	Direct Observation
Factor of organizational culture:					
Indicator 1:					
Indicator 2:					
Indicator 3:					

Process Evaluation

Evaluators can use RBE Worksheet 15, which may be photocopied for use within your organization, to develop a plan to collect and analyze information about a specific process, such as communicating standards and procedures or training. The worksheet asks a number of specific questions, such as who was involved or affected, what was achieved, when, and where. It also asks about successes, challenges, barriers, unexpected developments, and insights. By using the worksheet, evaluators can determine the best means of answering these questions.

	Interviews	Focus Groups	Surveys	Document Review	Direct Observation
Who: **Stakeholders involved in activity** **Stakeholders affected by activity**					
What: **Activities** **Output produced**					
When: **Timeline** **Milestones**					
Where: **By location** **By division** **By region**					
Developments **Successes** **Challenges** **Barriers** **Unexpected developments** **Insights**					

RBE WORKSHEET

16   Outcomes Evaluation

Evaluators can use RBE Worksheet 16, which may be photocopied for use within your organization, to develop a plan to collect and analyze information about the expected program outcomes developed through the Program Logic Model (RBE Worksheet 1). For each expected program outcome, evaluators should work with the enterprise to determine which measurable factors indicate the extent to which an outcome has been realized. When indicators for each expected program outcome have been identified, evaluators can design a plan using the five methods of collecting data across the top of the worksheet: interviews, focus groups, surveys, document review, and direct observation.

	Interviews	Focus Groups	Surveys	Document Review	Direct Observation
Expected program outcome					
Indicator 1:					
Indicator 2:					
Indicator 3:					

APPENDICES

A   SAMPLE ETHICAL DECISION-MAKING MODEL

B   BASIC GUIDELINES FOR CODES OF BUSINESS CONDUCT

C   SAMPLE INTEGRITY PACT

D   SAMPLE DECLARATION OF INTEGRITY IN BUSINESS CONDUCT

E   SAMPLE SUPPLY CHAIN MANAGEMENT QUESTIONNAIRE

F   BASIC INFORMATION ON THE U.S. FOREIGN CORRUPT PRACTICES ACT

G   FIGHTING CORRUPTION AND SAFEGUARDING INTEGRITY

H   EXTRACTS FROM U.S. FEDERAL SENTENCING GUIDELINES FOR ORGANIZATIONS

I   EXTRACTS FROM THE AUSTRALIAN CRIMINAL CODE

Appendix A Sample Ethical Decision-Making Model

This appendix outlines a step-by-step procedure for ethical decision-making by the responsible business enterprise. It is based on a number of approaches that are detailed in the works cited at the end of this appendix.

Preliminary Considerations

There are at least five matters that a decision-maker must be clear about in his or her own mind when beginning the formal process of ethics and policy decision-making:

1. What motivated the need for choice?
2. Is the decision-maker framing a question, developing an argument, or deciding how to act?
3. For purposes of this choice only, what can be reasonably assumed to be true?
4. What are the applicable enterprise core beliefs, standards, procedures, and expectations?
5. What will constitute a quality judgment or quality action under those circumstances?

Outcomes-Based Decision-Making

Step 1: Identify the desired result.

- A vision of a desired future?
- A question to pursue?
- An argument to support a position?
- A resolution of a dilemma?
- A solution to a problem?

Describe the desired result clearly. If it is to solve a problem, be sure there is a problem, not just a symptom.

Step 2: Describe the conditions or criteria that the result must meet to be satisfactory. List the essential criteria for a successful outcome, as well as the other conditions that it would be desirable for a result to meet:

- Minimum essential criteria include that the result be a quality judgment or quality action that is feasible, suitable, and cost-acceptable, specifically taking into account opportunity cost.
- An organizational essential requirement is that the result be consistent with the enterprise's core beliefs: its purpose, values, and envisioned future.

Include the specific enterprise standards, procedures, and expectations that might apply at all four levels of identity: compliance, risk management, reputation enhancement, and value added.

Step 3: Identify all stakeholders—that is, those who are involved in, affected by, or in a position to influence the decision-making process or the result.

- Determine their relationships.
- Analyze cultural differences, using Hofstede or another approach.
- Analyze organizational culture differences.
- If the decision is an organizational or community decision, categorize the stakeholders as either internal or external.
- Prioritize among the stakeholders.

Step 4: Search for all reasonably promising results and list them:

- Use brainstorming.
- Consider the points of view of as many stakeholders as possible.
- Use different frames of reference to develop new and better ways of looking at the decision.
- Ask, "What else is possible?"

Step 5: Obtain all the relevant facts concerning the extent to which each of the proposed alternatives would or would not meet the criteria for an acceptable result—or be likely to do so. Consider stakeholders' viewpoints:

- What are the stakeholders' perspectives?
- How do they understand the facts of the matter?
- What do they value concretely and in the abstract?
- What do they understand the key concepts to mean?

Step 6: Evaluate all the alternatives by examining them in terms of the criteria or conditions that a result must meet (*essentials*) and also in terms of those that are considered desirable (*desirables*):

- What alternatives best meet the criteria of the desired result?
- What are the numbers behind the alternatives? What will they cost? How probable are they? How long will they take? How long will they last?
- Are they feasible, suitable, and cost-acceptable?

After evaluating each alternative, ask, "And then what?" Expect there to be at least one unwanted consequence. Be prepared to support your evaluations with reasons and justifications.

Step 7: Compare the alternatives, and choose the one that best meets the essential and desired criteria:

- First, eliminate all the alternatives that do not meet the essential conditions.
- Then eliminate, progressively, those alternatives that meet the desirable conditions least satisfactorily.
- Remember that the object is to make a good choice with the information available, not to make a perfect choice.

Step 8: Carry the choice forward:

- Share the vision.
- Pursue the question.
- Make the argument.
- Act on the resolution.
- Begin implementing the solution.

Ethics and policy choices presume action, though a decision to do nothing when one has the power to act is also action. Find the courage to act on the hard choices. Take responsibility for the choice, the action required to take it forward, and the consequences. Be willing to be held accountable—and to hold others accountable.

Step 9: Reflect on the consequences of the choice and the actions implementing it. Learn from both the processes and the consequences:

- What questions are raised?
- What arguments can be made for staying the course or changing?
- What could have been done better in arriving at the result?
- What could have been done better in implementing the result?
- What did you learn from the processes and the consequences?

Works Consulted

Altier, William J. *The Thinking Manager's Toolbox: Effective Processes for Problem Solving and Decision Making*. Cambridge, United Kingdom: Oxford University Press, 1999.

Collins, James C., and Jerry I. Porras. *Built to Last: Successful Habits of Visionary Companies*. New York: HarperBusiness, 1994.

Eccles, Henry E. *Logistics in the National Defense*. Westport, Conn.: Greenwood Publishing Group, 1981.

Hardin, Garrett. *Filters against Folly: How to Survive Despite Economists, Ecologists, and the Merely Eloquent*. New York: Penguin Books, 1985.

Hofstede, Geert. *Cultures and Organizations: Software of the Mind*. London: McGraw-Hill, 1991.

Krolick, Sanford. *Ethical Decision-Making Style: Survey and Interpretive Notes*. Reading, Mass.: Addison-Wesley Training Systems, 1987.

Leavitt, Harold. "Management and Management Education in the West: What's Right and What's Wrong?" In *The Management of Organizations: Strategies, Tactics, Analyses*, edited by Michael L. Tushman, Charles O'Reilly, and David A. Nadler. New York: Harper & Row, 1989.

Likert, Rensis, and Jamie Gibson Likert. *New Ways of Managing Conflict*. New York: McGraw-Hill, 1976.

Paul, Richard W. *Critical Thinking: What Every Person Needs to Survive in a Rapidly Changing World*. 2nd rev. ed. Santa Ana, Calif.: Foundation for Critical Thinking, 1992.

Robertson, Chris, and Paul A. Fadil. "Developing Corporate Codes of Ethics in Multinational Firms: Bhopal Revisited," *Journal of Managerial Issues* 10, no. 4 (1998): 454, available at <http://www.questia.com>, accessed June 7, 2003.

Mises, Ludwig von. *Human Action: A Treatise on Economics*. 3rd rev. ed. Chicago: Contemporary Books, 1966.

BASIC GUIDELINES FOR CODES OF BUSINESS CONDUCT

This text, titled "Basic Guidelines for Codes of Business Conduct," was developed by the U.S. Department of Commerce in cooperation with the Russian Chamber of Commerce and Industry and the U.S.–Russia Business Development Committee. The guidelines are intended to assist organizations in developing their own codes of conduct. Questions may be addressed to Igor_Abramov@ita.doc.gov.

Basic Guidelines for Codes of Business Conduct

INTRODUCTION

In today's interconnected and interdependent world, where borders between states are becoming increasingly transparent, principles in business conduct are becoming criteria for building a good reputation in the international business community; they are the basis on which first impressions are formed and ongoing relationships maintained.

The purpose of this set of guidelines is to articulate general principles and standards that have been accepted in international business transactions. Although these principles apply generally, they are not intended to be an all-encompassing set of business practices and corporate principles. They must be adopted and implemented on a sector-by-sector and enterprise-by-enterprise[1] basis to take into account applicable laws, regulations, and other specific circumstances (such as the size of the enterprise).

PRINCIPLES IN PERSONAL AND PROFESSIONAL RELATIONS

No laws or contracts can anticipate the possible vicissitudes of life. Very often an entrepreneur must make a decision based on the prompting of common sense and conscience. The key is to embody ethical and moral principles into personal and professional relations, and remember to:

- always do business within one's means;
- have respect for the partners and participants in a shared business venture;

---

[1] "Enterprise" as used in this document means both a legal entity such as an "enterprise," "company," "firm," or "organization," and an individual or small entrepreneur.

- refrain from violence or the threat of violence as methods of achieving business success;

- resist crime and corruption, and do one's part to see that crime and corruption become unprofitable for everyone; and

- live up to the trust placed in you; trust is the foundation of entrepreneurship and a key to success;

- endeavor to earn a reputation for integrity, competency, and excellence.

CORPORATE GOVERNANCE: RELATIONSHIPS WITH SHAREHOLDERS

A trusting relationship between management and shareholders is critical. Investors and lenders must be satisfied with the manner in which shareholders oversee the performance of management and participate in key decisions.

Sound principles of corporate governance include the following:

- delineating in the company charter the respective roles and responsibilities of both management and shareholders;

- transparency of voting rules;

- respect for the rights of minority shareholders;

- open communications with shareholders through the provision of audited accounts, and information about the progress and operations of the company; and

- a well-functioning board of directors who have the skills, the time, and the access to information needed to discharge its responsibilities effectively. The board will act in a fiduciary capacity on behalf of all the shareholders.

RELATIONSHIP WITH EMPLOYEES

Enterprises have an important responsibility towards their employees. A number of basic principles typically guide the attitudes of successful enterprises toward their employees:

- due regard for labor laws;

- commitment to adequate standards of worker health and safety;

- non-discrimination in the recruitment, compensation, and promotion of employees;

- respect for the rights of workers to engage in union activity;

- effective systems for consultation with employees on employment conditions and other issues that affect the employees;

- clearly stated and transparent policies relating to compensation, benefits, promotions, and other employment conditions; and

- commitments by the enterprise for contributions to pension plans; and strict protection of the integrity of company-sponsored pension plans.

These principles do not limit the right of an enterprise to enforce discipline on its labor force or to terminate workers in accordance with applicable law.

RELATIONSHIP WITH OTHER ENTERPRISES

A relationship of mutual trust in which all parties benefit is the most significant aspect of relations between partners in joint ventures, contractual arrangements, or business relations with other enterprises. The reputation of a company is its most valuable asset. Once the reputation of an enterprise is tarnished, it is very difficult to gain trust with the same or other business relations. A number of basic principles that typically promote mutual trust in business relations include:

- commitment to excellence in products and services;
- commitment to gain respect and trust in all business relations;
- respect for the sanctity of contracts and business relations;
- in case of a commercial dispute, a willingness to negotiate and compromise in order to reach an amicable solution; and
- respect for the sanctity of rule of law, including abiding in a timely manner with decisions of any court, arbitral panels, or other administrative bodies.

RELATIONSHIP WITH THE GLOBAL COMMUNITY

As a company is an integral part of the community in which it operates, a sound relationship with the community is essential. Caring for the environment is a responsibility of the enterprise towards the immediate community, but it also extends to all communities and areas whose environment may be affected by the enterprise's activities. Enterprises must:

- be sensitive to concerns of the local population;
- communicate with the local population;
- abide by all applicable environmental laws and regulations; and
- show tolerance for people of other cultures, races, beliefs, and countries.

RELATIONSHIP WITH GOVERNMENT AUTHORITIES

Well-managed enterprises are law abiding enterprises. To maintain a sound relationship with governmental authorities, enterprises must:

- pay all taxes that are owed and due;
- abide by all mandatory government and local regulations;

- obtain all governmental permits, licenses, and approvals required to do business;
- deal with government authorities on an arm's length basis, and make no attempts to improperly influence governmental decisions;
- establish transparent procedures regarding transactions engaged in by enterprises with any government agency or official or in dealings with any enterprise owned or controlled by a government agency or official; and
- in transactions with any government agency or officials or with any enterprise owned or controlled by a government or government official, include appropriate provisions to ensure compliance with international or national codes against extortion and bribery.

PROPER CHECKS AND BALANCES

A proper system of checks and balances is necessary to ensure the ongoing integrity of the enterprise and of its relationship with its constituencies. Such a system must be based on the general principles of full disclosure, management accountability, separation of responsibility, and sound internal controls.

An enterprise should have a full disclosure policy concerning:

- statements of the enterprise's strategic aims and policies, how these have been achieved in the past reporting period, and how the enterprise will act in the future;
- prompt reports to the enterprise's constituencies on events that could have a material effect on the enterprise; and
- prompt disclosure of all important relationships between officials of the enterprise and other parties.

The key element of a system of checks and balances is that the shareholders are able to monitor management's performance and to condemn poor performance, including through the removal of management.

PREVENTION OF EXTORTION AND BRIBERY

Principles concerning prevention of extortion and bribery are intended as a method of self-regulation by businesses. The voluntary acceptance of these principles by enterprises will not only promote high standards of integrity in business transactions, whether between enterprises and public bodies or between enterprises themselves, but will also protect enterprises that are subject to attempts at extortion.

The business community objects to all forms of extortion and bribery. The highest priority should be directed to ending extortion and bribery involving politicians and senior officials. Bribery and extortion threaten democratic institutions and cause grave economic distortions.

All enterprises should observe both the letter and spirit of the following rules:

- no one may, directly or indirectly, demand or accept a bribe;
- no enterprise may, directly or indirectly, offer or give a bribe, and any demands for such a bribe must be rejected;
- enterprises should take measures reasonably within their power to ensure that any payment made to any agent represents no more than an appropriate remuneration for legitimate services rendered by the agent; that no part of any such payment is passed on by the agent as a bribe or otherwise in contravention of these principles;
- all financial transactions must be properly, accurately, and fairly recorded in appropriate books of account available for inspection by the board of directors as well as by auditors. Enterprises must take all necessary measures to establish independent systems of auditing in order to bring to light any transactions that contravene these principles. The enterprise must then take appropriate corrective action;
- the board of directors of the enterprise should periodically review compliance with these principles, and take appropriate action against any director or employee who acts in a manner inconsistent with these principles; and
- contributions to political parties or to individual politicians may be made only in accordance with applicable law, and in accordance with all applicable requirements for public disclosure of such contributions.

CREATION OF A CULTURE THAT FOSTERS SOUND BUSINESS STANDARDS AND CORPORATE PRACTICES

Ultimately, for an enterprise to live by sound business standards and ethical practices it must develop a culture that fosters such standards of integrity. This effort must be led by management and key shareholders. Steps that management and key shareholders may take to promote this positive attitude throughout the company include:

- the preparation and dissemination within the company of a code of conduct for employees;
- employee training;
- encourage proper conduct and sanctions against misconduct; and
- creation of an ethics office and ethics officers to advise and educate employees, and provide guarantees for confidential counseling.

RECOMMENDATIONS FOR IMPLEMENTATION OF THESE GUIDELINES

All enterprises that wish to become part of the international business community are recommended to:

- draft their own codes of business conduct consistent with these principles and apply them to the particular circumstances in which their business is carried out; and
- develop clear policies, guidelines, and training programs for implementing and enforcing the provisions of their codes.

The extent to which enterprises decide to incorporate the above listed guidelines may depend on the size, specific circumstances, and the business of the company.

This appendix contains the text of an integrity pact that was written with the help of Transparency International and subsequently signed with the government of Colombia in June 2000. Its purpose was to strengthen transparency in the bidding process for government-financed projects.

Integrity Pact for Strengthening Transparency in the Procurement Process No. 02/01 MDN–ARC for the Acquisition of Two Sea Bound Patrol Aircraft for the Ministry of Defense—National Navy of Colombia

Before domestic and international public opinion, we the undersigned, on one side, THE LEGAL REPRESNTATIVES AND MANAGING OFFICERS OF THE OFFERORS PARTICIPATING IN THE SUBJECT PROCUREMENT PROCESS acting on our own behalf and in representation of the legal entities that we represent as offerors, as well as in the name of all the officers and advisors who have either (1) directly, indirectly, formally or accidentally determined our participation in procurement process No. 02/01 MDN-ARC for the acquisition of two sea bound patrol aircrafts for the Ministry of National Defense—National Navy of Colombia (herein referred to as the "Subject Procurement"); (2) intervened in the preparation of our proposals to participate in the Subject Procurement; or (3) assessed our officers or companies in the Subject Procurement (hereinafter referred to individually or collectively as the "Participating Entities") and, on the other side, the OFFICERS AND ADVISORS OF THE COLOMBIAN MINISTRY OF DEFENSE, OF THE COLOMBIAN NAVY AND OF THE COLOMBIAN AIR FORCE, who directly, indirectly, formally or accidentally have participated in the technical, economical and legal structuring of the Subject Procurement or in its procedures, promotion, revision and definition, have together agreed to subscribe to this INTEGRITY PACT, upon having considered that in Colombia any and all corruption forms are illegal and that the Colombian Government prosecutes and will continue prosecuting transgressors.

Notwithstanding due compliance with Colombian laws, this Pact focuses upon a *non-bribery commitment for purposes of obtaining or retaining a contract or any other improper advantage. This includes the commitment not to collude with third parties for purposes of limiting competition in the award of this contract, as well as the obligation not to engage in unfair practices and acts contrary to free competition and an objective award within the procurement process* (hereinafter referred to as the "Non-bribery Commitment").

The Non-bribery Commitment includes any type of *payment, gift or other favor, whether offered or granted and whether, in a direct or indirect manner or through third parties,* to officials or advisors of the Colombian Ministry of Defense, the Colombian Navy and the Colombian Air Force, for purposes of:

1. Attempting to have the project, or segments of it, structured in such a way as to advantage one or more Participating Entity;

2. Securing any undue advantage to any Participating Entity in the evaluation and selection process leading to the award of the contract;

3. Being awarded the contract;

4. Achieving substantial changes in the contract through adjustment of its specifications, terms or any other material component thereof;

5. Having public officials, advisors or the receiver or supervisor of the contract (or their personnel, advisors and subcontractors) approve proposals for (or otherwise accept) substandard performance of parameters, which have been proposed by a Participating Entity and accepted by the Colombian Ministry of Defense

6. Having public officials, advisors or the receiver or supervisor of the contract (or their personnel, advisors and subcontractors) refrain from a) duly monitoring project implementation, b) reporting violations of contract specifications or other forms of non-compliance in a timely fashion, or c) holding contractors fully accountable for compliance with their legal obligations;

7. Evading taxes, duties, levies, rights, licenses or any other legal obligation;

8. Inducing any public officer to breach his official duties in any manner.

Within the above framework and in full compliance with Colombian laws, the undersigned fully commit to the following:

1. The Participating Entities and The Colombian Minstry of Defense place importance on the submission of proposals within a free, impartial, competitive and abuse-free environment. Within this scope, the Participating Entities are pleased to confirm that:

    a. They have neither offered to grant, granted or facilitated any improper inducement or reward nor attempted to offer, grant or facilitate any inducement or improper reward, nor will they offer, grant, or facilitate any inducement or improper reward, whether directly or indirectly through agents or third parties, to any official or advisor of the Colombian Ministry of Defense, the Colombian Navy or the Colombian Air Force, including their relatives or business associates, for purposes of being awarded this contract, or retaining it or any other undue advantage, and

    b. They have neither colluded with others, nor will so collude, for the undue limiting of competition for the award of this contract.

c. The Participating Entities understand the material relevance of the foregoing commitments for the COLOMBIAN MINISTRY OF DEFENSE and their consequent seriousness.

On their own behalf, the OFFICIALS AND ADVISORS OF THE COLOMBIAN MINISTRY OF DEFENSE—COLOMBIAN NAVY AND AIR FORCE confirm that they have neither requested nor accepted, nor shall they request or accept, whether directly or indirectly through third parties, any payment or favor from the Participating Entities in exchange for favoring them in the award of the contract or its retention. In this same sense, the abovementioned officers declare that the service has a present and actual need for goods meeting the precise technical specifications described in the Subject Procurement.

2. The Participating Entities hereby commit to performing their activities within a framework of principles for ethical behavior and to taking all necessary measures to ensure that this Non-bribery Commitment be observed by all their managers and employees as well as by all third parties working with the company on this project, including their agents, consultants and subcontractors. This framework shall be recorded in each Participating Entity's ethical code, which should demonstrate that each corresponding entity will perform under internal compliance systems capable of detecting corruption risks and preventing the payment of bribes. As a condition of participation, each Participating Entity shall file their corresponding ethics code with the COLOMBIAN MINISTRY OF DEFENSE.

3. This commitment is submitted in the name and on behalf of the Presidents and/or General Managers of each Participating Entity. All those participating as a Consortium ("consorcio" as defined in article 7 of the Law 80 of 1993) or temporary union ("unión temporal" as defined in article 7 of the Law 80 of 1993) do also subscribe to this Pact in their own name and on behalf of each and all the Presidents and/or General Managers of the associated companies.

4. Each international company participating in the Subject Procurement hereby assumes this commitment in the name and on behalf of the President and / or General Managers of the company's parent companies, and this commitment shall include all managers and personnel of their Colombian subsidiaries, should the latter exist.

5. Regarding the submission of bids, Participating Entities hereby commit to presenting a serious tender, including reliable information, and not to present an artificially low price seeking to compensate such price during the execution of the contract by claiming additional payments. This commitment is understood as not limiting the possibility that additions to the contracts for other items may be accepted, whenever they are fair and duly supported.

6. Regarding business-related payments, the Participating Entities agree that:

a. Payments to agents and other third parties will be limited to reasonable compensation for clearly business-related services.

b. In the event of a claim related to non-compliance of the Non-bribery Commitment made in this Pact and the existence of serious evidence of such non-compliance assessed for this purpose by the Arbitrator designated under number 10 herein, the involved or successful Participating Entities hereby commit to furnishing to the Arbitrator, if so demanded, all information under their control, directly or indirectly, on (1) payments relating to the preparation of the tender and/or contract, (2) contract beneficiaries, and (3) all other the contract-related documentation.

c. Upon the completion of the performance of the contract, the legal representative of the successful Participating Entity will formally certify that no bribes or other illegal fees have been paid in order to obtain or retain this contract. The final accounting shall include brief details of the goods and services provided sufficient to establish the legitimacy of the payments made.

7. In the event of non-compliance with the ethical commitments made herein by officials and Participating Entities, a decision shall be issued by an Arbitrator, called the "Tender's Transparency Defender," in order to achieve the purposes of this Pact. His or her decisions shall be fair pursuant to Law 446 of 1998.

The Arbitrator shall hear the above-mentioned matters upon request of the Government, Transparency International, or any of the Participating Entities.

The above-mentioned Arbitrator shall have the qualifications provided for in the National Constitution to hold the position of Supreme Court or Constitutional Court Justice and shall be selected from the list of arbitrators of the Chamber of Commerce of Bogotá, through the public impaneling system.

8. Should a declaration of guilt be issued by the Arbitrator for the default of any Participating Entity's under its Non-bribery Commitment, the following legal effects will be triggered, in addition to all other processes contemplated under Colombian legislation and under any legislation corresponding to the jurisdiction of the contractual process:

a. Should the defaulting Participating Entity be the party to whom the contract was awarded ("Defaulting Contractor"), any of the remaining parties to this Pact shall be entitled to request, before a competent Judge, total nullity of the underlying contract on the basis that it lacks licit cause;

b. Where the party involved is a Defaulting Contractor, the underlying contract will be terminated immediately for due cause attributable to that party. The Defaulting Contractor is hereby obligated to unconditionally and irrevocably accept termination of the contract for due cause immediately upon the declaration of default issued by the Arbitrators. The Defaulting Contractor will assume the contractual consequences derived from such termination.

c. Any defaulting Participating Entity shall be required to pay economic satisfaction equivalent to ten percent (10.00%) of the value of the contract, as an estimation of damages inflicted on the Participating Entities who have not defaulted under their Non-bribery Commitments. Should there be more than one complying Participating Entity, the resulting amount shall be distributed equally among them.

d. Any defaulting Participating Entity will abstain from participating in contracting processes of any nature with public entities of the Republic of Colombia for a period of five (5) years.

In order to ensure the effectiveness of the above-stated provisions, this Pact shall be included as an integral part of the contract to be signed by the chosen Participating Entity. The legal effects contemplated in letters a) and b) of this numeral shall solely be applicable to the Participating Entity awarded with the contract. The legal effects provided for in letters c) and d) shall be applicable to the awarded party or to any other Participating Entity.

9. All chiefs at the COLOMBIAN MINISTRY OF DEFENSE, the COLOMBIAN NAVY and the AIR FORCE, shall be obliged to undertake each and every action required to ensure that the competent entities promote and perform such investigations as may be required into the conduct of officers of any Participating Entity, or of their external advisors, who could have acted in default of the provisions of this Pact and of any applicable law.

10. In event of proven default to the Non-bribery Commitment, as established in numeral 8 of this Integrity Pact, the COLOMBIAN MINISTRY OF DEFENSE should exclude the defaulting Participating Entity from future eligibility for participation in direct contracting processes.

11. The Participating Entities hereby declare publicly that they know and accept the conditions of total transparency and equity, as established in the Documents of the Subject Procurement process and all their amendments. Thus, they commit not to seek to disqualify other Participating Entities using any argument concerning default of conditions not specifically included herein, throughout the period of evaluation of the proposals.

12. The Participating Entities do hereby accept that, throughout the period of evaluation of proposals, the criteria used will favor substantive aspects over formal ones, always seeking to favor free competition and the participation of the largest possible number of bids in the Subject Procurement process.

13. Additionally, the Colombian Government has established the Presidency's Program Against Corruption, with the purpose to serve as a channel for processing any investigation on any possible form of extortion or bribery

through public contracting. Participating Entities shall voluntarily report before this Program any information on irregular doings of which they have knowledge, which bears relation to the Subject Procurement process.

As evidence of acceptance of the foregoing, the officials of the Colombian Ministry of Defense, the Colombian Navy and the Colombian Air Force sign the present document on the _____

OFFICIALS AND ADVISORS OF THE COLOMBIAN MINISTRY OF DEFENSE

Colombian Minister of Defense and other senior officer's signatures appear.

OFFICERS AND ADVISORS OF THE COLOMBIAN NAVY

Names and functional position of additional signing officer follow.

AIR FORCE OFFICERS PARTICIPANT IN TECHNICAL ADVISORY OF THE PROJECT

Names and functional position of several Air Force officers follow.

LEGAL REPRESENTATIVES AND OFFICERS OF PARTICPITATING ENTITIES signing the present document on the date of submission of their respective proposals.

WITNESSES

Names and position of several senior government officials, the Executive Director of Transparencia por Colombia and the Director of the Presidency's Program Against Corruption.

SAMPLE DECLARATION OF INTEGRITY IN BUSINESS CONDUCT

This appendix reproduces the text of the Declaration of Integrity in Business Conduct in St. Petersburg, Russia. The Declaration was developed by the Center for Business Ethics and Corporate Governance with financial support from the U.S. Agency for International Development through the Eurasia Foundation. For more information about the declaration, see www.ethicsrussia.org/declaration.html.

Declaration of Integrity in Business Conduct in St. Petersburg, Russia

PRINCIPLES

The undersigned representative of the St. Petersburg business community ("Party to the Declaration") recognizes the following international principles of business conduct as the basis of this Declaration of Integrity in Business Conduct ("Declaration"):

Transparency. The functioning of a market economy presumes that each market participant conducts business with transparency, exchanging accurate information with other market participants on an efficient basis while respecting norms of confidentiality.

Sanctity of Contract. Respect for the sanctity of contract and the honoring of oral commitments lead to commercial ties built on goodwill, trust, and reputation for honesty.

Competition. A competitive economy provides transparent rules and opportunities for market participants, rewards quality of performance, and deters reproachable methods of obtaining advantages over other market participants.

Repudiation of Corrupt Practices. Corruption inflicts damage on market relations and on economy as a whole. Repudiation of corruption as a method of business facilitates the process of stabilizing the market.

Legal Settlement of Disputes. A civil market presumes the rejection of illegal and dangerous methods to defend economic interests. Any use of violence against a person in a business dispute, including the use of physical or psychological coercion, is impermissible.

DECLARATION

NOW, THEREFORE, in order to integrate the Declaration's principles fully into the business culture of St. Petersburg, by applying the principles consistently in concert with other members of the business community, each Party to the Declaration declares that:

ARTICLE I. CODE OF BUSINESS CONDUCT

A. The Party to the Declaration has adopted or shall adopt a Code of Business Conduct based upon the principles set forth in this Declaration ("Code").

B. The Party to the Declaration, which has adopted a Code, shall present the Secretary of the Governor of St. Petersburg's Council on Investment ("Depository") with a copy of the Code at the time of signing this Declaration.

C. The Party to the Declaration, which shall adopt a Code, shall present the Depository with a copy of the Code as soon as practicable but no later than ninety (90) days after signing this Declaration. In order to ensure that the Code conforms with the principles set forth in this Declaration, each Party to this Declaration which shall adopt a Code can utilize the Model Code of Ethics in Business Conduct attached to this Declaration.

D. The Party to the Declaration shall ensure that the Party's employees are familiar with the provisions of the Party's Code and systems of control that prevent actions by employees that are contrary to the provisions of the Party's Code.

E. The Party to the Declaration shall present the Depository a letter affirming that the Party has faithfully conducted business in accordance with the Party's Code on an annual basis.

ARTICLE II. PUBLICATION

A. By signing the Declaration, the Party to this Declaration hereby agrees to be included on a Register of Parties to the Declaration ("Register"), which shall be maintained and publicized by the Depository. The Register shall include the name of the Party to the Declaration and the dates the Party's representatives signed this Declaration.

B. The Depository shall update the Register regularly to include each new Party to the new Declaration.

ARTICLE III. MISCELLANEOUS

A. The Party to the Declaration is signing and executing the Declaration voluntarily.

B. Two duly authorized representatives of the Party to the Declaration shall sign and seal two (2) copies of this Declaration. One (1) copy shall remain with the Party to this Declaration and the second shall be submitted to the Depository.

SAMPLE SUPPLY CHAIN MANAGEMENT QUESTIONNAIRE

The U.S. company Hewlett-Packard requires its suppliers to answer the questions posed in this questionnaire regarding their compliance with the company's Supplier Code of Conduct. The company also requires its suppliers to complete three other self-assessment questionnaires: an environmental questionnaire, an occupational safety and health questionnaire, and a labor and employment questionnaire. (Text reproduced courtesy of Hewlett-Packard Company Supply Chain Operations. For more information, go to the Hewlett-Packard Web site, www.hp.com/hpinfo/globalcitizenship/environment/supplychain/index.html.)

HP Supplier Code of Conduct Questionnaire

Suppliers are requested to provide candid answers to the following questions. HP encourages its suppliers to accurately identify any areas in which their operations do not conform to the requirements of the HP Supplier Code of Conduct. As indicated in HP's Supplier Code of Conduct, HP expects to work collaboratively with its suppliers to achieve these standards.

Date:	
HP Contract Number(s), if applicable:	
Company Name:	Contact Name:
Address:	Position:
Telephone Number:	
Fax:	
E-mail:	

Purpose of the Questionnaire

This questionnaire is part of the annual performance report for HP suppliers under HP's Supplier Code of Conduct and Supplier Social and Environmental Responsibility Agreement. It provides a mechanism for HP to gather information about the environmental, occupational health and safety, and labor and employment practices and performance of its suppliers.

Scope of Questionnaire

Questions that ask for information about the "company" should be answered for the company as a whole.

Questions that ask for information about the "facility" should be answered for each company facility at which products supplied to HP are manufactured.

---

1. Does your company have a company representative for Corporate Social and Environmental Responsibility, or someone who otherwise has responsibility for addressing in your company the requirements set out in HP's Supplier Code of Conduct?

❏ Yes   ❏ No   If "yes," please provide contact information below.

Name: Position:

Address: Telephone Number:

Fax:

E-mail:

---

2. Does your company have procedures in place designed to ensure that the requirements set out in HP's Supplier Code of Conduct are met in your company?

❏ Yes   ❏ No

2.1 If yes, please attach copy of procedures or provide URL.

Attachment Title:
URL:

---

3. Does your company have procedures for internal reporting of any non-conformances with these requirements that may occur within your company? For correcting any non-conformances as they are identified by your company?

❏ Yes   ❏ No

3.1 If yes, please attach copy of procedures or provide URL.

Attachment Title:
URL:

4. Does your company have a code of conduct or similar standards to which you expect your suppliers to adhere? ❐ Yes ❐ No	
4.1 If yes, please attach copy of procedures or provide URL.	Attachment Title: URL:

5. Is your company currently subject to any enforcement action by any governmental authority for non-compliance with environmental, safety, or labor requirements at any facility at which products supplied to HP are manufactured? ❐ Yes ❐ No
5.1 If yes, please describe briefly the nature of the action and what steps your company is taking to resolve it.

BASIC INFORMATION ON THE U.S. FOREIGN CORRUPT PRACTICES ACT

This material appeared as Appendix A of Fighting Global Corruption: Business Risk Management, *a booklet published in May 2001 by the U.S. Department of State's Bureau for International Narcotics and Law Enforcement Affairs. (The full text of the booklet is available at* www.state.gov/g/inl/rls/rpt/fgcrpt/2001.*) For further information about the Foreign Corrupt Practices Act, see the US Department of Commerce and US Department of Justice websites:* www.ita.doc.gov/legal; www.usdoj.gov/criminal/fraud.html.

Appendix A: Foreign Corrupt Practices Act—Antibribery Provisions (U.S. Department of Justice and U.S. Department of Commerce)

The following information is intended to provide a general description of the FCPA and is not intended to substitute for the advice of private counsel on specific issues related to the FCPA. Moreover, this information is not intended to set forth the present enforcement intentions of the U.S. Department of Justice, the U.S. Securities and Exchange Commission (SEC), or any other U.S. government agency with respect to particular fact situations.

INTRODUCTION

The 1988 Trade Act directed the Attorney General to provide guidance concerning the Department of Justice's enforcement policy with respect to the Foreign Corrupt Practices Act of 1977 ("FCPA"), 15 U.S.C. §§ 78dd-1, et seq., to potential exporters and small businesses that are unable to obtain specialized counsel on issues related to the FCPA. The guidance is limited to responses to requests under the Department of Justice's Foreign Corrupt Practices Act Opinion Procedure (described below) and to general explanations of compliance responsibilities and potential liabilities under the FCPA. The following information constitutes the Department of Justice's general explanation of the FCPA.

U.S. firms seeking to do business in foreign markets must be familiar with the FCPA. In general, the FCPA prohibits corrupt payments to foreign officials for the purpose of obtaining or keeping business. The Department of Justice is the chief enforcement agency, with a coordinate role played by the Securities and Exchange Commission (SEC). The Office of General Counsel of the

Department of Commerce also answers general questions from U.S. exporters concerning the FCPA's basic requirements and constraints.

BACKGROUND

As a result of SEC investigations in the mid-1970s, over 400 U.S. companies admitted making questionable or illegal payment in excess of $300 million to foreign government officials, politicians, and political parties. The abuses ran the gamut from bribery of high foreign officials to secure some type of favorable action by a foreign government to so-called facilitating payments that allegedly were made to ensure that government functionaries discharged certain ministerial or clerical duties. Congress enacted the FCPA to bring a halt to the bribery of foreign officials and to restore public confidence in the integrity of the American business system.

The FCPA was intended to have and has had an enormous impact on the way American firms do business. Several firms that paid bribes to foreign officials have been the subject of criminal and civil enforcement actions, resulting in large fines and suspension and debarment from federal procurement contracting, and their employees and officers have gone to jail. To avoid such consequences, many firms have implemented detailed compliance programs intended to prevent and to detect any improper payments by employees and agents.

Following the passage of the FCPA, the Congress became concerned that American companies were operating at a disadvantage compared to foreign companies who routinely paid bribes and, in some countries, were permitted to deduct the cost of such bribes as business expenses on their taxes. Accordingly, in 1988, the Congress directed the Executive Branch to commence negotiations in the Organization of Economic Cooperation and Development (OECD) to obtain the agreement of the United States' major trading partners to enact legislation similar to the FCPA. In 1997, almost ten years later, the United States and thirty-three other countries signed the OECD Convention on Combating Bribery of Foreign Public Officials in International Business Transactions. The United States ratified this Convention and enacted implementing legislation in 1998.

The antibribery provisions of the FCPA make it unlawful for a U.S. person, and certain foreign issuers of securities, to make a corrupt payment to a foreign official for the purpose of obtaining or retaining business for or with, or directing business to, any person. Since 1998, they also apply to foreign firms and persons who take any act in furtherance of such a corrupt payment while in the United States.

The FCPA also requires companies whose securities are listed in the United States to meet its accounting provisions. See 15 U.S.C. § 78m. These accounting provisions, which were designed to operate in tandem with the antibribery provisions of the FCPA, require corporations covered by the provisions to make and keep books and records that accurately and fairly reflect the transactions of the corporation and to devise and maintain an adequate system of internal accounting controls. The information below discusses only the antibribery provisions.

ENFORCEMENT

The Department of Justice is responsible for all criminal enforcement and for civil enforcement of the antibribery provisions with respect to domestic concerns and foreign companies and nationals. The SEC is responsible for civil enforcement of the antibribery provisions with respect to issuers.

ANTIBRIBERY PROVISIONS

BASIC PROHIBITIONS

The FCPA makes it unlawful to bribe foreign government officials to obtain or retain business. With respect to the basic prohibition, there are five elements which must be met to constitute a violation of the Act:

A. **Who**—The FCPA potentially applies to *any* individual, firm, officer, director, employee, or agent of a firm and any stockholder acting on behalf of a firm. Individuals and firms may also be penalized if they order, authorize, or assist someone else to violate the antibribery provisions or if they conspire to violate those provisions.

Under the FCPA, U.S. jurisdiction over corrupt payments to foreign officials depends upon whether the violator is an "issuer," a "domestic concern," or a foreign national or business.

An "issuer" is a corporation that has issued securities that have been registered in the United States or who is required to file periodic reports with the SEC.

A "domestic concern" is any individual who is a citizen, national, or resident of the United States, or any corporation, partnership, association, joint-stock company, business trust, unincorporated organization, or sole proprietorship which has its principal place of business in the United States, or which is organized under the laws of a State of the United States, or a territory, possession, or commonwealth of the United States.

Issuers and domestic concerns may be held liable under the FCPA under either territorial or nationality jurisdiction principles. For acts taken within the territory of the United States, issuers and domestic concerns are liable if they take an act in furtherance of a corrupt payment to a foreign official using the U.S. mails or other means or instrumentalities of interstate commerce. Such means of instrumentalities include telephone calls, facsimile transmissions, wire transfers, and interstate or international travel. In addition, issuers and domestic concerns may be held liable for any act in furtherance of a corrupt payment taken *outside* the United States. Thus, a U.S. company or national may be held liable for a corrupt payment authorized by employees or agents operating entirely outside the United States, using money from foreign bank accounts, and without any involvement by personnel located within the United States.

Prior to 1998, foreign companies, with the exception of those who qualified as "issuers," and foreign nationals were not covered by the FCPA. The 1998 amendments expanded the FCPA to assert territorial jurisdiction over foreign companies and nationals. A foreign company or person is now subject to the FCPA if it causes, directly or through agents, an act in furtherance of the corrupt payment to take place within the territory of the United States. There is, however, no requirement that such act make use of the U.S. mails or other means or instrumentalities of interstate commerce.

Finally, U.S. parent corporations may be held liable for the acts of foreign subsidiaries where they authorized, directed, or controlled the activity in question, as can U.S. citizens or residents, themselves "domestic concerns," who were employed by or acting on behalf of such foreign-incorporated subsidiaries.

B. Corrupt Intent—The person making or authorizing the payment must have a corrupt intent, and the payment must be intended to induce the recipient to misuse his official position to direct business wrongfully to the payer or to any other person. You should note that the FCPA does not require that a corrupt act *succeed* in its purpose. The *offer or promise* of a corrupt payment can constitute a violation of the statute. The FCPA prohibits any corrupt payment intended to *influence* any act or decision of a foreign official in his or her official capacity, to *induce* the official to do or omit to do any act in violation of his or her lawful duty, to *obtain* any improper advantage, or to *induce* a foreign official to use his or her influence improperly to affect or influence any act or decision.

C. Payment—The FCPA prohibits paying, offering, promising to pay (or authorizing to pay or offer) money or anything of value.

D. Recipient—The prohibition extends only to corrupt payments to a *foreign official*, a *foreign political party* or *party official*, or any *candidate* for foreign political office. A "foreign official" means any officer or employee of a foreign government, a public international organization, or any department or agency thereof, or any person acting in an official capacity.

You should consider utilizing the Department of Justice's Foreign Corrupt Practices Act Opinion Procedure for particular questions as to the definition of a "foreign official," such as whether a member of a royal family, a member of a legislative body, or an official of a state-owned business enterprise would be considered a "foreign official." In addition, you should consult the list of public international organizations covered under the FCPA that is available on the Department of Justice's FCPA website.

The FCPA applies to payments to *any* public official, regardless of rank or position. The FCPA focuses on the *purpose* of the payment instead of the particular duties of the official receiving the payment, offer, or promise of payment, and there are exceptions to the antibribery provision for "facilitating payments for routine governmental action" (see below).

E. **Business Purpose Test**—The FCPA prohibits payments made in order to assist the firm in *obtaining* or *retaining business* for or with, or *directing business* to, any person. The Department of Justice interprets "obtaining or retaining business" broadly, such that the term encompasses more than the mere award or renewal of a contract. It should be noted that the business to be obtained or retained does not need to be with a foreign government or foreign government instrumentality.

THIRD-PARTY PAYMENTS

The FCPA prohibits corrupt payments through intermediaries. It is unlawful to make a payment to a third party, while knowing that all or a portion of the payment will go directly or indirectly to a foreign official. The *term "knowing" includes conscious disregard and deliberative ignorance.* The elements of an offense are essentially the same as described above, except that in this case the "recipient" is the intermediary who is making the payment to the requisite "foreign official."

Intermediaries may include joint venture partners or agents. To avoid being liable for corrupt third-party payments, U.S. companies are encouraged to exercise due diligence and to take all necessary precautions to ensure that they have formed a business relationship with reputable and qualified partners and representatives. Such due diligence may include investigating potential foreign representatives and joint venture partners to determine if they are in fact qualified for the position, whether they have personal or professional ties to the government, the number and reputation of their clientele, and their reputation with the U.S. Embassy or Consulate and with local bankers, clients, and other business associates.

In addition, in negotiating a business relationship, the U.S. firm should be aware of so-called "red flags," i.e., unusual payment patterns or financial arrangements, a history of corruption in the country, a refusal by the foreign joint venture partner or representative to provide a certification that it will not take any action in furtherance of an unlawful offer, promise, or payment to a foreign public official and not take any act that would cause the U.S. firm to be in violation of the FCPA, unusually high commissions, lack of transparency in expenses and accounting records, apparent lack of qualifications or resources on the part of the joint venture partner or representative to perform the services offered, and whether the joint venture partner or representative has been recommended by an official of the potential governmental customer.

You should seek the advice of counsel and consider utilizing the Department of Justice's Foreign Corrupt Practices Act Opinion Procedure for particular questions relating to third-party payments.

PERMISSIBLE PAYMENTS AND AFFIRMATIVE DEFENSES

The FCPA contains an explicit exception to the bribery prohibition for "facilitating payments" for "routine governmental action" and provides affirmative defenses which can be used to defend against alleged violations of the FCPA.

FACILITATING PAYMENTS FOR ROUTINE GOVERNMENTAL ACTIONS

There is an exception to the antibribery prohibition for payments to facilitate or expedite performance of a "routine governmental action." The statute lists the following examples: obtaining permits, licenses, or other official documents; processing governmental papers, such as visas and work orders; providing police protection, mail pick-up and delivery; providing phone service, power and water supply, loading and unloading cargo, or protecting perishable products; and scheduling inspections associated with contract performance or transit of goods across country.

Actions "similar" to these are also covered by this exception. If you have a question about whether a payment falls within the exception, you should consult with counsel. You should also consider whether to utilize the Justice Department's Foreign Corrupt Practices Opinion Procedure, described below.

"Routine governmental action" does not include any decision by a foreign official to award new business or to continue business with a particular party.

AFFIRMATIVE DEFENSES

A person charged with a violation of the FCPA's antibribery provisions may assert as a defense that the payment was lawful under the written laws of the foreign country or that the money was spent as part of demonstrating a product or performing a contractual obligation.

Whether a payment was lawful under the written laws of the foreign country may be difficult to determine. You should consider seeking the advice of counsel or utilizing the Department of Justice's Foreign Corrupt Practices Act Opinion Procedure when faced with an issue of the legality of such a payment.

Moreover, because these defenses are "affirmative defenses," the defendant is required to show in the first instance that the payment met these requirements. The prosecution does not bear the burden of demonstrating in the first instance that the payments did not constitute this type of payment.

SANCTIONS AGAINST BRIBERY

CRIMINAL

The following criminal penalties may be imposed for violations of the FCPA's antibribery provisions: corporations and other business entities are subject to a fine of up to $2,000,000; officers, directors, stockholders, employees, and agents are subject to a fine of up to $100,000 and imprisonment for up to five years. Moreover, under the Alternative Fines Act, these fines may be actually quite higher—the actual fine may be up to twice the benefit that the defendant sought to obtain by making the corrupt payment. You should also be aware that fines imposed on individuals may not be paid by their employer or principal.

CIVIL

The Attorney General or the SEC, as appropriate, may bring a civil action for a fine of up to $10,000 against any firm *as well* as any officer, director, employee, or agent of a firm, or stockholder acting on behalf of the firm, who violates the antibribery provisions. In addition, in an SEC enforcement action, the court may impose an additional fine not to exceed the greater of (i) the gross amount of the pecuniary gain to the defendant as a result of the violation, or (ii) a specified dollar limitation. The specified dollar limitations are based on the egregiousness of the violation, ranging from $5,000 to $100,000 for a natural person and $50,000 to $500,000 for any other person.

The Attorney General or the SEC, as appropriate, may also bring a civil action to enjoin any act or practice of a firm whenever it appears that the firm (or an officer, director, employee, agent, or stockholder acting on behalf of the firm) is in violation (or about to be) of the antibribery provisions.

OTHER GOVERNMENTAL ACTION

Under guidelines issued by the Office of Management and Budget, a person or firm found in violation of the FCPA may be barred from doing business with the Federal government. *Indictment alone can lead to suspension of the right to do business with the government.* The President has directed that no executive agency shall allow any party to participate in any procurement or nonprocurement activity if any agency has debarred, suspended, or otherwise excluded that party from participation in a procurement or nonprocurement activity.

In addition, a person or firm found guilty of violating the FCPA may be ruled ineligible to receive export licenses; the SEC may suspend or bar persons from the securities business and impose civil penalties on persons in the securities business for violations of the FCPA; the Commodity Futures Trading Commission and the Overseas Private Investment Corporation both provide for possible suspension or debarment from agency programs for violation of the FCPA; and a payment made to a foreign government official that is unlawful under the FCPA cannot be deducted under the tax laws as a business expense.

PRIVATE CAUSE OF ACTION

Conduct that violates the antibribery provisions of the FCPA may also give rise to a private cause of action for treble damages under the Racketeer Influenced and Corrupt Organizations Act (RICO), or to actions under other federal or state laws. For example, an action might be brought under RICO by a competitor who alleges that the bribery caused the defendant to win a foreign contract.

GUIDANCE FROM THE GOVERNMENT

The Department of Justice has established a Foreign Corrupt Practices Act Opinion Procedure by which any U.S. company or national may request a statement of the Justice Department's present enforcement intentions under the antibribery provisions of the FCPA regarding any proposed business conduct. The details of the opinion procedure may be found at 28 CFR Part 80. Under this procedure, the Attorney General will issue an opinion in response to a specific inquiry from a person or firm within thirty days of the request. (The thirty-day period does not run until the Department of Justice has received all the information it requires to issue the opinion.) Conduct for which the Department of Justice has issued an opinion stating that the conduct conforms with current enforcement policy will be entitled to a presumption, in any subsequent enforcement action, of conformity with the FCPA.

Appendix **G** **Fighting Corruption and Safeguarding Integrity**

This material appeared as Appendix C of Fighting Global Corruption: Business Risk Management, *a guide published in May 2001 by the U.S. Department of State's Bureau for International Narcotics and Law Enforcement Affairs. (The full text of the booklet is available at* www.state.gov/g/inl/rls/rpt/fgcrpt/2001.)

Appendix C: Guiding Principles for Fighting Corruption and Safeguarding Integrity among Justice and Security Officials

The following Anticorruption Principles were developed and approved by the United States Government in the preparation of the First Global Forum on Fighting Corruption and Safeguarding Integrity among Justice and Security Officials, held in Washington, D.C., in February 1999. Discussion at this Conference, among the many participants from around the world, addressed most of these principles. Today they continue to serve as an effective checklist in the fight against corruption and safeguarding integrity among government officials.

NOTE: Annotated Version. In this document, each of the practices is followed by a parenthetical letter or letters indicating from which source or sources the statement of the practice was derived, including agreements, documents, and other sources in existing international literature or experience regarding corruption, public integrity, or related matters of crime. Sources including those from the UN, OECD, OAS, GCA, EU, and CoE are identified in the listing at the end of this document.

Corruption, dishonesty, and unethical behavior among public officials represent serious threats to the basic principles and values of government, undermining public confidence in democracy and threatening to erode the rule of law. The aim of these Guiding Principles is to promote public trust in the integrity of officials within the public sector by preventing, detecting, and prosecuting or sanctioning official corruption and unlawful, dishonest, or unethical behavior.

It is anticipated that these guiding principles will be implemented by each government in a manner appropriately tailored to the political, legal, economic, and cultural circumstances of the country. Due to the different functions and missions of different judicial, justice, and security officials, not all practices are applicable in all categories. This document does not prescribe a specific solution to corruption among justice and security officials, but rather offers a list of potentially effective corruption-fighting practices for consideration.

The list of practices, which may apply to other sectors of government in addition to justice and security officials, is intended to help guide and assist governments in developing effective and appropriate means to best achieve their specific public integrity ends.

1. **Establish and maintain systems of government hiring of justice and security officials that assure openness, equity, and efficiency and promote hiring of individuals of the highest levels of competence and integrity.**

    Effective practices include:

    -   Systems for equitable compensation adequate to sustain appropriate livelihood without corruption (I, K, O);
    -   Systems for open and merit based hiring and promotion with objective standards (C, I, J);
    -   Systems which provide assurance of a dignified retirement without recourse to corruption (I, K, O);
    -   Systems for thorough screening of all employees for sensitive positions (M);
    -   Systems for probationary periods after initial hiring (M);
    -   Systems which integrate principles of human rights with effective measures for preventing and detecting corruption (M).

2. **Adopt public management measures that affirmatively promote and uphold the integrity of justice and security officials.**

    Effective practices include:

    -   An impartial and specialized institution of government to administer ethical codes of conduct (C, D, I, J, K);
    -   Training and counseling of officials to ensure proper understanding of their responsibilities and the ethical rules governing their activities as well as their own professionalism and competence (C);
    -   Training addressed to issues of brutality and other civil rights violations that often correlate with corrupt activity among justice and security officials (O, substantial international literature relating to human rights issues);
    -   Managerial mechanisms that enforce ethical and administrative standards of conduct (B, D, H, I, J, K);
    -   Systems for recognizing employees who exhibit high personal integrity or contribute to the anti-corruption objectives of their institution (O);
    -   Personnel systems that include regular rotation of assignments to reduce insularity that fosters corruption (B, D, J, K, O);
    -   Systems to provide appropriate oversight of discretionary decisions and of personnel with authority to make discretionary decisions (B, D, J, K, O);

- Systems that hold supervisors accountable for corruption control (B, D, J, K, O);
- Positive leadership which actively practices and promotes the highest standards of integrity and demonstrates a commitment to prevent and detect corruption, dishonesty, and unethical behavior (I, O);
- Systems for promoting the understanding and application of ethical values and the standards of conduct required (I, O);
- Mechanisms to support officials in the public sector where there is evidence that they have been unfairly or falsely accused (O).

3. **Establish ethical and administrative codes of conduct that proscribe conflicts of interest, ensure the proper use of public resources, and promote the highest levels of professionalism and integrity.**

   Effective practices include:

   - Prohibitions or restrictions governing officials participating in official matters in which they have a substantial direct or indirect financial interest (I, J, O);
   - Prohibitions or restrictions against officials participating in matters in which persons or entities with whom they are negotiating for employment have a financial interest (I, J, O);
   - Limitations on activities of former officials in representing private or personal interests before their former governmental agency or department, such as prohibiting the involvement of such officials in cases for which former officials were personally responsible, representing private interests by their improper use of influence upon their former governmental agency or department, or using confidential knowledge or information gained during their previous employment as an official in the public sector (O);
   - Prohibitions and limitations on the receipt of gifts or other advantages (F, I, J, O);
   - Prohibitions on improper personal use of government property and resources (C, F, O).

4. **Establish criminal laws and sanctions effectively prohibiting bribery, misuse of public property, and other improper uses of public office for private gain.**

   Effective practices include:

   - Laws criminalizing the giving, offer, or promise by any party ("active") and the receipt or solicitation by any official ("passive") of a bribe, and criminalizing or sanctioning the giving or receiving of an improper gratuity or improper gift (A, C, E, F, G, J, others);
   - Laws criminalizing or sanctioning the illegal use by officials of government information (C, F);

- Laws affirming that all justice and security officials have a duty to provide honest services to the public and criminalizing or sanctioning breaches of that duty (J);

- Laws criminalizing improper use of official power or position, either to the detriment of the government or for personal enrichment.

5. **Adopt laws, management practices and auditing procedures that make corruption more visible and thereby promote the detection and reporting of corrupt activity.**

Effective practices include:

- Systems to promote transparency, such as through disclosing the financial circumstances of senior officials (C, I, J, K).

- Measures and systems to ensure that officials report acts of corruption, and to protect the safety, livelihood, and professional situation of those who do, including protection of their identities to the extent possible under the law (F, I, J);

- Measures and systems that protect private citizens who, in good faith, report acts of official corruption (C, D, E, F, I, J, M);

- Government revenue collection systems that deter corruption, in particular by denying tax deductibility for bribes or other expenses linked to corruption offenses (B, C, D, K);

- Bodies responsible for preventing, detecting, and eradicating corruption, and for punishing or disciplining corrupt officials, such as independent ombudsmen, inspectors general, or other bodies responsible for receiving and investigating allegations of corruption (B, D, I, J);

- Appropriate auditing procedures applicable to public administration and the public sector (D, I, J, K);

- Appropriately transparent procedures for public procurement that promote fair competition and deter corrupt activity (B, C, D, F, I, K);

- Systems for conducting regular threat assessments on corrupt activity (O).

6. **Provide criminal investigators and prosecutors sufficient and appropriate powers and resources to effectively uncover and prosecute corruption crimes.**

Effective practices include:

- Empowering courts or other competent authorities to order that bank, financial, or commercial records be made available or be seized, and that bank secrecy not prevent such availability or seizure (C, E, K, L, M);

- Authorizing use under accountable legal supervision of wiretaps or other interception of electronic communication, or recording devices, in investigation of corruption offenses (E, F, K, M);

- Authorizing, where appropriate, the admissibility of electronic or other recorded evidence in criminal proceedings relating to corruption offenses (E, F, K, M);

- Employing where appropriate systems whereby persons charged with corruption or other corruption-related criminal offenses may secure more advantageous treatment in recognition of assisting in the disclosure and prosecution of corruption offenses (E, F, L, M);

- The development of appropriate information gathering mechanisms to prevent, detect, and deter official corruption and dishonesty (O).

7. **Ensure that investigators, prosecutors, and judicial personnel are sufficiently impartial to fairly and effectively enforce laws against corruption.**

   Effective practices include:

   - Personnel systems to attract and retain high-quality corruption investigators (O);

   - Systems to promote the specialization and professionalization of persons and organizations in charge of fighting corruption (D, E, K);

   - Establishment of an independent mechanism within judicial and security agencies with the duty to investigate corruption allegations, and with the power to compel statements and obtain documents from all agency personnel (I, O);

   - Codes of conduct or other measures that require corruption investigators, prosecutors, and judges to recuse themselves from any case in which their political, financial, or personal interests might reasonably raise questions about their ability to be impartial (O);

   - Systems that allow for the appointment, where appropriate, of special authorities or commissions to handle or oversee corruption investigations and prosecutions (O);

   - Standards governing the initiation of corruption investigations to ensure that public officials are not targeted for investigation for political reasons (O).

8. **Ensure that criminal and civil law provide for sanctions and remedies that are sufficient to effectively and appropriately deter corrupt activity.**

   Effective practices include:

   - Laws providing substantial criminal penalties for the laundering of the proceeds of public corruption violations (A, C, E, K, M);

   - Laws providing for substantial incarceration and appropriate forfeiture of assets as a potential penalty for serious corruption offenses (A, C, E, G, others);

- Provisions to support and protect whistleblowers and aggrieved private parties (B, D, I, K).

9. **Ensure that the general public and the media have freedom to receive and impart information on corruption matters, subject only to limitations or restrictions which are necessary in a democratic society.**

   Effective practices include:

   - Establishing public reporting requirements for justice and security agencies that include disclosure about efforts to promote integrity and combat corruption (D, H, J, K);

   - Enacting laws or other measures providing a meaningful public right of access to information about corrupt activity and corruption control activities (D, H, I, J, K).

10. **Develop to the widest extent possible international cooperation in all areas of the fight against corruption.**

    Effective practices include:

    - Systems for swift and effective extradition so that corrupt public officials can face judicial process (A, C, E, G, I, M, others);

    - Systems to enhance international legal assistance to governments seeking to investigate and prosecute corruption violations (A, C, E, G, I, M, others);

    - Systems to facilitate and accelerate international seizure and repatriation of forfeitable assets associated with corruption violations (A, C, E, F, G, I, M, others);

    - Inclusion of provisions on combating corruption in appropriate bilateral and multilateral instruments (I, O).

11. **Promote, encourage, and support continued research and public discussion in all aspects of the issue of upholding integrity and preventing corruption among justice and security officials and other public officials whose responsibilities relate to upholding the rule of law.**

    Effective practices include:

    - Appointment of independent commissions or other bodies to study and report on the effectiveness of efforts to combat corruption in particular agencies involved in justice and security matters (O);

    - Supporting the efforts of multilateral and non-governmental organizations to promote public integrity and prevent corruption (O);

    - Promoting efforts to educate the public about the dangers of corruption and the importance of general public involvement in government efforts to control corrupt activity (C, I, J, K, O).

12. **Encourage activities of regional and other multilateral organizations in anti-corruption efforts.**

Effective practices include:

- Becoming parties, as appropriate, to applicable multilateral legal instruments containing provisions to address corruption (I);

- Cooperating in carrying out programs of systematic follow-up to monitor and promote the full implementation of appropriate measures to combat corruption, through mutual assessment by governments of their legal and practical measures to combat corruption, as established by pertinent international agreements (A, E, L, I, O);

- Participating actively in future international conferences on promoting integrity and combating corruption among justice and security officials.

LISTING OF SOURCES FOR GUIDING PRINCIPLES

A. OECD Convention on Combating Bribery of Foreign Public Officials in International Business Transactions.

B. OECD Council Recommendations against Corruption, May 1997.

C. OAS Inter-American Convention against Corruption.

D. Council of Europe Committee of Ministers 20 Recommendations against Corruption, November 1997.

E. Council of Europe Criminal Law Convention on Corruption.

F. Council of Europe Conclusions of the Second European Conference of Specialized Services in the Fight against Corruption, October 1997.

G. European Union Convention on Corruption of EU or Member Officials, May 1997.

H. European Parliament Resolution on Combating Corruption in Europe, 1995.

I. Global Coalition for Africa, Principles to Combat Corruption in African Countries, February 1999.

J. United Nations Secretariat Manual: Practical Measures against Corruption, July 1990.

K. United Nations Commission on Crime Prevention and Criminal Justice: Report of Expert Group on Action against Corruption and Bribery, March 1997.

L. United Nations Convention against Illicit Trafficking in Narcotic Drugs or Psychotropic Substances.

M. United Nations Convention against Transnational Organized Crime, 2000.

N. Financial Action Task Force, 40 Recommendations.

O. Observed experience of governments ("common sense").

EXTRACTS FROM THE U.S. FEDERAL SENTENCING GUIDELINES FOR ORGANIZATIONS

These sentencing guidelines for organizational defendants were published as Chapter 8, "Sentencing of Organizations," in United States Sentencing Commission, Guidelines Manual *(Washington, D.C.: U.S. Sentencing Commission, November 2002). The full text of the manual can be found at* www.ussc.gov/2002guid/TABCON02.htm.

Chapter 8: Sentencing of Organizations

INTRODUCTORY COMMENTARY

The guidelines and policy statements in this chapter apply when the convicted defendant is an organization. Organizations can act only through agents and, under federal criminal law, generally are vicariously liable for offenses committed by their agents. At the same time, individual agents are responsible for their own criminal conduct. Federal prosecutions of organizations therefore frequently involve individual and organizational co-defendants. Convicted individual agents of organizations are sentenced in accordance with the guidelines and policy statements in the preceding chapters. This chapter is designed so that the sanctions imposed upon organizations and their agents, taken together, will provide just punishment, adequate deterrence, and incentives for organizations to maintain internal mechanisms for preventing, detecting, and reporting criminal conduct.

This chapter reflects the following general principles: First, the court must, whenever practicable, order the organization to remedy any harm caused by the offense. The resources expended to remedy the harm should not be viewed as punishment, but rather as a means of making victims whole for the harm caused. Second, if the organization operated primarily for a criminal purpose or primarily by criminal means, the fine should be set sufficiently high to divest the organization of all its assets. Third, the fine range for any other organization should be based on the seriousness of the offense and the culpability of the organization. The seriousness of the offense generally will be reflected by the highest of the pecuniary gain, the pecuniary loss, or the amount in a guideline offense level fine table. Culpability generally will be determined by the steps taken by the organization prior to the offense to prevent and detect criminal conduct, the level and extent of involvement in or tolerance of the offense by certain personnel, and the organization's actions after an offense has been committed. Fourth, probation is an appropriate sentence for an organizational defendant when needed to ensure that another sanction will be fully implemented, or to ensure that steps will be taken within the organization to reduce the likelihood of future criminal conduct.

SECTION 8A1.2 APPLICATION INSTRUCTIONS—ORGANIZATIONS

COMMENTARY

Application Notes:

3. The following are definitions of terms used frequently in this chapter:

. . .

(b) "High-level personnel of the organization" means individuals who have substantial control over the organization or who have a substantial role in the making of policy within the organization. The term includes: a director; an executive officer; an individual in charge of a major business or functional unit of the organization, such as sales, administration, or finance; and an individual with a substantial ownership interest.

(c) "Substantial authority personnel" means individuals who within the scope of their authority exercise a substantial measure of discretion in acting on behalf of an organization. The term includes high-level personnel, individuals who exercise substantial supervisory authority (e.g., a plant manager, a sales manager), and any other individuals who, although not a part of an organization's management, nevertheless exercise substantial discretion when acting within the scope of their authority (e.g., an individual with authority in an organization to negotiate or set price levels or an individual authorized to negotiate or approve significant contracts). Whether an individual falls within this category must be determined on a case-by-case basis.

(d) "Agent" means any individual, including a director, an officer, an employee, or an independent contractor, authorized to act on behalf of the organization.

(e) An individual "condoned" an offense if the individual knew of the offense and did not take reasonable steps to prevent or terminate the offense.

(f) "Similar misconduct" means prior conduct that is similar in nature to the conduct underlying the instant offense, without regard to whether or not such conduct violated the same statutory provision. For example, prior Medicare fraud would be misconduct similar to an instant offense involving another type of fraud.

. . .

(k) An "effective program to prevent and detect violations of law" means a program that has been reasonably designed, implemented, and enforced so that it generally will be effective in preventing and detecting criminal conduct. Failure to prevent or detect the instant offense, by itself, does not mean that the program was not effective. The hallmark of an effective program to prevent and detect violations of law is that the organization exercised due diligence in seeking to prevent and detect criminal conduct by its employees and other agents. Due diligence requires at a minimum that the organization must have taken the following types of steps:

(1) The organization must have established compliance standards and procedures to be followed by its employees and other agents that are reasonably capable of reducing the prospect of criminal conduct.

(2) Specific individual(s) within high-level personnel of the organization must have been assigned overall responsibility to oversee compliance with such standards and procedures.

(3) The organization must have used due care not to delegate substantial discretionary authority to individuals whom the organization knew, or should have known through the exercise of due diligence, had a propensity to engage in illegal activities.

(4) The organization must have taken steps to communicate effectively its standards and procedures to all employees and other agents, e.g., by requiring participation in training programs or by disseminating publications that explain in a practical manner what is required.

(5) The organization must have taken reasonable steps to achieve compliance with its standards, e.g., by utilizing monitoring and auditing systems reasonably designed to detect criminal conduct by its employees and other agents and by having in place and publicizing a reporting system whereby employees and other agents could report criminal conduct by others within the organization without fear of retribution.

(6) The standards must have been consistently enforced through appropriate disciplinary mechanisms, including, as appropriate, discipline of individuals responsible for the failure to detect an offense. Adequate discipline of individuals responsible for an offense is a necessary component of enforcement; however, the form of discipline that will be appropriate will be case specific.

(7) After an offense has been detected, the organization must have taken all reasonable steps to respond appropriately to the offense and to prevent further similar offenses—including any necessary modifications to its program to prevent and detect violations of law.

The precise actions necessary for an effective program to prevent and detect violations of law will depend upon a number of factors. Among the relevant factors are:

(i) **Size of the organization**—The requisite degree of formality of a program to prevent and detect violations of law will vary with the size of the organization: the larger the organization, the more formal the program typically should be. A larger organization generally should have established written policies defining the standards and procedures to be followed by its employees and other agents.

(ii) **Likelihood that certain offenses may occur because of the nature of its business**—If because of the nature of an organization's business there is a substantial risk that certain types of offenses may occur, management must have taken steps to prevent and detect those types of offenses. For example, if an organization handles toxic substances, it must have established standards and procedures designed to ensure that those substances are properly handled at all times. If an organization employs sales personnel who have flexibility in setting prices, it must have established standards and procedures designed to prevent and detect price-fixing. If an organization employs sales personnel who have flexibility to represent the material characteristics of a product, it must have established standards and procedures designed to prevent fraud.

(iii) **Prior history of the organization**—An organization's prior history may indicate types of offenses that it should have taken actions to prevent. Recurrence of misconduct similar to that which an organization has previously committed casts doubt on whether it took all reasonable steps to prevent such misconduct.

An organization's failure to incorporate and follow applicable industry practice or the standards called for by any applicable governmental regulation weighs against a finding of an effective program to prevent and detect violations of law.

SECTION 8C2.5 CULPABILITY SCORE

(a) Start with 5 points and apply subsections (b) through (g) below.

(b) Involvement in or Tolerance of Criminal Activity

If more than one applies, use the greatest:

(1) If —

(A) the organization had 5,000 or more employees and

(i) an individual within high-level personnel of the organization participated in, condoned, or was willfully ignorant of the offense; or

(ii) tolerance of the offense by substantial authority personnel was pervasive throughout the organization; or

(B) the unit of the organization within which the offense was committed had 5,000 or more employees and

(i) an individual within high-level personnel of the unit participated in, condoned, or was willfully ignorant of the offense; or

(ii) tolerance of the offense by substantial authority personnel was pervasive throughout such unit, add 5 points; or

. . .

(f) Effective Program to Prevent and Detect Violations of Law

If the offense occurred despite an effective program to prevent and detect violations of law, subtract 3 points.

Provided, that this subsection does not apply if an individual within high-level personnel of the organization, a person within high-level personnel of the unit of the organization within which the offense was committed where the unit had 200 or more employees, or an individual responsible for the administration or enforcement of a program to prevent and detect violations of law participated in, condoned, or was willfully ignorant of the offense. Participation of an individual within substantial authority personnel in an offense results in a rebuttable presumption that the organization did not have an effective program to prevent and detect violations of law.

Provided, further, that this subsection does not apply if, after becoming aware of an offense, the organization unreasonably delayed reporting the offense to appropriate governmental authorities.

EXTRACTS FROM THE AUSTRALIAN CRIMINAL CODE

Reproduced here are sections of the Australian Criminal Code relating to corporate criminal responsibility. The full text, prepared by the Office of Legislative Drafting, Attorney-General's Department, Canberra, is available at www.ausimm.com/ohs/ crimcode.pdf.

Part 2.5 Corporate criminal responsibility: Division 12

12.1 GENERAL PRINCIPLES

(1) This Code applies to bodies corporate in the same way as it applies to individuals. It so applies with such modifications as are set forth in this Part, and with such other modifications as are made necessary by the fact that criminal liability is being imposed on bodies corporate rather than individuals.

(2) A body corporate may be found guilty of any offence, including one punishable by imprisonment.

12.2 PHYSICAL ELEMENTS

If a physical element of an offence is committed by an employee, agent, or officer of a body corporate acting within the actual or apparent scope of his or her employment, or within his or her actual or apparent authority, the physical element must also be attributed to the body corporate.

12.3 FAULT ELEMENTS OTHER THAN NEGLIGENCE

(1) If intention, knowledge or recklessness is a fault element in relation to a physical element of an offence, that fault element must be attributed to a body corporate that expressly, tacitly, or impliedly authorised or permitted the commission of the offence.

(2) The means by which such authorisation or permission may be established include:

(a) proving that the body corporate's board of directors intentionally, knowingly, or recklessly carried out the relevant conduct, or expressly, tacitly, or impliedly authorised or permitted the commission of the offence; or

(b) proving that a high managerial agent of the body corporate intentionally, knowingly, or recklessly engaged in the relevant conduct, or expressly, tacitly, or impliedly authorised or permitted the commission of the offence; or

(c) proving that a corporate culture existed within the body corporate that directed, encouraged, tolerated, or led to non-compliance with the relevant provision; or

(d) proving that the body corporate failed to create and maintain a corporate culture that required compliance with the relevant provision.

(3) Paragraph (2)(b) does not apply if the body corporate proves that it exercised due diligence to prevent the conduct, or the authorisation or permission.

(4) Factors relevant to the application of paragraph (2)(c) or (d) include:

(a) whether authority to commit an offence of the same or a similar character had been given by a high managerial agent of the body corporate; and

(b) whether the employee, agent, or officer of the body corporate who committed the offence believed on reasonable grounds, or entertained a reasonable expectation, that a high managerial agent of the body corporate would have authorised or permitted the commission of the act.

(5) If recklessness is not a fault element in relation to a physical element of an offence, subsection (2) does not enable the fault element to be proved by proving that the board of directors, or a high managerial agent, of the body corporate recklessly engaged in the conduct or recklessly authorised or permitted the commission of the offence.

(6) In this section:

board of directors means the body (by whatever named called) exercising the executive authority of the body corporate.

corporate culture means an attitude, policy, rule, course of conduct, or practice existing within the body corporate generally or in the part of the body corporate in which the relevant activities takes [sic] place.

high managerial agent means an employee, agent, or officer of the body corporate with duties of such responsibility that his or her conduct may fairly be assumed to represent the body corporate's policy.

12.4 NEGLIGENCE

(1) The test of negligence for a body corporate is that set out in section 5.5.

(2) If:

(a) negligence is a fault element in relation to a physical element of an offence, and

(b) no individual employee, agent, or officer of the body politic has that fault element;

that fault element may exist on the part of the body corporate if the body corporate's conduct is negligent when viewed as a whole (that is, by aggregating the conduct of any number of its employees, agents, or officers).

(3) Negligence may be evidenced by the fact that the prohibited conduct was substantially attributable to:

(a) inadequate corporate management, control, or supervision of the conduct of one or more of its employees, agents, or officers; or

(b) failure to provide adequate systems for conveying relevant information to relevant persons in the body corporate.

12.5 MISTAKE OF FACT (STRICT LIABILITY)

(1) A body corporate can only rely on section 9.2 (mistake of fact [strict liability] in respect of conduct that would, apart from this section, constitute an offence on its part if:

(a) the employee, agent, or officer of the body corporate who carried out the conduct was under a mistaken but reasonable belief about facts that, had they existed, would have meant that the conduct would not have constituted an offence; and

(b) the body corporate proves that it exercised due diligence to prevent the conduct.

(2) A failure to exercise due diligence may be evidenced by the fact that the prohibited conduct was substantially attributable to:

(a) inadequate corporate management, control, or supervision of the conduct of one or more of its employees, agents, or officers; or

(b) failure to provide adequate systems for conveying relevant information to relevant persons in the body corporate.

12.6 INTERVENING CONDUCT OR EVENT

A body corporate cannot rely on section 10.1 (intervening conduct or event) in respect of the physical element of an offence brought about by another person if the other person is an employee, agent, or officer of the body corporate.

NOTES

CHAPTER 1 NOTES

[1] Peter F. Drucker, "The Delusion of 'Profits': A Company That Loses Money Is Socially Irresponsible," *OpinionJournal* (June 2, 2003), available at <http://www.opinionjournal.com/extra/?id=110003570>, accessed June 2, 2003.

[2] See, for example, Richard R. Ellsworth, *Leading with Purpose: The New Corporate Realities* (Stanford, Calif.: Stanford University Press, 2002), and James C. Collins and Jerry I. Porras, *Built to Last: Successful Habits of Visionary Companies* (New York: HarperBusiness, 2002).

[3] Ellsworth, *Leading with Purpose*, p. 122.

[4] The four levels of identity are developed in more detail in Chapter 3.

[5] See, for example, SustainAbility, *Developing Value*, available at <http://www.sustainability.com/developing-value/contents.asp>, accessed June 4, 2003.

[6] Maria Livanos Cattaui, "Responsible Business Conduct in a Global Economy," available at <http://www.iccwbo.org/home/global_compact/business_conduct.asp>, accessed May 23, 2003.

[7] See, for example, Muhammad Musleh-Ud-Din, *Economics and Islam*, 2nd ed. (Lahore, Pakistan: Islamic Publications, 1980).

[8] See, for example, Bodo B. Schlegelmilch and Diana G. Robertson, "The Influence of Country and Industry on Ethical Perceptions of Senior Executives in the U.S. and Europe," *Journal of International Business Studies* 26, no. 4 (1995), available at <http://www.questia.com>, accessed June 7, 2003.

[9] For a discussion of *riba*, "excess over the principal," and *mudaraba*, a type of agency relationship, see Musleh-Ud-Din, *Economics and Islam*, pp. 66–69.

[10] Cattaui, "Responsible Business Conduct."

[11] There are many definitions of the SME, especially the small enterprise. The World Bank definition of a *small enterprise* is fewer than 300 employees, whereas the U.S. Small Business Administration sets the limit at 500 employees. Uzbekistan, on the other hand, defines the *microfirm* (up to 10 employees in manufacturing and 5 in others); the *small enterprise* (not exceeding 40 in industry or 20 in construction, agriculture, and other manufacturing and not exceeding 10 in all others); and the *medium enterprise* (fewer than 100 in industry and fewer for other sectors). See International Finance Corporation, *Business Environment in Uzbekistan* (Washington, D.C.: International Finance Corporation, 2002), p. 15, available at <http://www1.ifc.org/pep/files/pdf/Uzbek_SME_ survey_eng.pdf> , accessed May 23, 2003.

[12] See, for example, Judith Kenner Thompson and Howard L. Smith, "Social Responsibility and Small Business: Suggestions for Research," *Journal of Small Business Management* 29, no. 1 (1991), available at <http://www.questia.com>, accessed June 6, 2003.

[13] Ibid., p. 23.

[14] Hubbards Foods Ltd., "CEO's Statement," Triple Bottom Line Report: Financial Web page, available at <http://www.hubbards.co.nz/triple_bottom_line/triple_financial.html>, accessed July 9, 2003.

[15] See Saul Estrin, "Competition and Corporate Governance in Transition," William Davidson Institute Working Paper Series 431 (William Davidson Institute, 2001), available at <http://eres.bus.umich.edu/docs/workpap-dav/wp431.pdf>, accessed May 23, 2003.

[16] The legacy of central planning was not identical in each country. It depended on (a) the extent and effectiveness of planning, (b) the openness of markets, and (c) the institutions and legal traditions. See Estrin, "Competition and Corporate Governance in Transition," pp. 5–7.

[17] Mark K. Dietrich, *Legal and Judicial Reform in Central Europe and the Former Soviet Union: Voices from Five Countries* (Washington, D.C.: World Bank, 2000), available at <http://www4.worldbank.org/legal/publications/LJR_ECA.pdf>, accessed May 23, 2003.

[18] Steven J. Norton and Lynda L. Maillet, "Mistakes Were Made: The 'Tabula Rasa Syndrome' and Russian Reform," reprint from *East–West Letter* 7 (September 1998), available at <http://www.okno.com/ewltr/archive/vol7/ru-trsyn.pdf>, accessed May 23, 2003.

[19] See, for example, Estrin, "Competition and Corporate Governance in Transition," Table 3: Cost of Entry.

[20] Ibid., p. 19. According to a survey cited by the author, latent entrepreneurship is highest in Poland (80 percent) compared with the United States (70.8 percent), Germany (64 percent), the United Kingdom (45 percent), the Czech Republic (36.8 percent), Russia (33.2 percent), and Norway (26.9 percent).

[21] Ellsworth, *Leading with Purpose*, p. 110.

[22] World Bank, *Anticorruption in Transition: A Contribution to the Policy Debate* (Washington, D.C.: World Bank, 2000), pp. xv–xvi, and Joel Hellman and Daniel Kaufmann, "Confronting the Challenge of State Capture in Transition Economies," *Finance & Development* (September 2001), p. 31.

[23] Dietrich, *Legal and Judicial Reform*, p. 18.

[24] See, for example, ibid.

[25] Ibid., p. 21.

[26] U.S. Department of Commerce, *Handbook on Commercial Dispute Resolution in the Russian Federation* (Washington, D.C.: U.S. Department of Commerce, 2000), p. 1.

[27] See, for example, Estrin, "Competition and Corporate Governance in Transition," p. 4.

[28] World Bank, *Anticorruption in Transition*, p. xvii.

[29] Ibid., p. 9.

[30] Ludwig von Mises, *Human Action: A Treatise on Economics*, 3rd rev. ed. (Chicago: Contemporary Books, 1963), pp. 257–59.

[31] Arthur Seldon, *Capitalism* (London: Basil Blackwell, 1990), p. 107.

[32] See discussion in Estrin, "Competition and Corporate Governance in Transition," pp. 16–17; Michael Camdessus, "Challenges Facing the Transition Economies of Central Asia," available at <http://www.imf.org/external/np/speeches/1998/052798.htm>, accessed May 23, 2003; and Carana Corporation, *The Environment for Business in Tajikistan—A Disincentive to Private Sector Growth and Investment* (Arlington, Va., March 2001).

[33] World Bank, *Anticorruption in Transition*, p. 25.

[34] See also Ellsworth, *Leading with Purpose*, pp. 30–34.

[35] Estrin, "Competition and Corporate Governance in Transition," p. 1.

[36] Stanley Kober, "The Purpose of NGOs," available at <http://www.civnet.org/journal/issue6/ftskober.htm>, accessed May 23, 2003.

[37] F. Neil Brady, *Ethical Managing: Rules and Results* (New York and London: Macmillan, 1990), pp. 2–3.

CHAPTER 2 NOTES

[1] There are too many variables in business for researchers to find conclusively that being a responsible business, as we have defined it, leads an enterprise to become more profitable. However, Paine has made a comprehensive survey of studies exploring various aspects of business ethics and business performance. See Lynn Sharp Paine, *Value Shift: Why Companies Must Merge Social and Financial Imperatives to Achieve Superior Performance* (New York: McGraw-Hill, 2003), Chapters 2 and 3.

[2] See, for example, Anita Roddick, "A Third Way for Business, Too," *New Statesman* (April 3, 1998), available at <http://www.questia.com>, accessed June 6, 2003.

[3] Paine, *Value Shift*, p. 8, citing Association of Certified Fraud Examiners, "Report to the Nation on Occupational Fraud and Abuse 1996," available at <http://www.cfenet.com/media/2002RttN>, accessed May 23, 2003. See also Joseph T. Wells, "Protect Small Business: Small Companies without Adequate Internal Controls Need CPAs to Help Them Minimize Fraud Risk," *Journal of Accountancy* 195, no. 3 (2003), available at <http://www.questia.com>, accessed June 2003.

[4] Paine, *Value Shift*, p. 36. Paine also notes the activity of customers as recorded by the Millennium Poll. See pp. 110–11.

[5] Gap Inc., "Our Vendor Code of Conduct," available at <http://www.gapinc.com/social_resp/sourcing/vendor_code.htm>, accessed May 23, 2003.

[6] Linda K. Treviño, et al., "Managing Ethics and Legal Compliance: What Works and What Hurts," *California Management Review* 41 (Winter 1999): 131–51, at pp. 142–43.

[7] Joshua Joseph, *National Business Ethics Survey 2000* (Washington, D.C.: Ethics Resource Center, 2000), pp. 42–44.

[8] These levels of social identity are adapted from Kenneth W. Johnson, "Ethical Complexity or Ethical Chaos? A Prescription for Integrating Applied Ethics," *Ethical Management* 7 (August 1997): 1, 3–4. Available at <http://www.Ethics-Policy.net/Integrating_Applied_Ethics.html>, accessed May 23, 2003.

[9] Susan A. Aaronson and James T. Reeves, *Corporate Responsibility in the Global Village: The Role of Public Policy* (Washington, D.C.: National Policy Association, 2002), p. 2.

[10] Komatsu Ltd., "Komatsu Code of Worldwide Business Conduct," available at <http://www.komatsu.co.jp/en/CompanyInfo/profile/conduct>, accessed May 23, 2003.

[11] See, for example, Muhammad Musleh-Ud-Din, *Economics and Islam*, 2nd ed. (Lahore, Pakistan: Islamic Publications, 1980), pp. 77–79.

[12] Stephen S. Cohen and Gary Fields, "Social Capital and Capital Gains in Silicon Valley," *California Management Review* 41 (Winter 1999): 108–130.

[13] Sociologist James Coleman as quoted in Francis Fukuyama, *Trust: The Social Virtues and the Creation of Prosperity* (New York: Free Press, 1995), p. 10. See also Robert D. Putnam, "The Prosperous Community: Social Capital and Public Life," *American Prospect* 13 (Spring 1993): 37–38.

[14] Fukuyama, *Trust*, p. 31.

[15] Paine, *Value Shift*, pp. 42–43.

[16] Ludwig von Mises, *Human Action: A Treatise on Economics*, 3rd rev. ed. (Chicago: Contemporary Books, 1963), p. 165; Paine, *Value Shift*, p. 79 ("a trusting community is a thief's paradise").

[17] *Enterprise*, as used in this guide, means both a legal entity (such as an enterprise, company, firm, or organization) and an individual or small entrepreneur.

[18] Caux Round Table, *Principles for Business*, available at <http://www.caux.org>, accessed May 23, 2003.

[19] International Chamber of Commerce, Web site available at <http://www.iccwbo.org>, accessed May 23, 2003.

[20] Coalition for Environmentally Responsible Economies, "CERES Principles," available at <http://www.ceres.org>, accessed May 23, 2003.

[21] International Electrical and Electronic Engineers, "Code of Ethics," available at <http://www.ieee.org/portal/index.jsp?pageID=corp_level1&path=about/whatis&file=code.xml&xsl=generic.xsl>, accessed May 23, 2003.

[22] International Electrical and Electronic Engineers, "Software Engineering Code of Ethics and Professional Practice," available at <http://computer.org/certification/ethics.htm>, accessed May 23, 2003.

[23] *An Interfaith Declaration: A Code of Ethics on International Business for Christians, Muslims, and Jews*, available at <http://astro.ocis.temple.edu/~dialogue/Codes/cmj_codes.htm>, accessed May 23, 2003.

[24] Task Force on Churches and Corporate Responsibility, "Principles for Global Corporate Responsibility: Benchmarks for Measuring Business Performance," available at <http://www.web.net/~tccr/benchmarks/index.html>, accessed June 7, 2003.

[25] Global Reporting Initiative, *Sustainability Reporting Guidelines*, available at <http://www.globalreporting.org>, accessed May 23, 2003.

[26] Social Accountability International, Web site available at <http://www.cepaa.org>, accessed May 23, 2003.

[27] "Global Sullivan Principles," available at <http://www.globalsullivanprinciples.org/>, accessed May 23, 2003.

[28] International Corporate Governance Network, Web site available at <http://www.icgn.org/>, accessed May 23, 2003.

[29] Institute of Directors in Southern Africa, Web site available at <http://www.iodsa.co.za>, accessed May 23, 2003.

[30] Institute of Social and Ethical AccountAbility, Web site available at <http://www.AccountAbility.org.uk>, accessed May 23, 2003.

[31] International Labor Organization, Web site available at <http://www.ilo.org/>, accessed May 23, 2003.

[32] For more detail, see Kathryn Gordon, *The OECD Guidelines and Other Corporate Responsibility Instruments: A Comparison*, available at <http://www.oecd.org>, accessed May 23, 2003, and David Grayson and Adrian Hodges, *Everybody's Business: Management Risks and Opportunities in Today's Global Society* (London and New York: DK Publishing, 2002), p. 294. A table of global corporate responsibility standards maintained by the Ethics & Policy Integration Centre for the Ethics Officer Association is updated periodically and available at <http://www.Ethics-Policy.net/global/index.html/>.

[33] Table 2.2 is provided courtesy of Kenneth W. Johnson. For more information and similar table, see <http://www.Ethics-Policy.net/SGO_questions.html>, accessed May 23, 2003.

CHAPTER 3 NOTES

[1] There appears to be a significant cultural component to setting business goals and objectives as well as to making ethical decisions. See, for example, Geert Hofstede and others, "What Goals Do Business Leaders Pursue? A Study in Fifteen Countries," *Journal of International Business Studies* 33, no. 4 (2002), available at <http://www.questia.com>, accessed June 6, 2003.

[2] See, for example, Judith Kenner Thompson and Howard L. Smith, "Social Responsibility and Small Business: Suggestions for Research," *Journal of Small Business Management* 29, no. 1 (1991), available at <http://www.questia.com>, accessed June 6, 2003. Thompson and Smith examined the relatively little research into SME social responsibility.

[3] The RBE Worksheets are provided courtesy of Kenneth W. Johnson, Ethics & Policy Integration Centre.

[4] Linda K. Treviño, et al., "Managing Ethics and Legal Compliance: What Works and What Hurts," *California Management Review* 41 (Winter 1999): 131–51 at p. 131.

[5] Ibid., pp. 141 (consistency) and 143–44 (reward systems).

[6] Ibid., p. 139.

[7] See, for example, Diana E. Murphy, "The Federal Sentencing Guidelines for Organizations: A Decade of Promoting Compliance and Ethics," 87 *Iowa Law Review* 697 (2002), available at <http://www.ussc.gov/corp/Murphy1.pdf>, accessed May 23, 2003.

[8] Treviño, et al., "Managing Ethics and Legal Compliance," pp. 135–38.

[9] Ibid., p. 139.

[10] The U.S. Department of Justice specifically considers whether a corporation has a corporate compliance program. In a memorandum dated Jan. 20, 2003, the department directs its prosecutors to ask two questions: (a) "Is the corporation's compliance program well designed?" and (b) "Does the corporation's compliance program work?" Although the department has no formal guidelines for corporate compliance, it specifically refers to the "Guideline for Sentencing Organizations" of the United States Federal Sentencing Guidelines, *Guidelines Manual*, §8A1.2, Commentary (n.3[k]) (November 1997). See also United States Sentencing Commission §8C2.5(f).

[11] Lori Tansey, "Corporate Compliance Programs: International Implications," *Corporate Conduct Quarterly* 4, no. 2 (1995). Cited in Dove Izraeli and Mark S. Schwartz, "What Can We Learn from the U.S. Federal Sentencing Guidelines for Organizational Ethics," available at <http://www.itci-lo.it/English/acttrav/telearn/global/ilo/code/whatcan.htm>, accessed May 23, 2003.

[12]　See, for example, Murphy, "The Federal Sentencing Guidelines for Organizations."

[13]　The enterprise must also voluntarily disclose any violations to the appropriate agency. Cooperation is encouraged, but not required. The FSGO have other, more specific requirements, but these have come to define what it means to have an effective program.

[14]　Australia Criminal Code (Criminal Code Bill 1994, Part 2.5, Division 12, Section 12.3[2] [c and d]). Australia has also established the AS 3086 Compliance Standard.

[15]　Dawn-Marie Driscoll and W. Michael Hoffman, *Ethics Matter: How to Implement Values-Driven Management* (Waltham, Mass.: Center for Business Ethics, 2000).

[16]　Linda K. Treviño and Katherine A. Nelson, *Managing Business Ethics: Straight Talk about How to Do It*, 2nd ed. (New York: John Wiley & Sons, 1999), pp. 33–35, 144–45.

[17]　See, for example, five recent works: Lynn Sharp Paine, *Value Shift: Why Companies Must Merge Social and Financial Imperatives to Achieve Superior Performance* (New York: McGraw-Hill, 2003); Sandra Waddock, *Leading Corporate Citizens: Vision, Values, Value Added* (Boston: McGraw-Hill, 2002); Simon Zadek, *The Civil Corporation: The New Economy of Corporate Citizenship* (London and Sterling, Va.: Earthscan, 2001); David Grayson and Adrian Hodges, *Everybody's Business: Management Risks and Opportunities in Today's Global Society* (London and New York: DK Publishing, 2002); and Malcolm McIntosh, et al., *Corporate Citizenship: Successful Strategies for Responsible Companies* (London: Financial Times Management, 1998).

[18]　John Carver with Caroline Oliver, *Corporate Boards That Create Value: Governing Company Performance from the Boardroom* (San Francisco: Jossey-Bass, 2002), pp. xxi–xxii.

[19]　Frances Hesselbein, "When the Roll Is Called in 2010," in *On Creativity, Innovation, and Renewal*, edited by Frances Hesselbein and Rob Johnson (San Francisco: Jossey-Bass, 2002), p. 2; James C. Collins and Jerry I. Porras, *Built to Last: Successful Habits of Visionary Companies* (New York: HarperBusiness, 2002); and James C. Collins, *Good to Great: Why Some Companies Make the Leap . . . and Others Don't* (New York: HarperBusiness, 2001).

[20]　David L. Bradford and Allan R. Cohen, *Power Up: Transforming Organizations through Shared Leadership* (New York: John Wiley & Sons, 1998), quoted in Janet Zich, "Ideas: We're All in This Together," available at <http://www.gsb.stanford.edu/community/bmag/sbsm9809/ideas.html>, accessed May 23, 2003.

[21]　Archie B. Carroll and Ann K. Buchholtz, *Business & Society: Ethics and Stakeholder Management*, 4th ed. (Cincinnati, Ohio: South-Western, 2000).

[22]　Robert C. Solomon, *A Better Way to Think About Business: How Personal Integrity Leads to Corporate Success* (New York and Oxford, England: Oxford University Press, 1999), p. 46. See also R. Edward Freeman, *Strategic Management: A Stakeholder Approach* (New York: Basic Books, 1984), and Brian K. Burton and Craig P. Dunn, "Feminist Ethics as Moral Grounding for Stakeholder Theory," *Business Ethics Quarterly* (April 1996): 133–47.

[23]　This approach to business ethics program design and implementation is an application of three of the better works in the field: David A. Nadler, *Champions of Change: How CEOs and Their Companies Are Mastering the Skills of Radical Change* (San Francisco: Jossey-Bass, 1998). Nadler's work is a very good guide to the theory of organizational change from a systems perspective. Tony Grundy, *Implementing Strategic Change* (London: KoganPage, 1993), which is a very good practical guide to organizational change. And, Robert W. Jacobs, *Real Time Strategic Change: How to Involve an Entire Organization in Fast and Far-Reaching Change* (San Francisco: Berrett-Koehler, 1994) suggests a process for involving an entire organization in strategic change.

CHAPTER 4 NOTES

[1] Joshua Joseph, "Integrating Business Ethics Programs: A Study of Ethics Officers in Leading Organizations," *Business and Society Review* (Fall 2002): 309–47, at p. 310.

[2] Ibid., pp. 310–11.

[3] Geert Hofstede, *Cultures and Organizations: Intercultural Cooperation and Its Importance for Survival* (New York: McGraw-Hill, 1997), p. 3.

[4] Kenneth W. Johnson, "The Role of Culture in Achieving Organizational Integrity, and Managing Conflicts between Cultures," available at <http://www.Ethics-Policy.net/quest_5.html>, accessed May 27, 2003.

[5] This list is based on the experience of the principal author. Certain of the items are more fully discussed in Linda K. Treviño, et al., "Managing Ethics and Legal Compliance: What Works and What Hurts," *California Management Review* 41 (Winter 1999): 131–51, at pp. 141–51; and Joshua Joseph, *National Business Ethics Survey 2003* (Washington, D.C.: Ethics Resource Center, 2003).

[6] These program outcomes are based on the experience of the principal author and are an adaptation and extension of those used in Treviño, et al., "Managing Ethics and Legal Compliance," and Joseph, *National Business Ethics Survey 2003.*

[7] Joseph, *National Business Ethics Survey 2003*, pp. 27–28.

[8] A plan of action and milestones integrates these into specific steps and includes the *when* element.

[9] This discussion of program logic models is adapted from University of Missouri Extension and Outreach, "Program Planning and Development—Program Logic Model," available at <http://outreach.missouri.edu/staff/programdev/plm>, accessed May 23, 2003.

[10] Bong-Ahn Yoo, "Korea's Police Anti-Corruption Plan," in *Progress in the Fight against Corruption in Asia and the Pacific* (Manila: Asian Development Bank, 2001), pp. 93–96.

[11] See, for example, Chris Robertson and Paul A. Fadil, "Developing Corporate Codes of Ethics in Multinational Firms: Bhopal Revisited," *Journal of Managerial Issues* 10, no. 4 (1998): 454, available at <http://www.questia.com>, accessed June 6, 2003.

[12] See, for example, Miroslav Prokopijević, editor, *Two Years of Reform in Serbia: A Wasted Opportunity* (Belgrade: Free Market Center Team, 2002), p. 8, available at <http://www.fmc.org.yu/studies/en/atlas-eng.pdf>, accessed May 23, 2003.

[13] Zygmunt J. B. Plater, Robert H. Abrams, and William Goldfarb, *Environmental Law and Policy: Nature, Law, and Society* (St. Paul, Minn.: West Publishing, 1992).

[14] Hofstede, *Cultures and Organizations*, pp. 13–14, 164–65. See also Christopher J. Robertson and James J. Hoffman, "How Different Are We? An Investigation of Confucian Values in the United States," *Journal of Managerial Issues* 12, no. 1 (2000): 34, available at <http://www.questia.com>, accessed June 7, 2003.

[15] See, for example, Richard D. Lewis, *When Cultures Collide: Managing Successfully across Cultures* (London: Nicholas Brealy, 1996).

[16] This table is updated periodically and is available at <http://www.Ethics-Policy.net/SGO_questions.html>, accessed May 23, 2003.

[17] See, for example, James C. Collins and Jerry I. Porras, *Built to Last: Successful Habits of Visionary Companies* (New York: HarperBusiness, 2002), pp. 46–79.

CHAPTER 5 NOTES

[1] This question is developed in detail in Chapters 2 and 4.

[2] See, for example, the worksheets in Chapter 4.

[3] See, for example, "Nucor's Management Philosophy," available at <http://www.nucor-fastener.com/nucor.html>, accessed June 5, 2003.

[4] See also Dawn-Marine Driscoll and W. Michael Hoffman, *Ethics Matters: How to Implement Values-Driven Management* (Waltham, Mass.: Center for Business Ethics, 2000), p. 78.

[5] John Carver with Caroline Oliver, *Corporate Boards That Create Value: Governing Company Performance from the Boardroom* (San Francisco: Jossey-Bass, 2002), p. 22. Referred to here as *responsible governance*, the approach ensures that all operating policies, decisions, and actions set, made, and taken by employees of the enterprise are consistent with the enterprise's core beliefs. See also Lynn Sharp Paine, *Value Shift: Why Companies Must Merge Social and Financial Imperatives to Achieve Superior Performance* (New York: McGraw-Hill, 2003), p. 142.

[6] Carver with Oliver, *Corporate Boards That Create Value*, p. 23 (Exhibit 2.2).

[7] The policy statements in Boxes 5.1 through 5.4 are provided courtesy of John Carver and Caroline Oliver. These statements are set forth in more detail in Carver with Oliver, *Corporate Boards That Create Value*, pp. 40–41 (Exhibit 3.2).

[8] Courtesy of John Carver and Caroline Oliver. See Carver with Oliver, *Corporate Boards That Create Value*, p. 53, extract from Exhibit 4.1, Board-Management Delegation Policy, "Delegation to the CEO."

[9] Ibid., p. 63.

[10] Ibid.

[11] Ibid.

[12] Ibid., pp. 74–75.

[13] Ibid., pp. 61–62.

[14] Ibid., pp. 66–67.

[15] Ibid., p. 67.

[16] See, for example, Chris Robertson and Paul A. Fadil, "Developing Corporate Codes of Ethics in Multinational Firms: Bhopal Revisited," *Journal of Managerial Issues* 10, no. 4 (1998): 454, available at <http://www.questia.com>, accessed June 6, 2003.

[17] James C. Collins and Jerry I. Porras, *Built to Last: Successful Habits of Visionary Companies* (New York: HarperBusiness, 2002), pp. 219–39.

[18] Ibid., p. 234.

[19] Ibid., pp. 226–27.

[20] Ibid., Chapter 11.

[21] "Guided by Values," available at <http://www.novonordisk.com/sustainability/sustainability_strategy/guided_by_values.asp>, accessed June 7, 2003.

[22] Collins and Porras, *Built to Last*, p. 237.

[23] The term *code of conduct* refers to written guidance to employees and agents that sets forth the standards they are to meet in making decisions and in acting on behalf of the enterprise with regard to the enterprise's core beliefs, commitments to stakeholders, and specific compliance requirements. Such guidance may be described by terms such as *standards of conduct, code of ethics, corporate credo,* or *code of business conduct.*

[24] Royal Dutch/Shell, "Statement of General Business Principles," available at <http://www.shell.ca/code/values/commitments/principles.html>, accessed May 23, 2003. These principles are augmented by "management primers" that "offer background on key commitments made in the [principles] and guidance on how to apply them."

[25] U.N. Global Compact, available at <http://www.unglobalcompact.org>, accessed May 23, 2003.

[26] Royal Dutch/Shell, "Statement of General Principles."

[27] Ibid.

[28] Ibid.

[29] Ibid.

[30] These concepts of social responsibility for businesses are developed in detail in Chapter 2.

[31] Royal Dutch/Shell, "Statement of General Principles."

[32] Amnesty International and Pax Christi Netherlands, press release, "Shell's Revised 'Statement of General Business Principles': A Significant but First Step Ahead," available at <http://www.paxchristi.net/PDF/AF02E97.pdf>, accessed May 23, 2003.

[33] Chiquita Brands International, "Corporate Responsibility: Living Our Core Values," available at <http://www.Chiquita.com>, accessed May 23, 2003.

[34] United Technologies Corporation, "Our Commitments," available at <http://www.utc.com/profile/profile/commitments/index.htm>, accessed May 23, 2003.

[35] Caux Round Table, "Principles for Business," available at <http://www.cauxroundtable.org/PRIN4.HTM>, accessed May 23, 2003.

[36] This subject is beyond the scope of this guide, but adopting a code is often a matter that must be negotiated under an individual employment contract or work council (European Union) or with organized labor (United States). For European Union considerations, see Lori Tansey Martens and William Miller, "Ethics and Compliance: European Update," *Ethikos* (July/August 1999): 4–5. For U.S. considerations, see American Electric Power Co., Decisions of the National Labor Relations Board, 302 NLRB No. 161 (1991).

[37] See, for example, M. Cash Mathews, *Strategic Intervention in Organizations: Resolving Ethical Dilemmas* (Thousand Oaks, Calif.: Sage, 1988); Joshua Joseph, *National Business Ethics Survey 2003* (Washington, D.C.: Ethics Resource Center, 2003); and Linda K. Treviño, et al., "Managing Ethics and Legal Compliance: What Works and What Hurts," *California Management Review* 41 (Winter 1999): 131–51.

[38] Phil Watts, a managing director at Royal Dutch/Shell, quoted in Ronald E. Berenbeim, *Global Corporate Ethics Practices: A Developing Consensus* (New York: Conference Board, 1999).

[39] For a matrix covering many of the European legislation and initiatives regarding corporate social responsibility as of October 2002, see United States Council for International Business, "Corporate Responsibility Initiatives in Europe," available at <http://www.uscib.org/docs/EUCSRMatrix.pdf>, accessed June 25, 2003.

⁴⁰ New York Stock Exchange, "Final NYSE Corporate Governance Rules," available at <http://www.nyse.com/pdfs/finalcorpgovrules.pdf>, accessed January 23, 2004. Demonstrating the close relationship between government regulation and free markets, these rules reflect the requirements of recent legislation in the United States known as the Sarbanes-Oxley Act of 2002, available at <http://news.findlaw.com/hdocs/docs/gwbush/sarbanesoxley072302.pdf>, accessed May 23, 2003.

⁴¹ NTT Group, "NTT Group Ethical Code on Environmental Issues," available at <http://www.ntt.co.jp/kankyo/e/2002report/qa/chapter1/q04_2.html>, accessed May 23, 2003.

⁴² See, for example, Robertson and Fadil, "Developing Corporate Codes of Ethics in Multinational Firms," p. 454.

⁴³ W. Michael Hoffman, "Writing a Company's Code of Ethics," available at <http://www.iit.edu/departments/csep/perspective/persp_v19_fall99_5.html>, accessed May 23, 2003.

⁴⁴ WMC Resources Ltd., "Code of Conduct," available at <http://www.wmc.com.au/about/conduct/index.htm>, accessed May 23, 2003.

⁴⁵ NTT Group, "NTT Group Ethical Code on Environmental Issues."

⁴⁶ Guardsmark LLC, "Ethics," available at <http://www.guardsmark.com/approach/approach_sec.asp?nav=1&subnav=3&content_id=8>, accessed May 23, 2003.

⁴⁷ HCA Inc., "Introduction to Ethics, Compliance and Corporate Responsibility," available at <http://ec.hcahealthcare.com>, accessed May 23, 2003.

⁴⁸ United Technologies Corporation, "Welcome to Social Responsibility," available at <http://www.utc.com/social/ethics>, accessed May 23, 2003.

⁴⁹ For more detail about code styles, see Driscoll and Hoffman, *Ethics Matters*, Chapter 8.

⁵⁰ Ronald E. Berenbeim, "Codes of Conduct," in *Compliance Programs and the Corporate Sentencing Guidelines: Preventing Criminal and Civil Liability*, edited by Jeffrey M. Kaplan, Joseph E. Murphy, and Winthrop M. Swenson (Deerfield, Ill., New York, and Rochester, N.Y.: Clark Boardman Callaghan, 1993–2003), Chapter 7, § 7.4.

⁵¹ William P. Birkett, "Ethical Codes in Action," in "Articles and Speeches," International Federation of Accountants, available at <http://www.ifac.org/Library/SpeechArticle.tmpl?NID=96261008030>, accessed May 23, 2003.

⁵² HCA Inc., "Code of Conduct," available at <http://ec.hcahealthcare.com>, accessed May 23, 2003. HCA's policies can be downloaded from the site.

⁵³ See also Stephen B. Page, *Establishing a System of Policies and Procedures* (Mansfield, Ohio: Bookmasters, 1998).

⁵⁴ These samples are included as representative examples. Each enterprise must decide for itself what specific provisions to include in its codes and policies.

⁵⁵ Motorola, "Code of Business Conduct," available at <http://www.motorola.com/code/code.html>, accessed May 23, 2003.

⁵⁶ See, for example, Berenbeim, "Codes of Conduct," § 7.5.

⁵⁷ Carver with Oliver, *Corporate Boards That Create Value*, pp. 66–67.

CHAPTER 6 NOTES

[1] This question is developed in detail in Chapters 2 and 4.

[2] HCA Inc., "Ethics and Compliance Web Site," available at <http://ec.hcahealthcare.com>, accessed May 23, 2003.

[3] Lori Tansey Martens and William Miller, "Ethics and Compliance: European Update," *Ethikos* (July/August 1999): 4–6.

[4] Joseph T. Wells, "Protect Small Business: Small Companies without Adequate Internal Controls Need CPAs to Help Them Minimize Fraud Risk," *Journal of Accountancy* 195, no. 3 (2003), available at <http://www.questia.com>, accessed June 6, 2003.

[5] Linda K. Treviño, et al., "Managing Ethics and Legal Compliance: What Works and What Hurts," *California Management Review* 41 (Winter 1999): 131–51, at pp. 141–42.

[6] In a 1996 opinion, *In re Caremark*, (C.A. 13670), the influential Delaware Chancery Court held that, "A director's obligation includes a duty to attempt in good faith to assure that a corporate information and reporting system . . . exists and that failure to do so under some circumstances may . . . render a director liable for losses caused by noncompliance with applicable legal standards." This standard has been adopted by the U.S. Department of Justice in deciding whether to prosecute an enterprise for misconduct on the part of its employees or agents. Department of Justice memorandum, "Principles of Federal Prosecution of Business Organizations," dated Jan. 20, 2003, available at <http://www.ethics-policy.net/prosecution_2003.html>, accessed May 23, 2003.

[7] The U.S. Securities and Exchange Commission has published regulations governing the conduct of the audit committee and a code of ethics for senior financial officers. Securities and Exchange Commission, "Final Rule: Disclosure Required by Sections 406 and 407 of the Sarbanes-Oxley Act of 2002, 17 CFR Parts 228, 229, and 249, Release Nos. 33-8177; 34-47235," available at <http://www.sec.gov/rules/final/33-8177.htm>, accessed May 23, 2003.

[8] Other committees that might be appointed include compensation and nominating committees.

[9] Box 6.2 is a policy statement adapted from an e-mail communication with John Carver, author (with Caroline Oliver) of *Corporate Boards That Create Value: Governing Company Performance from the Boardroom* (San Francisco: Jossey-Bass, 2002).

[10] See, for example, the International Corporate Governance Network. This principle also applies to compensation and nominating committees. Available at <http://www.icgn.org>, accessed May 23, 2003.

[11] Adapted from Christopher Martin Bennett and Graydon R. Wood, "Assigning Compliance Responsibility," in *Compliance Programs and the Corporate Sentencing Guidelines: Preventing Criminal and Civil Liability*, edited by Jeffrey M. Kaplan, Joseph E. Murphy, and Winthrop M. Swenson (Deerfield, Ill., New York, and Rochester, N.Y.: Clark Boardman Callaghan, 1993–2002), Chapter 8, §§ 8.1–8.5. See also Joshua Joseph, "Integrating Business Ethics and Compliance Programs: A Study of Ethics Officers in Leading Organizations," *Business and Society Review* (Fall 2003): 309–47.

[12] This is also a specific responsibility under the U.S. Federal Sentencing Guidelines for Organizations.

[13] Bennett and Wood, "Assigning Compliance Responsibility," § 8.4.

[14] Under the Federal Sentencing Guidelines for Organizational Defendants, the high-level person responsible may be a director, but that blurs the distinction made in this guide between governance and management.

[15] Adapted from Richard P. Kusserow and Andrew H. Joseph, *Corporate Compliance Policies and Procedures: A Guide to Assessment and Development* (Marblehead, Mass.: Opus Communications, 2000), p. 20. See also HCA Inc., "Policy on Business Ethics Offices," available at <http://ec.hcahealth-care.com/CPM/EC010.doc>, accessed May 23, 2003.

[16] Joseph, "Integrating Business Ethics and Compliance Programs," pp. 323–24.

[17] Ibid., pp. 330–31.

[18] Bennett and Wood, "Assigning Compliance Responsibility," § 8.8. See also Treviño, et al., "Managing Ethics and Legal Compliance," pp. 146–47.

[19] If the professional ethics council addresses issues that are of the essence of the RBE, a best practice is to design two separate councils—the general ethics, compliance, and responsibility council and the more specialized professional ethics council—each having overlapping membership and independent reporting to senior management and the board.

[20] Treviño, et al., "Managing Ethics and Legal Compliance," pp. 142–43.

[21] See, for example, Memorial Hermann Healthcare System, "Standards of Conduct," available at <http://www.mhhs.org/aboutus/StandardsofConduct100401.doc>, accessed May 23, 2003.

CHAPTER 7 NOTES

[1] Lyuba Zarsky, "Beyond Good Deeds: For Multinational Corporations to Adopt Socially Responsible Business Practices, Voluntary Measures Are Not Enough," *Forum for Applied Research and Public Policy* 16, no. 4 (2002), available at <http://www.questia.com>, accessed June 7, 2003.

[2] These questions are developed in detail in Chapters 2 and 4.

[3] See discussion in Chapters 4 and 10.

[4] "Corporate Recruiters Face the 'Enron Effect,'" available at <http://www.epolitix.com/data/companies/images/Companies/Work-Foundation/191202.htm>, accessed April 16, 2003.

[5] An example is the Better Banana Project of the Rainforest Coalition and Chiquita Brands: Rainforest Alliance, "Profiles in Sustainable Development Partnerships: Chiquita Reaps Better Bananas," available at <http://www.rainforest-alliance.org/programs/profiles/ag-chiquita-profile-11-14-02horizon.pdf>, accessed May 23, 2003.

[6] Jon Entine, "Shell, Greenpeace and Brent Spar: The Politics of Dialogue," in *Case Histories in Business Ethics*, edited by Chris Megone and Simon J. Robinson (London and New York: Routledge, 2002), pp. 59–95. This well-documented case study includes this quotation from a national Environmental Research Council report.

[7] British Broadcasting, "World: Europe Brent Spar Gets Chop," available at <http://news.bbc.co.uk/1/hi/world/europe/221508.stm>, accessed May 23, 2003.

[8] British America Tobacco, "Corporate Social Responsibility," available at <http://www.bat.com/oneweb/sites/uk__3mnfen.nsf/vwPagesWebLive/DO52AD7G?opendocument&TMP=>, accessed at May 23, 2003.

[9] These standard data collection devices are described in Chapter 10.

[10] Expected program outcomes are discussed in Chapters 4 and 10.

[11] Global Reporting Initiative, available at <http://www.globalreporting.org/>, accessed May 23, 2003. AA1000, developed by AccountAbility in the United Kingdom, is available at <http://www.accountability.org.uk>, accessed May 23, 2003.

[12] For European Union considerations, see Lori Tansey Martens and William Miller. "Ethics and Compliance: European Update," *Ethikos* (July/August 1999): 4–6. For U.S. considerations, see American Electric Power Co., Decisions of the National Labor Relations Board, 302 NLRB No. 161 (1991).

[13] Michael J. Marquardt, *Action Learning in Action: Transforming Problems and People for World-Class Organizational Learning* (Palo Alto, Calif.: Davies-Black, 1999), pp. 57–67.

[14] See, for example, Michael MacDonald, "A Framework for Ethical Decision-Making," available at <http://www.ethics.ubc.ca/mcdonald/decisions.html>, accessed May 23, 2003; Josephson Institute of Ethics, "The Seven Step Path to Ethical Decisions," available at <http://www.josephsoninstitute.org/MED/MED-4sevensteppath.htm>, accessed May 23, 2003; and Kenneth W. Johnson, "An Ethics and Policy Decision Making Tool," available at <http://www.Ethics-Policy.net/ethical_decisions.html>, accessed May 23, 2003.

[15] "Primary Sources," *Atlantic Monthly* 290, no. 4: 46, citing the Brookings Institution: "The Bigger They Are, the Harder They Fall: An Estimate of the Costs of the Crisis in Corporate Governance," available at <http://www.brookings.edu/views/papers/graham/20020722.htm>, accessed July 9, 2003.

[16] Lori Tansey Martens, "Transatlantic Perspectives on Business Ethics Training," International Business Ethics Institute unpublished working paper, accessed April 22, 2003.

[17] Several ethics games are described in Linda K. Treviño and Katherine A. Nelson, *Managing Business Ethics*, 2nd ed. (New York: John Wiley & Sons, 1999), pp. 265–67.

[18] See, for example, "Boeing Ethics Challenge," available at <http://active.boeing.com/companyoffices/ethicschallenge/cfm/initial.cfm>, accessed May 23, 2003.

[19] See, for example, Martens, "Transatlantic Perspectives on Business Ethics Training."

[20] Joshua Joseph, *National Business Ethics Survey 2000* (Washington, D.C.: Ethics Resource Center, 2001), pp. 22–23. See also Lori Tansey Martens and Amber Crowell, "Whistleblowing: A Global Perspective" (Part I), *Ethikos* (May/June 2002): 6–8.

[21] Christine A. Wardell and Jacqueline P. Minor, "Protecting Whistleblowers from Retaliation: The Corporate Ombuds Office," in *Compliance Programs and the Corporate Sentencing Guidelines: Preventing Criminal and Civil Liability*, edited by Jeffrey M. Kaplan, Joseph E. Murphy, and Winthrop M. Swenson (Deerfield, Ill., New York, and Rochester, N.Y.: Clark Boardman Callaghan, 1993–2002), Chapter 13, § 13.1.

[22] Joshua Joseph, *National Business Ethics Survey 2003* (Washington, D.C.: Ethics Resource Center, 2003), p. 42. The four elements used to differentiate among business ethics programs are discussed in Joseph, *National Business Ethics Survey*, Chapter 2. These positive associations between having a business ethics program and expected program outcomes held true for the following program outcomes as well: less feeling of pressure to compromise standards, more satisfaction with management's response to reported concerns, more sense that managers and supervisors are held accountable, and more satisfaction with the enterprise as a whole.

[23] Guy Dehn, cited in Lori Tansey Martens and Amber Crowell, "Whistleblowing: A Global Perspective (Part II)," *Ethikos* (July/August 2002): 9–12, at p. 10.

[24] Joseph, *National Business Ethics Survey 2000*, pp. 23–24.

[25] For a discussion of global approaches to protecting whistleblowers, see Martens and Crowell, "Whistleblowing: A Global Perspective (Part II)."

[26] See, for example, Kenneth W. Johnson, "Confidentiality, Privilege, and an Effective Ethics Program," available at <http://www.Ethics-Policy.net/confidentiality_Privilege.html>, accessed June 4, 2003.

[27] For more information about the organizational ombudsman, visit the Ombudsman Association Web site at <http://www.ombuds-toa.org/all_about_toa.htm>, accessed May 27, 2003.

[28] Anita Roddick, "A Third Way for Business, Too," *New Statesman* 3 (April 1998), available at <http://www.questia.com>, accessed June 6, 2003.

CHAPTER 8 NOTES

[1] See, for example, Larry Bossidy and Ram Charan, *Execution: The Discipline of Getting Things Done* (New York: Crown Business, 2002); James C. Collins and Jerry I. Porras, *Built to Last: Successful Habits of Visionary Companies* (New York: HarperBusiness, 2002), pp. 201–18; Joshua Joseph, *National Business Ethics Survey 2000* (Washington, D.C.: Ethics Resource Center, 2001); and Linda K. Treviño, et al., "Managing Ethics and Legal Compliance: What Works and What Hurts," *California Management Review* 41 (Winter 1999): 131–51, at pp. 141–44.

[2] These questions are developed in detail in Chapters 2 and 4.

[3] Treviño, et al., "Managing Ethics and Legal Compliance," pp. 141–42.

[4] Joshua Joseph, *National Business Ethics Survey 2003* (Washington, D.C.: Ethics Resource Center, 2003), p. 31. The elements used to differentiate among ethical actions of top management, supervisors, and co-workers are discussed in Joseph, *National Business Ethics Survey 2003*, Chapter 3.

[5] Ibid., p. 31. These associations between manager and supervisor ethics-related actions and expected program outcomes held true for feeling pressure to compromise standards (p. 37), being satisfied with management's response to reported concerns (p. 48), a sense that managers and supervisors are held accountable (p. 54), and employee satisfaction with the enterprise (p. 57).

[6] James C. Collins, *Good to Great: Why Some Companies Make the Leap . . . and Others Don't* (New York: HarperBusiness, 2001), p. 50.

[7] *Channel stuffing* is colluding with or offering improper incentives to clients to order products or services they would not ordinarily purchase at that time.

[8] Treviño and others, "Managing Ethics and Legal Compliance," p. 155.

[9] Joseph, *National Business Ethics Survey 2000*, pp. 22–23.

[10] Treviño, et al., "Managing Ethics and Legal Compliance," pp. 136–39. Most harmful, according to the authors' research, is an organizational culture of unquestioning obedience to authority. See pp. 136–37 and 143–44.

[11] Joseph L. Badaracco Jr., *Leading Quietly: An Unorthodox Guide to Doing the Right Thing* (Boston: Harvard Business School Press, 2002), p. 11.

[12] Anton R. Valukas and Robert R. Stauffer, "Investigation and Disclosure of Violations," in *Compliance Programs and the Corporate Sentencing Guidelines: Preventing Criminal and Civil Liability*, edited by Jeffrey M. Kaplan, Joseph E. Murphy, and Winthrop M. Swenson (Deerfield, Ill., New York, and Rochester, N.Y.: Clark Boardman Callaghan, 1993–2003), § 14.16.

[13] Lynn Sharp Paine, "Managing for Organizational Integrity," *Harvard Business Review*, (March/April 1994): 106–117, at p. 109.

[14] A link to its credo is prominently set on Johnson & Johnson's home page, and is accessible by national language from Argentina to Zimbabwe. Available at <http://www.jnj.com>, accessed May 23, 2003.

[15] Paine, "Managing for Organizational Integrity," p. 109.

CHAPTER 9 NOTES

[1] U.S. Department of State, "Recognizing and Making Anticorruption Issues Part of the Business–Government Dialogue," in *Fighting Global Corruption: Business Risk Management*, available at <http://www.state.gov/g/inl/rls/rpt/fgcrpt/2001>, accessed June 3, 2003.

[2] Joel S. Hellman and others, "Measuring Governance, Corruption, and State Capture: How Firms and Bureaucrats Shape the Business Environment in Transition Economies," Policy Research Working Paper 2312 (Washington, D.C.: World Bank, 2000), p. 36. Available at <http://www.world-bank.org/wbi/governance/pdf/measure.pdf>, accessed June 4, 2003.

[3] Legal services were also provided to several businesses whose rights were abused. In Azerbaijan, several business associations, including the Entrepreneurship Development Foundation and the Confederation of Entrepreneurs (Employees), lobbied for limitation of the number of licensed types of activities. As of Jan. 1, 2003, the number of such activities was reduced from 240 (including wild plant and berry picking) to 30.

[4] See, for example, Juliette Bennett, "Multinational Corporations, Social Responsibility, and Conflict," *Journal of International Affairs* 55, no. 2 (2002), available at <http://www.questia.com>, accessed June 7, 2003.

[5] Joel Hellman and Daniel Kaufmann, "Confronting the Challenge of State Capture in Transition Economies," *Finance & Development* (September 2001): 31.

[6] See, for example, Joel Hellman, Geraint Jones, and Daniel Kaufmann, "Seize the State, Seize the Day," Policy Research Working Paper 2444 (Washington, D.C.: World Bank Institute, 2000), available at <http://www.worldbank.org/wbi/governance/pdf/seize.pdf>, accessed May 23, 2003; Joel Hellman, Geraint Jones, Daniel Kaufmann, and Mark Schankerman, "Measuring Governance and State Capture: The Role of Bureaucrats and Firms in Shaping the Business Environment," World Bank Working Paper 2312 (Washington, D.C.: World Bank Institute, 2000); and Hellman and Kaufmann, "Confronting the Challenge of State Capture in Transition Economies." In general, see <http://www.worldbank/wbi/governance>, accessed May 23, 2003.

[7] Barry Z. Posner and Warren H. Schmidt, "The Values of Business and Federal Government Executives: More Different Than Alike," *Public Personnel Management* 25, no. 3 (1996), available at <http://www.questia.com>, accessed June 7, 2003.

[8] Ion Anton, "From Entrepreneurship Education to Policy Advocacy," available at <http://www.cipe.org/publications/fs/ert/e30/antoe30.htm>, May 23, 2003.

[9] Michael H. Wiehen, "Citizens against Corruption: Calling Government to Account," in *No Longer Business as Usual: Fighting Bribery and Corruption* (Paris: OECD Publications, 2000), pp. 199–213.

[10] Ibid., pp. 199–200.

[11] World Bank, "World Bank Procurement Policy," available at <http://www.worldbank.org/html/opr/propage.html>, accessed June 6, 2003. See also European Investment Bank, "Guide to

Procurements," available at <http://www.eib.org/Attachments/thematic/procure_en.pdf>, accessed July 21, 2003.

[12] The GPA can be found at <http://www.wto.org/english/docs_e/legal_e/grp-94.pdf>, accessed June 6, 2003.

[13] For a more detailed treatment of the integrity pact, see Wiehen, "Citizens against Corruption," pp. 206–8.

[14] For more information about the integrity pact, see "The Integrity Pact: The Concept, the Model, and the Present Applications—As of 31 December 2002," at <http://www.transparency.org/building_coalitions/integrity_pact/i_pact.pdf>, accessed May 23, 2003.

[15] See, for example, "A New Development Agenda: Outlining the Challenges to Development in the 21st Century," A Conversation with Louise Fréchette, *Harvard International Review* (Spring 2003): 40–41, at p. 40.

[16] Vijay Pothukuchi, et al., "National and Organizational Culture Differences and International Joint Venture Performance," *Journal of International Business Studies* 33, no. 2 (2002), available at <http://www.questia.com>, accessed June 7, 2003.

[17] Financial Action Task Force on Money Laundering, "Basic Facts about Money Laundering," available at <http://www1.oecd.org/fatf/MLaundering_en.htm#How%20does%20money%20laundering%20affect%20business?>, accessed June 6, 2003.

[18] See Todd Doyle, "Cleaning Up Anti-Money Laundering Strategies: Current FATF Tactics Needlessly Violate International Law," *Houston Journal of International Law* 24, no. 2 (2002), available at <http://www.questia.com>, accessed June 6, 2003.

[19] Lyuba Zarsky, "Havens, Halos, and Spaghetti: Untangling the Evidence about Foreign Direct Investment and the Environment," Nautilus Institute for Security and Sustainable Development, available at <http://www.nautilus.org/papers/enviro/zarsky_oecdfdi.html>, accessed May 23, 2003.

CHAPTER 10 NOTES

[1] Peter M. Senge, *The Fifth Discipline: The Art and Practice of the Learning Organization* (New York: Doubleday/Currency, 1990), p. 14.

[2] Peter Kline and Bernard Saunders, *Ten Steps to a Learning Organization*, 2nd rev ed. (Arlington, Va.: Great Ocean Publishers, 1998), p. 23.

[3] This question is developed in detail in Chapters 2 and 4.

[4] See, for example, Michael J. Marquardt, *Action Learning in Action: Transforming Problems and People for World-Class Organizational Learning* (Palo Alto, Calif.: Davies-Black, 1999), and Richard P. Nielsen, *The Politics of Ethics: Methods for Acting, Learning, and Sometimes Fighting with Others in Addressing Ethics Problems in Organizational Life* (New York: Oxford University Press, 1996).

[5] Discussed in detail in Chapter 5.

[6] Discussed in detail in Chapters 6 and 7.

[7] Discussed in detail in Chapters 8 and 9.

[8] Richard R. Ellsworth, *Leading with Purpose: The New Corporate Realities* (Stanford, Calif.: Stanford University Press, 2002), p. 129.

[9] See Kline and Saunders, *Ten Steps to a Learning Organization*, p. 24.

[10] Simon Zadek, "The Era of Stakeholder Engagement," *Ethical Corporation Magazine* (February 2003): 10–12.

[11] Jane Reisman and Richard Mockler, *A Field Guide to Outcome-Based Program Evaluation* (Seattle, Wash.: Evaluation Forum, 1994), p. 10. The approach we take to outcomes-based program evaluation is based on this work and its companion works, courtesy of the publisher. A source addressing the process of responsibility reporting is AccountAbility AA1000S, a stakeholder framework. See AA1000S, developed by AcccountAbility in the United Kingdom, at <http://www.accountability.org.uk>, accessed May 23, 2003 © 1994 The Evaluation Forum.

[12] These topics are developed in Chapter 4.

[13] Linda K. Treviño, et al., "Managing Ethics and Legal Compliance: What Works and What Hurts," *California Management Review* 41 (Winter 1999): 131–51, at p. 141.

[14] Global Reporting Initiative, available at <http://www.globalreporting.org>, accessed May 23, 2003.

[15] AccountAbility, AA1000S, available at <http://www.accountability.org.uk>, accessed May 23, 2003.

[16] Table 10.1 is adapted from Reisman and Mockler, *A Field Guide to Outcome-Based Program Evaluation*, p. 41, courtesy of the publisher.

[17] Box 10.4 is provided courtesy of Kenneth W. Johnson, Ethics & Policy Integration Centre.

[18] The Evaluation Forum, Seattle, Wash., has an excellent series on program evaluation: Reisman and Mockler, *A Field Guide to Outcome-Based Program Evaluation*; Jane Reisman and Judith Clegg, *Outcomes for Success* (Seattle, Wash.: Organizational Research Services and Clegg & Associates, 1999); and Marc Bolan, Kimberly Francis, and Jane Reisman, *How to Manage and Analyze Data for Outcome-Based Evaluation* (Seattle, Wash.: Organizational Research Services, 2000). See also Writing@CSU Web site, available at <http://writing.colostate.edu/references/research/survey/index.cfm>, accessed May 23, 2003.

[19] An excellent collection of corporate social responsibility reports can be found at the CSR Wire Web site, available at <http://www.csrwire.com/csr/home.mpl>, accessed May 23, 2003.

[20] Reisman and Mockler, *A Field Guide to Outcome-Based Program Evaluation*, adapted courtesy of the authors.

[21] Box 10.7 is adapted from Global Reporting Initiative, "Part C: Report Content," in *Sustainability Reporting Guidelines 2002*, available at <http://www.globalreporting.org/guidelines/2002/gri_2002_guidelines.pdf>.

GLOSSARY

Audit committee   In large, complex enterprises, and recently as a matter of joint-stock company law, the board of directors often creates an audit committee to ensure the financial integrity of an enterprise. An audit committee investigates an enterprise's financial records and ensures that its financial operations are conducted on a transparent and accurate basis. The committee provides members of the board of directors with information about the financial and business operations of the enterprise. This information enables the board of directors to supervise implementation of the enterprise's financial and business plan and to ensure the efficiency of its internal control and risk management systems—two key components of any business ethics program.

Board of directors   The board of directors of an enterprise is the primary body responsible for representing the shareholders and safeguarding their interests. The board creates special committees—such as audit, executive compensation, and ethics committees—to fulfill this function. Increasingly, corporations will also appoint a social responsibility committee. These committees issue reports to the board, which uses the reports to make decisions concerning the development, implementation, and modification of the ethics compliance program. The board of directors makes the final decisions concerning any policy, program, or initiative that an enterprise may make.

Bribery   Bribery is a form of corruption. In the case of political corruption, bribery is the direct or indirect provision of illegal compensation to—or any other action in favor of—any employee of a government body. In return, the government employee acts in a manner advantageous to the company or refrains from acting to the company's disadvantage. Enterprises use bribery to obtain or retain business, receive patronage, or obtain an unwarranted advantage over other businesses.

Business ethics   Business ethics are an integral part of responsible business conduct. They describe an organization's commitment to a set of commonly understood core values and principles, which provide a basis for business decisions and conduct. Typically, business ethics presume that decisions will conform to standards articulated in law and regulations; internal policy and procedures; a set of core values determined by owners and managers, including honesty, integrity, respect, and fairness; and commercial principles such as profitability, customer satisfaction, product quality, health, safety, and efficiency. Business ethics issues range from practical, immediate ones, such as an enterprise's duty to be honest with its employees and customers, to broader social and philosophical questions, such as a company's responsibility to contribute to the welfare of the community and to preserve the environment.

Channel Stuffing   Channel stuffing is the act of inducing customers or suppliers to increase purchases or decrease supplies or services that would be purchased or supplied in the ordinary course of business, solely to present a more favorable performance or financial picture to partners.

Code of ethics   A code of ethics is a blueprint for developing a culture of values in an organization. A code consists of a clearly stated and written set of guidelines that managers, employees, and agents of an organization must follow. A code of ethics is a reference tool that provides guidance to both employees and managers on how to implement and practice business ethics in the workplace. A code should embody both business standards (such as customer satisfaction, a high quality of products, safety, and employee rights) and values (such as mutual trust, respect, and honesty).

Conflict of interest   A conflict of interest occurs when the private interests of an individual who works for an enterprise interfere, or appear to interfere, in any way with the interests of the enterprise as a whole. A conflict arises when an employee, officer, or director of an enterprise performs an action that will interfere with that individual's ability to perform his or her official duties.

Core values   Core values are values shared by the leadership, the employees, and the stakeholders of a business that make the business special and determine its organizational culture.

Corporate governance   Corporate governance refers to the system that a corporation establishes to structure relations among managers, directors, and shareholders and between the enterprise and civil society. Such governance measures are necessary when government charters provide limited liability to shareholders, which separates ownership of the enterprise from responsibility for day-to-day operations. Corporate governance practices are built on the ethical premise that the leaders of an enterprise have an obligation to be fair, transparent, accountable, and responsible in their conduct toward shareholders and civil society.

Corruption   Corruption is any choice or action made or taken that intentionally violates the reasonable expectations of enterprise stakeholders for the profit or gain of one responsible to some degree for meeting those expectations. Public-sector corruption is easy to recognize when a politician or bureaucrat accepts large sums of cash to steer a government contract to a particular enterprise. However, corruption also exists when an owner or manager consciously chooses to fail to meet reasonable stakeholder expectations for personal gain. The damage done to the reputation of the enterprise and the social capital of its community may be as severe as in public-sector corruption. See **Enron** and **WorldCom.**

Declaration of integrity   A declaration of integrity is a public agreement among business enterprises in an industry or a locality that they will abide by an agreed-on set of norms, values, and standards with a view to improving the business climate of the industry or community. This term differs from an **integrity pact** in that the government is not necessarily involved and the agreement has broader application than with government procurement. Such a declaration, however, does not have the immediate risk of loss of an ability to bid on a contract that characterizes an **integrity pact.** A declaration of integrity might be particularly valuable when a community foundation intends to fund a community-driven development project.

Discipline   A discipline is a body of theory and practice that requires both reflection and action to be put into practice. The discipline of responsible business conduct is a study that will last a lifetime. This discipline requires an understanding that an enterprise is a system and part of yet wider systems. It recognizes that there are bodies of experience embedded in traditions, laws and regulations, industry best practices, and emerging global standards that practitioners will spend precious time acquiring and sharing. Ultimately, the practitioner of such a discipline generates new knowledge to further the discipline itself.

Economic progress   According to Peter Drucker, economic progress is "a steady rise in the ability of an economy to invest more capital for each job and thereby to produce jobs that yield better living as well as a better quality of work and life." (Peter F. Drucker, "The Delusion of 'Profits': A Company That Loses Money Is Socially Irresponsible," *OpinionJournal*, available at *www.opinionjournal.com/extra/?id+110003570.*)

Employee survey   An employee survey is a mechanism that an enterprise may use to secure feedback from employees and to evaluate the effectiveness and impact of the enterprise's ethics program. Such a survey sets forth questions concerning the enterprise's organizational culture, the way the enterprise's ethics program works in practice, and the measurable expected program outcomes, such as observed misconduct, willingness to seek advice and report misconduct, issue awareness, and employee satisfaction and commitment to the enterprise. Owners and managers use the survey data along with other data to determine whether they have set and communicated the proper standards and procedures and have fostered reasonable stakeholder expectations.

Enron and WorldCom   Business scandals and failures are not new, but it is a sign of how closely connected the global economies are that these two companies in the United States have become symbolic of much that is wrong with businesspeople. Researchers calculate that the loss of confidence following the collapse of Enron and WorldCom will cost the U.S. economy $37 billion to $42 billion in reduced gross domestic product. Enron, in particular, went from being the seventh largest company in the United States to bankruptcy in a matter of months as confidence in its leadership faded.

Ethics committee   In large, complex enterprises, an ethics committee is often created and assigned overall responsibility for the ethics and compliance program. The ethics committee helps develop and implement the ethics program and the code of ethics of an enterprise. The committee ensures that ethical, regulatory, and policy standards have been established within the enterprise and that they are widely and consistently communicated to all. The committee also monitors and improves the processes of the ethics program and works closely with all parties responsible for supervising and managing the ethics program, including the ethics office, the ethics officer, and the board of directors.

Ethics office   Many enterprises create an ethics office, which is responsible for the day-to-day management and implementation of the enterprise's ethics program. The office provides clarity and guidance on compliance with the code of ethics and the enterprise's policies and procedures regarding reporting and investigation of alleged misconduct. This office normally includes an ethics officer, support staff, and a help-line.

Ethics officer   The position of ethics officer is created to accomplish the day-to-day operations of the business ethics program. The ethics officer may or may not be the person with high-level responsibility for the business ethics program. He or she provides advice on ethical behavior and on how to report ethics concerns, investigates and monitors investigations of possible misconduct, monitors the development of the ethics program, and works with other bodies in the enterprise to promote compliance. The ethics officer ensures that all levels of the organization meet or exceed ethical, legal, and civil society expectations on a day-to-day basis. The ethics officer generally has the right to report directly to both the chief executive officer and the board of directors, and often to the audit committee.

External stakeholders   The external parties that have a stake in an enterprise's success include customers and consumers, suppliers and service providers, civil society organizations, nongovernmental organizations, government agencies, local community representatives, the media, and the environment. External stakeholders share the objective of having business succeed in a manner that strengthens both the economy and civil society. These stakeholders can provide feedback on values and political, economic, and social considerations that an enterprise should integrate into its ethical identity.

Feedback mechanism   A feedback mechanism is a tool that an enterprise may use to obtain timely information pertaining to the implementation and effectiveness of its ethics program. A feedback mechanism could take the form of a survey, a focus group, a one-on-one interview, or a help-line.

Fiduciary duties   Each member of the board of directors of an enterprise is a fiduciary who owes a duty of loyalty and duty of care to the enterprise. The duty of loyalty requires a board member to place the best interests of the enterprise first and to avoid advancing the member's personal, financial, or professional interests at the expense of the enterprise. The duty of care requires a board member to act as a reasonable and diligent businessperson would to help the enterprise create maximum shareholder value with minimum risk.

Focus groups   A focus group is a feedback mechanism that brings together a small group of employees and an outside party to gather information about life in the enterprise. A focus group is a particularly useful device in evaluating a business ethics program. During a focus group, the outside party asks detailed questions and receives in-depth responses from employees about the ethics program.

Good corporate governance   Good corporate governance is the process by which the leadership of an enterprise, especially a limited liability enterprise, sets standards and procedures for employees and agents, fosters reasonable expectations among stakeholders, and meets those expectations. Good corporate governance expresses itself through a sound set of core beliefs, standards and procedures, and expectations. It requires understanding the relevant context of the enterprise, its organizational culture, and its strengths and weaknesses. Good corporate governance exercises those strengths and reforms the weaknesses through infrastructure, including a business ethics program. Good corporate governance is more likely when there is a transparent relationship between the government and the private sector.

Good public governance   Good public governance, in the context of this manual, is the process by which the leadership of a country makes and implements decisions concerning the market. There are eight characteristics of good governance: consensus building, participation of all interest, accountability, transparency, responsiveness, effectiveness and efficiency, equality and inclusiveness, and finally the rule of law. Good public governance occurs when there is a transparent relationship between the government and the private sector.

Help-line   A help-line or hot-line is a secure telephone line that is connected to an ethics office or the office of an ombudsman. Employees use this tool to contact the ethics office or ombudsman to report a violation or receive advice on matters that concern them. A current best practice is that no call to a help-line is refused except for grievance matters under a labor–management bargaining agreement.

Industry standards   Industry standards are standards that different enterprises in a specific industry develop and agree on with one another or that are so common as to be considered a custom of the industry or profession. Such standards go beyond laws and regulations to promote free, fair, and honest competition among the members of the industry.

Integrity pact   An integrity pact is an agreement among a group of businesses that obligates them to participate in a government tender or procurement process in a legal and transparent manner. Under an integrity pact, the parties may pledge not to offer, pay, accept, or seek bribes of any kind during the tender. The key component of an integrity pact is transparency. A business in the pact also abides by any and all sanctions placed on it by the other members of the pact.

Internal stakeholders   The internal parties that have a stake in an enterprise's success include the shareholders, the board of directors, the executive management, and the employees.

Learning organization   A learning organization is an enterprise adept at generating, acquiring, and sharing knowledge about its relevant context, its organizational culture, and the expectations of its stakeholders and at using that knowledge so that its owners, managers, employees, and agents can live the lives they truly want to live.

Money laundering   Under the process of money laundering, one conceals the existence, illegal source, or illegal application of income, and disguises that income to make it appear legitimate. From Andrew J. Camelio and Benjamin Pergament, "Money Laundering," *American Criminal Law Review* 35, no. 3 (1998), available at *www.questia.com*.

Ombudsman   The office of ombudsman is designed to be completely independent from enterprise management and to provide a safe place where employees and agents can seek advice and report concerns. The position of an organizational ombudsman in a business ethics program has evolved to be an independent, neutral, and alternative position. The position is independent because the ombudsman is not a part of day-to-day staff or operations management. It is neutral because the ombudsman does not function as an advocate for the enterprise or individual. It is alternative because the ombudsman does not duplicate any other enterprise function, such as investigations. With few exceptions, the ombudsman is authorized only to refer reports of misconduct for investigation with the express consent of the reporting source.

One-on-one interviews   One-on-one interviews of employees are used to secure detailed feedback for enterprise management and to allow management to conduct intensive questioning of individuals that is designed to improve the ethics program. An interview provides a forum in which an employee can identify and address issues that employee surveys may not bring to the surface.

Organizational culture   Organizational culture can be understood in the same way as the culture of a society, nationality, or country. Organizational culture is shaped by the enterprise's origin and history, as well as by the values, norms, and attitudes of its leaders and stakeholders. The culture is reflected in the organization's decision-making and communication procedures, production methods, and policies regarding servicing customers and clients. Organizational culture is the primary predictor of business ethics program success or failure. There are several measurable elements of culture that should be a part of the regular evaluation of the business ethics program by owners and managers.

Parade of horribles A parade of horribles often consists of news headlines and stories about enterprises that failed and senior executives who went to prison for breaking the law. It is one way to encourage an enterprise and its owners, managers, employees, and agents to embrace the discipline of responsible business conduct. See, for example, **Enron** and **WorldCom**.

Purpose statement The fundamental reasons for an enterprise's existence beyond profit are noted in the purpose statement. A purpose, unlike a vision of a desired future, is broad, essential, enduring, and even spiritual. A purpose inspires and guides employees and agents. It is pursued but never fully captured. Researchers suggest that the way to surface the purpose of an enterprise is to describe what the enterprise does, or intends to do, and ask, "Why is that important?" five times.

Relevant context All enterprises strive to meet enterprise goals and objectives in a context of legal, economic, political, environmental, socio-cultural, and technological elements. Each element in an enterprise's "relevant context" may cause threats, opportunities, demands, constraints, and uncertainties that owners, managers, workers, and agents must recognize and address.

Responsible business conduct Responsible business conduct reflects an understanding of the relevant context of the enterprise, its organizational culture, and the reasonable expectations of its stakeholders. In one sense, responsible business conduct is very practical and rooted in the particular situation of the individual and enterprise. In another, however, responsible business conduct is a recognition that we are all in this situation together and that one does not cease to be a member of a community simply because one goes into business.

Responsible business enterprise A responsible business enterprise is a learning organization that is adept at understanding its relevant context, its organization culture, and its core beliefs. From these understandings, the owners, managers, employees, and agents of such an enterprise are able to build an enterprise that has the appropriate standards, procedures, and expectations; has structures and systems; has communication and feedback; and has an enterprise alignment that is able to foster reasonable expectations among its stakeholders and meet those expectations. By meeting reasonable expectations, the responsible business enterprise is able to improve its business performance, to make a profit, and to contribute to the economic progress of its community.

Responsible officer A responsible officer is a high-level person who is responsible for overseeing the business ethics program. The responsible officer should be an owner, director, or senior manager. This person may or may not be the ethics officer for the enterprise. Indeed, where the enterprise is large or complex, the responsible officer often has executive responsibilities and relies on the ethics officer to run day-to-day operations.

Reward system   Through a system of rewards, an enterprise provides rewards to employees who uphold core values and fulfill ethical goals in their day-to-day activities. These rewards may be formal, taking the form of promotions, pay raises, bonuses, and public recognition. The rewards may also be informal, taking the form of private praise or a special meeting with the president of the enterprise. A reward system reinforces the enterprise's commitment to ethics and encourages its employees and managers to conduct themselves according to the guidelines of the enterprise's code of ethics.

Risk management   The risk management process helps the owners and managers of an enterprise plan, organize, and control the day-to-day operations of the enterprise to minimize risks to capital and earnings. Risk management includes, but is not limited to, the management of risks associated with accidental losses, financial mismanagement, fraud and embezzlement, corruption, loss of reputation, and employee health and safety, as well as other operational risks.

Social capital   Social capital is the mutual trust and shared values among individuals within an organization and between an organization and external stakeholders that enables those parties to work together on a cooperative basis. Social capital accrues through performance at the grassroots level within an enterprise and through the creation of civil society organizations, such as trade groups, business associations, service clubs, charities, and nongovernmental organizations.

State capture   State capture is an effort by an enterprise to shape the laws, policies, and regulations of the state to its own advantage by providing illicit, illegitimate, and nontransparent private gains to public officials.

Triple bottom line   Triple bottom line reporting requires enterprises to evaluate their social and environmental performance to the same degree they evaluate and report economic performance.

Values statement   A values statement sets forth in a clear and consistent form the core values that make an enterprise special in the market. Each value is explained in the relevant context and culture of the enterprise. The process of establishing core values requires an enterprise's leaders to consider the values and expectations of internal and external stakeholders.

Vision statement   A vision statement expresses a view of what success for the enterprise will look like. This statement incorporates the enterprise's short- and long-term objectives and provides the enterprise the opportunity to publicly declare its role in the market and in civil society and to set a standard that it can be expected to meet.

RESOURCES AND FURTHER READING

PART I: THE RESPONSIBLE BUSINESS ENTERPRISE

Aaronson, Susan A., and James T. Reeves. *Corporate Responsibility in the Global Village: The Role of Public Policy*. Washington, D.C.: National Policy Association, 2002.

AccountAbility Web site. Available at <http://www.AccountAbility.org.uk>. (Accessed August 22, 2003.)

American Society of International Law. "ASIL Guide to Electronic Resources for International Law." Available at <http://www.asil.org/resource/humrts1.htm>. (Accessed May 27, 2003.)

BISNIS. "US–Russia Code of Conduct Basic Guidelines." Available at <http://www.bisnis.doc.gov/bisnis/country/codebusen.htm>. (Accessed August 22, 2003.)

Business for Social Responsibility. Available at <http://www.bsr.org>. (Accessed August 22, 2003.)

Cattaui, Maria Livanos. "Responsible Business Conduct in a Global Economy: Companies Are Now Subject to Intense Public Scrutiny. How Should They Respond?" Available at <http://www.oecdobserver.org>. (Accessed August 22, 2003.)

Caux Round Table. "Principles for Business." Available at <http://www.cauxroundtable.org>. (Accessed August 22, 2003.)

Coalition for Environmentally Responsible Economies. Available at <http://www.ceres.org>. (Accessed August 22, 2003.)

Codes of Conduct. "Interest Groups—Nongovernmental Organizations." Available at <http://www.codesofconduct.org/interest.htm>. (Accessed May 27, 2003.)

Collins, James C., and Jerry I. Porras. *Built to Last: Successful Habits of Visionary Companies*. New York: HarperBusiness, 2002.

Ellsworth, Richard R. *Leading with Purpose: The New Corporate Realities*. Stanford, Calif.: Stanford University Press, 2002.

Global Reporting Initiative. "Sustainability Reporting Guidelines." Available at <http://www.globalreporting.org>. (Accessed August 22, 2003.)

Global Sullivan Principles Web site. Available at <http://www.globalsullivan-principles.org>. (Accessed August 22, 2003.)

Gordon, Kathryn. "The OECD Guidelines and Other Corporate Responsibility Instruments: A Comparison." Available at <http://www.oecd.org>. (Accessed August 22, 2003.)

Grayson, David, and Adrian Hodges. *Everybody's Business: Management Risks and Opportunities in Today's Global Society*. London and New York: DK Publishing, 2002.

Institute of Directors in South Africa Web site. Available at <http://www.iodsa.co.za>. (Accessed August 22, 2003.)

Interfaith Center on Corporate Responsibility, Taskforce on Churches and Corporate Responsibility. "Principles for Global Corporate Responsibility: Benchmarks for Measuring Business Performance." Available at <http://www.web.net/~tccr/benchmarks/index.html>. (Accessed June 7, 2003.)

International Chamber of Commerce Web site. Available at <http://www.iccwbo.org>. (Accessed August 22, 2003.)

———. "The Business Charter for Sustainable Development—16 Principles." Available at <http://www.iccwbo.org/home/environment_and_energy/sdcharter/charter/about_charter/about_charter.asp>. (Accessed August 22, 2003).

International Corporate Governance Network Web site. Available at <http://www.icgn.org>. (Accessed August 22, 2003.)

International Electrical and Electronic Engineers. "Code of Ethics." Available at <http://www.ieee.org/portal/index.jsp?pageID=corp_level1&path=about/whatis&file=code.xml&xsl=generic.xsl>. (Accessed August 22, 2003.)

———. "Software Engineering Code of Ethics and Professional Practice." Available at <http://computer.org/certification/ethics.htm>. (Accessed August 22, 2003.)

International Labor Organization Web site. Available at <http://www.ilo.org>. (Accessed August 22, 2003.)

Joseph, Joshua. *National Business Ethics Survey 2000*. Washington, D.C.: Ethics Resource Center, 2000.

———. *National Business Ethics Survey 2003*. Washington, D.C.: Ethics Resource Center, 2003.

Micklethwait, John, and Adrian Wooldridge. *The Company: A Short History of a Revolutionary Idea*. New York: Modern Library, 2003.

Monks, Robert A. G., and Nell Minow. *Corporate Governance*. 2nd ed. Oxford, U.K.: Blackwell, 2001.

Organization for Economic Cooperation and Development. "Home: Corporate Social Responsibility." Available at <http://www.oecd.org/oecd/pages/home/

displaygeneral/0,3380,EN-home-126-3-no-no-no,00.html>. (Accessed June 6, 2003.)

————. "Home: Guidelines for Multinational Enterprises." Available at <http://www.oecd.org/EN/home/0,,EN-home-93-3-no-no-no,00.html>. (Accessed June 6, 2003.)

Paine, Lynn Sharp. *Value Shift: Why Companies Must Merge Social and Financial Imperatives to Achieve Superior Performance*. New York: McGraw-Hill, 2003.

Roddick, Anita. "A Third Way for Business, Too." *New Statesman*, April 3, 1998. Available at <http://www.questia.com>. (Accessed June 8, 2003.)

Social Accountability International Web site. Available at <http://www.cepaa. org>. (Accessed August 22, 2003.)

Stiglitz, Joseph. *Globalization and Its Discontents*. New York: W. W. Norton, 2002.

SustainAbility. "Developing Value." Available at <http://www.sustainability. com/developing-value/contents.asp>. (Accessed June 4, 2003.)

Treviño, Linda K., and others. "Managing Ethics and Legal Compliance: What Works and What Hurts." *California Management Review* 41 (Winter 1999): 131–51.

United Nations Global Compact Network. "The Global Compact." Available at <http://www.unglobalcompact.org/Portal>. (Accessed August 22, 2003.)

United Nations Office of the High Commissioner on Human Rights. "The International Bill of Human Rights." Available at <http://www.unhchr. ch/html/menu6/2/fs2.htm>. (Accessed May 27, 2003.)

Waddock, Sandra. *Leading Corporate Citizens: Vision, Values, Value Added*. Boston: McGraw-Hill, 2002.

Zadek, Simon. *The Civil Corporation: The New Economy of Corporate Citizenship*. London and Sterling, Va.: Earthscan, 2001.

PART II: THE BUSINESS ETHICS PROGRAM

Carroll, Archie B., and Ann K. Buchholtz. *Business and Society: Ethics and Stakeholder Management*. 4th ed. Cincinnati, Ohio: South-Western, 2000.

Carver, John, and Caroline Oliver. *Corporate Boards That Create Value: Governing Company Performance from the Boardroom*. San Francisco: Jossey-Bass, 2002.

Collins, James C. *Good to Great: Why Some Companies Make the Leap ... and Others Don't*. New York: HarperBusiness, 2001.

Freeman, R. Edward. *Strategic Management: A Stakeholder Approach*. New York: Basic Books, 1984.

Grundy, Tony. *Implementing Strategic Change*. London: KoganPage, 1993.

Hesselbein, Frances. "When the Roll Is Called in 2010." In *On Creativity, Innovation, and Renewal*, edited by Frances Hesselbein and Rob Johnson. San Francisco: Jossey-Bass, 2002.

Hofstede, Geert. *Cultures and Organizations: Intercultural Cooperation and Its Importance for Survival*. New York: McGraw-Hill, 1997.

Hofstede, Geert, and others. "What Goals Do Business Leaders Pursue? A Study in Fifteen Countries." *Journal of International Business Studies* 33, no. 4 (2002). Available at <http://www.questia.com>. (Accessed June 7, 2003.)

Jacobs, Robert W. *Real Time Strategic Change: How to Involve an Entire Organization in Fast and Far-Reaching Change*. San Francisco: Berrett-Koehler, 1994.

Johnson, Kenneth W. "The Role of Culture in Achieving Organizational Integrity, and Managing Conflicts between Cultures." Washington, D.C.: Ethics and Policy Integration Centre. Available at <http://www.Ethics-Policy.net/quest_5.html>. (Accessed May 27, 2003.)

Kotter, John P., and James L. Heskett. *Corporate Culture and Performance*. New York: Free Press, 1992.

Nadler, David A. *Champions of Change: How CEOs and Their Companies Are Mastering the Skills of Radical Change*. San Francisco: Jossey-Bass, 1998.

Robertson, Christopher J., and James J. Hoffman. "How Different Are We? An Investigation of Confucian Values in the United States." *Journal of Managerial Issues* 12, no. 1 (2000): 34. Available at <http://www.questia.com>. (Accessed June 7, 2003.)

University of Missouri Extension and Outreach. "Program Planning and Development—Program Logic Model." Available at <http://outreach.missouri.edu/staff/programdev/plm>. (Accessed August 22, 2003.)

U.S. Department of Health and Human Services. "Corporate Responsibility and Corporate Compliance: A Resource for Health Care Boards of Directors." Available at <http://oig.hhs.gov/fraud/docs/complianceguidance/040203Corp RespRsceGuide.pdf>. (Accessed June 7, 2003.)

PART III: STRUCTURING THE BUSINESS ETHICS PROGRAM

Boeing. "Boeing Ethics Challenge." Available at <http://www.boeing.com/companyoffices/aboutus/ethics>. (Accessed August 22, 2003.)

Chiquita Brands International. "Corporate Responsibility: Living Our Core Values." Available at <http://www.Chiquita.com>. (Accessed August 22, 2003.)

Driscoll, Dawn-Marie, and W. Michael Hoffman. *Ethics Matter: How to Implement Values-Driven Management*. Waltham, Mass.: Center for Business Ethics, 2000.

EthicsWeb.ca. "Applied Ethics Resources on the Web." Available at <http://www.ethicsweb.ca/ resources>. (Accessed June 7, 2003.) [An excellent source for codes of ethics and a collection of ethical decision-making models.]

HCA Inc. "Introduction to Ethics, Compliance and Corporate Responsibility." Available at <http://ec.hcahealthcare.com>. (Accessed August 22, 2003.)

Hoffman, W. Michael. "Writing a Company's Code of Ethics." Available at <http://www.iit.edu/departments/csep/perspective/persp_v19_fall99_5.html>. (Accessed August 22, 2003.)

Howmet Castings. "Code of Ethics and Standards of Business Behavior." Available at <http://www.howmet.com/home.nsf/files/booklet/$file/booklet.pdf>. (Accessed August 22, 2003.)

International Standards Organization. "The Magical Demystifying Tour for ISO 9000 and ISO 14000." Available at <http://www.iso.ch/iso/en/iso9000-14000/tour/magical.html>. (Accessed June 6, 2003.)

Joseph, Joshua. "Integrating Business Ethics Programs: A Study of Ethics Officers in Leading Organizations," *Business and Society Review* (Fall 2002): 309–47.

Josephson Institute of Ethics. "The Seven Step Path to Ethical Decisions." Available at <http://www.josephsoninstitute.org/MED/MED-4sevensteppath.htm>. (Accessed August 22, 2003.)

Kaplan, Jeffrey M., Joseph E. Murphy, and Winthrop M. Swenson. *Compliance Programs and the Corporate Sentencing Guidelines: Preventing Criminal and Civil Liability*. Eagan, Minn.: West Group, 2002.

Kusserow, Richard P., and Andrew H. Joseph. *Corporate Compliance Policies and Procedures: A Guide to Assessment and Development*. Marblehead, Mass.: Opus Communications, 2000.

LeClair, Debbie Thorne, O. C. Ferrell, and John P. Fraedrich. *Integrity Management: A Guide to Managing Legal and Ethical Issues in the Workplace*. Tampa, Fla.: University of Tampa Press, 1998.

Machan, Tibor R., and James E. Chester. *A Primer on Business Ethics*. Lanham, Md.: Rowman & Littlefield, 2002.

Martens, Lori Tansey, and Amber Crowell. "Whistleblowing: A Global Perspective" (Part I). *Ethikos* (May/June 2002): 6–8.

———. "Whistleblowing: A Global Perspective" (Part II). *Ethikos* (July/August 2002), 9–12.

Murphy, Diana E. "The Federal Sentencing Guidelines for Organizations: A Decade of Promoting Compliance and Ethics." 87 *Iowa L. Rev.* 697, 2002. Available at <http://www.ussc.gov/corp/Murphy1.pdf>. (Accessed August 22, 2003.)

NTT Group. "NTT Group Ethical Code on Environmental Issues." Available at <http://www.ntt.co.jp/kankyo/e/2002report/qa/chapter1/q04_2.html>. (Accessed August 22, 2003.)

Ombudsman Association Web site. Available at <http://www.ombuds-toa.org/all_about_toa.htm>. (Accessed May 27, 2003.)

Page, Stephen B. *Establishing a System of Policies and Procedures*. Mansfield, Ohio: Bookmasters, 1998.

Rainforest Alliance. "Profiles in Sustainable Development Partnerships: Chiquita Reaps Better Bananas." Available at <http://www.rainforest-alliance.org/programs/profiles/ag-chiquita-profile-11-14-02horizon.pdf>. (Accessed August 22, 2003.)

Robertson, Chris, and Paul A. Fadil. "Developing Corporate Codes of Ethics in Multinational Firms: Bhopal Revisited." *Journal of Managerial Issues* 10, no. 4 (1998): 454. Available at <http://www.questia.com>. (Accessed June 7, 2003.)

Royal Dutch/Shell. "Statement of General Business Principles." Available at <http://www.shell.ca/code/values/commitments/principles.html>. (Accessed August 22, 2003.)

Solomon, Robert C. *A Better Way to Think about Business: How Personal Integrity Leads to Corporate Success*. New York and Oxford, U.K.: Oxford University Press, 1999.

Treviño, Linda K., and Katherine A. Nelson. *Managing Business Ethics: Straight Talk about How to Do It*. 2nd ed. New York: John Wiley & Sons, 1999.

U.S. Department of Justice. "Principles of Federal Prosecution of Business Organizations." Available at <http://www.usdoj.gov/dag/cftf/business_organizations.pdf>. (Accessed May 23, 2003.)

PART IV: PUTTING BUSINESS ETHICS INTO PRACTICE

Agreement on Government Procurement. Available at <http://www.wto.org/english/docs_e/ legal_e/gpr-94.pdf>. (Accessed June 6, 2003.)

Badaracco, Joseph L. Jr. *Leading Quietly: An Unorthodox Guide to Doing the Right Thing*. Boston: Harvard Business School Press, 2002.

Bennett, Juliette. "Multinational Corporations, Social Responsibility, and Conflict." *Journal of International Affairs* 55, no. 2 (2002). Available at <http://www.questia.com>. (Accessed June 2003.)

Bossidy, Larry, and Ram Charan. *Execution: The Discipline of Getting Things Done*. New York: Crown Business, 2002.

Financial Action Task Force on Money Laundering. "Basic Facts about Money Laundering." Available at <http://www1.oecd.org/fatf/MLaundering_en.htm

#How%20does%20money %20laundering%20affect%20business?>. (Accessed June 6, 2003.)

Naim, Moises. "The Five Wars of Globalization." *Foreign Policy* (January/February 2003). Available at <http://www.questia.com>. (Accessed June 7, 2003.)

Paine, Lynn Sharp. "Managing for Organizational Integrity." *Harvard Business Review* (March-April 1994): 106–17.

Transparency International. "Bribe Payers Index." Available at <http://www.transparency.org>. (Accessed May 27, 2003.)

Wiehen, Michael H. "Citizens against Corruption: Calling Government to Account." In *No Longer Business as Usual: Fighting Bribery and Corruption*, 199–213. Paris: OECD, 2000.

PART V: ACHIEVING RESPONSIBLE BUSINESS CONDUCT

AccountAbility. "AA1000S Framework." Available at <http://www.accountability.org.uk>. (Accessed August 22, 2003.)

Bolan, Marc, Kimberly Francis, and Jane Reisman. *How to Manage and Analyze Data for Outcome-Based Evaluation*. Seattle, Wash.: Organizational Research Services, 2000.

Kline, Peter, and Bernard Saunders. *Ten Steps to a Learning Organization*. 2nd ed. Arlington, Va.: Great Ocean, 1998.

Lusthaus, Charles, and others. *Organizational Assessment: A Framework for Improving Performance*. Washington, D.C.: Inter-American Development Bank, 2002.

Marquardt, Michael J. *Action Learning in Action: Transforming Problems and People for World-Class Organizational Learning*. Palo Alto, Calif.: Davies-Black, 1999.

Nielsen, Richard P. *The Politics of Ethics: Methods for Acting, Learning, and Sometimes Fighting with Others in Addressing Ethics Problems in Organizational Life*. New York: Oxford University Press, 1996.

Reisman, Jane, and Judith Clegg. *Outcomes for Success*. Seattle, Wash.: Organizational Research Services and Clegg & Associates, 1999.

Reisman, Jane, and Richard Mockler. *A Field Guide to Outcome-Based Program Evaluation*. Seattle, Wash.: Evaluation Forum, 1994.

Senge, Peter M. *The Fifth Discipline: The Art and Practice of the Learning Organization*. New York: Doubleday/Currency, 1990.

Tansey, Lori A., Gary Edwards, and Rachel E. Schwartz. "Compliance Program Modification and Refinement." Chapter 5 in *Compliance Programs and the Corporate Sentencing Guidelines: Preventing Criminal and Civil Liability*, edited by Jeffrey M. Kaplan, Joseph E. Murphy, and Winthrop M. Swenson. Eagan, Minn.: West Group, 2002.

PERMISSIONS

Permission has kindly been granted to the U.S. Department of Commerce by the respective authors, publishers, or copyright holders to reprint the following material in this book: on pages 4, 189, and 267, Hewlett-Packard Corporation; on pages 5 and 231, Stanford University Press; on page 6, Earthscan Publications Ltd.; on page 8, Journal of International Business Studies; on page 9, ICC Publishing Inc.; on page 11, The World Bank; on page 22, United Parcel Service; on page 23, New Statesman; on pages 24 and 132, The Journal of Accountancy; on page 28, The McGraw-Hill Companies; on page 25, Gap Inc.; on page 29, Komatsu Ltd., on page 44, Journal of Small Business Management; on page 51, Nestlé Inc.; on page 54, Jossey-Bass; on page 56, John Wiley & Sons; on page 95, Nucor Fastener; on pages 104 and 135, Novo Nordisk; on page 105, Sony Corporation; on pages 107 and 122, Royal Dutch/Shell; on page 108, Chiquita Brands; on pages 108 and 217, United Technologies Corporation; on pages 110 and 136, The Boeing Company; on page 111, the New York Stock Exchange; on pages 113, 119, and 172, Motorola, Inc.; on page 115, WMC Resources Limited; on pages 126 and 127, Howmet Corporation; on pages 121 and 143, Alcatel; on page 137, HCA, Inc.; on page 142, the Raytheon Company; on pages 148 and 167, Forum for Applied Research and Public Policy; on page 163, © 1999 the Lockheed Martin Corporation; on page 170, The Atlantic Monthly, Used with Permission; on page 193, Herman Miller Inc.; on page 196, Guardsmark LLC.; on page 203, Johnson & Johnson; on page 211, Columbia University Press; on page 213, International Public Management Association for Human Resources; on page 219, Harvard International Review; on page 240, © 1994 The Evaluation Forum; on pages 259–264, Transparency International.

INDEX

A

AA1000S standard, 32, 35, 235, 238, 239
accountability systems in business ethics
    infrastructure, *see* responsibility
    functions
action planning and action learning,
    161–62
administration of training programs, 165
agents, *see* employees and agents
AIDS/HIV, 28
Alcatel Group, 121, 143
alignment, 185–206
    see also dealing with problems; "the
      right people in the right places"
      (under *r*)
    business ethics programs, 186
    checklist, 205
    encouraging employees to follow
      standards, procedures, and expec-
      tations, 95, 101–2, 186, 194–98
    fundamental questions regarding, 186
    RBE worksheets, 206
anti–money laundering (AML) provi-
    sions, 49, 221–22
approval process, design and implemen-
    tation of business ethics program, 62,
    123
auditing
    audit committee, 134
    enforcement of standards, proce-
      dures, and expectations, 167–68
    integration of business ethics
      infrastructure with internal auditing
      systems, 142
Australia, 49
authority, delegating, 55–56, 97, 132–34
authority systems in business ethics
    infrastructure, *see* responsibility
    functions

B

baselines, 69–70
*Basic Guidelines for Codes of Business
    Conduct*, 32, 109, 235
benchmarking, 69–70
Bennett, Juliette, 211
best practices, 7, 37–38
board of directors, 96–97, 132, 134
The Body Shop, 23, 175
Boeing Company, 110, 136
Brabeck-Letmathe, Peter, 51
Bradford, David L., 56
bribes and kickbacks, 9, 24, 208–11, 221
brochures, availability of, 154–55
business associations, 32–34
business conduct representatives, 141–42

business ethics council, 140
business ethics infrastructure, 129–46
    checklist, 145
    communication, 166, 181
    importance of, 130
    LCEs, 129
    leadership elements, 132
    NGOs, 129, 131
    owners and owner representatives,
      132–34
    RBE worksheet, 146
    responsibility functions and systems,
      see responsibility functions
    SMEs, 129, 131, 133, 140
business ethics officer, 138–40, 143
business ethics personnel, *see* responsibil-
    ity functions
business ethics programs
    see also design and implementation of
      business ethics program; evaluat-
      ing business ethics programs;
      more specific entries
    alignment, 186
    communicating, 45–47, 59
    evolving market economies, 6–7
    good management, responsible
      business conduct viewed as,
      31–32
    identity levels, 6, 47–51, 68
    list of issues to be covered by, 123
    process of developing responsible
      business conduct, 21
    reporting program performance,
      237–40
    resources, 123
    structural components, 52–53
Business Partnership of Seversk, 210

C

capital
    expanded access through ethics, 26
    social capital, *see* social capital,
      29
generating
Carver, John, 54, 96–100
case studies in training programs, 162,
    163, 164
Cattaui, Maria Livanos, 9
Caux Round Table, 32–33, 108, 235
central planning legacies, transition to
    market economy, 12–16
CEO (chief executive officer), 97, 132
CERES (Coalition for Environmentally
    Responsible Economies), 32, 33
charitable foundations, 220
checklists
    alignment, 205

business ethics infrastructure, 145
communication, 177
design and implementation of
    business ethics program, 63, 77
evaluating business ethics
    programs, 242
evolving market economies, 20
government officials and agencies,
    224
process of becoming a responsible
    business, 40
standards, procedures, and
    expectations, 124
chief executive officer (CEO), 97–98,
    132
chief financial officer, 142
chief legal officer, 143
Chiquita Brands International, 108
clarification of responsibilities, 102
Coalition for Environmentally
    Responsible Economies (CERES),
    32, 33
codes of conduct, 109–17
    adaptations, revision, updates, and
      improvements, 116
    aspirational *vs.* obligatory provisions,
      115–16
    cultural norms, 112–13
    design, review, and approval process,
      123
    developmental guidelines, 114–15
    disclaimers, 118–19
    environmental protections, 111–12
    formats, 116, 118
    industry standards, compliance with,
      111
    introductory materials, 118
    law, compliance with, 110
    policies related to, 116–17
    sample outline, 125–26
    typical provisions, 117–23
Cohen, Allan R., 56
Collins, James C., 105
command economy's evolution to market
    economy, *see* evolving market
    economies
communication, 147–55
    see also feedback
    audience knowledge, 149–51
    brochures, availability of, 154–55
    business ethics infrastructure, 166,
      181
    business ethics programs, 45–47, 59
    checklist, 177
    developing communications
      programs, 148–52

document distribution, 153, 154–55
management speeches, 152–53
needs assessment, 151–52, 178
posted materials, 153–54
public feedback mechanisms and media involvement, 174–76
published materials, 154
RBE worksheets
infrastructure, 181
needs assessment, 178
standards, procedures, and expectations, 101, 152–55
training, *see* training programs
Web site, 154
community, *see* social capital, generating
competition
central planning legacies, 12–13
enhancement through ethics, 25–26
relationships and responsibilities between enterprise and, 121
compliance level of RBE identity, 6, 48–49, 187–88
confidentiality, ensuring, 172
consultants, stakeholders as, 59
consumers, *see* customers and consumers
contents
program evaluation reports, 239–41
training programs, 156–58
context of enterprise, scanning, 74–75, 80–81
continuous improvement, incorporating, 56–57
contracting and procurement, governmental, 215–18
cooperation with government, 201–2
core beliefs and values
Herman Miller Japan Ltd. statement on, 193
mobilizing enterprise around, 55
narrative used to project, 158
personal values, 159–60
standards, procedures, and expectations for RBEs, 102–4
training programs, 155–56, 158–59
corporate social responsibility (CSR), and SMEs, 44
corrective actions, 202
corruption, 9, 24, 201, 208–11, 221
cost reduction and responsible business conduct, 23–24
councils
business ethics council, 140
professional ethics councils, 141
credibility of evaluation reporting, 238–39
credit, expanded access to, 26
CSR (corporate social responsibility), and SMEs, 44
culture and business ethics, *see also* organizational culture
codes of conduct and respect for cultural norms, 112–13
compliance level of business ethics

programs, 49
evolving market economies, 8–9
socio-cultural element of relevant context, scanning, 73–74
standards, procedures, and expectations, 100–101
customers and consumers
evolving market economy, 13
public feedback and involvement in ethics enforcement, 174–76
relationships and responsibilities between enterprise and, 119–20
senior personnel *vs.* lower-level personnel, perception of misconduct by, 190–91
social responsibilities of RBEs, 28

D

data collection plan, evaluating business ethics programs, 236–37
dealing with problems, 186, 198–204
see also enforcement of standards, procedures, and expectations
cooperation with government, 201–2
corrective actions, 202
discipline systems, 198–99
learning from failures and mistakes, 198–99
misunderstandings and misperceptions, 202–3
model policy statement, 199
modifying business ethics programs due to, 203–4
senior personnel *vs.* lower-level personnel, perception of misconduct by, 190–91
stakeholders, misconduct or serious harm to, 199–201
unethical behavior/misconduct of employees and agents, 24–25, 70
voluntary disclosure of violation of law, 200–201
declarations of integrity, 218–19
delegation of authority, 55–56, 97, 132–34
design and implementation of business ethics program, 43–64, 65, 77, 123
see also RBE worksheets
adoption of design, 62
approval process, 62, 123
checklists, 63, 77
communicating program, 45–47, 59
consultants, stakeholders as, 59
defining nature of program, 45–47
goals and purposes, determining, 65–70
identity levels for RBEs, 6, 47–51, 68
infrastructure, designing, *see* business ethics infrastructure
internal structure and dynamics of enterprise, 75–76, 84–85
organizational culture, 66–67
orientation of program, 46
principles of planning process, 53–57

program catalyst, 58
program logic model, 70–71, 78–79
project networks, 59
project officer, 58
relevant context, scanning, 71–75
resource teams, 59
review process, 62, 123
stakeholders, engagement of, 57–61
strategic planning, 43–45
strengths and weaknesses of organization, 52, 54–55
structural components, 52–53
table of development process, 62
working groups or task forces, 58–59, 60–61
design and implementation of training programs, 155–58
direct observation, data collection plan for evaluating programs, 237
discipline systems, 197–98
disclaimers in codes of conduct, 118–19
document distribution, 153, 154–55
document reviews, data collection plan for evaluating programs, 237
due diligence in hiring, 188–89

E

economic element of relevant context, scanning, 72–73
education, *see* learning; training programs
eight questions for RBEs, 37–39, 86–89
Ellsworth, Richard F., 5, 231
employees and agents
business conduct representatives, 141–42
central planning legacies, 13
communicating business ethics plan to, 45–47
discipline systems, 197–98
enforcement of ethical behavior, role in, *see* enforcement of standards, procedures, and expectations
hiring, 188–89
personnel issues distinguished from ethics issues, 172–73
recognition, need for, 194
relationships and responsibilities between enterprise and, 119–20
retaliation, protection from, 171
retention of, 192–93
reward systems, 195–97
satisfaction with organization, correlates with, 192
standards, procedures, and expectations, 95, 101–2, 186, 194–98
unethical behavior/misconduct, 24–25, 70
ends, policies defining, 98–99
enforcement of standards, procedures, and expectations, 165–76
see also dealing with problems
confidentiality, ensuring, 172
employees and agents, 168–73
confidentiality and security,

ensuring, 172
help-lines, 171–72
personnel issues distinguished
from ethics issues, 172–73
reporting violations, 169–71
retaliation, protection from, 171
seeking advice and reporting
concerns, 168–69
external stakeholders engaged in,
174–76
feedback, importance of, 165–66
investigations, policies and procedures for, 173–74
monitoring behavior, 166–67
ombudsmen, 173
security, maintaining, 172
Enron, 160
entry into market, 13
environment
codes of conduct, 111–12
foreign governments and businesses,
222–23
relevant context, scanning, 73
Ethics Resource Center, 70
European Union (EU) codes of conduct,
110
evaluating business ethics programs,
65–70, 229–45
checklist, 242
credibility, establishing, 238–39
data collection plan, 236–37
importance of, 231–32
organizational culture, 234, 235, 243
organizational learning, 229–31,
240–41
outcomes evaluation, 233, 235–36,
245
process evaluation, 233, 234–35, 244
purpose of evaluation, determining,
233
RBE worksheets, 243–45
relevant context, scanning, 234
reporting program performance,
237–41
SMEs, 232
evolving market economies, 3–20
business ethics program, 6–7
central planning legacies, 12–16
checklist, 20
global marketplace, 7–9
improvement of business
performance, 18
individual businesses, 17–19
institutional framework, development
of, 16–17
leaders, working with, 19
reasonable business conduct in, 4–6
SMEs, 9–11
social capital, developing, 18–19
solution *vs.* problem, RBE as part
of, 9
exit from market, 12
expectations, *see* standards, procedures,

and expectations
external stakeholders, *see* stakeholders
extortion, 201, 208–11

F
failures, dealing with, 198–99
see also dealing with problems
fairness, concept of, 143, 198
FCPA
(*see* Foreign Corrupt Practices Act)
Federal Sentencing Guidelines for
Organizations (FSGO), United
States, 34, 49
feedback, 147–48,
see also communication
importance of, 165–66
public feedback mechanisms, 174–76
training programs, 164–65
Foreign Corrupt Practices Act (FCPA),
United States, 221
foreign governments and businesses,
relationship to, 220–23
foreign investment, expanded access
to, 26
formats
codes of conduct, 116, 118
report of program evaluation, 239–40
fraud
employee fraud and abuse, 24
small business owner detection of, 132
Fréchette, Louise, 219
FSGO (*see* Federal Sentencing Guidelines
for Organizations),
future, vision of, 104–5

G
games used in training programs, 163
The Gap Inc., 25
gift-giving practices, 113
global business standards and organizations
adoption of, 37–39
emergence of, 32–36
table, 37
global marketplace and evolving market
economies, 7–9
Global Reporting Initiative (GRI), 32,
34, 157, 234, 241
Global Sullivan Principles, 34
goals and purposes
business ethics programs, 65–70
evaluation of programs, 233
RBEs, 4, 5–6, 9, 27
good corporate governance, 7
good public governance, 208
goodwill, 22
governance
good corporate governance, 7
good public governance, 208
management differentiated from,
53–54
responsible governance, 96–100
government officials and agencies
checklist, 224

contracting and procurement,
215–18
cooperation with, 201–2
corrective actions required by, 202
corruption, bribery, and extortion,
201, 208–11, 221
evolving market economies, 7, 14–15,
19
foreign governments and businesses,
relationship to, 220–23
international governmental organizations, 35–36
leaders, RBEs working with, 19, 31
private sector's role in regulatory
process, 212–15
RBE worksheets, 225
relationships between RBEs and,
208–12
relevant context, scanning, 71–73
standards, procedures, and expectations, encouraging, 211–12
voluntary disclosure of legal violations to, 201
GPA (WTO Agreement on Global
Procurement), 216
GRI (Global Reporting Initiative), 32,
34, 157, 234, 241
Guardsmark LLC, 114, 196

H
HCA Inc., 114, 117, 130, 137
help-lines for employees and agents
reporting violations, 171–72
Herman Miller Japan Ltd., 193
Hewlett-Packard, 4
hiring employees, 188–89
HIV/AIDS, 28
Hoffman, W. Michael, 114
Hubbard Foods Ltd., 6

I
ICC (International Chamber of
Commerce), 9, 33
identity levels for RBEs, 6, 47–51, 68,
187–88
IEEE (Institute of Electrical and
Electronics Engineers), 33–34
illegal activity, climate of, 16
ILO (International Labour
Organization), 14, 35
improvement of business performance
through ethics
capital, credit, and foreign
investment access, 26
continuous improvement,
incorporating, 56–57
cost reduction, 23–24
employees and agents, behavior of,
24–25
evolving market economies, 18
increased profit and sustained
long-term growth, 26
international respect, 26–27
performance, productivity, and

competitive position, 25–26
reputation and goodwill, 22, 26–27
responsible business conduct contributing to, 21–27
risk reduction, 22–23
inclusivity, AA1000S definition of, 238
independent directors, 134
Indonesia, 211
industry-based professional ethics councils, 141
industry standards, compliance with, 111
infrastructure, *see* business ethics infrastructure
Institute of Directors in Southern Africa, 35
Institute of Electrical and Electronics Engineers (IEEE), 33–34
Institute of Social and Ethical AccountAbility, 35, 232, 235, 238, 239
institutional market-oriented framework, development of, 16–17
integrity, declarations of, 218–19
integrity pacts, government contracting and procurement, 217–18
Interfaith Declaration, 32, 34
internal structure and dynamics of enterprise, 75–76, 84–85
International Center for Entrepreneurial Studies, 214
International Chamber of Commerce (ICC), 9, 33
International Corporate Governance Network, 34–35
international governmental organizations, 35–36
International Labour Organization (ILO), 14, 35
International Organization for Standardization (ISO), 134
international respect, 26–27
Internet
    communication via Web sites, 154
    training programs, 163
interviews, data collection plan for evaluating programs, 237
investigations
    government, cooperation with, 201–2
    internal policies and procedures for, 173–74
investing, 14
Islamic culture, 8–9
ISO (International Organization for Standardization), 134

J

job position and placement, 190–92
Johnson & Johnson, 202–3

K

kickbacks and bribes, 9, 24, 208–11, 221
Komatsu Ltd., 28, 29

L

labor unions, 14
large, complex enterprises (LCEs)
    business ethics infrastructure, 129
    design and implementation of business ethics program, engagement of stakeholders in, 57–59
    evolving market economies, 10
    global business standards, adopting, 37
    ombudsmen, 173
    wrong people, dealing with, 194
lateness, ways of dealing with, 198
laws and regulations
    categories of laws affecting business, 48
    codes of conduct requiring compliance with, 110
    compliance level of business ethics programs, 6, 48–49
    cooperation with government investigations, 201–2
    corrective actions, 202
    important role of, 14–15
    private sector's role in, 212–15
    relevant context, scanning, 72
    voluntary disclosure of violation, 200–1
LCEs, *see* large, complex enterprises (LCEs)
leadership
    business ethics infrastructure, 132
    business, government, and civil society leaders, RBEs working with, 19, 31
    corporate, 54
learning
    see also training programs
    action planning and action learning, 160–62
    failures and mistakes, learning from, 198–99
    organizational learning, 229–31, 240–41
lending, 14
lobbying, 212–15
Lockheed Martin Corporation, 163
long-term growth, ethical behavior sustaining, 26

M

management
    see also standards, procedures, and expectations
    board-management linkage policy, 134
    communication via management speeches, 152–53
    governance differentiated from, 53–54
    limitations policies, 99–100
    responsible business conduct viewed as good management, 31–32
    "the right people in the right places," 187–88
    senior personnel *vs.* lower-level personnel, perception of misconduct by, 190–91
    training programs, 155, 159
means, policies defining, 99–100
misconduct, mistakes, and misunderstandings, dealing with, *see* dealing with problems
Mochler, Richard, 240
money laundering, 49, 221–22
Motorola Corporation, 113, 118–19, 172
mudaraba, 8

N

needs assessment and communication, 151–52, 178
nepotism, 9
Nestlé, 51
New York Stock Exchange, 111
Newmont Mining Corporation, 211
NGOs, *see* nongovernmental organizations (NGOs)
Nippon Telegraph & Telephone (NTT Group), 112, 114
nongovernmental organizations (NGOs)
    business ethics infrastructure, 129, 131
    corruption, bribery, and extortion, 210
    environmental concerns, 112
    evolving market economies, 7, 11, 19
    external stakeholders engaged in enforcement of ethics requirements, 174
    extortion, help in dealing with, 201
    global stakeholder groups, 34–35
    leaders, working with, 19, 31
    management principles, 108
    regulatory process, private sector's role in, 214–15
Novo Nordisk, 104, 135
NTT Group (Nippon Telegraph & Telephone), 112, 114
Nucor Fastener Division, 95

O

OECD (Organization for Economic Cooperation and Development), 35, 221, 235
Oliver, Caroline, 54, 96, 97, 99, 100
ombudsmen, 173
Organization for Economic Cooperation and Development (OECD), 35, 221, 235
organizational culture
    design and implementation of business ethics program, 66–67, 75–76, 84–85
    evaluating business ethics programs, 234, 235, 243
    RBE worksheets, 243
    training programs, 155–56
organizational learning, 229–31, 240–41
outcomes evaluation, 233, 235–36, 245
owners

business ethics infrastructure for
owners and representatives,
132–34
central planning legacies, 13–14
management performance
expectations, 98–100
relationships and responsibilities
between enterprise and, 119
"the right people in the right places,"
187–88
training programs, 159

P

Packard, David, 4
"parade of horribles," 160
partners, relationships and responsibilities between enterprise and, 120–21
performance
evaluating, *see* evaluating business
ethics programs
improving, *see* improvement of business performance through ethics
personnel and business ethics, *see*
employees and agents; management;
owners; responsibility functions;
supervisors
personnel issues distinguished from
ethics issues, 172–73
planning business ethics programs, *see*
design and implementation of business ethics program
policies and procedures
board–management linkage policy,
134
codes of conduct or guiding princi
ples, policies related to, 116–17
employee responsibility and
management support, 199
ends, defining, 98–99
governance commitment statement,
96
governance model delegation of
authority statement, 97
government anti-corruption policies,
U.S. Department of State, 209
investigations, 173–74
management limitations, 99–100
means, defining, 99–100
voluntary disclosure of legal
violations, 201
political element of relevant context,
scanning, 72–73
Porras, Jerry I., 105
Posner, Barry Z., 213
posted materials, 153–54
private sector's role in regulatory
process, 212–15
problems, dealing with, *see* dealing with
problems
procedures, *see* policies and procedures;
standards, procedures, and expectations
process evaluation, 233, 234–35, 244
procurement of government contracting,

215–18
productivity enhancement through
ethics, 25–26
professional ethics councils, 141
profits
increased profits through ethics, 26
role of, 4, 6
trust, values, and profitability, 30
program catalyst, 58
program logic model, 70–71, 78–79
project networks, 59
project officer, 58
public feedback mechanisms, 175, 176
public perception of misconduct by senior *vs.* lower-level personnel, 190–91
published materials, 154
purposes and goals, *see* goals and
purposes

R

RBE worksheets, 60–61
alignment, 206
business ethics infrastructure, 146
code of conduct, sample outline for,
125–26
communication
infrastructure, 181
needs assessment, 178
eight questions for RBEs, 86–89
evaluating business ethics programs,
243–45
external context by stakeholder
category, 74–75, 82–83
government officials and agencies,
225
internal structure and dynamics of
enterprise, 75–76, 84–85
organizational culture, 243
outcomes evaluation, 245
process evaluation, 244
program logic model, 70–71, 78–79
relevant context, scanning, 74–75,
80–81
standards, procedures, and expectations, 127–28
training programs, 179–80
RBEs, *see* responsible business enterprises (RBEs)
recognition, need for, 194
regulations, *see* laws and regulations
Reichheld, Frederick, 28
Reisman, John, 240
relevant context, scanning, 74–75,
80–81, 234
reporting program performance, 237–41
reputation, 22, 26–27, 50, 51
reputation-enhancement level of RBE
identity, 6, 50, 188
resource teams, 59
responsibilities
clarification of, 102
fostering climate of acceptance of,
198–99
government-related challenges faced

by, 207–25
responsibility functions, 131–44
business conduct representatives,
141–42
business ethics council, 140
business ethics officer, 138–40, 143
high-level responsibility officer
(individual or group), 134–38
individual responsibility, 143–44
integration with other executive and
departmental functions, 142–43
owner–board level, 132–34
seven levels of responsibility, 131
responsible business enterprises (RBEs), 3
see also more specific entries
differentiated from other enterprises,
93–94
eight questions for, 37–39, 86–89
good management, responsible
business conduct viewed as,
31–32
government-related challenges faced
by, 207–8
identity levels, 6, 47–51, 68, 187–88
process of becoming a responsible
business, 21
purpose and goals, 4, 5–6, 9, 27
social responsibilities of, 27–29
stakeholders, 5
worksheets, *see* RBE worksheets
responsible governance, 96–100
retaliation, protecting employees and
agents from, 171
retention of employees and agents,
192–93
review process, design and implementation of business ethics program,
62, 123
reward systems, 195–97
"the right people in the right places,"
186, 187–94
hiring employees, 188–89
identity levels of RBEs, 187–88
owners, managers, and supervisors,
187–88
placing people in the right job
positions, 190–92
retention, 192–93
wrong people, dealing with, 193–94
risk management level of RBE identity,
6, 50, 188
risk reduction, 22–23
Robertston, Diana G., 8
Roddick, Anita, 23, 28, 175
Royal Dutch/Shell, 106–9, 122
Russia
Business Partnership of Seversk, 210
Chamber of Commerce and
Industry, 36

S

SA8000 standard, 32, 34
SAI (Social Accountability
International), 34

satisfaction of employees with organization, correlates with, 192
satisfaction of stakeholders, 28
scenarios used in training programs, 162
Schlegelmilch, Bodo B., 8
Schmidt, Warren H., 213
security, maintaining, 172
self-paced studies, 163
service providers, *see* vendors, suppliers, and service providers
Seversk, Business Partnership of, 210
shadow economy, 12, 16
shareholders, 13–14
Sharia, 8
small to medium-sized enterprises (SMEs)
    business ethics council, 140
    business ethics infrastructure, 129, 131, 133, 140
    CSR (corporate social responsibility), 44
    defining and communicating business ethics programs, 46–47
    design and implementation of business ethics program, engagement of stakeholders in, 57
    evaluation of programs for, 232
    evolving market economies, 9–11, 14
    global standards, adopting, 37
    RBE worksheets, 60
    relevant context, scanning, 74
    strategic planning, 44
    wider commercial network, developing, 32
    wrong people, dealing with, 193
Smith, Howard L., 44
Social Accountability International (SAI), 34
social capital, generating, 27–31
    charitable foundations, 220
    CSR (corporate social responsibility) and SMEs, 44
    defining an RBE's social responsibilities, 27–29
    development of community, private sector voluntary participation in, 219–20
    evolving market economies, 18–19
    relationships and responsibilities between enterprise and community, 122
    reporting program evaluations, 238
    trust, 29–30
    ultra-social responsibilities of RBEs, 28–29
    voluntary actions by private sector, 218–20
socialism, transition to market economy from, *see* evolving market economies
socio-cultural element of relevant context, scanning, 73–74
Sony Corporation, 105
staffing and business ethics, *see* employees

and agents; management; owners; responsibility functions; supervisors
stakeholders,
    see also customers and consumers; employees and agents; management; owners; vendors, suppliers, and service providers
    communications programs, developing, 149
    dealing with misconduct or serious harm to, 199–201
    design and implementation of business ethics program, engagement in, 57–61
    enforcement, engagement of external stakeholders in, 174–76
    external context by stakeholder category, RBE worksheet for, 74–75, 82–83
    global stakeholder groups, 34–35
    list of, 4
    producers' lack of contact with as central planning legacy, 13–14
    reporting program evaluations to external stakeholders, 238
    satisfaction of, 28
standards, procedures, and expectations, 93–95
    see also codes of conduct
    checklist, 124
    clarification of responsibilities, 102
    communication, 101, 152–55
    core beliefs and values, 102–4
    cultural considerations, 100–1
    employees and agents, 95, 101–2
    enforcement, *see* enforcement of standards, procedures, and expectations
    future, vision of, 104–5
    global, *see* global business standards and organizations
    governments, encouraging standards for, 211–12
    guiding principles, 100–2, 105–9
    higher standards, striving for, 100
    industry standards, compliance with, 111
    management, 105–17
        owner expectations of management performance, 98–100
        principles, 100–2, 105–9
        vision for enterprise, 102–5
    policies related to codes of conduct and guiding principles, 116–17
    RBE worksheets, 127–28
    responsible governance, 96–100
strategic owners, 13
strategic planning, 43–45
strengths and weaknesses of organization, 52, 54–55
structural components of business ethics program, 52–53
Sullivan, Leon H., 34

supervisors
    employee satisfaction correlated with actions of, 192
    "the right people in the right places," 187–88
    senior personnel *vs.* lower-level personnel, perception of misconduct by, 191
suppliers, *see* vendors, suppliers, and service providers
surveys, data collection plan for evaluating programs, 236–37

T

tardiness, ways of dealing with, 198
task forces or working groups, 58–59, 60–61
technological element of relevant context, scanning, 74
Thompson, Judith Kenner, 44
training programs, 155–65
    action planning and action learning, 160–62
    administration of, 165
    case studies, 162, 163, 164
    comprehensiveness of, 160–61
    content and structure, 156–58
    core beliefs and values, 155–56, 158–59
    delivery of, 158–62
    design and implementation, 155–58
    feedback, 164–65
    games, 163
    lectures and presentations, 162
    management involvement and commitment, 155, 159
    modes of training, 162–64
    organizational culture, 155–56
    owner involvement, 159
    personal values of trainees, 159–60
    RBE worksheets, 179–80
    scenarios, 162
    self-paced studies, 163
    updating and modifying, 164–65
    videos, 163
transparency, governmental, 210, 211, 215, 216–17
Transparency International, 216–17
triple bottom line, 6, 7, 238
trust
    laws and regulations, important role of, 14–15
    social capital, generating, 29–30

U

U.N. Global Compact, 36, 106, 235
unions, 14
United Parcel Service Inc., 22
United States
    AML (anti–money laundering) provisions, 49, 222
    codes of conduct, 110
    compliance level business ethics programs, 49

Department of Commerce, 36, 235
Department of State on government anti-corruption policies, 209
FCPA (Foreign Corrupt Practices Act), 221
FSGO (Federal Sentencing Guidelines for Organizations), 34, 49
government contracting and procurement policy of United Technologies Corporation, 217
United Technologies Corporation, 108, 114, 217

V

value-added level of RBE identity, 6, 50–51, 188
values, *see* core beliefs and values
vendors, suppliers, and service providers
    central planning legacies, 13
    monitoring behavior, 167
    relationships and responsibilities between enterprise and, 120–21
    sample vendor conduct code, 25
videos used in training programs, 163
vision
    management vision for enterprise, 102–5
    translation of vision, responsibility for, 135
voluntary actions by private sector, 218–20
voluntary disclosure of legal violations to authorities, 201

W

weaknesses and strengths of organization, 52, 54–55
Web sites
    communication via, 154
    training programs, 163
Wells, Joseph T., 24, 132
WMC Resources Ltd., 114, 115
working groups, 58–59, 60–61
worksheets, RBE, *see* RBE worksheets
World Bank, 11, 213, 216
World Trade Organization (WTO)
    Agreement on Global Procurement (GPA), 216
WorldCom, 160
wrong people, dealing with, 193–94
WTO (World Trade Organization)
    Agreement on Global Procurement (GPA), 216

Z

Zarsky, Lyuba, 148, 167